A VOLUME OF ESSAYS
TO COMMEMORATE
THE
QUINCENTENARY OF THE FOUNDATION
OF THE COLLEGE

Main Gate and Court

ST CATHARINE'S COLLEGE

CAMBRIDGE

1473 1973

A Volume of Essays

TO COMMEMORATE THE

Quincentenary

OF THE FOUNDATION OF
THE COLLEGE

Editor:

E. E. RICH, LITT.D.

Master

PRINTED IN ENGLAND
BY W. S. MANEY AND SON LTD, HUDSON ROAD, LEEDS LS9 7DL

CONTENTS

PAGE

PREFACE — vii

Origins; Robert Wodelarke and St Catharine's — I
DR A. B. COBBAN
of Trinity College; University Lecturer, Liverpool University

Ad Honorem Sanctae Katerinae Virginis — 33
DR S. C. ASTON
Fellow and Bursar, University Lecturer in French

Catharine Hall and The Reformation, 1500–1650 — 59
DR H. C. PORTER
Cambridge University Lecturer in History

Church and College, 1660–1745 — 110
DR RICHARD LUCKETT
Fellow, University Assistant Lecturer in English

Fellow Commoners and the College Plate, 1473–1875 — 138
DR SYDNEY SMITH
Fellow and Tutor, University Lecturer in Zoology

The Nineteenth Century — 164
PROFESSOR E. E. RICH
Master. Emeritus Professor of Naval and Imperial History

The Nineteenth-Century College; Rise, Decline and
Resurgence — 248
PROFESSOR OLIVER MACDONAGH
*Former Fellow, Professor-elect of History, Institute of
Advanced Studies, Australian National University,
Canberra*

The College, 1919–70 — 266
T. R. HENN
Fellow Emeritus, Reader Emeritus in English

INDEX — 303

ILLUSTRATIONS

FRONTISPIECE, Main Gate and Court

page

PLATE I   Reproduction from the facsimile   *facing* 48
           edition of P. Franchi de'
           Cavalieri, *Il Menologio di Basilio
           II*, Turin, 1907, p. 207

II   Label-stops in King's College Chapel   ,,   49
      A, St Catharine; B, St Margaret

III   Thomas Sherlock, by J-B. Vanloo   ,,   112

IV   Benjamin Hoadly, by Wm. Hogarth   ,,   113

V   Some College Silver   *following* 144

VI   Some College Silver   ,,   144

VII   The College in 1688.   *facing* 164
      The buildings recently set up, as
      well as those which, today only
      planned, in a short time will
      be actually constructed.
      By David Loggan

VIII The College in mid-nineteenth   ,,   165
      century

PREFACE

THIS volume is not intended to be a *History of St Catharine's*. The standard works by G. Forrest Browne and W. H. S. Jones are available; they still stand, they are much quoted in the Essays, and most of what they say would have to be repeated if another full-scale *History* were embarked upon. These are essays, in which scholars — not all of them members of the College — have written on subjects and episodes which build up to a historical understanding without pretence at continuous narrative or exhaustive exposition.

The result has been that emphasis has been on persons rather than on sites and buildings. Sites and buildings have, in any case, already been very fully treated by Dr Jones, and Dr Sydney Smith's article in the College Magazine (1963) has supplemented and amended the earlier work. The Ramsden Bequest, too, although it is mentioned many times, receives much less explicit attention than it would deserve in any narrative history of the College — as do numerous other episodes.

The volume has been some ten years a-brewing; and inevitably there have been some losses. It must be the poorer because Canon C. H. E. Smyth eventually decided against filling out a most understanding Commemoration Sermon into a full essay. Otherwise there would have been two essays on the Eighteenth Century, as there are on the Nineteenth — a treatment which offers alternative approaches, and variations in emphasis. The volume must be the poorer, too, by the death of Professor John Hutton. He undertook an essay on the College's pictures which would have been the counterpart of Dr Sydney Smith's essay on the silver; and in view of the way in which the essay on the silver complements and illustrates other essays it must cause great regret that John Hutton died shortly after he had sent in the first draft of his essay, and before it had taken definite shape. The cost of illustrating it would have been intimidating, but the fact that he would not be at hand to supervise the revision needed to fit his draft into the pattern of the other essays was the consideration which weighed most heavily as I decided against inclusion.

To an editor who, in other projects, has suffered the frustrations and difficulties of bringing out a co-operative study at an agreed date the appearance of this volume in time to take its place in the Quincentenary celebrations of the College is the source of considerable satisfaction. The authors are all men with many claims upon their time, and I am grateful for the way in which they have responded to exhortations (and admonitions) from a Master on the verge of retirement. Readers will judge for themselves how much they are indebted to the printers for the quality of the production; as Editor I can assure them that Messrs W. S. Maney and Company have anticipated and have met all the demands made upon them by an exacting timetable.

E. E. RICH
Master.

18.ii.73

Origins

Robert Wodelarke and St Catharine's

By Dr A. B. Cobban

Trinity College, University Lecturer, Liverpool University

THE opening of St Catharine's College in November 1473 may have occasioned mild interest and even some surprise in Cambridge academic circles. There must have been cynics who had predicted that Robert Wodelarke's projected college would never materialize. It had certainly been unusually long in the making. The acquisition of the site had begun as early as 1459 when Wodelarke purchased two tenements on the east side of Milne Street situated, in the words of Thomas Fuller, 'over against the late Carmelites then newly Queens' College'. Over the next fourteen years Wodelarke advanced very gradually towards the completion of the St Catharine's site:[1] this frustrating and intricate task was made even more exacting because it had to be carried through in conjunction with Wodelarke's time-consuming and harassing duties as Provost of King's College during one of the most troubled phases of its history. When, at last, St Catharine's emerged in embryonic form in November 1473 it possessed a complement of only two fellows, augmented by an indeterminate number of fellow commoners. A new society had unquestionably arrived, but a society so small that contemporaries might be forgiven for dismissing it as of little account.[2]

By any yardstick Robert Wodelarke must be reckoned an enigmatic figure. Whether or not he was an enigma to his

---

[1] For details of the acquisition of the site see R. Willis and J. W. Clark, *The Architectural History of the University of Cambridge and of the Colleges of Cambridge and Eton* (4 vols, Cambridge, 1886), II, 69 ff.

[2] See the discussion below, pp. 26–7.

fifteenth-century colleagues, he most assuredly is to us because although we can furnish a skeletal outline of his career without too much difficulty,[3] the medieval records of St Catharine's yield little insight into Wodelarke's character or objectives. It is particularly galling that the earliest college register, a large folio volume of sixty-nine parchment leaves, should contain only one piece of personal commentary about the founder. And while it may be reassuring to discover that Robert Wodelarke was 'vir benignus mansuetus et humilis'[4] this kind of stereotyped panegyric is of slight biographical aid.

One might reasonably expect to find revealing personal detail in the celebrated manuscript known as the *Memoriale Nigrum*.[5] This is a small paper folio volume of fifty-four numbered leaves, being a descriptive list of Wodelarke's possessions and containing the extremely valuable and much quoted account of the circumstances pertaining to the foundation of St Catharine's. It is tempting to suppose that this business notebook is written in Wodelarke's own hand. Such an assumption cannot be proven and all that may be affirmed from the handwriting and internal evidence is that the document seems mainly to be a late fifteenth-century production. But although our understanding of the origins of St Catharine's would be greatly impoverished were it not for the survival of the *Memoriale Nigrum*, Wodelarke's narration is almost entirely of an impersonal business nature, disclosing only incidental sidelights on the founder's character and motivation.

No further personal data may be gleaned from the extant charters and property deeds to be found among the medieval muniments of St Catharine's. The same holds true for the documentation arising from Wodelarke's twenty-seven year

---

[3] Details of Wodelarke's career are given in A. B. Emden, *A Biographical Register of the University of Cambridge to 1500* (Cambridge, 1963), pp. 645–6; see also C. Hardwick, 'Robert Woodlark, founder and first Master of St Catharine's Hall', *Cambridge Antiquarian Society Communications*, 1 (1850–9), no. xxxvii, 329 ff. and N. Moore's article in *The Dictionary of National Biography*, lxii (1900), 277 ff.

[4] College Register, St Catharine's Muniments, XL/8, p. 63.

[5] *Memoriale Nigrum*, St Cath. Mun., XL/18; printed by H. Philpott, ed., *Documents relating to St Catharine's College in the University of Cambridge* (Cambridge, 1861), pp. 1 ff. A transcription made by E. A. B. Barnard in 1930 is deposited in the Muniment Room.

tenure of the Provostship of King's College, Cambridge, between 1452 and 1479. His register, the *Registrum Roberti Wodelarke*, consists mainly of deeds relating to the property of King's and contains little of personal interest and nothing on the St Catharine's project.[6] Wodelarke's accounts as Provost of King's are far more engrossing, their chief value being their detailed coverage of the itemized expenditure on travel undertaken by the Provost on behalf of the college. It appears, however, that Wodelarke kept wholly separate accounts for King's and St Catharine's and I have not alighted upon a single reference to expenditure on the latter in the King's domestic records.[7] Accepting the severe limitations of the medieval evidence, it has to be admitted that it is in no wise possible to present a biographical study of Robert Wodelarke in the round. He will ever be a shadowy figure, lost beyond recall, and all that one can hope to achieve is to eke out the bare bones of his career with speculative inference. This is not as pessimistic an enterprize as it may sound: for the probability is that Wodelarke has a pronounced historical importance as a participant in a significant academic splinter movement in late medieval society.

The main events in Wodelarke's life and career are reasonably well established.[8] He was born in the village of Wakerley, near Stamford in Northamptonshire, the son of Richard and Joan(na) Wodelarke. The year of his birth and the circumstances of his parents are unknown, his early education is wrapped in oblivion, nothing has been discovered of his pre-Cambridge career, and Wodelarke's undergraduate phase at Cambridge University is still a complete blank. By 1441, however, he had taken an M.A. degree, and he later acquired a doctoral degree in theology, generally regarded as one of the most prized academic distinctions that a medieval university could award. It now seems probable that Wodelarke was

---

[6] *Registrum Roberti Wodelarke*, Muniment Room, King's College, Cambridge.
[7] The first volume of King's College accounts contains much interesting data on Wodelarke's journeys to and from London with details of persons visited en route.
[8] See above, p. 2, note 3.

admitted as a fellow of Clare Hall *c.* 1440, although this remains a highly obscure episode.[9] Presumably, the Clare fellowship was vacated on his appointment in February 1441 as a foundation fellow of Henry VI's new Cambridge society originally styled the College of St Nicholas. In 1443 Henry VI modified his collegiate plan and set in motion the erection of the revised College of St Mary and St Nicholas, otherwise King's College. The members of the first foundation were to continue as members of the second, and Wodelarke was appointed one of the foundation fellows of King's in July 1443. Nine years later, in June 1452, Wodelarke succeeded John Chedworth as third Provost of King's on Chedworth's promotion to the Bishopric of Lincoln. In December of this eventful year Wodelarke was made master of the works at King's, following in that arduous office Nicholas Close, an original fellow of King's and later Warden of the King's Hall, Chancellor of the University and Bishop of Carlisle. He made vigorous efforts to promote the languishing building operations at King's: but his endeavours were curtailed through a chronic shortage of funds which became an insuperable obstacle after Henry VI's deposition in 1461. On the testimony of an official auditor, Thomas Betts, it was declared that King's stood indebted to its Provost for the sum of £328 10s. 4d. paid from his own income.[10] It seems that Wodelarke was accused of misappropriating revenues of King's College for his own St Catharine's project: he replied to this allegation in the *Memoriale Nigrum* with the forthright statement that not a farthing of King's money had been spent on St Catharine's.[11] Who had levied this charge? Was it circulated by disgruntled fellows of King's who could not understand why their Provost should

---

[9] See W. J. Harrison, *Notes on the Masters, Fellows, Scholars and Exhibitioners of Clare College, Cambridge* (Cambridge, 1953), with additional notes by A. H. Lloyd, p. 160. Clare Hall was established in 1359 by Elizabeth de Burgh, Lady of Clare, and grand-daughter of Edward I, on the basis of the earlier University Hall, founded in 1326 by Richard de Badew, Chancellor of Cambridge University. See A. C. Chibnall, *Richard de Badew and the University of Cambridge 1315–1340* (Cambridge, 1963).

[10] *Memoriale Nigrum*, St Cath. Mun., XL/18, fo. 51; Philpott, ed. cit., p. 4. The sum is underlined in the original text.

[11] *Memoriale Nigrum*, fo. 50; Philpott, p. 3.

divert his energies into founding a new college when the one of which he was the head had scarcely got off the ground? One can certainly imagine the disquiet caused by Wodelarke's implacable decision to press on with his St Catharine's scheme regardless of the incomplete state of King's buildings, the depletion of both its revenues and its complement of fellows, and the general problem of Yorkist hostility towards a Lancastrian enterprise.

In addition to his absorbing burdens as Provost of King's and director of its building works, Wodelarke had special responsibilities for the royal College of the King's Hall, Cambridge, whose origins date from *c.* 1317. In the 1440s Henry VI had decided that the King's Hall required to be severely disciplined and overhauled: he considered that this task could be most conveniently accomplished under the auspices of his splendid new collegiate foundations of Eton and King's.[12] The punitive regime for the King's Hall was inaugurated in 1446 when Henry VI transferred the Crown's right of nomination of the King's Scholars (i.e. King's Hall fellows) to the joint control of the Provosts of Eton and King's. In 1447 there was added the right of appointment to the King's Hall Wardenship. And in 1448 the Provosts were charged with plenary powers to examine and reform the King's Hall statutes, to enforce the observance of new or reformed statutes upon the Warden and fellows, on pain of expulsion if necessary, and to hold disciplinary visitations. This process of reformation was completed by the imposition of a most humiliating oath of obedience upon the King's Hall Warden, who was thereby reduced to little more than a cypher. There is not the slightest doubt that these patronage arrangements were intended to be permanent, but the accession of Edward IV in 1461 brought about the reversal of this inequitable Lancastrian settlement and in 1462 the former independent status of the King's Hall under the Crown was restored. It can be seen that most of the period of the King's Hall's temporary loss of independence coincided

[12] On this episode in the history of the King's Hall see A. B. Cobban, *The King's Hall within the University of Cambridge in the Later Middle Ages* (Cambridge, 1969), pp. 188–92.

with Wodelarke's Provostship of King's College. This meant that in the decade between 1452 and 1462 Wodelarke, in conjunction with the Provost of Eton, had direct responsibility for all appointments to the King's Hall and ultimate responsibility for the administrative and disciplinary arrangements in that college. In view of the fact that the King's Hall remained the largest college in Cambridge until the foundation of King's College, Wodelarke's involvement in the affairs of the King's Hall must have been an undertaking of no mean proportions.

It is impressive that Wodelarke's multiple collegiate commitments did not exhaust his energies. On two occasions he was Chancellor of the University, in 1458–9 and again in 1462–3, and he seems to have given many years of service as a justice of the peace for Cambridge. It was in the midst of all these taxing labours that Wodelarke took the first positive steps towards the founding of St Catharine's.[13] He remained Provost of King's College during the birth pangs and post-natal period of St Catharine's and retired from the Provostship in October 1479 on an annual pension of £46 13s. 4d. There is some slight evidence to suggest that a long and crowded life had finally taken its toll and that Wodelarke's mental faculties began to fail in his twilight years.[14]

By founding St Catharine's while still Provost of King's Robert Wodelarke established a notable English academic record. To quote the garrulous Thomas Fuller, in one of his more succinct moods, 'Herein he stands alone, without any to accompany him, being the first and last who was master of one college, and at the same time founder of another.'[15] This is not to deny other striking instances of

---

[13] Wodelarke began the acquisition of the St Catharine's site in September 1459 by purchasing the two Milne Street tenements from John Botwright and others.
[14] See the letter of Simon Grene, master of Corpus Christi College 1477–87, relating to a dispute between Corpus and King's over property at Barton, Cambridgeshire, in R. Masters, *History of the College of Corpus Christi and the Blessed Virgin Mary in the University of Cambridge* with additional material by J. Lamb (London, 1831), p. 60, note g, in which Grene has occasion to remark: '. . . Mr Woolark that was Profest, and by age and seknes noth holle of mynde . . .' The letter is also printed by C. Hardwick, art. cit., pp. 335–6.
[15] T. Fuller, *The Worthies of England* (ed. J. Freeman, London, 1952), p. 446.

academic pluralism. For example, Henry Bost, said to have been confessor to Edward IV's mistress, Jane Shore, was currently Provost of Eton when he was appointed by the Crown to the Wardenship of the King's Hall in 1477. He remained Provost of Eton until his death in 1504 and Warden of the King's Hall until 1485. In 1483 he was also created Provost of Queen's College, Oxford, and thus for two years he was the head of three colleges, a case of academic pluralism not easily paralleled in English university history.[16] Wodelarke did not quite emulate this performance, but his career furnishes the only example in medieval England of the head of one college who was simultaneously the founder of another.

The intriguing circumstance of a reigning head of a college bringing into being a new collegiate society might suggest a measure of constitutional nexus between the two academic establishments. In the event, however, this did not materialize and there is no evidence to indicate that Wodelarke had ever envisaged such an association. It is natural that one should formulate the image of a mother and daughter relationship with respect to King's and St Catharine's but it is unlikely that Wodelarke saw the situation in these quasi-monastic terms. The founding of St Catharine's was for him a truly personal venture carried through independently of King's and his own position as its Provost. Any notion that St Catharine's was destined to serve as a perpetually small academic cell functioning under the surveillance of King's and basking in its reflected glory is entirely contrary to the evidence of the surviving records. It is not known whether Wodelarke had the blessing of the King's fellows for his enterprise. Some of the fellows of King's may have accused their Provost of misappropriating college revenues for the St Catharine's scheme. This is purely an inference but, on balance, seems a fairly probable one.

It is sometimes conjectured that St Catharine's was designed to be little more than an elaborate chantry for the profit of the founder's soul. Such a view necessarily carries with it the

[16] For the case of Bost see Cobban, op. cit., p. 288.

corollary that the College was intended as more of a personal spiritual investment than an institution of learning, an interpretation which might account for St Catharine's seeming non-alignment with current collegiate trends in the English universities. This possibility deserves closer investigation.

The later middle ages were much preoccupied with the problem of death, as can plainly be seen from the literature and art of the period. The fragility of life was an ever-pervasive reality in any medieval society. In the England of the fourteenth and fifteenth centuries it was starkly intensified. The Black Death and successive visitations of plague, the effects of the Hundred Years' War, and internal strife all served to accentuate this melancholy obsession with the transience of the human condition. Current mystical trends in religion may well have contributed to this mental absorption by stressing the role of individualism in society, the role of individual experience in the contemplative quest for union with God and the soul's salvation. This preoccupation with thoughts of death and the post-mortem judgment led to a sharper focus upon the need to provide for the salvation of one's own soul and those of the family circle. Increasingly, this need came to be met by the provision of institutionalized arrangements for the saying of special masses and other prayers. The institutional means at hand was the chantry foundation. Chantries came in all shapes and sizes according to the status, predilection, and financial position of the founder. They ranged from the humble endowment of a single chantry priest to a large collegiate church or an academic college.

In a sense, every academic college was a chantry foundation in that devotional duties were imposed upon the fellows of all the secular colleges at the universities. These services would be for the soul of the founder, his relatives, and perhaps also for those of the king and his near dependants. Some colleges were more obviously utilized as chantries than others. For example, at Eton and King's College, Cambridge, and Queen's, New College and All Souls, Oxford, the fellows or scholars had heavy chantry functions to perform: by contrast, the statutes of the King's Hall, Cambridge, enjoin only a minimal stress upon the religious duties of its fellows.[17] It is indisputable that the chantry motive was pronounced in Wodelarke's thinking. His chantry arrangements for St Catharine's are too extensive to be in any way minimized. On the contrary, one feels that they are of fundamental importance for the founder. About one-sixth of the original statutes of St Catharine's comprise elaborate instructions on the prayers to be offered for the soul of the founder and his kindred. It is true that prayers are to be said for the souls of Wodelarke's parents, Henry VI and other benefactors; but the overwhelming concentration is to be upon the founder himself. The heavily obtrusive way in which Wodelarke insures himself spiritually in his statutes is rather exceptional for a secular college and leads one to suspect that the founder was inordinately preoccupied with death. However this may be, it is manifest that Wodelarke was determined to use St Catharine's as a personal academic chantry to an extent that marks him out from the generality of founders of English secular colleges.

Are we then to infer from this that the chantry motive was Wodelarke's primary objective in launching St Catharine's? Was it for this alone that Wodelarke incurred crippling financial sacrifice and personal calumny? This seems inherently improbable. Without in any way detracting from the importance of the chantry element, it is unlikely that this was to be the predominant emphasis in Wodelarke's scheme of things. If Wodelarke had been concerned first and foremost with chantry considerations, the likelihood is that he would not have selected the secular academic college as his vehicle. This would have been such a needlessly complicated way of going about matters that one cannot believe that the personal chantry ideal provides the principal *raison d'être* for St Catharine's. A straightforward non-academic form of chantry would surely have been the answer if Wodelarke's concern with salvation had been his only motivation. While he undoubtedly injected more of the chantry ingredient into his college than did the majority of founders, it is nevertheless probable that his

[17] See ibid., p. 227.

spiritual wants were to be combined with an urgent educational purpose, and that it is this educational motive that has the primacy of place in the St Catharine's enterprize.

But the *Memoriale Nigrum* does not leave us entirely in the dark in our search for Wodelarke's motives. In this personal business notebook Wodelarke delineates both the dedication and the purpose of St Catharine's. His foundation, to be popularly styled 'Saynt Kateryns hall of Cambrige', is dedicated 'to the honour of God, the Blessed Virgin Mary and Saint Katerine the Virgin'.[18] After stressing that St Catharine's was a product of his own resources, Wodelarke gives a devastatingly simple (but far from illuminating) motive for his society, declaring that it was founded 'for the glory and praise of God and the stability of the faith'.[19] This kind of phraseology is a commonplace among medieval founders of English secular colleges. But it is reinforced at St Catharine's by a memorandum at the end of the *Memoriale Nigrum* which adds the information that the College was intended for fellows studying philosophy and theology. Apart from these references, this document provides no further lead on the vexed problem of motivation.

The charter of Edward IV of 16 August 1475, by which St Catharine's was legally incorporated as a college within the University with full right of mortmain, merely duplicated the *Memoriale*'s dedication (with slight variations) and reference to philosophical and theological studies. It omits even the general statement on the purpose of the foundation,[20] and thus affords no elucidation on motive.

But the original statutes go further than anything else in helping to establish the founder's motives. Although the statutes were compiled between 1475 and 1481, when Richard Roche was Master, they are the founder's statutes and embody his intentions. In the preamble to the statutes Wodelarke announces that he has established St Catharine's to aid 'in the exaltation of the Christian faith and the defence and furtherance

[18] *Memoriale Nigrum*, fo. 49v; Philpott, p. 2.
[19] '. . . ad gloriam et laudem Dei et stabilimentum fidei . . .', loc. cit.
[20] See copy of charter, St Cath. Mun., XL/8; printed by Philpott, pp. 8 ff.

of holy Church by the sowing and administration of the word of God, and in the increase of the disciplines of philosophy and theology'.[21] For want of anything better, this laconic declaration must serve as the most explicit surviving statement of Wodelarke's aims. In isolation, it is informative only in the broadest of terms, but the import of Wodelarke's intentions becomes clearer when some aspects of the Church and society in late fifteenth-century England are considered in relation to the detailed rules set out in the statutes.

The fear of heresy in England was still something of a spectre during Wodelarke's lifetime. It is true that Lollardy was no longer a semi-respectable force: it had lost its initial measure of intellectual and aristocratic support. But the movement continued to be significant in the second half of the fifteenth century, and indeed right up to the Reformation, surviving sporadically among the lower orders in society in small communities scattered throughout the country, apparently without prominent leaders and with little organization.[22] It would be misleading to argue that Lollardy embodied a coherent set of doctrines: nonetheless, it presented a threat to the secular and ecclesiastical powers by virtue of the consistently anti-authoritarian and anti-sacerdotal tenor of its attitudes. Although the most stringent efforts had been made to purge Oxford University of its Wyclifite and Lollard associations, the stigma of heresy lingered there throughout the fifteenth century. Oxford's murky reputation as 'the University of heresies' (Archbishop Courtenay) seems to have redounded to the profit of Cambridge. Because of its orthodoxy, because of its freedom from the taint of Lollardy, Cambridge came to be regarded as a sound investment and was used to counter the heretical tendencies of her sister university. It is almost certain that Oxford's involvement with heresy was one of the considerations which prompted Henry VI to choose Cambridge for the

[21] '. . . in exaltionem Christiane fidei, Ecclesie sancte defensam et profectum per seminationem et administrationem verbi Dei, in augmentum scientiarum et facultatum philosophie et sacre theologie . . .': original statutes, St Cath. Mun., XL/10, fo. 2v; Philpott, p. 11.
[22] See J. A. F. Thomson, *The Later Lollards 1414–1520* (Oxf. Hist. Series, 1965).

academic project that eventually became King's College;[23] and the founders of later Cambridge secular colleges in the fifteenth century, those of Queens', St Catharine's and Jesus, appear to have shared in this objective of reinforcing the University as a bastion of orthodoxy in the community. For although colleges could hope to exert little missionary influence in countering heresy in society at large, at least a founder might take all reasonable steps to ensure that his college was not utilized to subsidise fellows with heretical notions, as had clearly happened at Oxford. And the collegiate movement at Cambridge in the later fifteenth century in some measure institutionalized this aim. Robert Wodelarke does not refer specifically to the need to combat heresy in his declared statutory motive for his foundation, but his stress on the defence and furtherance of holy Church by the sowing and administration of the word of God ('defensam et profectum per seminationem et administrationem verbi Dei') is probably best interpreted in this sense. The point is strengthened by the fact that the crime of heresy is placed first among the statutory reasons for which a fellow is to be deprived of his fellowship.[24] There was a similar emphasis at Queens' and Jesus Colleges on the conservation of the purity of the faith.[25]

It is not suggested that the heresy issue was a primary concern of Cambridge college founders of the fifteenth century. It was not: their vision was a wider one. The urgent need to eliminate heretical tendencies was only a subsidiary, though integral, part of the more expansive, more positive functions that they hoped to ascribe to their collegiate foundations as vitalizing

[23] See H. Rashdall, *The Universities of Europe in the Middle Ages* (3 vols, ed. by F. M. Powicke and A. B. Emden, Oxford, 1936), III, 316; also the letters patent of Henry VI of 10 July 1443 in *Documents relating to the University and Colleges of Cambridge* (3 vols, ed. by the Queen's Commissioners, London, 1852), II, 471, where the king's intention is stated that the college should aid in the extirpation of heresy.

[24] For the reasons for which a fellow is to be removed see original statutes, St Cath. Mun., XL/10, fos. 12v, 13; Philpott, pp. 24-5.

[25] With reference to Queens' (and its earlier prototypes) this point is discussed by E. F. Jacob, *The Fifteenth Century 1399-1485* (Oxford, 1961), pp. 671-2 and J. B. Mullinger, *The University of Cambridge* (3 vols, Cambridge, 1873-1911), I (1873), 313-14. For Jesus see e.g. A. Gray, *The Earliest Statutes of Jesus College, Cambridge* (Cambridge, 1935).

entities within the University and the community. They were concerned with the state of society as a whole, with the general deep-rooted malaise that so troubled contemporaries: and the collegiate movement in fifteenth-century Cambridge, insofar as it had an identity of motive, embodied a concerted attempt to provide an academic move towards the amelioration of the ills of the age. This could be no more than a humble gesture because of the restricted scale of the operation. But if, as some came to believe, the regeneration of society depended on a positive lead from the universities in its midst, then the secular colleges could play a crucial part in creating that academic stimulus. And it is within this context that Robert Wodelarke's foundation has much of its importance and historical significance.

It was accepted in some fifteenth-century circles that the main cause of contemporary social evils in England was the dearth of men of spiritual capacity within the Church. In the later middle ages the ecclesiastical structure in England had become increasingly complex, with an ever-growing maze of courts and officials to implement delegated episcopal functions. By the fifteenth century, most of a bishop's diocesan work was carried out by deputies: and, more often than not, the bishop was a remote non-resident dignitary who rarely appeared in his diocese. An analysis of the fifteenth-century episcopal bench[26] reveals the extent to which considerations of materialism rather than spirituality prevailed in the upper ranks of the ecclesiastical hierarchy. The distribution of sees appears to have been dictated by monetary values. The richer sees of Winchester, Bath and Wells, Exeter, Lincoln, and Ely were normally parcelled out as rewards for service in the secular sphere. Their recipients, absorbed in the heavy demands of state affairs, were frequently permanent absentees. This category of bishop accounted for the greater proportion of the episcopal bench, controlling at any one time more than half the country.

---

[26] See R. L. Storey, 'Diocesan Administration in the Fifteenth Century', *St Anthony's Hall Publications*, no. 16 (1959), especially pp. 3, 4.

For a successful career in ecclesiastical administration the essential qualification appears to have been a degree in canon or civil law, or both.[27] As an enormously wealthy and multi-structured corporation, the later medieval Church required an army of personnel to serve as its judges and administrators. And the universities responded to this need by turning out a flood of law graduates for absorption in the church establishment. The faculties of civil and canon law at Oxford and Cambridge were the largest of the superior faculties and this doubtless reflects the realization that a legal training held out the best prospect for a satisfactory and lucrative position within the Church.

It is evident that throughout fifteenth-century England there were few resident bishops to provide spiritual leadership for the secular clergy and ordinary parishioners. Only a handful of the bishops were trained theologians. Theology at the English universities was pursued more by members of the religious orders than by secular clerks. The number of secular theologians who gained high advancement within the Church in the fifteenth century was small, and seculars would not ordinarily proceed to a theological degree if their sights were set on rapid promotion in the ecclesiastical hierarchy. But a reaction set in against the dominance of the legalistic outlook that pervaded the Church. For example, the Oxford chancellor, Thomas Gascoigne, was a stringent critic of a system that seemed so openly to prefer legal skills to matters of the faith, that seemed to prize legal dexterity at the expense of religious zeal, that seemed to turn out priests more fitted to give a legal ruling than a spiritual lead.[28] His concern was echoed within the universities by a mounting body of disquiet at the overwhelmingly utilitarian emphasis in the ecclesiastical sphere. It is only fitting that criticism should emanate from the quarter that furnished the main staffing for the ecclesiastical machine. While there had been acute difficulties over the

[27] See e.g. ibid., p. 22; also J. R. Lander, *Conflict and Stability in Fifteenth-Century England* (London, 1969), p. 125.

[28] Lander, op. cit., p. 127. A recent valuable analysis of the state of the English clergy in the later middle ages is provided by P. Heath, *English Parish Clergy on the eve of the Reformation* (London and Toronto, 1969).

promotion of graduates in the early part of the fifteenth century, these appear to have subsided in the period following *c.* 1450, and few unbeneficed graduates are then to be found although the competition for the better positions remained as fierce as ever.[29] A recent analysis of English parish clergy in the late fifteenth and early sixteenth centuries reveals that, in terms of spirituality, the Church's increasing employment of graduate legal personnel was a somewhat Pyrrhic gain: for the greater proportion of graduate incumbents seems to have been absentee clergy with little or no interest in parish affairs.[30] The standing of the graduate secular clergy was therefore of paramount importance for those who felt that however competently the Church might manifest itself in external legal forms it was nonetheless suffering from a spiritual atrophy; and a minority section of university opinion came to regard this spiritual poverty as not only symptomatic of the troubles of the fifteenth century but a primary cause of community malaise.

The collegiate movement in fifteenth-century Cambridge is inseparably bound up with this diagnosis insofar as it represents an attempt, on however small a scale, to stimulate spiritual values in English society. This objective probably lies at the core of Robert Wodelarke's St Catharine's scheme. In company with other Cambridge college founders, Wodelarke appears to have believed that the spread of legal studies at the universities must be checked by making provision for a less utilitarian, more 'spiritually uplifting' educational content. In practical collegiate terms, this could only mean a reduction in places available for law fellows and a corresponding increase in the number of theological fellowships.

Such a pattern is clearly detectable in Henry VI's foundation, King's College. According to the founder's statutes, that college was to consist of a Provost and seventy fellows and scholars, the latter to be recruited from Eton.[31] The college was designed primarily for the training of theologians, only ten of

[29] Heath, op. cit., p. 35.
[30] Ibid., p. 82.
[31] See the excellent analysis of the detailed statutes of King's College by J. Saltmarsh, 'King's College', *Victoria History of the County of Cambridge and the Isle of Ely*, III (ed. J. P. C. Roach, London, 1959), 382 ff.

its fellows being permitted to study outside the confines of theology and arts. Of these, two were allowed to study civil law, four canon law, two medicine and two astronomy. The rest were to apply themselves to theology and were required to take priests' orders within three years of beginning their study of theology: it was further stipulated that the jurists must also take priests' orders within nine years of beginning their legal studies.

A similar emphasis on theology was embodied at Queens' College, Cambridge.[32] This foundation was probably due mainly to the initiative of Andrew Doket(t), rector of St Botolph's, Cambridge, principal of St Bernard's Hostel, first President of Queens' and a friend of Wodelarke. In 1446 he obtained a royal charter for the incorporation of a 'College of St Bernard'. It was refounded by Queen Margaret of Anjou in 1448 under the title of the 'Queen's College of St Margaret and St Bernard' but in 1475 it was again refounded, this time by Elizabeth Woodville, consort of Edward IV. The statutes of 1475 are the earliest known code issued for the college. By these, it was enacted that the college was to be for a President and twelve fellows, all of whom would normally be in priests' orders and who were required to study in philosophy and theology. On becoming masters of arts fellows might teach arts subjects for three years. Afterwards, they were to proceed to theological studies although a special dispensation to study law or medicine might be granted. As this concession required the consent of the President and the majority of the fellows, one must conclude that dispensations would be exceptional and would not seriously qualify the overwhelmingly theological complexion of the college.

Jesus College, founded in 1496 or 1497 by John Alcock, Bishop of Ely, exhibits the same pronounced academic concentration.[33] The earliest statutes did not emerge until the

---

[32] For the early arrangements at Queens' see R. G. D. Laffan, 'Queens' College', *V.C.H.* (Cambridge), III, 408 ff.; also Jacob, *The Fifteenth Century*, cit., pp. 671–2. The statutes of 1475 are discussed by Mullinger, op. cit., I, 321–2.
[33] On the early situation at Jesus see J. G. Sikes and F. Jones, 'Jesus College', *V.C.H.* (Cambridge), III, 421 ff.; also Mullinger, op. cit., I, 321–2.

opening years of the sixteenth century. They were drawn up by the then Bishop of Ely, James Stanley: they are undated, but it is now known that they belong to between 1513 and 1515. The foundation charter had envisaged a complement of a Master and six fellows: in Stanley's statutes, however, the number of fellows was fixed at five. They were all to be priests, four of them were to be theologians and one was allowed to be a legist. The study of canon law was not permitted.

St Catharine's, the only other new secular collegiate foundation in fifteenth-century Cambridge apart from Godshouse (an exceptional institution founded in 1439 for the training of grammar school teachers), embodied this reaction against the dominance of legal studies in the English universities in explicit terms. Wodelarke's views may be gathered from the extremely restrictive regime of study which he imposed on his fellows. The founder is insistent that study for a degree should be limited entirely to philosophy and theology. This provision is set forth in the statutes with unusually repetitive force. The Master is to swear not to permit any fellow to pursue a course of study other than in philosophy and theology,[34] and the fellows themselves are to swear never to consent to one of their number following courses outside the two prescribed disciplines.[35] It is laid down that the Master himself must confine his own studies to theology.[36] It is further enacted that the fellows are to participate in weekly philosophical and theological disputations[37] in which they may be joined by fellow commoners living in the College.[38] These disputations were formal debates conducted according to strict procedural rules and were basic academic exercises in the medieval universities. Clearly, Wodelarke's intention was to prevent his fellows from diverting themselves to the subjects of canon or civil law, or medicine, at any serious or sustained level. The allure of medicine would

---

[34] Statutes, St Cath. Mun., XL/10, fo. 5v; Philpott, p. 15.
[35] Ibid., fo. 7v; Philpott, p. 18.
[36] Ibid., fo. 5; Philpott, p. 14.
[37] Ibid., fo. 7; Philpott, p. 17.
[38] Ibid., fo. 9; Philpott, p. 19.

not perhaps have been much of a temptation at a fifteenth-century English university, and the supposition must be that the founder was primarily concerned with ensuring that the St Catharine's fellows did not pursue a legal discipline.

The extremely conservative nature of the academic arrangements at St Catharine's is underlined by its almost exclusively graduate composition during the first phase of its life. According to the original statutes the fellows were to be native Englishmen of M.A. status or, failing this, they were to be selected from among the better bachelors of arts: all were to be at least in deacons' orders and preferably they were to be priests.[39] It was further stipulated that no more than two fellows from the same county might be elected at any one time.[40] The Master of the College was required to be a graduate in theology.[41] The one possible allusion to an undergraduate element in the statutes derives from the provision authorizing that a boy be appointed to serve as a Bible-clerk to read to the fellows during meals.[42] As it is known that the College later employed students for domestic duties[43] it is certainly conceivable that the Bible-clerk of the statutes would be a university undergraduate. But if this was indeed so, it constituted only a minor qualification to the graduate nature of the society in its early years. The fellow commoners, of whom mention has been made, were provided for in the founder's statutes.[44] It is not there specifically stated that commoners (*commensales*), admitted to live in college at their own expense by permission of the Master and fellows, must be graduates: however, as they are to be engaged in the same kind of studies as those prescribed for the fellows, philosophy and theology, one has to assume that only

[39] Ibid., fo. 6v; Philpott, p. 16.
[40] Loc. cit.; Philpott, pp. 16–17.
[41] Ibid., fo. 3; Philpott, p. 12.
[42] Ibid., fo. 9; Philpott, pp. 19–20. The readings are to be delivered '. . . per unum puerum sive clericum ad id deputatum qui biblista sive biblicus vocitetur'.
[43] This matter is discussed by W. H. S. Jones, *A History of St Catharine's College* (Cambridge, 1936), pp. 65–9.
[44] Statutes, fo. 9; Philpott, p. 19.

those of graduate status would be considered for admission. In this respect, the St Catharine's commoners would accord very well with what has been discovered about the commoner class elsewhere in English secular colleges of the medieval period. For it seems that until undergraduate commoners began to permeate the colleges from the fifteenth century onwards the normal type of academic commoner was of mature years and usually of graduate status.[45]

Why should Robert Wodelarke be concerned to graft a graduate commoner element on to his small collegiate society? It is generally supposed that the English colleges looked on pre-Reformation commoners as a means towards augmenting their revenues.[46] The profit motive behind the maintenance of commoners was doubtless a very real one in the English universities, just as it was at Paris: from what evidence we have of the detailed working of the commoner system, however, it is unlikely that much financial benefit was in fact realized. The efficiency with which the commoner system was administered varied considerably from college to college but, in general, the admission of commoners does not appear to have been a lucrative practice, yielding at most only a marginal profit. Wodelarke's statutes are silent on the reasons for the admission of commoners to St Catharine's. It is certainly stated that the money accruing from the room rents of the *commensales* is to be used for the common good of the College:[47] but this is hardly tantamount to affirming that a profit motive underlay commoner entry. There is a strong likelihood that Wodelarke's purpose was largely academic. This is indicated by his statutory limitation of commoner studies to philosophy and theology. In other words, the *commensales* are to be the academic counterparts of the fellows: indeed, from their highly privileged status within the College, they must have been in every way closely identified with the fellows except for the obvious circumstance that they were not on the foundation. Wodelarke probably reasoned that good

[45] See the discussion of ex-fellow pensioners, commoners and semi-commoners by Cobban, *The King's Hall*, cit., pp. 259 ff.
[46] Ibid., pp. 272-3 with notes.
[47] Statutes, fo. 9; Philpott, p. 19.

advantage was to be derived from a cautious diversification
of his college complement. It was not altogether healthy for
his fellows to live in complete isolation. A moderate degree of
intellectual and social contact with more mobile associates of
like-minded interests could have only a broadening and
salutary effect. Moreover, it was inevitable that some of the
more prominent of the *commensales* would come to be viewed
as potential fellows. At least two of the *commensales* who had
entered the College when it first opened in November 1473
were later promoted to fellowships,[48] and although extant records
do not allow us to follow through the situation in detail in the
fifteenth century it is likely that the practice would have
continued. Whatever the case, it is only right, when considering the composition of the original society of St Catharine's,
that a due stress be given to its graduate commoner element,
as Robert Wodelarke himself had undoubtedly intended that
commoners should form an integral part of his scheme from
the start.

Apart from its graduate composition and restriction of
serious study to philosophy and theology, the third distinguish-
ing feature of St Catharine's in its early years is its smallness.
At a time when English secular colleges were being planned on
an increasingly grandiose scale, commensurate with their
developing importance as teaching units within the university,
St Catharine's is readily conspicuous by its dwarfish proportions. It seems that Wodelarke had originally envisaged a
college for a Master and ten fellows[49] but had been forced to
revise his ideas because of financial difficulties stemming from
Henry VI's deposition in 1461. However this may be, both
the charter of incorporation of Edward IV of 16 August 1475
and the first code of statutes (between 1475 and 1481) allow

---

[48] Both James Wylborde and Edmund Bacton entered the College as *commensales*
in November 1473 and became fellows shortly afterwards. A. B. Emden, *A Biographical Register of the University of Cambridge*, cit., pp. 30, 656 assumes that both
were foundation fellows of St Catharine's: this is not strictly true as is evident
from the entry in the *Memoriale Nigrum*, fo. 49v, printed by Philpott, p. 2. On
Wylborde's status as a fellow commoner see Jones, op. cit., p. 196.

[49] See the memorandum at the end of the *Memoriale Nigrum*, printed by Philpott,
p. 6.

for a complement of a Master and three or more fellows:[50] when, in fact, the College had opened in November 1473 there had been only two fellows and a number of fellow commoners.[51] Such a niggardly complement would seem to be more in tune with an earlier tentative phase of collegiate development than with the expansive buoyancy that underlay the foundation and growth of colleges in the fifteenth century.

Extant records do not permit us to derive much information about the size of the St Catharine's fellowship in the years immediately following the foundation of the College. The revised statutes of Edward VI of 1549, however, fix the complement of fellows at six with the proviso that this number may fluctuate according to the current state of college revenues.[52] Judging from entries in Cambridge University histories such as those of John Caius, Richard Parker and Gerard Langbaine, six appears to have remained the normal number of fellows in the hundred years following the issue of the Edwardian statutes.[53] This figure refers only to fully-fledged fellows and excludes both the significant company of graduate commoners attached to the College from its earliest years and the undergraduate members who began to infiltrate into the society in the sixteenth century. But even if we take fellow commoners and undergraduates into account when reckoning the complement, it is still abundantly clear that St Catharine's was one of the smallest collegiate societies at the English universities until well after the Reformation. It was also one of the least financially endowed. In the valuation of the Cambridge colleges by royal commissioners in 1534 St Catharine's was valued at only £39 2s. 7¼d., the lowest figure

[50] See charter of Edward IV conveniently printed by Philpott, pp. 8 ff. at p. 8; also copy of charter in St Cath. Mun., XL/8. See founder's statutes in Philpott, pp. 11 ff. at pp. 12, 16; also copy of statutes in St Cath. Mun., XL/10, at fos. 3, 6.
[51] See *Memoriale Nigrum* printed by Philpott, p. 2; also original, St Cath. Mun., XL/18, fo. 49v.
[52] Edwardian statutes printed in *Documents relating to the University and Colleges of Cambridge*, cit., III, 78 ff. at pp. 78, 81.
[53] See J. Caius, *Historiae Cantebrigiensis Academiae ab urbe condita, Liber primus* (London, 1574), p. 72; R. Parker, *The History and Antiquities of the University of Cambridge* (London, 1721(?)), p. 114; G. Langbaine, *The Foundation of the Universitie of Cambridge* (London, 1651), p. 11.

for any of the colleges. The next lowest was Trinity Hall estimated at £72 0s. 10d., and the highest valuation was set on King's at £751 7s. 0d.[54]

St Catharine's, by virtue of its smallness, its wholly graduate composition and exclusive limitation of degree studies to philosophy and theology, has no exact parallel at either of the English universities in the fifteenth century. It is unique: it is decisively at odds with the type of collegiate society that was evolving in the English university world in the fifteenth and sixteenth centuries. And yet, however singular and set apart from the mainstream of late medieval collegiate development, it may be justifiably argued that St Catharine's was a striking representative of that splinter academic trend dedicated to the advancement of an educational ethos that cared nothing for lucrative rewards or social success in the community and which was partially institutionalized in the new Cambridge foundations of the fifteenth century. To a varying degree, King's, Queens', and Jesus Colleges all share in this ideal through their primary concern with a study-regime of theology and philosophy and their severe curtailment of facilities for legal or medical disciplines. On the other hand, it must be remembered that these colleges were teaching bodies from the start, and the presence of an undergraduate element would ensure that they did not have an entirely graduate focus. With St Catharine's, however, free from the undergraduate distraction, this ideal is incorporated in its purest form, no concession whatever being permitted in favour of the disciplines of civil or canon law or medicine.

Robert Wodelarke's project, then, is probably best viewed as an episode in a more general movement in fifteenth-century Cambridge, characterized by a partial return to a contemplative, quasi-monastic educational ideal, having at its heart the rejection of secular utilitarian values and with a pronounced stress on a 'spiritually ennobling' concept of study. This highlights the conflict between the utilitarian and non-utili-

---

[54] For these valuations see C. H. Cooper, *Annals of Cambridge* (4 vols, Cambridge, 1842–53), I, 370.

tarian principle which is fundamental to most educational systems and which is crucial for an understanding of medieval European education. The fifteenth-century collegiate movement in Cambridge stands etched in relief as one of those recurrent, if short-lived, endeavours to qualify the utilitarian emphasis which usually predominated at the average medieval educational level. Whether a university can successfully or meaningfully function on a purely technical or professional diet was a problem that engaged the minds of Wodelarke and his circle just as much as it has those of later centuries. As St Catharine's could make provision for only a handful of theologians, it must have been realized that even in association with those colleges with similar academic concentrations the practical impact outside the University would be negligible. Wodelarke himself put no limitations upon the tenure of his college fellowships and was not therefore particularly anxious to turn his fellows loose in the world, was not especially concerned with any minimal influence for good they might have in a concrete ecclesiastical situation. This was not the essential purpose. The aim was rather to effect a change in the climate of educational opinion, to set an example for the way that education should be directed if the universities were to produce graduates of sufficient calibre and in sufficient quantity to raise the 'spiritual average' of the secular clergy. College founders such as Wodelarke could not possibly assume an undertaking of these proportions. They could only hope that others would follow where they led, so that their acorn movement might swell to be a significant one in the universities, making some visible impact on the wider community. To view this nascent movement as an academic expression of the current mysticism of northern Europe might not be altogether without justification.

The Oxford collegiate scene does not manifest a comparable reaction against the primacy of legal studies. At Oxford, only three colleges were founded in the fifteenth century, all of them in the first half. Only at the earliest of these, Lincoln College, founded by Richard Fleming in 1429, is there a stress on theology at all similar to that of the late fifteenth-century

Cambridge foundations.[55] Archbishop Chichele's foundation of All Souls (1438) was intended for twenty-four artists and sixteen jurists. Although it was hoped that regent masters in arts (masters officially lecturing in the university schools as opposed to nonregent masters who were not currently employed as lecturers) would pursue theological studies, there was clearly not here the same preoccupation with non-utilitarian values as in the new fifteenth-century colleges of Cambridge.[56] William Waynflete's Magdalen College (1448) was designed for fellows of at least B.A. status who, upon admission, were to proceed in arts and then in theology, but who could also embrace legal and medical studies if granted licence to do so.[57] No colleges were founded at Oxford in the remainder of the century; that is to say, not a single new secular college was begun at Oxford during the productive period of Cambridge's second wave of collegiate expansion launched by King's College in the early 1440s.

It would therefore seem fair to conclude that the utilization of college establishments for the advancement of non-utilitarian studies was a movement of greater dimensions at fifteenth-century Cambridge than at Oxford. One cannot seriously believe that the 'degree factory' approach to education was any the less at Oxford and that Cambridge stood in greater need of salvation. It is difficult to discover much in the way of contemporary educational commentary before 1500 apart from the humanist treatises that begin to spring up in the fifteenth century and which are not really germane to the present subject: but there is an extremely valuable collection of over five hundred letters for Oxford University, extending from 1421 to 1509,[58] which contains sentiments that would have been echoed by Wodelarke and his circle. A central theme coursing through this collection is that the ills of society might be cured by a spiritual regeneration that would emanate

[55] See Rashdall, op. cit., ed. cit., III, 225–6.
[56] Ibid., III, 227; also E. F. Jacob, *Archbishop Henry Chichele* (London and Edinburgh, 1967), p. 79.
[57] Rashdall, III, 230.
[58] See *Epistolae Academicae Oxon.* (2 vols, ed. by H. Anstey, Oxf. Hist. Soc., xxxv, xxxvi, 1898).

initially from the universities. For do not the universities harbour the 'light by which kings rule their subjects, the morals of Christians are reformed, and the twin evils of heresy and error are extirpated?'.[59] Are not Oxford and Cambridge the 'eyes and blazing lights of the kingdom?',[60] 'the mother, lantern and well of the clergy?'.[61] By a concentration upon 'true learning' the universities have the capacity to inject into the community values of a salutary and ennobling nature, necessary to counteract the damage caused by those meaner spirits, of ill education and blinkered attitudes, who act as a drag upon the loftier aspirations of society. Such is the tenor of this academic letter collection and one can readily appreciate that notions of this kind must have permeated the college scene of late fifteenth-century Cambridge. Why they failed to find an adequate collegiate expression at Oxford is an intriguing problem to which there is as yet no satisfactory solution.

Robert Wodelarke's concept did not survive intact into the sixteenth century. It fell before the combined impact of humanist and Reformation educational drives. St Catharine's was converted from a society of student priests into a mixed teaching body, developing along orthodox academic lines, its curriculum transformed to meet its changing functions within the University. Although Wodelarke had been Provost of King's, a college which, after the King's Hall, had done so much to pioneer undergraduate teaching in Cambridge, he had not seemingly been interested in undergraduates for St Catharine's. This transformation of St Catharine's into a teaching institution marks the decisive movement away from that insular, almost rarefied, type of collegiate society brought into being by the founder.

---

[59] (The Universities) '. . . in quibus oritur lumen sciencie, quo reges regunt subditos, mores reformantur Christianorum, et horrenda extirpantur genimina heresium et errorum'. (The University of Oxford to the Archbishop of York, 1443: *Epistolae Academicae*, I, no. 160, pp. 219–20 at p. 220.)

[60] '. . . in hoc regno . . . (Oxford and Cambridge are) . . . oculi, due lucerne ardentes . . .'. (The University of Oxford to the Archbishop of Canterbury and other members of the Council at London, 1438, ibid., I, no. 125, pp. 154–7 at p. 157.)

[61] See letter of University of Oxford to the Commons, 1450, ibid., I, no. 208, pp. 293–4 at p. 294.

Clearly, the quasi-monastic collegiate pattern was alien to the university world of the sixteenth century; and this might explain why the founding of St Catharine's caused scarcely a ripple among literary commentators of the fifteenth and sixteenth centuries, attuned as they were to the notion of colleges as residential teaching institutions for undergraduates.

St Catharine's earned no place in the late fifteenth-century writings of our earliest English antiquaries, William Worcestre and John Rous, although the former knew Cambridge well and the latter displayed a deep interest in the history of the University and its component establishments.[62] John Leland's *Itinerary* of the first half of the sixteenth century also leaves us unaware of the existence of St Catharine's, probably because the author was content to rely largely upon Rous for his notes on Cambridge foundations.[63] It is even more puzzling to find that the Tudor historian, Polydore Vergil, passes over St Catharine's in silence. Vergil had a sustained interest in educational matters and added to the first printed edition of his *Anglica Historia* of 1534 more than a dozen passages on the English universities which are not incorporated in the original manuscript of *c.* 1512–13.[64] While this additional material provides a fairly detailed survey of the Cambridge collegiate scene, St Catharine's is strangely absent, though the later fifteenth-century foundation, Jesus College, is duly publicised. This 'conspiracy of silence' over St Catharine's is maintained generally in histories and chronicles throughout the sixteenth century, including those works which have significant entries on the English universities such as the *De Antiquitate Britannicae Ecclesiae* of Archbishop Matthew Parker.[65] The earliest printed reference in a history to the foundation of the College and to its founder appears to be the notice by John Caius in his *Historiae*

---

[62] See the relevant parts of *William Worcestre Itineraries* (ed. J. H. Harvey, Oxford Medieval Texts, 1969) and J. Rous, *Historia Regum Angliae* (2nd ed. by T. Hearne, Oxford, 1745).
[63] See appropriate entries on English universities in J. Leland, *The Itinerary in England* (4 vols, ed. L. Toulmin Smith, London, 1907–10).
[64] On this point see D. Hay, *Polydore Vergil* (Oxford, 1952), p. 119, with details in appendix II, pp. 187 ff.
[65] M. Parker, *De Antiquitate Britannicae Ecclesiae* (ed. S. Drake, London, 1729).

Cantebrigiensis Academiae ab urbe condita, Liber primus of 1574.[66]
There is here valuable information on the numbers present in
the College that year; but the entry, taken as a whole, is not
particularly revealing. Following the lead of Dr Caius, however,
St Catharine's was regularly included in seventeenth-century
histories of Cambridge University, for example in those of
Richard Parker,[67] Gerard Langbaine[68] and Thomas Fuller.[69]
Also, and perhaps surprisingly, the College wins a paragraph
entry in John Stow's *Annales of England*, written near the
beginning of the century.[70]

There can be little doubt that St Catharine's was a consistent
victim of the selective processes of Yorkist and Tudor historio-
graphy. From the standpoint of contemporary observers who
were aware of what was going on in the English universities,
however, it is perhaps understandable why St Catharine's
failed to make much of an initial impact since, both in terms of
size and intent, the College seemed to be at variance with the
main collegiate trends in the later middle ages. For, considerations of piety apart, the English collegiate movement of the
late thirteenth, fourteenth, and early fifteenth centuries was
designed to bridge a gap in the academic community by
enabling promising graduate students to pursue advanced
courses of study in the university.

The dangers of overestimating the importance of the secular
colleges in writing the history of the medieval English universities have long been recognized.[71] With one or two notable
exceptions, such as Merton and New College, Oxford, and the
King's Hall, Cambridge, the thirteenth and fourteenth-
century colleges tended to be small communities of limited
financial means providing, generally speaking, for only a few

---

[66] See J. Caius, op. cit., p. 72.
[67] R. Parker, op. cit., pp. 113–15.
[68] G. Langbaine, op. cit., pp. 10–11.
[69] T. Fuller, *The Church History of Britain from the birth of Jesus Christ until the
year 1648* incorporating *The History of the University of Cambridge since the Conquest*
(London, 1656), pp. 83–4 (of latter work).
[70] J. Stow, *Annales of England* (London, 1615), p. 1059.
[71] See e.g. H. E. Salter, *Medieval Oxford* (Oxf. Hist. Soc., 1936), pp. 95–102,
and idem, 'The Medieval University of Oxford', *History*, xiv (1929), 57 ff.

selected graduate scholars. In an age bereft of state post-
graduate assistance it was often extremely difficult, and sometimes financially impossible, for the B.A. or M.A. of moderate
means to remain at university to take a degree in one of the
superior faculties of law, theology or medicine. The trouble
lay in the length of the courses leading to the higher degrees.
Because of the duration and expense of courses in the superior
faculties there was a need to provide accommodation and
financial support for secular scholars capable of study beyond a
first degree: and this, initially, was the *raison d'être* for the English secular college. Oxford led the way with Walter de Merton's foundation of 1264, which ranks as the prototype of the
English 'graduate' college: at Cambridge the first college,
Peterhouse, was established by Hugh de Balsham, Bishop of
Ely, in 1264.

This was the pattern of collegiate development to which
St Catharine's, in its own way, conformed. But it was a pattern
which was changing as undergraduates became more important
in the collegiate structure. English colleges and undergraduates
are relatively late bedfellows. In the early stages of university
history the undergraduates lived a separate existence wherever
they could find accommodation compatible with their means,
either in halls or hostels, in taverns, or in private houses in the
town. These arrangements proved unsatisfactory. The main
disadvantage of the halls or hostels was that they were un-
endowed societies with no security of tenure beyond the year
for which the premises had been leased.[72] They were therefore
unstable units, a situation exacerbated by an unedifying
mercenary competition among their governing principals for
the custom of the fee-paying undergraduates. In these circumstances, halls or hostels proved unequal to the task of
maintaining discipline over the younger and more unruly
members of the universities.

---

[72] On medieval academic halls and hostels see A. B. Emden, *An Oxford Hall in
Medieval Times* (Oxford, 1927) and H. P. Stokes, 'The Mediaeval Hostels of the
University of Cambridge', *Cambridge Antiquarian Society* (Octavo Publications),
xlix (1924).

It became clear that the long-term solution was to house the undergraduates in the colleges,[73] but this could not be achieved overnight. Economic pressures acting upon the colleges, however, led them to adopt a course of action that ended in their absorption of the undergraduate population. Inflationary trends of the late fifteenth and early sixteenth centuries forced the colleges, whose revenues derived in the main from fixed rents, to find alternative ways of augmenting their finances. One such method was to open up their exclusive societies to undergraduates: the heart-searchings and traumatic effects of such a step can well be imagined.

Nevertheless, considerations of finance prevailed over the insular feelings of the fellows, especially when they realized that they could supplement their incomes with tutoring fees. For the halls did not possess comparable tutorial facilities, lacking, as they did, not only stability but also a sufficiently large graduate teaching element. As a result, the colleges were able to attract a steady stream of undergraduates on the strength of the tutorial advantages they could now offer. With the evolution of tutorial facilities in the colleges[74] the undergraduates felt less inclined to attend the ordinary lectures[75] of the regent masters in the university schools; and the regency system of public instruction, which had been the mainstay of university teaching for over two centuries, fell into progressive abeyance. The final blow to university teaching was dealt by the establishment of college lectureships whereby fellows of a college, or others from outside, were appointed to deliver a definite course of lectures within a college at an agreed salary.[76] These endowed college lectureships, which were mostly, though not always, of a public nature, and open to all

[73] A discussion of the reasons behind the gradual infiltration of undergraduates into the colleges will be found in Emden, op. cit., introductory.
[74] For the growth of early tutorial facilities in English colleges see Cobban, *The King's Hall*, pp. 66 ff.
[75] Ordinary lectures were the formal university lectures given by the regent (i.e. teaching) masters in the mornings at fixed hours. They were concerned with the expounding of the set texts and with the more difficult questions arising from them. The ordinary lectures were supplemented by informal lectures (cursory lectures) and by other academic exercises of which the most important was the disputation.
[76] On the emergence of college lectureships see Cobban, *The King's Hall*, pp. 79 ff.

comers in the university, became a permanent feature of the English collegiate scene after their inception at Magdalen College, Oxford, in 1479. Thereafter, nearly every new college foundation made provision for lectures; and, at the same time, most of the older colleges revised their constitutions to keep pace with this new development. Indeed, by the beginning of the reign of Elizabeth the colleges had become, to a lesser or greater extent, self-contained teaching units.[77] Attempts by the universities to prop up the moribund system of university teaching proved ineffective.[78] The course of events in favour of the colleges had gone too far to be reversed and, by the third quarter of the sixteenth century, the colleges had recognizably become the only teaching organs within the universities.

St Catharine's, the twelfth college to be founded in Cambridge,[79] was the antithesis of the type of collegiate society that was evolving in the late fifteenth century. It is evident that the Mertonian 'graduate' pattern of college organization had led to the divorce in university society between the senior graduate members domiciled in the colleges and the mass of the undergraduate population living an extra-collegiate existence. The piecemeal transference of the undergraduates to the colleges, a movement largely completed by the Reformation, had firmly deflected the Mertonian collegiate tradition into those channels which produced the 'mixed' or consciously balanced societies that have been the hallmark of college life since the sixteenth century: that is to say, 'mixed' societies in which undergraduates studying for a first degree share a life in common with graduate members of the community. Although this vitalizing movement was well under way by the 1470s, Robert Wodelarke set his face against it, and St Catharine's was conceived wholly in the Mertonian 'graduate' mould. Undergraduates had no place in Wodelarke's original scheme: St Catharine's was designed to be a foundation for senior members of the University. This also applied to Wodelarke's commoners (*commensales*)

---

[77] Ibid., pp. 81–2.
[78] See e.g. M. H. Curtis, *Oxford and Cambridge in Transition* (Oxford, 1959), p. 101 with notes.
[79] Including Godshouse (1439), later Christ's College.

who were to be students in philosophy and theology, participating in the weekly academic exercises of the fellows and sharing some of their privileges.[80] Accordingly, they are to be reckoned as commoners of graduate status and not undergraduate commoners introduced into the College for tutorial purposes. There is nothing to suggest that Wodelarke envisaged his foundation as a teaching establishment within the University. Clearly, the absence of undergraduates in the St Catharine's scheme would make this a lesser priority than in 'mixed' colleges; but the provision of formal instruction in philosophy and theology for the fellows and commoners would have been a valuable asset. Perhaps the founder's resources would not stretch to this: it is probable, however, that not even the idea was entertained at this early juncture. St Catharine's was founded a few years before the appearance at Magdalen College, Oxford, of what appears to be the first endowed college lectureship. Although the college lectureship made rapid inroads in university society, we hear nothing of this for St Catharine's during its initial phase of life.[81]

It would therefore seem legitimate to describe the college of Wodelarke's making as a small conservative community cast in an outworn Mertonian 'graduate' tradition and standing firmly apart from the exciting educational metamorphosis that was transforming the English collegiate movement. At first sight, St Catharine's would appear to have a completely anomalous and almost irrelevant position within late medieval university society. For its age, however, it gave expression to an educational gesture against current utilitarian values. Wodelarke and his fellow college founders at Cambridge were convinced of the necessity of providing an institutional antidote to the grasping materialism of society in which the universities were so obviously implicated. It was an honourable ideal and Robert Wodelarke's St Catharine's was a small but complete embodiment of it.

St Catharine's, moreover, can scarcely be regarded as the creation of a remote recluse out of touch with the pulse of

---

[80] Statutes, fo. 9; Philpott, p. 19.
[81] See Cobban, *The King's Hall*, p. 81.

academic life. As Provost of King's College from 1452 and twice Chancellor of the University, Wodelarke was better placed than most to understand the changing forces at work in the English universities. Nevertheless, in planning his St Catharine's project, he patently refused to swim with the tide and turned away from all that seemed to be progressive in the academic sphere. But such a contemplative, introspective vision of university life, centring entirely on the speculative pursuits of philosophy and theology, had insufficient substance to sustain it in a situation wherein the universities were increasingly orientated towards the professional concerns of the community. The irresistible tide of university-community supply and demand swept over the late fifteenth-century Cambridge college scene, sapping its vital forces and leaving its educational ideal in fragments. This is no reason, however, to dismiss this movement as of no account. Quite the reverse. Every generation benefits from those enlightened spirits who keep alive educational notions that transcend the short term and the immediately consumable. Robert Wodelarke was such a one. Retrospectively, his ideal may seem tarnished and negative; but given the circumstances of his time, the apparently crumbling fabric of society, the misappropriation of educational talent, learning commonly prostituted for money, it assumes a more positive and challenging aspect.

The St Catharine's scheme was far from being the outgrowth of a reactionary spirit: on the contrary, the origins of the College seem to be inseparably bound up with a constructive objective that could truly be called an educational ideal. The ideal may have been acceptable to only a minority in educated society. But as a gesture against prevailing utilitarian educational values in late medieval English society Wodelarke's academic enterprise, however humble, has a long-term significance that commends itself to the historian of education.

Ad Honorem Sanctae Katerinae Virginis

By S. C. ASTON

Fellow and Bursar, St Catharine's College

WHEN, on 16 August 1475, King Edward IV granted the royal charter which formally conferred a legal and corporate identity (*unum collegium perpetuum et una societas et comitiva perpetua*)[1] upon the little community of scholars who had entered commons (*intrarunt communas*) on 26 November 1473 as Fellows and Fellows Commoner in the *aula sanctae Katerinae*, certain features of the new foundation were noteworthy in the educational context of the time.[2] In two respects, however, Robert Wodelarke had followed tradition; neither his decision to dedicate the embryonic College to a saint,[3] nor the choice of patron saint he made would have greatly surprised his contemporaries. The early medieval universities, for the most part sprung from the earlier monastic or cathedral schools, retained throughout the Middle Ages a close connection with the Church and remained to some extent quasi-religious institutions. In essence they were a formal guild or corporation of scholars, of which the cap and gown were the distinctive livery. They possessed special privileges which they strove to maintain and increase, often in opposition to the lay authority. They ensured their succession by admitting to their corporation *magistri* who had given proof of their competence by acquiring the degree which was their

[1] Royal Charter of Incorporation (College Muniments). In the charters of the early colleges of Oxford and Cambridge the word College (*collegium*) designates a corporate community of scholars brought together for a common purpose; the word does not relate to the building itself, which is an *aula* or *domus*. Hence the establishment in which the corporate body resides is a *domus scholarium* or *aula scholarium*. The distinction is clearly indicated in Bishop Bateman's Statutes of 1350 for Trinity Hall.
[2] See Chapter 1, p. 10.
[3] It should be noted, however, that the Royal Charter, the Founder's Statutes and the *Memoriale Nigrum* all state that the College was founded ... *ad honorem (Dei et) beatissimae virginis Mariae et sanctae Katerinae virginis (et martiris)*.

33

licencia docendi, and the prime function of these *magistri*, apart from individual private study, was to teach, through the medium of lectures in the schools, those who cared to come and listen to them. For the junior students, how they lived and how they fared, the University itself in the early days had little concern beyond exacting in principle from time to time certain standards of discipline and morals, and establishing a surveillance on the rents paid by students for their lodgings. It was only from the latter part of the thirteenth century that the conditions of life and behaviour of the students themselves, and in particular of the poor students who formed the majority, began to attract attention and to lead to the provision of places of residence for them. Such residences were of two kinds: the first and earlier, hostels (*hospitia*) rented from a town landlord and managed by a Principal who was, at first, independent of any higher authority; the second, the endowed *domus* or *aula*.[4]

The *domus* or *aulae* themselves, primarily intended as places of ordered residence for the often disorderly students who were thus to be placed under the watchful eye of presumedly more sober *magistri*, were the foundations of benefactors whose concern for the diligence and well-being of the younger generation was no doubt often tempered by their laudable desire to lay up treasure for themselves in Heaven. Within the wider corporation of the University the Colleges formed confraternities which, like their lay counterparts, often had their patron saints chosen by their pious founders. Thus, of the eight modern collegiate foundations which already existed in Wodelarke's day, although some might bear, and be known by, the name of their benefactors, the majority were placed under a collective or individual holy patronage; Peterhouse (1285), while being at the same time *aula scholarium Episcopi Eliensis*, was the *domus Sancti Petri*; Gonville Hall (1348) was the College of the Annunciation of the Blessed Virgin Mary; Trinity Hall (1350) the College of scholars of the Holy Trinity of Norwich;

---

[4] In later years some of the hostels were absorbed in the new college foundations; others attached themselves to the colleges, which used them as college lodging-houses, while others again were founded by the colleges, or given to the colleges by benefactors for the same purpose. Hostels still existed in the sixteenth century.

Corpus Christi (1352), also called Bene't (i.e. St Benedict's) College, was the College of Corpus Christi and the Blessed Virgin Mary; King's College (1441) that of St Mary and St Nicholas; and Queens' College (1448) that of St Margaret and St Bernard. Similarly, Michael House (1324) and God's House (1446), later to be absorbed into Trinity and Christ's Colleges. Many of the hostels, too, which existed in Wodelarke's day[5] or which had been absorbed by the earlier colleges or belonged to them, were similarly titled; thus, St Austin's (King's), St Benedict's (Corpus Christi), St Bernard's (Queens'), St Botolph's (Pembroke), St Katherine's,[6] St Clement's, St Edmund's, St Edward's, St Gerard's (Garret), St Hugh's, St Margaret's,[7] St Mary's, St Nicholas,[8] St Paul's, St Thomas's (Pembroke).

In dedicating his new foundation to a patron saint Wodelarke thus followed a long-established usage and probably the main decision which confronted him was the selection of a particular saint. Here the choice was wide. Outside the ranks of the Apostles and the Biblical saints, a number of later saints, sometimes for quite fortuitous reasons, inspired particularly widespread devotion among clerics and laymen alike. Some of the most popular had already been pre-empted by the earlier foundations, but if popularity had been the sole criterion, a number still remained.[9] It may be assumed, therefore, that in selecting St Catharine, Wodelarke had some particular reason in mind.

[5] For full list of Hostels and Inns, see R. Willis and J. W. Clark, *The Architectural History of the University of Cambridge* (Cambridge, 3 vols), 1886, Vol. 1, xxv–xxviii.

[6] For St Katherine's Hostel, see below, p. 54.

[7] In Trinity Lane, and the property of Gonville Hall in 1467.

[8] There were two hostels of this name; one in Milne Street, which was absorbed into King's College; the other, a lawyer's inn and the property of Queens' College, lay between the present Christ's and Emmanuel Colleges, and was still functioning in the sixteenth century, its scholars being 'eminent for hard study, infamous for their brawlings by night' (Dr Caius).

[9] To judge by the dedication of existing medieval English churches, St Catharine came twenty-sixth in the order of popularity. Dedications to the Blessed Virgin Mary total 2335, followed by All Saints (1255), St Peter (1140), St Michael (687), St Andrew (637), St John Baptist (550), St Nicholas (437), St James the Elder (414), St Paul (326); St Margaret, whose cult was particularly popular, possibly because she was the patron saint of women in childbirth, comes eleventh, with 261. St Catharine herself has 63 dedications. See F. Bond, *Dedications and Patron Saints of English Churches*, Oxford U.P., 1914, and F. Arnold-Forster, *Studies in Church Dedications*, London, Skeffington, 3 vols, 1899.

Few saints inspired throughout the Middle Ages such wide-spread devotion and affection as St Catharine of Alexandria and, although her cult has waned since the sixteenth century, it is by no means certain that her recent official demotion by the Church of Rome — which marks the present terminal stage of a long controversy — will completely oust her from the position she occupied so long in popular favour all over Europe. Yet few saints are so ill-authenticated, few have origins and identity so shrouded in the obscurity of time. Her story, as it ultimately crystallized, derives from two lines of tradition, both devoid of historical foundation, the *Passio*, reporting the events at Alexandria and her martyrdom, and the *Conversio*, recounting her mystical espousal with Christ in a vision; it is found in Greek and Latin texts of the ninth and tenth centuries and subsequently in most of the vernacular languages of Western Europe. The legend is too well-known to need detailed treatment here but it will be convenient to extract the salient points from the version given in the *Legenda Aurea*, written by Jacobus de Voragine about 1290, a narrative which is itself at once a recapitulation of earlier western versions and the source of many later ones.

According to this version, Catharine was the eighteen-year-old daughter of King Costus; instructed in all the liberal arts, she was as wise and learned as she was beautiful. The Emperor Maxentius (Maximinius) having summoned all men to Alexandria to offer sacrifices to the pagan idols and having decreed the punishment of the Christians who refused to obey, Catharine defended them before the tyrant who, unable to contend with her arguments, ordered fifty orators, grammarians and rhetors, who surpassed all others in wisdom, to dispute with her. These she overcame in the ensuing philosophical and theological debate; they confessed themselves vanquished in argument, declared themselves Christians and were promptly burned at the stake on the command of the discomfited Emperor, who ordered the virgin to be beaten and thrown into prison without food. Here she was sustained and nourished by angels and when the Empress, who in the temporary absence of her husband had gone to visit her, saw this she, too, was converted to Christianity, along with Porphyrius and the two hundred soldiers of his guard. When the Emperor returned, he summoned Catharine and tried to win her over by offering to make her his wife, an offer she refused. Whereupon the furious Emperor ordered four wheels to be made, set with sharp blades and nails, which would revolve in different directions and cut the virgin to pieces; at the critical moment, however, an angel descended from Heaven and destroyed the wheels. The Empress, seeing the miracle, reproached the Emperor for his cruelty, confessed her own conversion to Christianity and was promptly mutilated and executed by order of her wrathful husband, who wreaked a similar vengeance on the converted soldiers. Again he offered to make Catharine his wife if she would recognize the pagan gods; again she refused and the Emperor ordered her to be beheaded. Comforted from Heaven, she died; and from her mutilated body came not blood but pure milk and precious oils, which cured the sick who touched them. Angels took up the head and body of Catharine and bore them to Mount Sinai where they were buried, and where later the Emperor Justinian I (527–65) founded a nunnery and named it in her honour.

Such, in outline, is Catharine's story. It is a story which may vary in detail in different versions of different periods: for example, in details of her pedigree the general 'of noble birth' or 'of royal birth' in early Greek and Latin versions is made more specific by making her the daughter of King Costus, who is later localized as a King of Cyprus, whence further pseudo-historical details of his connection with Maximinius and Alexandria (this detail of royal descent may have given rise to the common representation of the saint with a crown on her head); in the number of wheels (one, two or four); in the extension and elaboration at an early date of the philosophical disputations, which probably reflect the incorporation of material derived from Christian apologists.[10] Nevertheless, it

---

[10] See J. Rendel Harris, 'A New Christian Apology', *Bulletin of the John Rylands Library*, vii, viii, ix, 1923–5, whose view that the Catharine story embodied the lost apology of Quadratus, Bishop of Athens, is not, however, endorsed by later critics.

remains remarkably constant in the numerous Latin and early
vernacular medieval renderings, whence it may safely be
inferred that the story had developed and become fixed at an
early date through the medium of written documents which
were subsequently copied and widely disseminated. It is
evident, too, that the story contains many features which are
not peculiar to St Catharine. The legends of many other saints
contain similar details, which are almost standard elements in
hagiographical literature, such as the persecution of Christians,
the saintly protestor, the appearance before a cruel pagan
tyrant, the immediate conversion of soldiers, guards and
onlookers, the miraculous interventions, the theological
discussions, the virginity motif, and so on. Even the wheel is
not associated only with St Catharine; at least ten other saints
were reputedly subjected to the same torture. Nearly all the
heroines of medieval saints' lives have the same characteristics
as she; they are usually young, beautiful and highly born, are
usually ladies who, before or even after marriage, are concerned to preserve their virginity and purity. There seems little
doubt that the story is a composite blend of standard elements
and features present in many hagiographical legends.

To say this is not to decry the honesty and good faith of the
pious writers who have so frequently set down the story of
St Catharine in different languages throughout the centuries;
still less is it intended to deny that it is one of many such stories
which have afforded comfort and inspiring *exempla* to devout
Christians in all ages. Nevertheless, the legend indicates a
process which underlies the development of many medieval
romances, both secular and ecclesiastical,[11] and which leads,
whatever the original basic elements, to a type of elaborate
written story in which real or presumed fact is obscured
beneath a mass of amplification and rhetoric. In the Catharine
story, a number of elements may have played their part. It

---

[11] For a full discussion of these points in connection with Saints' legends, see a
number of important works by H. Delehaye; in particular, *Les Légendes hagiographiques*, 3rd ed., Brussels, 1927 (English trans. by D. Attwater, *The Legend of the
Saints*, London, Chapman, 1962); *Les Passions des Martyrs et les genres littéraires*,
Brussels, 1921; *Les martyres d'Egypte*, Brussels, 1923; *Etude sur le légendaire romain*;
les saints de novembre et de décembre, Brussels, 1936; *Sanctus*, Brussels, 1927, etc.

may possibly contain the vestiges of myth, the explanation in concrete terms of a natural phenonemon which occurs to a society in a primitive stage of development; or again of the oral tale, the invented story not associated with any particular place or person but which, when it is localized and linked with time, place and person develops into legend. When legend is expanded by the inclusion of fictitious inventions it passes into romance; and, if the romance is intended to depict the life, adventures and *exemplum* of a saintly personage it becomes the hagiographical romance, of which so many literary examples survive from the medieval period. At the root of hagiographical romance, however, lies the written legend,[12] and that legend itself may be varied in different versions by the inclusion of extra biographical details, frequently imagined or supposed, by an elaboration of the details of the recitals, by the inclusion of additional extraneous elements, or by the inclusion or substitution of local material. In this context, details may again develop as a result of the confusion of people of the same name, by an ignorance of historical or geographical fact, by the reputed discovery of relics or of historical documents, and so on. The medieval world had, too, a liking for the eye-witness account; thus there is more than one medieval writer who, although composing many years and even centuries after the event described, claims to have been present or to have been personally associated with the central figure of the story.

Many of these processes appear to have entered into the story of St Catharine as it was disseminated in medieval Europe.[13] Its origins are lost in obscurity; they can only be surmised, and the development of the legend traced, from the tangible evidence which has fortuitously survived, above all from the written learned texts which are almost certainly the point of departure for the later popular cult of the saint. If one strips

[12] The word legend, indeed, comes from hagiography; it derives from *legenda*, the story of a saint which was to be read on his feast-day.
[13] The medieval vernacular versions appear to derive primarily, *via* Latin translations and adaptations, from the account given by Simeon Metaphrastes. The present essay is concerned primarily with the development of the legend in England. For a comprehensive treatment of the literary texts in English, see T. Wolpers, *Die englische Heiligenlegende des Mittelalters*, Tübingen, Niemeyer, 1964.

off from the story the common features and elaborations which enter into many other hagiographical legends of the medieval period, if one comes down, in short, to the basic facts, the story is reduced to two simple elements; first, a lady, converted to Christianity, who suffered death during one of the many persecutions of the early Christians; secondly, to judge by the testimony of the earliest accounts, the location of this event in the early fourth century in Alexandria. Much learned work over the past three centuries has centred on these elemental points, but all efforts to identify a historical Catharine have been in vain.

A passage in Eusebius,[14] Bishop of Caesarea (267–340), alludes to a certain unnamed Christian, one of the most noble ladies of Alexandria, who was coveted for her beauty, wealth and learning by the tyrant Maximinius, whom she resisted. Unwilling, by reason of his affection, to put her to death, Maximinius confiscated her property and banished her. This account has been held by some,[15] from its resemblance to the basic elements of the legend, to contain the germ of Catharine's story, but two difficulties arise. The first, though not necessarily conclusive in itself since later generations may conceivably have elaborated on the original, is that Eusebius, a historian worthy of respect, records, not the death, but the banishment of the lady; the second, and more weighty, is that a Latin version of Eusebius written by Rufinus of Aquileia about the year 400, less than a century after the historical Maximinius, specifically gives to the lady in question the name of Dorothea. Catharine has also been identified with the celebrated pagan woman philosopher Hypatia, renowned for her eloquence and intellect as well as for her beauty, who was born in Alexandria c. 370 and murdered there in March 415 by a fanatical Christian mob.[16] Quite apart from these conjectures one is tempted to wonder whether the Catharine story

[14] *Hist. Eccl.*, VIII, 14. For the Greek text of Eusebius and facing Latin text of Rufinus see T. Mommsen (ed.), *Eusebius Werke; II, Die Kirchengeschichte; Die lateinische Übersetzung des Rufinus*, Leipzig, 1908, pp. 784–5.

[15] Joseph Simon Asserani (1687–1768) appears to have been the first to identify the lady of Eusebius' story with Catharine.

[16] According to Socrates (*Hist. Eccl.*, VII, 15) she was cut to pieces with oyster shells and subsequently burnt.

has evolved, as did so many medieval legends, by a process of confusion or contamination of one legend with another. The life of St Charitina,[17] for example, has a number of features which parallel that of Catharine while the life of the historical St Peter of Alexandria (Bishop of Alexandria, martyred on 24 or 25 November 311 during the persecutions of Maximinius) may perhaps have been of some relevance to her localization in Alexandria.[18]

Whatever the validity of this shadowy evidence from the late Imperial period, it is not until some four centuries later that direct evidence relating specifically to St Catharine is forthcoming; it is then of two kinds, pictorial and written. The earliest evidence of the veneration of St Catharine is provided by a painting, dating perhaps from the eighth century, discovered in the oratory in the Pelagian Basilica of S. Lorenzo all'Agro Verano, representing the saint beside the Virgin and bearing the inscription S. Ecaterina. There is also a painting, dating from the end of the eighth century, in the catacomb of S. Gennaro at Naples.[19] Her legend, like that of other eastern saints such as Saint Nicholas, St George and St Margaret, may have come to Western Europe during the eighth century in the wake of eastern monks who had fled from the persecution which broke out in full force in the middle of that century as a result of the Iconoclasm movement in the Byzantine Empire. Its acceptance and dissemination may then have been aided by the development and elaboration in the west of the Church ritual and services, which established an increasing number of saints' days to be observed, created a need for additional liturgical material and gave rise, not only to new compositions, but also to the compilation of anthologies which formed the reading library of the monastic communities.[20] The need

---

[17] *Acta Sanctorum*, Vol. III, Antwerp, 1770 under 5 October (pp. 21–8) and *Dictionary of Christian Biography*, London, 1877, Vol. I, 453–4.
[18] The feast day of Peter of Alexandria was variously inscribed in Eastern breviaries for 23, 24, 25, 26 November; in the West it was transferred from 25 to 26 November, as a result of the greater popularity of St Catharine (see *Propylaeum ad Acta Sanctorum decembris*, Brussels, 1940, p. 546). Athanasius (see below) gives St Catharine's festal day as 24 November.
[19] See *Enciclopedia Cattolica*, Vatican City, 1949, Vol. III, 1139–42.
[20] See R. W. Southern, *The Making of the Middle Ages*, London, Hutchinson, 1953.

found expression *inter alia* in Latin Lives of Saints which indicate a literary development of basic material derived in some measure from written sources but doubtless augmented by oral tradition, by the inclusion of extraneous material and standardized elements and also, perhaps, by invention. The texts all speak of the miraculous translation of the body of St Catharine to Mount Sinai, but this legend is not mentioned in the itineraries of the earliest pilgrims to the monastery there. It appears that at some time in the eighth century the monks on Mount Sinai disinterred a body which they supposed to be that of a Christian martyr; nothing would have been easier than to identify it with a real or supposed person, and so to endow it with a name.[21]

It is impossible, given the paucity of evidence, to trace a precise development of the Catharine legend at this time, but extant texts afford an indication of the growth of her cult.[22]

The oldest surviving texts of St Catharine's story are in Greek and date from the latter part of the tenth century. The earliest version was for long held to be that contained in the *Menologium Basilianum*,[23] a collection of pious legends made, it was thought, for the Emperor Basil I the Macedonian (867–86);

[21] The name Catharine itself probably derives from a diminutive of the Greek *Καθαρός* = pure). The Greek form of her name in the earliest versions (see below) is Aikaterina.

[22] A reference to a *Passio Ecaterine virginis* in an index contained in a MS of the late eighth–early ninth century (Munich, Claramontano 4554) suggests that the legend of St Catharine was known in Western Europe at the beginning of the Carolingian epoch; this lost Passion may be identical with the version contained in the *Bibl. Hagiographica Latina*, 1657 (Brussels, 1898–1901). Another attestation is found in a Greek Saint's life of *c.* 975 (published, with Latin translation, H. Delehaye, 'Vita S. Pauli Iunioris in Monte Latro', *Analecta Bollandiana*, XI, 1892, 5–14, 136–82, see Sec. 39, p. 153; see also H. Delehaye, 'La Vie de St Paul le Jeune (+955) et la Chronologie de Métaphraste', *Revue des questions historiques*, LIV (n.s.X), 1893, 49–85). A tenth-century calendar at Monte Cassino records her feast day as 25 November, and an eleventh-century legendary there contains her Passion (*Bibl. Hag. Lat*, 1658, 1662). Alfanus, Archbishop of Salerno (1058–86) composed three hymns in her honour (Migne, *Patrologia Latina*, CXLVII, 1240–1). See also H. Knust, *Geschichte der Legenden der h. Katharina von Alexandrien*, Halle, Niemeyer, 1890.

[23] Fac. ed. P. Franchi de'Cavalieri, *Il Menologio di Basilio II* (Cod. Vat. Graeco, 1613), 2 vols, Turin, 1907; see reproduction, Plate I. The erroneous attribution was corrected three centuries ago (by L. Allacci, *De Libris ecclesiasticis Graecorum*, Paris, 1645, pp. 83 ff., and by others subsequently) but has persisted down to the twentieth century.

the Emperor concerned is, in fact, Basil II (976–1025). The version, of which the following English translation is that by the Reverend Charles Hardwick,[24] Fellow and Chaplain of St Catharine's Hall, is short: 'Aecaterina was a martyr of Alexandria and the daughter of a rich and noble chieftain. Being distinguished by talent as well as by beauty, she devoted herself to Grecian literature and the study of philosophy, and was moreover master of the languages of all nations. On a Grecian festival in honour of the idols, she was moved by the sight of so many slaughtered animals and came into the presence of Maximinius and expostulated with him in these words: "Why hast thou left the living God to worship before idols?" Whereupon the Emperor gave her into custody and punished her severely. He then fetched fifty orators and bade them reason with Aecaterina and confute her, adding "If ye fail to overpower her I shall consign every one of you to the flames". But they, seeing themselves vanquished in the contest, were all baptised and forthwith burnt. She, on the contrary, was beheaded.'

On the basis of the erroneous attribution of the *Menologium* to Basil I, it has been mistakenly held[25] that this story, which is itself possibly a *résumé* of an unknown text, was the basis of the elaborate Life in Greek composed in the second half of the tenth century by Simeon Metaphrastes[26] and of another, slightly later, version, also in Greek, by a certain Athanasius,[27] self-styled stenographer of Catharine. These two latter narratives are the principal sources of Latin translations[28] and thence of vernacular versions in the West.

Evidence of the further and wider dissemination of the Catharine legend is found in a history of the relics of the Saint reputedly preserved in the Benedictine monastery of La

---

[24] In his *Historical Enquiry touching Saint Catharine of Alexandria*, Cambridge, 1849.
[25] For example, by E. Einenkel (ed.), *The Life of St Katherine*, London, E.E.T.S., 1884.
[26] Text in Migne, *Patrologiae Graecae*, cxvi, 276–302.
[27] Text in Abbé J. Viteau, *Passions des Saints Ecaterine et Pierre d'Alexandrie, Barbara et Anysia*, Paris, Bouillon, 1897, pp. 4–22.
[28] For the relationship of Greek and Latin texts see H. Varnhagen, *Zur Geschichte der Legende von Katharina von Alexandrien*, Erlangen, Junge, 1891.

Trinité-au-Mont at Rouen; this history[29] is the work of an anonymous monk writing between 1054 ('after the death of Abbot Isembert') and 1090 and comprises two parts, a history of the relics and a list of miracles occasioned by them. After summarising her life, the author relates how her body was carried by angels to Mount Sinai where, at the convent bearing her name, the monks celebrated Mass every Sunday at her tomb, leaving two of their number to collect the balm miraculously flowing from her coffin. One day a certain monk Simeon was on duty and received, together with the balm, three small bones which he concealed. Shortly afterwards Simeon was chosen as one of a four-man embassy sent by the monks to Normandy to seek the favour of Duke Richard II, who had a wide reputation for generosity. The embassy was lodged by the Duke at the house of one of his nobles, Joscelin d'Arques and his wife Emmeline, both renowned for their piety; they revealed to Simeon their plans to found an abbey. Simeon promised to give his relics to the new foundation which was consecrated to the Holy and Undivided Trinity on 26 August 1030, the first abbot being Isembert who received the relics from Simeon. After staying for two years Simeon decided to return to Sinai but fell ill and died at Trier. Then follows a list of miracles.

The story told here has been shown[30] to be a mixture of fact and fiction, as indeed are most medieval accounts of the origins of relics venerated in sanctuaries. Nevertheless it indicates the presence in Rouen in the mid-eleventh century of the reputed relics of St Catharine and confirms also that the story of the Saint's interment at Mount Sinai was widely current by this time. The relics were certainly there when Ainard, Abbot of Saint-Pierre-sur-Dives, a disciple of Isembert and sometime monk at the Abbey of La Trinité-au-Mont, composed his lost

---

[29] Publ. Père Poncelet, 'Sanctae Catharinae virginis et martyris translatio et miracula Rothomagensia saec. XI', *Analecta Bollandiana*, XXII, 423–38. This text is known as the *Miracula*.

[30] See R. Fawtier, 'Les reliques rouennaises de Sainte Cathérine d'Alexandrie', *Analecta Bollandiana*, XLI, 1923, 357–68.

Latin *historia*,[31] and probably there in the time of Abbot Isembert, since the *Miracula* record that he was cured by them of an illness.

The Rouen relics may have been the starting point of the popular cult of St Catharine in the West, and it seems probable that her fame was brought to England by the clerics who followed in the wake of William the Conqueror. Her name does not seem to appear in Anglo-Saxon Calendars and a mention of her in Bede's *Martyrology* under 'vii *Kalend. decembris*', devoted to St Peter of Alexandria ('*eodem die passio S. Catherinae virginis et martyris Christi et aliorum*') appears to be a later interpolation. After the Conquest, however, her popularity in England seems to have developed rapidly. Towards 1119 a certain Norman Geoffrey, called to the Abbey of St Albans but finding on his arrival that the office had been given to another, lectured at Dunstable while waiting for the next vacancy and there composed a *ludus de Sancta Katerina*,[32] possibly the first record of a theatrical composition in English history. In 1148 Matilda, wife of King Stephen, founded the Royal Hospital and Church of St Catherine near the Tower of London, and similar dedications followed.[33] About the same time Robert Chesney, Bishop of Lincoln (1148–66) founded the important Gilbertine priory of St Katharine without Lincoln.[34]

To judge from extant Anglo-Norman MSS it was in the twelfth and thirteenth centuries that Saints' Lives in the vernacular were composed in considerable numbers by clerkly writers working for pious lay patrons ignorant of Latin, the Anglo-Norman aristocracy being instrumental in their composition.[35] Of the score of MSS of Lives of Saints in French

[31] Mentioned by Ordericus Vitalis, writing 1120–40, in his *Hist. Eccl.*, II, 292. The Abbey of La Trinité was known in his time in popular parlance as the Abbey of Ste-Cathérine-au-Mont.
[32] H. T. Riley (ed.), *Gesta Abbatum Monasterii S. Albani*, London, 1867 (Rolls Series), I, p. 73.
[33] The City parishes of St Katherine Coleman and St Katherine Cree were also of early date. The present St Catherine's Docks in London derive their name from the ground cleared when the hospital was moved to Regent's Park in 1825.
[34] J. W. F. Hill, *Medieval Lincoln*, Cambridge U.P., 1948, pp. 346 ff.
[35] S. C. Aston, 'The Saint in Medieval Literature', *Modern Language Review*, LXV, 1970, xxv-xlii.

which have survived from the twelfth century, two-thirds are written in the Anglo-Norman dialect, while of some fifty MSS from the thirteenth century almost one-half are of similar provenance. Of these lives several deal with St Catharine. The earliest is a fragment[36] dating from the late eleventh, or early twelfth century, which starts with the visit of the Empress to Catharine in prison and concludes with the statement that three bones are preserved in the Abbey of La-Trinité-au-Mont at Rouen, a detail which may indicate the MS's affinity with Ainard's version. The poem may have been intended to be mimed.[37] More important, however, is the *Life*[38] composed in the latter part of the twelfth century by Clemence, a nun in the Benedictine Abbey of Barking, a rhymed version of 2700 lines which appears to derive from Athanasius *via* an eleventh-century Latin adaptation known as the *Vulgata*. Clemence states that she is translating, but she has added numerous commentaries and a good deal of apologetic material to her original source. That her work was well-known and of some importance and duration may be deduced from the fact that three MSS of it have survived.[39]

The Manchester fragment and Clemence's *Life* are only two of the eight lives in French surviving, in whole or in part, from the twelfth to the fourteenth centuries. No less numerous are the English versions of the story. Of these the oldest is a twelfth-century composition in the prose *Hali Meidenhad* group which, written in a West Midland dialect, possibly derived originally from Athanasius. Another Life is found in the thirteenth-century verse *South English Legendary*, a work of collaborative authorship which possibly originated in Gloucester. Two further Lives, both deriving from the *Legenda Aurea*, survive from the fourteenth century, one in the *North English*

---

[36] John Rylands Library, Manchester, MS Fr. 6. See R. Fawtier and E. C. Fawtier-Jones, *Romania*, XLIX, 1923, 321–42.
[37] See E. C. Fawtier-Jones, 'Les vies de Ste Cathérine d'Alexandrie en ancien français', *Romania*, LVI, 1930, 80–104.
[38] Ed. W. Macbain, *The Life of St Catherine*, Oxford, Anglo-Norman Text Society, XVIII, 1964.
[39] Two at the BN in Paris, dating from *c.* 1200 and the late thirteenth century, and a third in the well-known Welbeck collection, dating from the thirteenth–fourteenth century.

Legendary, probably compiled at Durham early in the century, the other, and later, in the *Scottish Verse Legendary*. The fifteenth century saw the production of further works. The *Gilte Legende*, an abbreviated version of the *Legenda Aurea*, dates from about 1430; more important, however, in the present context, because of their connection with Cambridge, are Osbern Bokenham's *Lyf of Seynt Kateryne*, one of thirteen poems contained in his *Legendys of Hooly Wummen*,[40] and the major version, extending to 8372 lines in rhyme royal, *The Life of St Katharine of Alexandria*,[41] composed about 1445 by John Capgrave.[42] Catharine's story finally reached print in England when Caxton, in 1485, included it in *The Golden Legend: the Legende of Sayntes.*

It is evident that over a period of more than five centuries there is in Western Europe a continuous and unbroken literary

---

[40] Ed. M. S. Serjeantson, London, E.E.T.S., 1938. Bokenham (*c.* 1392–*c.* 1447) an Augustinian friar of the convent of Stoke-by-Clare in Suffolk and a Doctor of Divinity, composed his *Life* about 1443–5. A note at the end of the unique MS. states that it was 'translatyd in to englys be a doctor of dyvynite clepyd Osbern Bokenham, a suffolks man, frere Austin of the convent of Stokclare, and was doon wrytyn in Canebryge by hys soun Frere Thomas Burgh': apparently the author himself feared harsh criticism from the 'capcyows wyttys' of Cambridge and so kept his name secret and had his work presented posthumously by Thomas Burgh. In 1447 the latter was in a house of friars at Cambridge; the MS. was presented to a convent of nuns in Cambridge. The *Lyf of Seynt Kateryne* is dedicated to Katherine, wife of John Denston, and to Katherine, wife of John Howard of Stoke-by-Nayland. The name of John Denston, apparently a man of some importance in the Clare area, appears in a number of local records between 1441 and 1463; there is a memorial window to him and to his daughter in the Church of Long Melford, about ten miles east of Stoke-by-Clare. It may be noted that one of the earliest documents in the St Catharine's College archives is the composition of William Cotte and Clement Denston (28 June 1475). Clement Denston, a priest who held a number of livings, was a canon of Stoke-by-Clare from 1437 to 1447 and died about 1452 (see A. B. Emden, *A Bibliographical Register of the University of Cambridge to 1500*, Cambridge U.P., 1963, p. 183).
[41] Ed. C. Horstmann, London, E.E.T.S. no. 100, 1893.
[42] Capgrave was born at King's Lynn in 1394. Nothing is known of his early education but he may have gone to Cambridge (Leland, *Com. de Script, Brit.*, ed. 1709, p. 453). He was ordained priest in 1416 or 1417 and preached in 1422 at least seven sermons in Cambridge. After a visit to Rome he returned to the Austin Friary at King's Lynn, where he became Prior and subsequently (by 1456 at latest) Prior of his Order, with jurisdiction extending as far as Oxford. In his *Liber de illustribus Henricis*, Capgrave states that he knew Master William Millington, the first Provost of King's College, and, in the same work, that he met Henry VI, for whom he attested frequently his profound admiration and devotion, when the King visited Lynn on 1 August 1456. Capgrave died at Lynn on 12 August 1464 and was buried there.

tradition associated with St Catharine and one which must have been well-known to the educated members of the community as well as to the ecclesiastics. The written texts are a source of the wider cult of the saint; at the same time they are a testimony to it. Catharine's legendary skill in debate, her learning and her wisdom, offered an immediate appeal to the medieval academic and she was the obvious choice as the guardian saint of philosophers and theologians. As early as the beginning of the thirteenth century the Faculty of Theology of the University of Paris recognized her as patroness, an example followed by numerous other institutions in Europe. Similarly, her cult extended steadily in the Church; and if, on a higher plane, she was mystically elevated to become the Bride of Christ, a development widely reflected in the art of the fourteenth and fifteenth centuries, she was equally venerated by the lowly as one of those saints who, through their purity, simplicity and human appeal became by the fourteenth century an object of veneration and appeal for all Christians. She is numbered, together with Saints Barbara and Margaret, among the Fourteen Holy Helpers, a cult first advanced by the Dominicans and developed especially in Germany, where their Feast was celebrated on 8 August.

With the rise of the artisan guilds in the thirteenth and fourteenth centuries, her popularity developed in the lay world. The Saint's emblem of the wheel led to her adoption as the patron saint of many groups, such as wheel-wrights, turners, spinners, potters, mariners, etc. Her virginal sanctity made her, too, the natural protector of the unmarried woman, of the nun and of the female student. In the latter connection her cult appears to have developed particularly in Nuremberg; it was especially fostered by the Dominican sisters of St Catharine and spread throughout Germany and Western Europe to receive an additional impulse in France in the first half of the fifteenth century, when it was rumoured that she had appeared to Joan of Arc and, together with St Margaret, had been divinely appointed Joan's advisor. It is, indeed, in the fifteenth century that St Catharine attains her full popular saintly stature and enters most fully into the hearts, minds, and vision

Plate I

τῆ ἀυτῆ ἡμιρα. ἀθλησις τῆς αγιας μεγαλομάρ
τυρος αικατερίνης.

Η μάρτυσ αι καντερίνα. ἀρμῶτο λᾶος ἀρέξανδρείασ. θυ
γατηρ μαξιλίου λεου τι ροσ. ηρουσίου καὶ ἐνδόξου.
ἀμορφοσ σάμιν. ἀρ η νολέ υσπαρχουσα. ὅμα θχ
Ἑλληνικὰ γράμματα. καὶ ἀρμῶτοσ ΦΚ. λαθουσα
Καὶ γλῶσσαι. σπάντα ρτόμε θμῶν. ὄυβ τ6 λει το
Δε υορτι τοις ειδώλοιο. σπαρ ἀ τῶ μ6 Αλί μων. Καὶ
ν καρθουσα ται ζῶα σ ἀ ραβ ὸμ6ναι. ὁ λυω λί θι. καὶ ἀ
πολι ηθμ εισ το μ μαξιλ θαμμα β όμ τίομ. καὶ ἐ Φι λο
μ εικ κ η ὀβμ ἀυτόμ. ἐι σπουσα σα ὅτι δια τί ἀγ καταλιπὸ
Θ ῦ ζ ῶρ ται. καὶ σπρο σκυμ εισ ἐι δώλοι σ ἀ υ ηρ οισ.
ὁκ ε ι μ ο ο δ6 ὅ τ μ ἀπ ο θμ ἀ υτλιυ. καὶ ἐξι μμ ο ρ ησα το]ο χ ρα ο σ.
Καὶ μ6 ἀυτου το. ὁ Φ6 ρ β ρ ο μαξιλ δο σ πθμ τῆ κο μ τ ά ρ η τ ο ρ α σ.
Καὶ ἐι πβμ ἀυτοι σ. ὅτι δια ρ6 Χ λ τ6 σπρο ο τὴμ αι καντερίμα.
Καὶ π εισα σ ἀ υτῆμ. ὁ α μ γαρ μλή μικ η ολ τ6 ἀ υτῆ μ. πάμ Τα σ
ν μα ο κ ατα υ λίω σο πυρί. ὁκ ἐι μοι δ6 ι δ ο ρ τ6 ὅτι6μ ικ η θμ σα.
ὁ υ α π τι ο θμ σα μ κ αὶ ὁ υ πω σ ὁκ α ι κ σα μ. ἀπ ε κε φ α λ ί ο θ η δ6 σ α υ τή.

Reproduction from the facsimile edition of P. Franchi de' Cavalieri,
Il Menologio di Basilio II, Turin, 1907, p. 207.

PLATE II

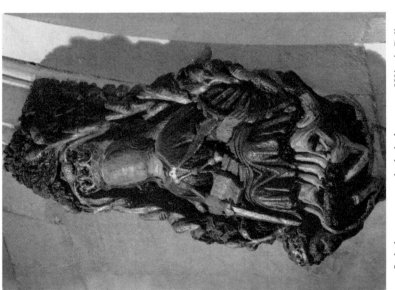

B. Label-stops on south choir doorway of King's College, Chapel, Cambridge, showing St Margaret

Photos: E. Leigh, Cambridge (by kind permission of the Provost and Fellows of King's College)

A. Label-stops on south choir doorway of King's College Chapel, Cambridge, showing St Catharine, with emblems (crown, wheel, sword, book, palm, and tyrant) beneath her feet

of all sections of the communities of all countries of Western
Europe. The devotion and veneration she had long inspired in
scholars, clerics and laymen find wider expression. Artists,
miniaturists, illuminators and sculptors alike, inspired by a
new humanism and a new realism, combine to depict her
beauty, her wisdom and her saintliness in tangible form. She is
frequently, and like many other saints, shown with a book, the
emblem of learning; a sword, indicating death by decapitation;
a crown or sceptre, indicating either royal birth on earth or the
martyr's crown in heaven; a palm, the emblem of heavenly
reward; a dove, the symbol of purity and innocence. More
specifically, she is shown with a wheel; and sometimes with the
pagan tyrant beneath her feet, symbolically portraying the
triumph over tyranny and persecution.

In England, the growth of the cult of St Catharine is revealed
by similar developments and may be indicated by a few specific
examples. Her introduction during the Norman period has
been noted above. In the mid-thirteenth century her festival
was promoted from the second class, that is from a day on
which agricultural labour, but no other, was permitted, to the
first class of holy days on which no work was permitted.[43]
In the fourteenth century she has entered into the Canon of the
Mass, as is shown, for example, by a passage in a Cambridge
University MS. (Dd. 1.1) of the fourteenth century:

> Katerine, Mergrete and Agace
> Deyden for this bred of grace,
> Ther for it is riht her name to be
> Nemened in the canone;
> Ffor alle these deyde in good entent
> For to mayntene this sacrement.

> (p. 38v, ll. 29–34)

Among the trades in England which adopted St Catharine as
patron saint may be noted in particular the bell-founders,[44]
especially those of London, many of whose bells, dedicated to
St Catharine, still exist, particularly in Essex (20), Kent (11)

---

[43] *Concilium Oxoniense* (1222), cap. 8, and *Synodus Wigorniensis* (1240), cap. 54.
In J. D. Mansi, *Concilia*, Venice, 1798, Vol. 22, p. 1154 and Vol. 23, p. 548.
[44] See H. B. Walters, *Church Bells of England*, Oxford U.P., 1912.

and Somerset (19); in particular, William and Robert Burford
(1350–1420) inscribed on a number of their bells *Sancta
Katerina ora pro nobis*. Although St Catharine, as indicated
above, comes twenty-sixth in the list of dedications, among the
saints who have bells named after them she is third, with 160
dedications, following the Virgin Mary (900) and St John
Baptist or Evangelist (260). The most charming of all the
examples is that at Shapwick in Dorset:

> I KATERY(N)E GODDES DERLYNG
> TO THE(E) MARI SHAL I SY(N)G

The adoption of Catharine as patron saint by the bell-founders
dates from the time when bells began to be rung by wheel and
rope. In the fifteenth century the appearance (1438) of an
English version of the *Legenda Aurea*, containing, apparently for
the first time, an account of the mystical marriage of Catharine
and Christ, appears to have served as a stimulus for the
artistic expression of the story. A further direct impetus to the
popularity of St Catharine in the fifteenth century seems to
have been given by the grant in 1442 of a new charter by
Henry VI to the Hospital of St Catherine in London, which
exempted the neighbouring land from all ecclesiastical and
similar jurisdiction except that of the Lord Chancellor and the
Master of the Hospital.[45] As a testimony to the consequent
enhanced popularity of the cult of St Catharine, Browne[46]
cites a passage from Reginald Pecock's *The Repressor of overmuch
blaming of the Clergy* (1455), which in view of its value as contemporary evidence, is worth repeating here,[47] not merely
because, as Browne observes, Wodelarke's first purchase of
property for his future College is only four years later, but also

---

[45] Henry's grant of land was made *ad laudem gloriam et honorem Crucifixi et beatissime
Virginis Marie matris ejus necnon gloriose virginis et martyris Katerine*. Compare the
preamble to the Founder's Statutes for St Catharine's College; *Ego Robertus
Wodelarke . . . unum collegium sive aulam . . . erexi, fundavi et stabilivi ad laudem, gloriam et
honorem Domini nostri Jesu Christi, gloriosissimae virginis Mariae matris ejus et sanctae
Katerinae virginis . . .* Given the formal and even stereotyped nature of both dedications, it is not suggested, of course, that there is necessarily anything here more
than a fortuitous parallel.

[46] In his *St Catharine's College*, London, Robinson, 1902, p. 9.

[47] Reginald Pecock, *The Repressor . . . Clergy*, London, Rolls Series, 2 vols, 1860;
Pt 2, chap. XI, 208 ff.

because of the reaction against Pecock in Cambridge and, in particular, in King's College. Defending images and pilgrimages against the arguments of the Lollards and pointing out that visible signs, no less than books, are profitable to Christians for whom writings are less available, Pecock observes that images and pictures serve in a more special manner than books, continuing: 'Confirmacioun into this purpos mai be this: Whanne the dai of Seint Kateryn schal be come, marke who so wole in his mynde alle the bokis whiche ben in Londoun writun upon Seint Kateryn's lijf and passiouns, and y dare weel seie that though ther were x. thousind mo bokis writun in Londoun in thilk day of the same Seintis lijf and passioun, thei schulden not so moche turn the citee into mynde of the holi famose lijf of Seint Kateryn and of her dignitee in which sche now is, as dooth in ech year the going of peple in pilgrimage to the College of Seint Kateryn bisidis Londoun, as y dare putte this into iugement of whom ever hath seen the pilgrimage doon in the vigil of Seint Katheryn bi persones of Londoun to the seid College. Wherfore right greet special commoditees and profitis into remembraunce making ymagis and pilgrimagis han and doon, which writingis not so han and doon.' Pecock's theological views, and in particular his defence of bishops, attracted considerable opposition in the Universities; one of his most formidable adversaries in Cambridge was William Millington, first Provost of King's College, who preached a sermon against him in St Paul's. In Henry VI's Statutes for King's College there is a prohibition against the residence there of any disciple of Wyclif or Pecock, whence perhaps an indication of Wodelarke's own attitude towards Pecock.[48]

Thus, when Wodelarke came to choose a patron saint for his little foundation he may have been influenced by any one, or by any combination, of a number of considerations. It has been suggested[49] that the name of the new College may have been

[48] For the dating of the Founder's Statutes of King's College, see J. Saltmarsh, 'The Founder's Statutes of King's College, Cambridge', *Studies presented to Sir Hilary Jenkinson,* Oxford U.P. 1957, pp. 337–60. I offer my thanks to Mr Saltmarsh for his helpful advice on this point, and on several other matters affecting the early domestic history of King's College.

[49] W. H. S. Jones, *A History of St Catharine's College,* Cambridge U.P., 1936, p. 46.

an accident, in that, if the College buildings became ready to
receive their first occupants just before St Catharine's Day, the
name may have presented itself. Against this suggestion three
major objections can be raised. First, Wodelarke's own appointments, responsibilities and achievements indicate that he was a
competent and well-organized administrator and, as such, one
who would be unlikely to leave an important detail like this to a
chance completion-date of the local builder. Secondly, prepara-
tions for the new College had been in hand for fourteen years.
Thirdly, the texts of the *Memoriale Nigrum* (*Quod opus praedictum
in festo sanctae Katerinae virginis anno domini MCCCCLXXIII
consummatum et ad perfectum deventum est*) and the Founder's
Statutes (*Fundatum et stabilitum fuit hoc collegium in festo sanctae
Katerinae virginis anno domini MCCCCLXXIII*) both indicate a
firm intent and a deliberately chosen opening day. An accidental nomenclature hardly enters, therefore, into serious
consideration.

An obvious, but none the less real, possibility is that Wodelarke chose the name for purely private reasons. He may have
felt a personal devotion to St Catharine; for this possibility some
evidence may be found (. . . *Cum tu ob specialem devotionem,
quam ad sanctam Katerinam virginem et martirem habeas et geras* . . .)
in the licence, dated 26 September 1478, for divine worship in
the College Chapel, although in the context this passage may
have a general, as well as a personal, application. The reasons
for such a devotion must be conjectural. It might have been
occasioned either by personal circumstances or by past experience, or yet again by fortuitous events or by a contemporary
climate. It was not unusual for a medieval man to appropriate
to himself a special saintly patron; the day of his birth might be
deemed to place him under the protection of a particular
saint no less than under a particular star.[50] Wodelarke might

---

[50] In a collection of omens (ed. D. Bassi and E. Martin, Brussels, 1903, pp. 158–9)
the invocation of various saints, among them Catharine, is recommended. The
saints listed are apparently those whose names were given to the stars from which
portents were read. H. Delehaye (*Les Légendes hagiographiques*, p. 125) suggests
that the practice may represent, in a Christian setting, a survival from pagan
antiquity.

conceivably have wished to recall an earlier personal association with, for example, a church[51] or an academic institution.[52] In the complete absence of information about Wodelarke's early life, factors of this kind, although not necessarily
irrelevant or unimportant, are a matter of pure speculation
and it is more prudent to consider other possibilities[53] of a
more specific nature.

A particular personal consideration is advanced by Browne.
Remarking on the fact that Wodelarke had stood high in the
favour of Henry VI, for whom indeed his affectionate memory
is well attested by the *Memoriale Nigrum* and the Founder's
Statutes, Browne observes that the King's mother, Catherine
of Valois, bore the name of the saint. Henry himself was
royally commemorated at King's College, while Queens'
College, the foundation of his wife Margaret of Anjou, was
dedicated to St Margaret. Might not St Catharine's, therefore,
commemorate the mother? Browne offers no evidence for his
suggestion, but some circumstantial support for it could be
adduced. The Founder's Statutes of King's College ordain that
Masses are to be celebrated daily for Henry VI's father and
mother and also each year, on the anniversary of their deaths,
for his father, mother, and wife. On the South choir doorway
in King's College Chapel are two label stops, depicting St
Catharine and St Margaret, which are believed to allude to
the two ladies and which were carved before 1461, at a time
when Wodelarke was directly concerned with the building of
the Chapel. There is some possibility, therefore, that a further

[51] The church in his native Wakerley is dedicated to St John Baptist. St Catharine is not associated with any of the churches and livings in Cambridgeshire
which Wodelarke is known to have held; from 1453 to 1460, the free chapel at
Whittlesford; from 1457–8, the rectory of Kingston (All Saints and St Andrew),
from 1471–to 1470 the rectory of Coton (St Peter); and from 1474 the rectory of
Fulbourn (St Vigor).

[52] Nothing is known of Wodelarke's early life, but he might have studied theology,
as so many of his contemporaries did, at the University of Paris. In this context it
may be noted that the first Fellow of St Catharine's, Peter Welde, admitted on
26 November 1473, is styled *Picardus natione*. The designation may indicate that
Welde had been a member of one of the four 'nations' (Picard, Norman, English,
French) in that University.

[53] A number of these, further discussed here, are considered by, for example,
G. F. Browne, op. cit., pp. 6–11; W. H. S. Jones, op. cit., pp. 45–6, and Id., *The
Story of St Catharine's College*, Cambridge, Heffer, 1951, pp. 4–5.

and more specific commemoration of Catherine of Valois may not have been absent from Wodelarke's mind and that his purchase in 1459 and 1460 of the three tenements in Mylstrete were intended, at least at that time, to be the first steps in the realisation of this design. By 1473, however, certain practical difficulties had obtruded. After the death of her husband Henry V in 1422, Catherine had married two years later an obscure Welsh gentleman, Owen Tudor. She had died in 1438, without leaving any great mark on English history, while her second husband had been killed in 1461, fighting on the Lancastrian side against the Yorkists. Two years before the foundation of St Catharine's Henry VI had been finally ousted by the Yorkist Edward IV and murdered. Bearing in mind the difficulties with which the change of régime had faced the Provost of King's College it is questionable whether Wodelarke would have been well-advised publicly to under-line an attachment to the House of Lancaster. Further, while his Statutes for St Catharine's ordain a weekly requiem Mass for the repose of the soul of Henry VI, there is no similar in-junction in respect of the King's mother, as there surely would have been if the new College had been intended to honour her memory. On balance, therefore, it seems probable that a commemoration of Catherine of Valois was at most a supple-mentary, and silent, factor in Wodelarke's choice of a name for his his new foundation.

Browne also hazards a general suggestion, although not very strongly, that a connection may have existed between Wode-larke's new foundation and the already existing hostel of St Katherine, and advances a few tenuous details of a possible relationship. This hostel occupied a site in St Michael's Lane (now Trinity Lane) on what is now the South-East corner of Trinity Great Court. Michaelhouse had acquired the property in 1349 and the estate was first known as Refham's messuage and later as the Mighell Angel or St Katherine's Hostel. In 1476 it was sold to Matthew Chambers and others, but was again left to Michaelhouse in 1494 by a widow Edith Chambers, who left a life interest in the property to a relative, Thomas Ayeray; he used it as a 'grammar hostel'. It was still called St Katherine's

Hostel in 1494; in 1508 it was designated as 'the grammar hostel now in the tenure of Maister Thomas Ayeray, clerke', subsequently as Edith Chambers House, a name ultimately corrupted into Edith's Chambers, under which title it was leased in 1552 for forty years to Trinity College. The fact that its name and style varied so frequently might have been due to the fact that the new St Catharine's had come into existence; but a dual nomenclature might equally well have continued. The dedication of King's College to St Nicholas and of Queens' College to St Margaret did not terminate the existence of St Nicholas' Hostel[54] nor of St Margaret's Hostel (which, in fact, was located next door to St Katherine's Hostel). In short there seems at present no real evidence to link the name of St Catharine's with that of the older Hostel.

Another possibility, although again perhaps no more than a supplementary factor, is that Wodelarke was influenced by the contemporary climate of mid-fifteenth-century England. The wide popularity of St Catharine among all sections of society at this time has been noted, and even the learned academic is not necessarily detached from current trends. Within the wider context, moreover, certain individual events or contacts might conceivably have acted as a particular focus. The notable grant made by Henry VI to the Royal Hospital and Church of St Catherine in London may not have gone unnoticed by his admirer Wodelarke and such an interest might have been specifically sharpened on the one hand by the *Lives* of Capgrave and Osbern Bokenham, and on the other by an opposition to the views of Reginald Pecock.[55] Capgrave was personally acquainted with the first Provost of King's College, of which College Wodelarke was himself an original Fellow and hence may also have known Capgrave. He may also have known, if not the man himself, at least Bokenham's work,

---

[54] See note 8, *supra*.

[55] The opposition to Pecock's views in Cambridge, especially by the Provost of King's College, has been noted. Wodelarke's choice of St Catharine as the patron saint of a learned institution concerned with 'holi bokis' could indicate the deliberate reaction of a serious scholar against the popular and unlearned veneration of St Catharine indicated in the passage quoted from Pecock.

either through Thomas Burgh or through the Denston connection. It may be noted that in the list of *Libri in Capella ex dono Fundatoris et aliorum*[56] are three texts devoted to St Catharine: *unum pervum Gradale cum missis de sancta Katrina* . . .; an *Istoria Ste Katrine cum notis in tribus libellis*; and a *Legenda Ste Katrine cum istoria sine notis*. There were a number of Latin Lives available in fifteenth-century England, but one is tempted to wonder whether the three-volume history of Saint Catharine may have been a copy of Capgrave's *Life* and the smaller volume one of Bokenham's.

In the absence of sure evidence to support these various conjectures it is safer to rely on the testimony of authentic documents; that is to say, on the Charter of 1475, on the Founder's account of the foundation of the College, and above all on the Founder's Statutes. Here, four points are of importance. First, that Wodelarke founded a College or Hall in Mylstrete not only *ad laudem, gloriam et honorem Domini nostri Jesu Christi*, etc., and in *augmentum scientiarum et facultatum philosophiae et sacrae theologiae*, but also *in exaltationem Christianae fidei, Ecclesiae sanctae defensam et profectum per seminationem et administrationem verbi Dei*, and drew up his Statutes 'after taking the advice of learned men'. Secondly, the foundation provides for a Master and three Fellows, with no mention of undergraduates; hence the new College is a community of scholars divorced from teaching and dedicated to study, not a hall or residence nor place of instruction for the junior students of the University. Thirdly, the Fellows take an oath not to consent to any Fellow proceeding to a degree other than in philosophy and sacred theology. Fourthly, Wodelarke gives instructions at some length as to the prayers and masses to be said for the repose of his soul. In short, the College is at once a chantry and a place where the ancient higher studies were to be maintained to the exclusion of all others. For such a foundation the nomination of St Catharine as its patron saint would be, whatever the influence of any personal devotion or of any

[56] See G. E. Corrie, *Catalogue of Books given to the Library and Chapel by Wodelarke*, Cambridge Antiquarian Society, 1840, reprinted by W. H. S. Jones, *A History* . . ., pp. 367–81.

contemporary vogue or event, the obvious and even logical choice. It would continue the old academic tradition of St Catharine as the patron saint of theologians and philosophers; it acknowledged her special position as a patron saint of all devout Christians and as a shining luminary of the old and true faith; and it recognized her reputation as one of the supremely powerful intercessors in Heaven for the forgiveness of sins and for the eternal repose of the soul in Paradise.

In making his choice, Wodelarke may have had one further major consideration in mind. The traditional curriculum and outlook of the medieval university were being progressively eroded in the fifteenth century by the new approach to learning represented by the current of Humanism which, along with new attitudes of mind engendered by a growing awareness of the needs and claims of the contemporary lay world, cast doubt upon the usefulness and validity of the old learning and of long-established studies and methods. Of this new trend and its growing impact on the fifteenth-century universities new collegiate foundations at Oxford were already the tangible recognition, and the provision they made for new approaches and the emphasis they placed on other and more worldly branches of learning must have seemed, as all new trends and ideas do, undesirable and even potentially dangerous to older and more conservative academic minds. Wodelarke, as his Statutes indicate, seems to have remained, in outlook as well as in sympathies, devoted to the old order, a conservative man whose private thoughts turned towards salvation rather than to the exploration of the material world, and whose views of academic life inclined to the medieval ideal of contemplation and of study rather than to a participation and a leadership in the new ideas stirring in the contemporary world without, an Ancient in an emerging world of Moderns. He sought to establish, in opposition to the new-fangled trends, a collegiate community of scholars who would uphold the pure traditions of the past, who would maintain the time-honoured disciplines and who would perpetuate the medieval belief that the proper object of all study was the quest for God. And of that community St Catharine of Alexandria by reason of her

5

long-established cult, her legendary learning and her exemplary devotion to the faith, would be at once the mirror, the patron and the inspiration.

It was a choice which, however noble and honourable in conception, was probably dis-advantageous for at least the immediate development of the College. The pre-occupation with venerable studies tended to isolate the College from the main currents of thought in the new academic world of the sixteenth century, leaving it as a kind of backwater and defender of the past and hence unfashionable; this in its turn may have contributed to the failure of the College to enlist the support and benefactions of the coming men in the new and turbulent society of the Reformation period who might have ensured a participation in the distribution of the land and wealth wrenched from the old monastic orders. And while St John might continue to find favour in the eyes of the pro-tagonists of the Protestant revolution, St Catharine would remain in those same eyes associated with the old faith and become, together with a host of other saints of the ancient church, a target for the iconoclast and the popular preacher.

Catharine Hall and The Reformation
1500 – 1650

By H. C. PORTER

Cambridge University Lecturer in History

THE Oxonian John Evelyn visited Cambridge in September 1654. Although he admired the 'very ample' Market Place, he thought the town 'situated in a low dirty unpleasant place, the streetes ill paved, the aire thick, as infested by the fenns'. No church, even Great St Mary's, was 'anything considerable in compare to *Oxford* which is doubtlesse the noblest Universitie now in the whole World'. He visited eleven Colleges: King's Chapel did not disappoint expectation, Clare was 'noble', Peterhouse 'neate', Sidney Sussex 'fine', Emmanuel 'zealous', Jesus 'one of the best built', Christ's 'of exact Architecture'. The Great Court of Trinity was 'in truth far inferior to that of *Christ-Church*'. '*Kathrine*-hall', Evelyn found, was of 'meane structure': 'yet famous for the learned *B:Andrews* once Master'.[1]

The diarist's charity in giving credit where credit was due was suspiciously ill-informed. Bishop Lancelot Andrewes had been Master of Pembroke.

Condescension mitigated by inaccuracy was perhaps appropriate for a community which even by the 1650s could properly be considered only as among the minor Cambridge colleges. David Loggan's engraving of Catharine Hall, published in 1690, but perhaps drawn a dozen years before, tactfully added an East block to the court then under construction — a range which in the event was never to be built. Loggan wished to

---

[1] *The Diary of John Evelyn*, ed. E. S. de Beer, III (1955), 139. The description of Cambridge is on pages 136–40.

show both 'the buildings newly erected' and 'those at present only projected, but which it is hoped may shortly be completed'. The 'fragmentary remains' of the 'ancient housing' he declined to depict, being 'a spectacle too hideous to find a place among the Colleges of the University' :'a confined hovel, ill-timbered and frail from the very beginning'.[2] Thomas Fuller, a Queens' man, writing in 1634 — when Richard Sibbes was nearing the end of his Mastership — had been kinder.[3] Catharine Hall, he said, if not a 'proper' Hall, was a 'pretty' one; and he quoted Martial, to the effect that small things are most flatteringly called pretty. For Fuller, the architecture of the College was 'proportionably most complete in chapel, cloisters, library, hall, etc.' The hindrance had been 'lowness of endowment and littleness of receipt' — and therefore shortage of accommodation; lately remedied by the new buildings begun in 1631.

In Elizabethan Cambridge, Catharine Hall and Magdalene had been, architecturally, the two least spacious colleges. University fire regulations of 1575 laid down the number of buckets appropriate to each college: King's, Trinity and St John's needed eight, Clare and Queens' five; four were required for Jesus, Peterhouse, Pembroke, Corpus, Clare, Trinity Hall, and Caius; Catharine Hall, like Magdalene, could make do with only two — plus one scoop and two ladders.[4]

[2] From the caption to Loggan's engraving of St Catharine's, translated by J. W. Clark (Loggan, *Cantabrigia Illustrata*, ed. Clark, 1905, Plate xxiii). The caption may have been written by Eachard.
[3] Thomas Fuller, *The History of the University of Cambridge from the Conquest to the year 1634*. First edition 1655. Edited M. Prickett and T. Wright, 1840, pp. 168–9.
[4] Charles Henry Cooper, *Annals of Cambridge*, ii, 356–7. Volume i of Cooper's *Annals* (1842) goes to 1546; Volume ii (1843) to 1602; Volume iii (1845) to 1688. The majority of my quotations can be found in the *Annals*, under the appropriate year. Another collection of original documents I have used is J. Heywood and T. Wright, *Cambridge University Transactions during the Puritan Controversies of the 16th and 17th Centuries*, 2 vols, 1854. Biographical information is found in J. Venn and J. A. Venn, *Alumni Cantabrigienses*, Part i (to 1751), 4 vols, 1922–7; C. H. Cooper and T. Cooper, *Athenae Cantabrigienses*, 1500–1609, 3 vols, 1858–1913; and the *Dictionary of National Biography*. J. B. Mullinger's *The University of Cambridge* is a neglected Victorian classic: Volume i, to 1535, 1873; Vol. ii, 1535–1625, 1884; Vol. iii, 1625 to the Restoration period, 1911. G. F. Browne's *St Catharine's College* was published in 1902. In 1936 appeared W. H. S. Jones's *A History of St Catharine's*

The 'old' or 'little' Court of the College, measuring about fifty-six feet by forty-five feet, had two stories, and was made of stone and wood — not the resplendent brick of Queens', across the street, or of St John's (to be praised by Evelyn). The entrance gate, with the porter's room above it, was in Milne (or Mill) Street, now Queens' Lane: probably where 'D' staircase now stands. In addition to the residential 'chambers' (or sets: which could be partitioned into separate studies and bedrooms) there were, on the north side (towards King's) the Hall, kitchen and buttery, and perhaps a 'parler'. (Evelyn in 1654 was to think it worthy of note that Emmanuel had a 'Parler for the fellows'.) The library was at the far end of that range, maybe with a cloister below it. This library at the beginning of the sixteenth century had about 140 volumes of manuscripts, presented by Woodlark, kept in seven cases or 'stalls'; about the size of the Pembroke library, quite respectably large — Peterhouse had over three hundred volumes, and so did the University Library, but probably no other library in the University had more than two hundred. The range opposite the entrance gate contained the Treasury (with the muniments) and the rooms of the Master, probably four of them, from one of which he could look into the Chapel, which was towards Silver Street (then Small Bridge Street). The College stable was probably behind this range. On the Silver Street side of the court (now the Master's Lodge garden) was a garden/orchard belonging to Queens', with some sheds in it, and maybe a cottage or two. To the east of the court were the gardens and back premises of the properties on the High Street (now Trumpington Street). In 1517, when Thomas Green was Master, a 'new structure of four chambers' was built on Milne Street, towards the Queens' garden. But for the rest of the sixteenth century the only substantial addition to the fabric was the gallery built by an Elizabethan bursar (demolished in favour of new buildings in the early seventeenth century).

College; in 1951 his abridged version of this, *The Story of St Catharine's College*; and in 1959 his essay on the College in Victoria County Histories: *The City and University of Cambridge*, ed. J. P. C. Roach, pp. 415–20.

Thus the inhabitants of Tudor Catharine Hall were relatively undisturbed by masons, carpenters, joiners, plumbers, and tilers. The windows were probably glazed in the Elizabethan period.[5]

In 1534 (part of the 'Tudor Revolution in Government') the colleges in England were valued, together with religious houses, bishoprics and archbishoprics, with a view to possible taxation: not, it transpired, to be levied on colleges — Henry VIII was fortunately fonder of dons than of bishops. If we discount King's and St John's, disgustingly rich, the average value of the fourteen Cambridge Colleges was about £100. Catharine Hall, valued at £39, was the poorest. The next most lowly was Trinity Hall, at £72 (Magdalene was not founded until 1542). Corpus, Clare, Jesus, and Gonville Hall were also valued at less than £100. Between £100 and £200 came (the wealthiest first) Christ's, Pembroke, Peterhouse, and Michaelhouse. King's Hall was set at £211; Queens', £230; St John's, £507; King's, £751. King's was thus eighteen times wealthier than Catharine Hall (Trinity was founded in 1546, incorporating King's Hall and Michaelhouse). In 1542 there was a Cambridge assessment for contributions to military expenses. Catharine Hall, at ten shillings, was the only college assessed at less than £1. The next poorest — a group of three: Trinity Hall, Gonville Hall, and Clare — were each assessed at twenty-four shillings (and King's at £4). Four years later, in 1546, there was a survey of Cambridge Colleges, which put the annual income of Catharine Hall at nearly £56. Magdalene was now on the scene; and the fact that its annual income was less than £44 meant that Catharine Hall was now for the moment promoted to *second* poorest — from henceforth the College had a companion in desolation. The next poorest colleges in 1546 had £119. The

[5] On the College buildings the basic authority is R. Willis and J. W. Clark *The Architectural History of the University of Cambridge and of the Colleges of Cambridge and Eton*, Volume II, 1886, pp. 69–110. This chapter was prepared by Robert Willis, helped by Henry Philpott (Master, 1845–61), and edited by Clark, with the advice of C. K. Robinson (Master, 1861–1909) and G. F. Browne. There are further suggestions, and more illustrations, in Jones's *History*, and *Story*. In *Story*, p. 53, Jones has a good 'Plan of the College in 1634'; his 'Conjectural View' of the College in 1634, p. 57 — with a superimposed drawing of the College in 1951 — is less authoritative, but interesting.

average yearly income of a Cambridge don was about £5 (some King's dons got £10): the Fellows of Catharine Hall received £4. The Master got £5; the average college stipend of a Cambridge Master was about £8.

Later Tudor and Stuart statistics confirm these comparative valuations. Colleges were assessed in 1554 for their contribution to a new silver cross for the University (this was in the reign of Mary). Magdalene paid 10/-, Catharine Hall 16s. 8d.; the next lowest was 33s. 4d. (Trinity was now the financial star, with £5. 6s. 8d.: King's paid £4). Over a century later, in 1657, the sixteen colleges were rated for a poor relief levy. Trinity was to raise over £5, King's and St John's over £4. The average contribution of the other thirteen was over 30/-. Catharine Hall was expected to provide 8/-. The next lowest contributions, of £1. 1s. 4d., were to come from Magdalene, Corpus, Pembroke, Trinity Hall, and Sidney Sussex (founded 1596).[6]

It is only fair to add that in the following year, 1658, money was collected from each of the colleges for the relief of Protestants in Poland.[7] Trinity and St John's each gave over £8. The average contribution of the other colleges was £2. 15s. 0d. The Catharine Hall of John Lightfoot gave £3. 5s. 0d.; being fifth on the scale of generosity (exceeded by Trinity, St John's, Clare, and Caius). The College could rise to the evangelical occasion. Money can mysteriously be raised when necessary for a college image.

The original establishment at Catharine Hall of a Master and three priests was enlarged. The number of Fellows was raised to six after an endowment of 1515, under Green — this sixth Fellowship (a gift of £124 ensuring an annual payment of £4) was the last to be founded until 1919. In 1503 Richard Nelson, Vicar of Sawston, a Cambridge B.A. of 1469, had given £100 for a Fellowship — with a preference for Westmorland men. And in 1506 the income from three estates had been channelled by a former Fellow of Peterhouse, Dr William Stockdale, into a fund for a new Fellowship at Catharine Hall. Thus, in the 1546 Cambridge survey, six dons were recorded at the College.

---

[6] Heywood and Wright, *Transactions*, II, 584.
[7] Heywood and Wright, *Transactions*, II, 600–1.

In its Fellowship, Catharine Hall was the second smallest college: Magdalene had only four Fellows. St John's and King's had each about fifty: Trinity, to be founded in December, was to have sixty. Queens' had twenty-one; Peterhouse and Pembroke fifteen each; Clare and Christ's twelve each; Gonville Hall eleven; Trinity Hall ten; Corpus nine; and Jesus seven. Michaelhouse had eleven and King's Hall twenty-five, at the end of their separate existences — the eve of their merger into Trinity.

The 1546 survey gives details also about college servants. The Catharine Hall of Reginald Bainbridge was appropriately modest, with a cook, butler, and laundress. A laundress had first been mentioned in 1517; the first paid professional servant, it seems, in the history of the College. She lived in the town. In other Cambridge colleges at the end of the reign of Henry VIII were to be found grooms, stable lads, cellarers, bell ringers, and other lowlier 'ministers', from brewers to scullions — all counted as 'privileged' persons, within the jurisdiction of the University: a constant source of friction, this, with the borough. The Catharine Hall 'butler' may have been a student: there was certainly a student butler in Elizabethan times, and a student cook — and the College had student porters until the middle of the eighteenth century (and again in World War II). A good idea, probably; undergraduate barmen in modern college bars can be as reliable as, and pleasanter than, salaried professionals.

The word 'undergraduate' was not common until the 1630s. The Tudor and Stuart word was 'scholar' (used of all junior members, not, as today, only of award holders): or, more frequently, 'student'. The modern tendency, deplored by some, to call students 'students' is thus traditional. The nomenclature can be confusing, because M.A.s were often called 'students', and 'scholar' could mean anything from a freshman to a Doctor of Divinity. The distinction between *socius* (Fellow), *scholaris* (B.A.), *discipulus* (foundation scholar) was not rigidly adhered to in college surveys. *Discipulus* was often used of any student. Fourth year men (the degree course was four years) were *sophistae seniores*, third year men *sophistae juniores*: 'second year' and 'first year' were normal usage. More conversationally, undergraduates were called 'the younger sort of scholars', 'young gentlemen and scholars' (1594: education and gentility had become synonomous), 'the boys', or (more frequently in the seventeenth century) 'the lads'.

The 1546 Cambridge survey made no mention of any fee-paying students: pensioners (*pensio*: a payment). Figures were given only for subsidized 'scholars' (in the modern sense); and it is not always clear whether these were undergraduates or B.A.s. Magdalene and Catharine Hall each had one such. Richard Nelson had given money in 1517 for a Bible Clerk at Catharine Hall: *bibliotista*, to read aloud during meals, and act as waiter (how he did both is not clear); he also sang in chapel, and was rather like a modern Choral Scholar. This was the earliest junior member of the College to receive money: we have seen that the butler, the cook and the porter may also have been 'in statu pupillari'. University matriculation records began in 1544, and it appears that for the next half century about ten junior members entered Catharine Hall every year (many would leave without completing the four-year course). In 1558, apparently, Catharine Hall had four pensioners (some of whom may have been Fellow Commoners: eating at the Fellows' table), and eight *discipuli* (these appear to include the cook and the butler, as well as the Bible Clerk). It is indeed possible that there had always been Fellow Commoners at Catharine Hall, who were really junior members.

The statistics, it will be perceived, can be puzzling. But we have what appear to be reliable figures for the early 1570s and the early 1630s.[8] In 1573 Catharine Hall was the smallest college, with just over thirty resident members: the Master, six Fellows, the Bible Clerk, the three servants, and twenty-one pensioners. There were nearly 1,800 members of the University in 1573, as against 1,300 twenty years earlier. (The population of the borough was around 5,000.) About 320 Fellows; over 400 Foundation Scholars; and over 1,000 pensioners. Catharine

[8] 1573 figures from John Caius, *Historiae Cantabrigiensis Academiae*, published 1574; in Cooper's *Annals* under 1573 (II, 315–16). 1634: in Fuller, ed. Prickett and Wright (in his accounts of each separate College).

Hall had the fewest pensioners. Above it, in ascending order and with approximate figures, came Trinity Hall (thirty), Caius (thirty-five), Magdalene (forty), Pembroke (fifty), Corpus (fifty), Peterhouse (sixty), Clare (seventy), Queens' (eighty), Jesus (ninety), Christ's (ninety), St John's (125), Trinity (250).

By 1634 there were over 3,000 members of the University. Catharine Hall, of course, still had only six Fellows. (Magdalene now had eleven.) So far as the Fellowship went, it remained the smallest college. But, in relation to the thirteen of the sixteen colleges for which figures were given (Sidney, King's, and Christ's were given no numerical details), regarding under-graduate population Catharine Hall was ninth down the scale, with ninety-three junior students — the same size as Jesus. Peterhouse, Pembroke, Clare, and Trinity Hall were smaller. Caius, Queens', Magdalene, St John's, and Corpus were larger; and Emmanuel and Trinity much larger (Emmanuel, founded in 1584, was the fashionable puritan college). Those figures were given by Thomas Fuller. As we have seen, he commended the new buildings at Catharine Hall. The College, he thought, had been too long 'town bound'; that is, hemmed in by town properties. The gift to the College of the Bull Inn and Yard by Dr John Gostlin, the Master of Caius, who died in 1626, had changed all that. And now, under Richard Sibbes (Master since 1626) the College 'hath flourished with numbers and students'. The regimes of Sibbes and Ralph Brownrigg, covering 1626 to 1645, mark one of the few peak periods of student expansion in the history of Catharine Hall. In 1627 there were twenty-four new members; in 1630, twenty-eight; in 1638, thirty-two; in 1641, thirty-four. (There should also be mentioned such benefactions as that in 1610 by Mrs Rosamund Payne: £100 to endow a Scholarship.)

The emergence of the undergraduate: this was a sixteenth-century development in England. True, there were those before 1500 who had visions of an academic collegiate community with junior members (Lady Elizabeth de Clare, for instance, in the middle of the fourteenth century). Again, sons of the nobility sometimes joined colleges at their own expense in the Middle

Ages. Magdalen, Oxford, had twenty such in the 1450s; and William Blount, Lord Mountjoy, studied at Cambridge — probably at Queens' — in the 1490s: later in the 1490s he met Erasmus in Paris, and presumably told him of the delights of Cambridge.[9] Such noble youths would have been Fellow Commoners. The statutes of Peterhouse in the mid-fourteenth century had allowed the possibility of two or three 'younger scholars'; but it was not until the early sixteenth century, under a far-seeing Master, that Peterhouse developed as an under-graduate institution — the years 1500 to 1518, when Cambridge became as 'flourishing' as the Schools of Europe, and received the New Learning, as Erasmus said: Erasmus lived in Queens' from August 1511 to January 1514, teaching Greek in his college chamber and lecturing in the Old Schools on St Jerome, whose letters he was engaged in editing. By 1516 Peterhouse had eight 'poor scholars'. The Tudor government required lay civil servants, and educated M.P.s and J.P.s: education, in an increasingly lay-orientated society, became both necessary and fashionable. So we have the thesis that in the sixteenth century the 'medieval clerks' were largely replaced by 'well born successors'.[10] We have cited the 1594 phrase 'young gentlemen and scholars'. A man with a degree had the status of 'gentle-man', whatever his social origins. Education came to be on a par with birth. This was not untraditional; but the Tudor conception of lay public service gave a vital boost to the tradition. The King of Bohemia salutes a Lord of Sicilia thus in *The Winter's Tale* (1611):[11]

> As you are certainly a gentleman, thereto
> Clerk-like experienced, which no less adorns
> Our gentry than our parents' noble names.

And one of the strands in the intellectual history of Europe in our period is the attention drawn in published works to the education of the gentleman: noble youths, reared in good letters, piety and the social graces. In England this was a theme

---

[9] D. F. S. Thomson and H. C. Porter (eds), *Erasmus and Cambridge*, 1963, p. 216.
[10] M. H. Curtis, *Oxford and Cambridge in Transition*, 1959, Chapter III: 'Well-born successors to the medieval clerks.'
[11] *The Winter's Tale*, Act I, scene 2, line 391.

from Thomas Elyot's *The Governor* (1531) to Milton's *Of Education* (1642). The real university for the gentry was the Inns of Court in London.[12] But most people (Clarendon for instance) though not all (for example Milton) thought that 'noble and generous lads', 'the children of persons of quality', could profitably spend two or three years at Cambridge or Oxford before proceeding to the expensive, chic and central 'third university'.[13] And a mid-seventeenth-century Cambridge tutor, preparing a reading list which included *The Praise of Folly*, *Utopia*, Camden's history of the reign of Elizabeth, and *The Anatomy of Melancholy*, recognized that many young men came to Cambridge 'to get such learning as may serve for delight and ornament, and such as the want thereof would speak a defect in breeding rather than scholarship'. A far cry from the statutes of Catharine Hall; but there is no reason to suppose that the tutors under Sibbes, Brownrigg, or William Spurstowe would have been unsympathetic to that realism.

In origin, Catharine Hall was a tiny pious foundation. As Dr. Cobban has stressed, the educational purpose, though urgent, was restricted. Compare Trinity, seventy years later: a grandiose Henrician gesture — with its more than fifty graduates, and its sixty students. Trinity Great Court (fashioned by the end of the century) is the product of a different attitude to education from that which designed the old court of Catharine Hall (or, to mention a similar structure which survives today, the old court of Corpus). Before the dissolution of the religious houses in England in the late 1530s (and there were houses of monks and friars and canons in Cambridge) the Colleges, Halls and Hostels of Cambridge and Oxford were grouped in the same family as monasteries, friaries and chantries. There was nothing very monastic about Trinity; apart from the contributions made to its revenues and fabric by

---

[12] There is an excellent recent book on the Inns, a model for a College History. Wilfred R. Prest, *The Inns of Court under Elizabeth and the Early Stuarts*, 1590–1640, 1972.
[13] Clarendon was an Oxford B.A. in 1626. His *Dialogue concerning Education* was first printed in 1727. The *Miscellaneous Works*, 2nd ed. 1751, 313–48. William Harrison in the 1570s called the Inns the third University of England: *The Description of England*, ed. Georges Edelen, 1968, p. 65.

confiscated monastic estates and filched monastic bricks and stones. The set of values behind higher education had changed. Woodlark's aims had been 'the exaltation of the Christian faith', 'the defence and furtherance of Holy Church', and 'the growth of the sciences and faculties of philosophy and sacred theology'. King's at the end of the fifteenth century was described as having been founded for 'the increase of virtue, cunning and Christian faith'; but the prospectus, besides 'holy divinity' and 'liberal sciences', included 'astronomy, physics, civil and canon law' (and the students were provided with servants). By the 1530s Divinity had become primarily scriptural: the New Learning in theology, said Hugh Latimer of Clare, is the Bible. In 1536 Henry VIII assumed the purpose of Cambridge and Oxford to be 'the advancement of the sincere and pure doctrine of God's Word' (a characteristically Erasmian sentiment), and 'the increase of knowledge in the seven liberal sciences, and the three tongues of Latin, Greek, and Hebrew' — such linguistic study being 'necessary not only for the understanding of scripture, but also for the conservation and maintenance of policy and common justice'. At the two Universities, 'youth and good wits be educated and nourished in virtue and learning'. The 1546 statutes of Trinity were similar: with their stress on the amplification of Christian faith against heresy (the only provision in the Catharine Hall tradition), their equating of Divine Learning and Good Letters (again in the Erasmus vein), their requiring the knowledge of the three tongues, and their provision for the relief of the poor (another Erasmian theme: better help the poor than subsidize monks or chantry priests). Divine Learning, as Archbishop Cranmer emphasized when he recommended Martin Bucer to Cambridge in 1549, meant 'pure understanding of Holy Scripture'. Edwyn Sandys and John Bradford of Catharine Hall were among the Cambridge men who took that thesis to heart (and who took Bucer under their wing).

Moreover, Divine Learning was having to find its place in a free market. The Duke of Somerset, Chancellor of the University, worried in 1549 by the relative lack of recruits for the diplomatic service, argued for less Divinity and more Roman

Law (useful in official dealings with foreigners). Every college, he thought, should have at least one Fellow in Civil Law. The new statutes of Catharine Hall in 1549, while assuming that parsons make the best dons, laid down that of the six Fellows *at least* three should be in orders: 'inasmuch as the University and Colleges thereof are bound not only to teach letters but also to promote piety'. These statutes repeated the earlier provision for philosophy and theology; but added the phrase 'other arts'. Elizabeth I in 1561 could still refer to colleges as 'societies of learned men professing study and prayer'; and for John Whitgift, Master of Trinity in the early 1570s, dons and students were properly considered as persons 'for the most part ecclesiastical'. But such phrases had a slightly archaic ring. The Privy Council in 1575 had a more alertly balanced plea for 'good and godly learning', financial support for M.A.s who 'teach all liberal sciences and exercise the study and profession of divinity', and recognition that colleges were 'instituted principally for the nurture and education of a multitude of youth in good manners, learning and Christianity'.[14] From the 1570s also came an official nod to 'good learning, godliness, virtue and manners', and a reminder that graduates should serve 'in all the places of public government' — 'as well in the Church as in the Civil Estate' (an interestingly nervous balance of priorities). William Harrison, discussing the Universities in his *Description of England*, first published in 1577, praised their attention to 'use of the tongues', 'philosophy' and 'the liberal sciences'; besides the 'profound studies of the civil law, physic and theology'.[15] It is true that the statutes of Emmanuel in 1585[16] contained no provision for law and medicine — Emmanuel was meant to do for Elizabethan Cambridge what Catharine Hall had intended to do in the fifteenth century (although the orientation was now very protestant: puritan). It is also true that to the mind of the clerical Establishment Cambridge and Oxford were primarily

---

[14] Heywood and Wright, *Transactions*, II, 35–7; I, 216.
[15] Edited Edelen, 1968. Chapter III, 'Of Universities'.
[16] Selections from the Emmanuel Statutes, in a new translation by Dr Frank Stubbings, in H. C. Porter (ed.), *Puritanism in Tudor England*, 1970, 182–94.

for training clergymen; law and medicine were *fairly* respectable; the rest were trifles — and mathematics and scientific experiment rather suspect. But the official academic mind can be surprisingly unfocussed. Sidney Sussex was to develop as a puritan college; but the will of the foundress referred to the proposed institution only as a 'good and godly monument for the maintenance of good learning'. In 1626 the Chancellor wrote of Cambridge as a 'nursery of literature and good manners': Charles I, a few months earlier, had been more traditional in his linking of 'religion and learning'.[17]

It may be noted that by 1600, 34 per cent of M.P.s had been to Cambridge or Oxford; two-thirds of that group had also been to the Inns of Court.[18]

Latimer, in a sermon before the court of Edward VI in 1549, lamented that divinity students were avoiding Cambridge, partly because of rising costs: 'none now but great men's sons in Colleges' — and 'gentlemen' tend not to do theology.[19] This 'sons of rich men' complaint became increasingly common. By the 1570s it was established as orthodoxy that once upon a time in Cambridge there had been an 'ancient and comely usage' of 'modesty and honest frugality', nowadays (1578) undermined by 'sundry young men being the children of gentlemen and men of wealth', whose attire, for example, was fit only for 'riotous, prodigal and light persons'.[20] William Harrison regretted that although colleges had been originally for the poor, such now 'have the least benefit of them, by reason the rich do so encroach' — and study only 'histories, tables, dice and trifles'. The effects of luxury were apparently not confined to the undergraduates. Chancellor Burleigh complained in 1587 of the vast stipends of tutors, who price out the poorer boys and cater for the young bloods, 'corrupt with liberty and remissness'.

The very detailed admission registers of Caius College have been remorselessly analysed for the period 1580 to 1640 in an

---

[17] Heywood and Wright, *Transactions*, II, 335, 337.
[18] J. E. Neale, *The Elizabethan House of Commons*, 1949.
[19] Latimer, *Sermons*, Parker Society, 1844, p. 179.
[20] Heywood and Wright, *Transactions*, I, 217–18.

attempt to sustain such Tudor grumbles. (The registers of Catharine Hall begin only in the reign of Sibbes, and are even then a mere list of names.)[21] The most recent contribution to the debate, by David Cressy, suggests that the complaints were exaggerated. The sons of gentry accounted for about one-third of the entry at Caius, the sons of yeomen and farmers for about 15 per cent — and these percentages remained fairly stable throughout the sixty-year period.[22] At any rate, recent writing on University History has interestingly dwelt upon the changes and varieties of educational purpose, the relation of the Universities to the national awareness, purpose, and quality of life, and the statistics of educational and social mobility.[23]

Official regulations indicate that Tudor and Stuart students and dons were very lively. The college ideal, of course, was of Uniformity and Discipline. 'We are joined together in a very straight society', said a don in 1576; and Robert Cecil, soon after becoming Chancellor in 1602, stressed the value in a University of 'conformity to things established'; that 'a good conformity be had and observed in all the members of the

---

[21] The St Catharine's Admission Register begins in the late 1620s, but is a mere list of names. Caius has a particularly detailed admissions Register from the 1560s, and Sidney from 1598; and Emmanuel -less full- from 1584. The St Catharine's Audit Book survives from 1622. Thus the sixteenth-century documentation in St Catharine's is very weak. The College has documents relating to property, leases, title deeds, and so on. The University Archives (now in the University Library) have a volume of St Catharine's material: Registry Guard Book Number 90. There are thirty-seven original manuscripts for the period 1580–1650 (nothing before): material on Fellowship disputes under Hound, some items concerning Hills and Buck, and eleven items about the election of Overall as Master — which thus becomes one of the few College episodes in the period which has substantial original documentation. There are two or three other Tudor snippets, unbound, which can be looked up in the card index to the University Archives, in the Manuscripts Reading Room of the University Library: under University Internal Administration: Colleges.

[22] D. Cressy, *The Social Composition of Caius College*, Past and Present, Number 47, May 1970. A refutation of Joan Simon, *The Social Origins of Cambridge Students 1603–40*, Past and Present, Number 26, November 1963.

[23] Recent books include: K. Charlton, *Education in Renaissance England*, 1965; W. T. Costello, *The Scholastic Curriculum at early 17th Century Cambridge*, 1958; M. H. Curtis, *Oxford and Cambridge in Transition 1558–1642: an essay on changing relations between the English Universities and English Society*, 1959; C. Hill, *Intellectual Origins of the English Revolution*, 1965; H. Kearney, *Scholars and Gentlemen: Universities and Society in Pre-Industrial Britain 1500–1700*, 1970; J. Simon, *Education and Society in Tudor England*, 1966; L. Stone, *The Educational Revolution in England 1560–1640*, Past and Present, Number 28, July 1964.

University, with the avoiding both of distraction in opinion and diversity in practice'. (Henry VIII had made it clear in 1530 that there should be in England 'unity and agreement in one persuasion of faith and religion, the dissension wherein, as being ground and fundament, moveth, confoundeth and totally subverteth all the rest': that was true of all Public Weals, whether Catholic, Protestant or Puritan.) Cecil also thought that 'there can be no greater enemy to all good order than the liberty in the education of young gentlemen'; rather in the spirit of his father Burleigh, who at the beginning of his own Chancellorship had been much exercised by the difficulty of 'the ruling of inordinate youth'.

The average freshman in the sixteenth and early seventeenth centuries was sixteen: in the 1970s he is nineteen. It is true that Francis Bacon entered Trinity when he was 12.3 (1573), Thomas Nashe St John's at 14.11, and John Dee St John's at 15.5. Thomas Goodwin went up to Christ's in 1614 when he was 13.6 (and was much excited by the thought that he might go to heaven with the Fellows): he was elected a Fellow of Catharine Hall when he was nineteen (1620). But Oliver Cromwell's second son, also called Oliver, came up to Catharine Hall when he was just nineteen (1642); John Caius was 18.11 when he entered Gonville Hall in 1529; John Harvard was twenty as an Emmanuel freshman in 1627. Milton was 16.3 (Christ's, 1625) and Marlowe 16.6 (Corpus, 1580) — they were typical.

Certainly Cambridge was then more youthful than it is now. Marriage meant the forfeiture of a Fellowship: so the normal member of the Fellows' Table was under thirty. Complaints echo from the 1560s about the lack of discipline among young M.A.s: 'younger than in times past' (1564), and moreover (1572) 'not only younger in age, but more youthful and intractable': 'cockish against their superiors'. The Regent House (now the University Combination Room, adjacent to the Squire Law Library) was largely for young M.A.s, and it was a tumultuous place. It was a site for sit-ins, as it was to be again in 1972; but in Tudor Cambridge it was the dons, not the students, who were addicted to sitting-in. Apart from being young, our academic ancestors were proud. There was a Tudor proverb: 'A Royston horse and a Cambridge M.A. are a couple of creatures that will give way to nobody'.

In our period the oldest Master of Catharine Hall, at the time of election, was Lightfoot, who was forty-eight; Sibbes was forty-six, Hills forty-four, Brownrigg forty-three; Balderston, Hound, Overall, and Spurstow were in their thirties; and Sandys and May in their late twenties.

Life in many ways was hard. The fact that in 1530 Catharine Hall received a gift of eight shillings a year for a fire in the hall and the parlour reminds one of the picture of Cambridge student life given in 1550 by Thomas Lever, who had gone up to St John's in 1538: a busy working day (rising at 4.30 a.m.) with bed-time between nine and ten — preceded by a thirty minute run in the Court 'to get a heat on their feet when they go to bed'. Dinner, Lever tells us, was at 10 a.m., a 'penny piece of beef amongst four' (plus beef broth and oatmeal); supper, at 5 p.m., was no better.[24] Burleigh noted that some students in Elizabethan Cambridge were under-nourished. And in the 1590s about 15 per cent of students were in severe financial difficulty.[25]

On the other hand, it was assumed in Elizabethan Cambridge that some students had guns, bows and swords, kept horses, and had their private servants and boys. They lodged and ate in the town, and explored the countryside with their dogs. They wore silk, satin and velvet, ruffs, hose Italian-style, coloured jackets, and 'light and gay attire'. They wore their hair very long, and elaborately coiffeured, not 'polled, notted or rounded, after the accustomed manner of the gravest scholars' (1560). A student, it was thought, should be Grave; his clothes of 'sad colour and plain stuff'. There should be 'one uniformity of comeliness and modesty', according to Degree. Again, the assumption was that there had existed a 'fashion of old time'. In the time, maybe, of Woodlark. But to Robert Cecil most

---

[24] Thomas Lever, Paul's Cross Sermon, 14 December 1550; in Lever, *Sermons*, ed. E. Arber, 1870, pp. 91–143. Lever became Master of St John's in 1551 at the age of twenty seven.
[25] Calculations from 1597 figures in Heywood and Wright, *Transactions*, II, 156.

undergraduates and some dons looked more like courtiers than scholars. Brownrigg in the 1630s found himself helping to issue decrees in favour of 'clerical or scholastical habit', and against 'long or excessive hair hanging over the foreheads or ears'. Woodlark would not have felt much at home in Caroline Catharine Hall.

And what would the founding fathers of Catharine Hall have made of the fact that in 1597 the bursar of the College, a clergyman in his sixties, found himself before the town J.P.s accused of raping a girl of nine — at the same time as a Cambridge matron named him as the father of her child.[26] (W. H. S. Jones tactfully described the bursar as 'an active man, with a taste for novelty'.)

The crucial fact is that before the 1530s the courtier-type student would have resided not in a college but in a hostel. In medieval Cambridge, colleges were for the minority. (Nothing shows this better than the early history of Catharine Hall.) Erasmus praised the 'sobriety of living in Cambridge Colleges, with their religious regime (so much more disciplined than Paris)'.[27] But in Erasmus's day there were in Cambridge, apart from the colleges, some thirty hostels. In all, from the thirteenth to the early sixteenth century the names of about 140 hostels have come down to us. There was a Catharine Hostel, which since the middle of the fourteenth century belonged to Michael-house, and was still in use in Woodlark's Cambridge. Some hostels were tiny, with half a dozen students; one or two had over 100. Some — though not all — were for the rich. Some were attached to colleges, others independent. Cambridge had been in existence as a *studium* for at least eighty years before anyone thought of founding a college, and not for another two centuries did the colleges begin to achieve primacy (a primacy which they are tending to lose in the 1970s, as the Faculties, on their new sites, become more important in student life). The colleges replaced the hostels for various reasons. One was financial: colleges could claim tax exemptions. Another was

---

[26] Heywood and Wright, *Transactions*, II, 132–3.
[27] Erasmus to Servatius Rogerus, July 1514. Thomson and Porter, *Erasmus and Cambridge*, p. 183.

concerned with power in the University. Catharine Hall was officially granted the status of a college about 1500: in 1501 Richard Balderston, Fellow and later Master, was accordingly eligible to be a University Proctor. More important was the fact that colleges provided good teaching. By the 1450s there were college lectures at King's, and at Godshouse, which became Christ's in 1506 — the new college statutes also provided for college lectures in Hall. The importance of the Latin and Greek Renaissance has been emphasized by some: languages require direct personal teaching (such as that provided by Erasmus in Queens'). By the late 1530s it was assumed that college lectures were as important as University lectures (in the Old Schools). Indeed, college 'exercises' became the training for the appearance of the student in the Schools, for the university routine of determinations, disputations, and declamations. St Catharine's has a brief document, a seventeenth-century copy of a mid-sixteenth-century sheet, which outlines the college routine of 'keeping problems': *Problemata observare*.[28] At Corpus in the 1580s there were over thirty lectures and 'exercises' a week in the Hall and Chapel.[29] John Dee, at St John's in the 1540s, tells us he worked sixteen hours a day.[30]

Thomas Cromwell's University Injunctions of 1535, which are traditionally taken as marking the end of the medieval University, advocated daily lectures in Latin and Greek in every college: except, we must note, Catharine Hall. Expert lecturers: not the earlier stint of young graduates. At the University level, a Reader in Greek was appointed in 1518 (Erasmus's University post had been in the Divinity Faculty). There were University Lecturers in Latin (1492), Mathematics (1501), Philosophy, Logic and Rhetoric (all three in 1518). And in 1540 came the foundation of the five Regius Professorships: Greek, Hebrew, Divinity, Civil Law, and Medicine.

Erasmus made some (though not many) friends in Cambridge. One of them was the Master of Catharine Hall: Thomas Green. In two letters of 1514, written to Cambridge

---

[28] Document discussed in Jones, *Story*, pp. 24–5.
[29] Corpus manuscripts of the 1570s in private possession.
[30] *Autobiographical Tracts of Dee*, ed. J. Crossley, 1851, p. 5.

shortly after his final departure,[31] Erasmus asked to be remembered to Green; his 'friend' and 'patron' (Erasmus was always in need of reliable patrons, but found few). Green was a wealthy man, who financed the building of the Milne Street range in 1517. The sixth Master of the College, he reigned from 1507 to 1529, and was the first Master to be Vice-Chancellor (1523). He was from Cumberland, and went up to Cambridge in the early 1480s. His college is not recorded. He became one of the early Fellows of Jesus in 1498; and would have known Thomas Cranmer, who went up to Jesus about 1503. In Erasmus's day Dr Green (he became Doctor of Divinity in 1512) was Commissary of the University: that is, presiding over the Consistory Court, which dealt with cases concerning B.A.s and undergraduates and 'privileged' persons such as college servants. In effect he was deputy Vice-Chancellor. The Commissary was customarily a Doctor of Civil Law — Green's legal learning was a novelty for Catharine Hall. One of Erasmus's undergraduate friends was Thomas Lupset of Pembroke, who was to lecture in Greek at Oxford in the 1520s. In 1524 Lupset's father, a wealthy Londoner, gave £10 to Catharine Hall (double Green's annual stipend from the College). Green's Mastership was a good period for the College: the new building, the fixing of the Fellowship at six, the purchase of properties (at Coton, Fulbourn, and Wilbraham, for instance), some acknowledgement of junior members — and the appointment of the laundress.

Of the thirteen Masters between 1506 and 1675, none had been an undergraduate at the College. Four had been Fellows: Balderston, Bainbridge, Cosyn, and Spurstowe (and Hills had studied for his M.A. at Catharine Hall). Three were members of King's Hall, three of St John's; and Queens', Trinity, Pembroke, Emmanuel, and Christ's each provided one Master of Catharine Hall. Four were from Suffolk, and six, including Green and Sandys, from the north. Indeed, the College had a decidedly northern bias. The Bible Clerk was required to be from Lancashire, Yorkshire, or Westmorland. Catharine Hall

31 Thomson and Porter, *Erasmus and Cambridge*, 179–80.

men would have appreciated the comment of a seventeenth-century Master of Emmanuel on a Fellowship candidate at his college: the Master would have respected him, 'had he not been southern, and therefore in my judgement uncapable'.[32] (In 1582 William Camden decided to visit Lancashire, 'which I go unto (God speed me well) after a sort somewhat against my will, but I will proceed, in the hope that God's assistance, which hitherto hath been favourable unto me, will not now fail me'.[33])

Four of the thirteen Masters held office for over twenty years: Lightfoot, Green, Hound, and Hills. May and Bainbridge each reigned for eighteen years. Continuity is important in the history of an institution. In the period 1500 to 1640 Catharine Hall had eleven Masters; the lowest total of the pre-Elizabethan foundations — except Gonville and Caius, which had ten. St John's had nineteen, Queens' seventeen. The Elizabethan reign of Hound puts him in a longevity class with Barwell of Christ's, Legge of Caius, Duport of Jesus, Perne of Peterhouse, and Harvey of Trinity (though not with Laurence Chaderton, first Master of Emmanuel from 1584 to 1622 — he died in 1642).

Eight of the thirteen were to be considered worthy of inclusion in the *Dictionary of National Biography*; and Sandys, Overall, Sibbes, and Lightfoot were allowed lengthy treatment.

Reginald Bainbridge, the seventh Master, was a Westmorland man, who had been a Fellow of King's Hall. He succeeded Green in 1529: the year of the fall of Wolsey, the summoning of the 'Reformation' Parliament, and the developing dominance of 'the King's Great Matter' — the desired nullification of the marriage to Catharine of Aragon. In 1529 also there was an attempt by the Parliament to have two Bishops visit Cambridge: 'for examination, reformation and correction of such errors as then seemed, and were reported, to reign amongst the students and scholars as well touching the Lutheran sect and opinions as otherwise'. (The Chancellor was John Fisher, conservative member — he was Bishop of Rochester — of the House of

---

[32] Heywood and Wright, *Transactions*, II, 587.
[33] Quoted, from the English version of *Britannia*, by Christopher Morris, The Historical Journal, Vol. VIII, Number 3, 1965, p. 293.

Lords.) Luther's works had been burnt in Cambridge by the University authorities in 1520. But his books continued to circulate, as the Parliamentary disquiet indicates; in what Gordon Rupp has called a 'forbidden Book-of-the Month Club'. Hugh Latimer, Thomas Bilney, Robert Barnes, and George Stafford were prominent in the group, which probably had about ten other directing members. John Foxe later said that members of seven colleges were conspicuously attracted by the German and Swiss Reformation. He did not include Catharine Hall; though he did name the neighbouring colleges of Queens', King's and Corpus (and also St John's, Peterhouse, Pembroke, and Gonville Hall). Members of the group were later said to have met in the White Horse Tavern, between Catharine Hall and King's; a property, technically called 'Fordham's Place', bought by Woodlark in 1455 and conveyed to King's. The sparsity of reliable documentation on this aspect of Cambridge in the 1520s and 1530s makes any historical reconstruction invalid. There is no evidence whatever about the reaction of members of Catharine Hall. But early in 1530 there was an official University debate in the Regent House about the legality of Henry's marriage to the wife of his brother, and among those who spoke in favour of Henry's case, with Latimer, was the Master of Jesus, William Capon, who had become a Fellow of Catharine Hall in 1509, at the age of about thirty. (He was sometimes called William Salcot, being born in Salcot, Essex.) Capon was the only man associated with Catharine Hall to be involved in the debate. Bainbridge, however, might well have supported the former Fellow, for Bainbridge, becoming a prebendary of Wells in 1535, was one of the conforming clerics who supported the Henrician Reformation. The recipe for survival in Tudor England was, imitate the willow, not the oak.

In 1536 it was ordered that all those proceeding to a Cambridge degree were to take an oath recognizing the King as Supreme Head of the Church: 'so help me God, all saints, and the holy evangelists'. The matters at issue in the 1530s were increasingly argued on a scriptural basis. This led to the questioning of other doctrinal points, besides the supremacy of the Pope. But for the moment the techniques of piety remained traditional. In 1535 there was to be a monthly mass in Great St Mary's, attended by all the members of the University, to pray for the souls of the founders of the University and the colleges, and for the prosperity of Henry and Anne Boleyn 'his lawful wife'. From 1536 masses were to be 'solemnly sung' in every college each May and October for Henry, Anne, and the Princess Elizabeth — and at the same dates after Henry's death, with a requiem. The Chapel vestments and ceremonies were the same under Bainbridge as they had been under Woodlark; indeed in 1535 a former Fellow of Peterhouse presented to Catharine Hall a set of vestments, and an altar cloth.

But one medieval ideal was ended in the late 1530s with the dissolution of the monasteries and friaries, in Cambridge as elsewhere. The dissolved house of the Carmelites, the White Friars, was opposite Catharine Hall, next to Queens'.

Cranmer's English liturgy, the Book of Common Prayer, was in use from June 1549, the idea being enforced that there was to be in England 'one uniform order, rite and ceremony in the mass, matins and evensong'. By then Bainbridge had retired as Master, presumably because he disapproved of the new regime. In 1547, the year of the accession of Edward VI, Edwin Sandys became Master of the College. (Bainbridge lived until 1555.) Sandys was a Johnian, who had come up to Cambridge in 1535, the year of the Cromwell University Injunctions. His great friend was Edmund Grindal: both were born at St Bees, near the coast of western Cumberland. Grindal became Master of Pembroke at the end of Edward's reign; a college which Nicholas Ridley was to describe as being from the 1520s 'studious, well learned, and a great setter forth of Christ's gospel and of God's true word' (pacing the college orchard, he had learned by heart all the New Testament epistles in Greek).[34]

In the early summer of 1549 there was a nine-week Visitation of the University, to root out 'papistry' and to encourage 'God's word and true learning' (a significant parity). The visitors inspected Catharine Hall on 18 May. The report makes no comment on the occasion; except to point out the consideration

[34] Ridley, *Works*, Parker Society, 1843, pp. 406–7.

of the Visitors in departing before evening supper, so as not to put the College to expense — they merely drank beer at four o'clock. So Sandys had reformed the College well enough. Also in 1549 all colleges were given new statutes. Those of Catharine Hall survived until 1860. The comparison with Woodlark's statutes is revealing. The College continued to be devoted to 'the praise, glory and honour of our Lord Jesus Christ'; but references were deleted to 'the most glorious Virgin Mary His Mother' and to 'the holy virgin Katharine'. The phrase 'the defence and furtherance of Holy Church' became 'the advantage of His Church'. The 'exaltation of the Christian Faith' became the 'administration of the sacred Word of God'. Until 1549 prayers had been said for the soul of Woodlark at dinner and supper; a requiem mass was said weekly on the day of his death; and four further requiem masses were held for him each year. These ceased. Masses were replaced by 'common prayer' and 'pious exercises'. At dinner, the Bible was to be read aloud; not, as formerly, the Bible or the Fathers. From henceforth in Cambridge, gifts given on condition of requiems (spiritual insurance for the donors) were to be converted into scholarships. (The first new scholarship to Catharine Hall thereafter was in 1587.) Money previously devoted to 'choristers' and 'chanters' in Cambridge was now to be given 'to the support of scholars in literature or philosophy'. (The Visitors also had plans for converting one of the existing colleges into a community exclusively for the study of medicine). W. H. S. Jones considered such changes a progression from Morbidity to 'virile common sense'.

The fact that the Master and Fellows of Catharine Hall had their stipends raised by 20 per cent presumably prevented overmuch nostalgia.

Sandys became a confidant of the Strasbourg Reformer Martin Bucer, who died in Cambridge in March 1551 after being resident for fourteen months as Regius Professor of Divinity, and a member of the Trinity Fellows' Table. Bucer, like Erasmus, approved of the Cambridge collegiate ideal; the endowments, the statutes, the financial aid to poor students, the emphasis on theology and the training of 'swarms of faithful ministers'. But the dons of 1550 dismayed him. They seemed largely (he wrote to Calvin) 'either most bitter papists, or profligate epicureans, who, as far as they are able, draw over the young men to their way of thinking and imbue them with an abhorrence of sound Christian doctrine and discipline'.[35] Bucer meant the Discipline of 'The Kingdom of Christ' — the title of an influential book he completed in Cambridge: the Protestant — and later the Puritan — Utopia. Sandys of course was sympathetic. And so was John Bradford.

Bradford entered Catharine Hall in the summer of 1548 at the age of thirty-seven, and in 1548 was by special license given the M.A. degree. A Manchester man, who had been an army paymaster (which gave scope, which apparently he had taken, for financial chicanery) Bradford had been decisively influenced by the London sermons of Latimer. Early in 1548, at the Middle Temple, he decided that 'a tumbling stone gathereth no moss' and decided to be a 'minister of God's Word'. He was to be ordained in 1550. Three of his letters from Catharine Hall survive. He wrote of the spiritual comfort of 'the Cause'; to one such as he, 'a refuse, an abject, a hireling of this naughty and wretched world, yea, a worse than so, one of the most wretched sinners living'. He had been promised a Fellowship by Sandys. But there was 'contention' for him between Sandys and Ridley of Pembroke, and in the autumn of 1549, after seventeen months at Catharine Hall, he accepted a Fellowship at Pembroke. The election demonstrated 'the Lord's carefulness for me'; a Fellowship at Pembroke was worth £7 a year, as against £5 at Catharine Hall. At Pembroke, his pupils included John Whitgift. As tutor 'he used in the morning to go to the common prayer in the College where he was, and after that he used to make some prayer with his pupils in his chamber'. He left Cambridge in 1551, to become a prebendary of St Paul's, and then chaplain to the boy King. He was burnt in 1555.

Bradford was the author of several sermons and tracts, some published posthumously, all to be reprinted in the nineteenth century by the Parker Society, in two volumes (Cambridge

[35] Porter, *Puritanism in Tudor England*, p. 61.

University Press). He remains a fine guide to the emphases of the Protestant spiritual life.

Before his death, Bradford wrote a farewell to Cambridge.[36] This was an appeal to the members of the University to come out of Babylon. The University had 'the truth of God's Word plainly manifested unto thee by reading, disputing and preaching, publicly and privately'. 'O ye Doctors, Bachelors and Masters repent. O mayor, aldermen and town dwellers repent, repent, repent, that you may escape the near vengeance of the Lord'. His impact in tiny Catharine Hall must have been rather shattering.

Sandys became Vice-Chancellor in 1552; the first Master to hold the office since Green. (In the period before 1660 seven Masters of Catharine Hall were Vice-Chancellor: Green, Sandys, Edmund Cosyn (1558), John May (1569), John Hills (1616), Ralph Brownrigg (1637, 1643) and John Lightfoot (1654).) Edward VI died on 6 July 1553, aged 15.10 (he could have been a freshman). John Dudley, Duke of Northumberland, Chancellor of the University, and High Steward of the borough, arrived in Cambridge on Saturday 15 July with a force of troops. That evening he had supper with some Heads of Houses sympathetic to Lady Jane Grey and opposed to Mary. Sandys was there, and Thomas Lever of St John's and Matthew Parker of Corpus. The next day Sandys preached the University Sermon in Great St Mary's, taking his text from the first chapter of the Book of Joshua:

And they answered Joshua, saying, All that thou commandest us we will do, and whithersoever thou sendest us, we will go. According as we hearkened unto Moses in all things, so will we hearken unto thee: only the Lord thy God be with thee, as he was with Moses. Whosoever he be that doth rebel against thy commandment, and will not hearken unto thy words in all that thou commandest him, he shall be put to death: only be strong and of a good courage.

Joshua was Northumberland: Edward VI Moses (a burden for a boy). On the Monday Northumberland and his men left

---

[36] Bradford: Letters, in Parker Society, *Letters*, pp. 18, 22–7; the farewell, Parker Society, *Sermons*, pp. 442–6; as tutor, *Sermons*, p. 34. Extracts from his 1553 Sermon of Repentance were printed in 1971 in John Chandos's anthology, *In God's Name: examples of preaching in England 1534–1662*.

Cambridge to challenge Mary and her troops in East Anglia. Thomas Lever prepared to ride to London with the text of the Sandys sermon. But the cause of the Kingdom of Christ was ill-fated. Northumberland's men were useless, and on the Tuesday he retreated back to Cambridge. In that week Mary was proclaimed to be Queen by a herald on Market Hill. Northumberland was arrested in his chamber at King's. A mob attempted to invade Catharine Hall to take possession of the University keys and Statute Book. Sandys had withdrawn from the College on that day; but hearing that without his authorization a Congregation had been summoned in the Regent House, he hurried there and insisted on taking his Vice-Chancellor's seat. Some M.A.s tried to drag him out of it; and he reached for his dagger. (Sandys was a quick-tempered man. On the occasion of his election as Proctor in the Regent House in 1542 — probably after he had canvassed for the office and bribed another candidate to withdraw — he had drawn his dagger to wound a rival M.A.; and the then Master of Catharine Hall had urged one of Sandys' Johnian friends to assault the Vice-Chancellor.) But the winds of change were blowing strong. Sandys resigned as Vice-Chancellor, turned over his books and keys, and swept back to Catharine Hall, closely followed by Marian agents, who made an inventory of his effects and stole four horses from the College stable. On Tuesday 25 July Sandys and Northumberland left under escort for London: the destination was the Tower.[37]

The Chancellor was executed in August; being the fourth of five Tudor Chancellors of Cambridge to meet death on the scaffold. Sandys was released (apparently at the suggestion of Mary) and left for Germany and Switzerland with his family.

In all, seventy-six Cambridge graduates left England as exiles during the reign of Mary, including forty-four Fellows or former Fellows: the Master of St John's and the Provost of King's among them. One Fellow of Catharine Hall was an exile, James Taylor, and one student, Edward Frencham.

[37] The story was told in the 1560s by John Foxe in the *Acts and Monuments*: 'A Brief Discourse concerning the Troubles and Happy Deliverance of Dr Sandys': ed. G. Townsend, VIII, 1849, 590–8. A brief recent treatment of the national background is D. M. Loades, *The Oxford Martyrs*, 1970, pp. 100–12.

Sandys and Frencham went to Zurich. Mrs Sandys and one of the children died there: and Frencham, a wayward hypochondriac, died abroad in 1559. Taylor, ten years' Sandys' junior, and a Lancashire man, went to Geneva, as did about 25 per cent of the nearly 500 male Marian exiles. The Geneva of Calvin: praised by John Knox as 'the most perfect School of Christ that ever was in earth since the days of the Apostles'. The English exiled community in Zurich (about two dozen males) took as their centre the house of a printer.

Bradford exhorted England to remember the exiles. And the exile experience was vital to the development of English puritanism: the sense of the little flock, the persecuted but godly remnant. This paralleled the sufferings of imprisoned Saints in England such as Bradford, who found comfort in the Augustinian theme of Predestination and Election; being, as Bradford said, in 'the very dungeon of despair'. The shock to English Protestantism of the triumph of Mary was traumatic. Can Antichrist triumph? Can the Deity be mutable? For Bradford Predestination became 'the University' of the pilgrim's progress, Justification by Faith Alone the mere 'grammar school'. The exiles who returned to England in the 1560s looked back with nostalgia to the pure air of Zurich, and the community of 'the little flock who were hidden *in Germania*'. Bullinger of Zurich dedicated a book of his in 1565 to Sandys and other Zurich Englishmen. Matthew Parker, Elizabeth's first Archbishop of Canterbury, who disliked things European, was suspicious of Sandys' 'Germanical nature'. But the former Master of Catharine Hall became an important prelate in Elizabethan England: Bishop of Worcester in 1559 (one of the twelve returned exiles appointed to Bishoprics in the first two years of Elizabeth's reign); Bishop of London (succeeding Grindal) in 1570; and Archbishop of York from 1577 until his death in 1588 at the age of about seventy. Sandys was the only Master of Catharine Hall in our period to become an Archbishop. May, Overall, and Brownrigg were to become Bishops.

Sandys' noteworthy published work was a collection of twenty-two sermons, which appeared in 1585, and was reprinted by the Parker Society in 1842. (Five of our thirteen

Masters of the College were famous for their printed sermons;
all save Sandys were seventeenth century — Sibbes, Brownrigg,
Spurstowe, and Lightfoot.) Sandys's sermons were an eloquent
guide to left-of-centre Elizabethan Anglicanism, and a concise
and moderate expression of many Elizabethan commonplaces.
(True to the spirit of Woodlark, he is especially direct in his
criticism of lawyers.) He also deserves memorial because it was
on his recommendation that Richard Hooker was appointed
Master of the Temple in 1585. Hooker had been tutor to one
of his sons at Oxford. The only one of his seven boys he sent to
Cambridge went to Peterhouse.

Sandys's successor as Master of Catharine Hall during the
reign of Mary was Edmund Cosyn; a Bedfordshire man, a
graduate of King's Hall, and one of the initial Fellows of
Trinity in 1546. His election as Master was engineered by
Stephen Gardiner, the conservative Master of Trinity Hall, and
Mary's Bishop of Winchester. Cosyn also became chaplain to
Bishop Bonner of London, the *bête noire* of English Protes-
tantism. The 1549 College Statutes were revoked, and for five
years Catharine Hall, like England, reverted — so far as that
was possible — to the state of affairs before the death of
Henry VIII (or, in matters concerning the Pope, before 1534).
Cosyn had five ecclesiastical livings, and during his period as
Master seems to have spent a great deal of time in Norfolk.
Indeed, one wonders how much attention some Masters were
able to devote to the College. Most of them in our period had
livings elsewhere. Also, Overall was Dean of St Paul's, Brownrigg a prebendary of Durham and then Bishop of Exeter, Hills
a prebendary of Lincoln and then Archdeacon, Sibbes a weekly
preacher at Gray's Inn, Spurstowe — and Brownrigg —
members of the Assembly of Divines at Westminster in the
1640s. However, Cosyn condescended to return to Catharine
Hall from time to time, most notably for the Visitation of the
University, by five Visitors, in 1557.

This Marian Visitation began with a sung mass in King's
Chapel, followed by a Latin sermon in Great St Mary's
denouncing the errors of Cambridge Protestants. Cosyn was
personally questioned on 13 January: the Visitors dealt with

three other Heads of Houses on the same day. It was his duty as Master to compile a list of all the books owned by all the resident members of Catharine Hall; suspected literature was to be carried away in baskets. Cosyn also took part in such formalities as a procession through Cambridge of town and gown, with, as conclusion, a mass in Great St Mary's with 'pricksong and organs': as a Head of House he carried a torch in the march (one such torch set fire to the canopy over the Sacrament, carried at the head of the procession). On Tuesday 19 January Catharine Hall was formally visited by the Bishop of Chester and the Provost of Eton. They arrived at 7 a.m. and left at 10 a.m.; hearing mass, inspecting the Chapel (to check, for instance, whether the Sacrament was reserved over the altar), searching the archives, and touring the chambers, with a special eye for suspected literature (spiritual pornography, it would have seemed to them). Cosyn and the six Fellows were before the Visitors again on 11 February — together with the dons of Gonville Hall, Jesus, Clare, Trinity Hall, and Corpus. There are not — there never are — many details of the situation at Catharine Hall. This presumably indicates that Authority was satisfied.

The succession of Elizabeth on 17 November 1558 meant another spin of the wheels in Cambridge, including the Catharine wheel. Cosyn was especially implicated, because he had become Vice-Chancellor on 8 November. He resigned seventeen days later, on 25 November. He also resigned the Mastership. His reign of five years is the shortest in our period (except for Balderston, who died in 1507 after one year in office). Cosyn rented a room in Caius, and lived until the late 1570s, first in Cambridge and then abroad. At the beginning of Elizabeth's reign four Heads of Houses resigned; one fled; three conveniently died; two hung on, and left later; and two survived the change of regime. In only two colleges was there a technical 'deprivation'. The new government was comparatively courteous.

Cosyn's successor was John May, in his early thirties, graduate, Fellow, and bursar of Queens', and amateur playwright, who had lived in Cambridge during the reign of Mary, taking the oaths and subscribing to the articles: the willow again, rather than the oak. May was Master for eighteen years. While Master, he also became rector of livings in Buckinghamshire, Norfolk, and London, a prebendary of Ely, and Archdeacon of the East Riding. He became Bishop of Carlisle, and left Cambridge, in 1577, holding the see until his death in 1598: 'this barbarous country', he called it. Matthew Parker was his friend and patron. No doubt Parker had put in a word for him at Catharine Hall.

In 1564 Cambridge had a visit from the Queen and her entourage. She lodged in King's. There were nine noblemen in the party, farmed out between five colleges: Trinity, St John's, Trinity Hall, Clare — and Catharine Hall. Thomas Ratcliffe, Earl of Sussex, lodged in the College — though his retinue of one hundred servants was put up in the town.

The central position of Catharine Hall, not for the first or last time, was the attraction

On the fifth day of the visit, Wednesday 9 August, Elizabeth toured ten of the fourteen Colleges. Not, in the event, Catharine Hall. By the time she arrived at Queens' and Milne Street it was nearly one o'clock, past the dinner hour. She merely 'perused' the façade of Catharine Hall; and William Howgrave, who had become a Fellow Commoner of the College via King's and Eton, was deprived of the opportunity of delivering his prepared Latin Oration (he was careful to see, nonetheless, that it got into print). However, the members of the College had seen the royal party on the afternoon of Saturday 6 August, when Elizabeth had made her entry down Milne Street to King's Chapel — the street strewn with rushes and hung with flags and lined with the twelve hundred members of the University in academic attire and echoing with the sounds of the trumpeters.

The 1560s saw the development of effective Puritanism in Cambridge. May became Vice-Chancellor in 1569, the year in which Thomas Cartwright, Fellow of Trinity, was elected Lady Margaret Professor of Divinity. Cartwright's lectures concentrated on a comparison of the condition of the apostolic Church with that of the contemporary Church of England, to the grave disadvantage of the latter. By June 1570 the authorities were alert. Grindal, the new Archbishop of York, recommended to Chancellor William Cecil that a proposed grace for Cartwright's Doctorate of Divinity be vetoed by May as Vice-Chancellor. On 29 June there was another stormy meeting in the Regent House. Cartwright's supporters — nearly half the dons — voted against most of the candidates proposed for the University Governing Body. May retaliated by vetoing the Doctorate: 'for which my doing I have suffered this day no small troubles at Cartwright's and his favourers' hands.' In the following weeks petitions and counter petitions proliferated. John Whitgift, Master of Trinity, prepared a new and more disciplinary set of University Statutes; helped by some other Heads of Houses, including May. These Statutes received the royal assent at the end of September. And in November Whitgift succeeded the no doubt relieved May as Vice-Chancellor. In December Cartwright was deprived of his Professorship by nine Heads, again including May, and he went to Geneva. But the argument about the Statutes continued. In May 1572, 164 dons signed a petition against them: these protestors included Edmund Hound of Caius, later Master of Catharine Hall, and two members of Peterhouse who were Catharine Hall men by origin — Edmund Messenger and William Stanton. Archbishop Sandys, with Parker and Grindal, was called upon to investigate the complaints of the 'young men'. The three decided, predictably, that 'these younger men have been far overseen to seek their pretended reformation by disordered means'. (New 'reformations' are always '"pretended" reformations' to ageing radicals.) In these months May was attacked as a man of 'small consistency' in life or religion; quite mild, really, when other Heads of Houses were characterized as 'enemies unto Christ's Gospel'. May was an average and fairly inoffensive member of the Clerical Establishment.

The most interesting Fellow of Catharine Hall in May's period was John Maplet, a sizar of Queens' in 1560, Fellow of Catharine Hall from 1564 until about 1568. In a way, he was a precursor of John Ray. In 1567 Maplet — 'M. of Arte, and student in Cambridge' — published a book which W. H. Davies

7

(*The Autobiography of a Super Tramp*) was to describe in 1930 as 'curious and wonderful'. This was *A Green Forest*, dedicated to Thomas Ratcliffe, Earl of Sussex.[38]

A greene Forest, or a naturall Historie, wherein may bee seene first the most sufferaigne vertues in all the whole kinde of stones & mettals: next of plants, as of herbes, trees & shrubs, lastly of brute beastes, fouls, fishes, creeping wormes & serpents, and that alphabetically.

Maplet — a clergyman — intended that 'God might especially be glorified: and the people furdered'. His information was based on the standard classic authors: Aristotle, Pliny, Cicero, and so on. But he would find a place in any history of scientific enquiry in Tudor Cambridge (a topic never yet investigated). Maplet's second book appeared in London in 1581:

The Diall of Destiny. A booke very delectable and pleasaunt: wherein may be seene the continuall and customable course, disposition, qualities, effects and influence of the seven Planets on all kyndes of Creatures here belonging to the severall and sundry Kingdomes. Compiled and discussed Briefly, as well Astrologically, as Poetically and Philosophically.

Maplet died in 1592.

A letter from the Queen in 1577 recommended Edmund Hound as the next Master of Catharine Hall. Hound had gone up to Trinity in 1558, and by now was Fellow (and sometime President) of Caius; he was Elizabeth's chaplain, too — and also chaplain to Robert Dudley Earl of Leicester. He was less 'safe' than May; as we have seen, he had petitioned in 1572 against the new university statutes. In fact he was a controversial figure. At Caius he had been an ally of the erratic Master, Thomas Legge, a suspected papist. Hound's chamber was said to have been the scene of 'great and continual disorder', of students' singing the Roman *sanctus*, and also 'lewd ballads, with heads out of the windows, and so loud voices that all the House wondered thereat, to the very evil example of the youth'. (Legge had been equally musically inclined, using 'continual and expressive loud singing and noise of organs, to the great

[38] Reprinted at the Cambridge University Press, and published by the Hesperides Press, London, in 1930, with an introduction by W. H. Davies.

disturbance of our studies'. A tradition of complaints in Tudor Cambridge about excessive musical activity suggests that the modern neighbour with his hi-fi is not without academic precedent.) The Caius complainers also said that in general in their College 'godly peace, through evil and uncharitable dealing, is daily disturbed, our minds much disquieted, our studies almost wholly neglected, that we were better to live in any society than in such a College'.[39] Better, no doubt Dr Hound thought in reply, to live in the comparative calm of Catharine Hall.

Comparative; for in Hound's reign of twenty years there were several commotions in the College. Disputes about Fellowships, which occasioned ugly publicity; wranglings about finance — these may have been the fault of the Bursar, the efficiency-expert John Cragg, Fellow from 1574, and also Rector of Coton until his death in 1605: we have already encountered him on a rape charge in 1597 — he was acquitted, and the informer imprisoned for slander.

From 1583 Hound was also a rector in Dorset. A man of melancholy humour, in the end he committed suicide in his parsonage.

Two B.A.s from Catharine Hall under Hound were to become prelates. Nehemiah Donellan from Galway, by origin a King's man, took his B.A. from Catharine Hall in 1582; he was to be Archbishop of Tuam from 1595 to 1609, and to supervise a translation of the New Testament into Irish. William Foster went up to Catharine Hall in 1589, and was a Fellow from 1594 until about 1618, when he became a prebendary of Chester; he was consecrated Bishop of Sodor and Man in March 1634 — but died in February 1635.

Academic Cambridge in the 1590s was much concerned with the developing conflict between the rather old-style High Calvinism of men like William Perkins, Fellow of Christ's, and William Whitaker, Master of St John's, and a more liberal, humanist and sacramental tradition, represented by, for instance, Lancelot Andrewes, Master of Pembroke since 1589,

---

[39] Heywood and Wright, *Transactions*, I, 325.

and John Overall, Fellow of Trinity, who was significantly elected Regius Professor of Divinity in succession to Whitaker in 1596: a crucial appointment in the story of the progress of Cambridge from Puritanism to the Age of Reason. The Catharine Hall of Hound appears to have been of a similar flavour to Andrewes' Pembroke. In 1595 sixty Cambridge dons signed a pro-Calvinist petition: there is no one from Catharine Hall or Pembroke in the list. Also, no Catharine Hall men had signed a petition of 1589 in favour of the Christ's puritan Francis Johnson (later a religious exile to Holland).[40]

The Mastership election after Hound's suicide in March 1598 was tense. The three Senior Fellows, led by Cragg, voted for Overall, who was in the good books of Archbishop Whitgift. But the three Juniors preferred a Dr Simon Robson of St John's. Cragg declared Overall to have been elected, and the Juniors appealed to the Vice-Chancellor. There were four days of inquiry, and then Robson was declared to be the successful candidate. He was in office for only one week: the Queen and the Archbishop intervened, and finally, in mid-April, Overall was admitted as Master. It would be an obvious comment to say that the tangled tale of Robinson's vote comes to mind; however, the tale of Robinson's vote does come to mind.

Overall, twelfth Master of the College, had an intellect more distinguished than any of his predecessors. His Mastership laid the foundation for the flourishing Catharine Hall of the reign of Charles I. His tenure of the Regius Chair was predictably controversial. In 1599 complaints were made about his unsoundness concerning what some took to be English Protestant Orthodoxy. Among other things, he was said to have taught the real and substantial presence of Christ in the Communion bread and wine. But his star was in the ascendant. In 1602 he became Dean of St Paul's, and for five years combined that office with the Mastership and the Professorship. In 1606 he was president of the Lower House of the Convocation of Canterbury, at a time when the Convocations were debating

---

[40] 1589 Petition in British Museum Lansdowne MSS, Vol. 61, No. 16. 1595 Petition in Trinity College, Cambridge MSS No. B-14-9. I have discussed the latter in *Reformation and Reaction in Tudor Cambridge*, 1958, 346–7.

Canons about political theory; in the event James vetoed the publication of the final Canons, and 'Bishop Overall's Convocation Book' was only to be published by Archbishop Sancroft in 1690, as Dr Luckett points out. (Overall did not become a Bishop until 1607: he died in 1618 as Bishop of Norwich.)[41]

Mrs Overall had become notorious when her husband was Dean of St Paul's. John Aubrey was to describe her as 'so tender hearted that she could scarce deny any one'; and to print a verse which by the mid-seventeenth century had become almost traditional:

> The Dean of St Paul's did search for his wife
> And where d'ee think he found her?
> Even upon Sir John Selby's bed
> As flat as any flounder.

She was 'the greatest beauty of her time in England'; but she was most at home at the court or the theatre, and there is no record of her opinion of Catharine Hall.

Appropriately perhaps, Overall's successor as Master in 1607, John Hills, was rather a nonentity (although he was to have quite a vigorous row with the Fellows about money in 1623). Hills was born in Fulbourn, entered Jesus in 1579, but took his M.A. from Catharine Hall under Hound in 1586; he then returned to Jesus. He was a competent cleric, a prebendary of Ely at the time of his election as Master. He later became an Archdeacon, first of Stow, then of Lincoln; and never rose higher. He was elected Vice-Chancellor in 1616, the year after King James and Prince Charles had made a visit to Cambridge, when a Fellow of Catharine Hall was appointed one of the five Masters of Ceremonies. (The University, whether by accident or design, neglected to invite the Queen; James's roving eye for glamorous young men was given a scope in Cambridge which might have worried her.) The royal party, the report runs, visited 'all the Colleges save two or three': whether Catharine Hall was among the spurned does not appear. At any rate, the

---

[41] Bishop Overall's Convocation Book was reprinted at Oxford in 1844 in *The Library of Anglo-Catholic Theology*.

College was 'new be-painted' — every College was, a contemporary versifier tells us (except the 'pure house of Emmanuel' which as its contribution to the festivities 'conceived a tedious mile of prayer').

There was more to see at Catharine Hall than there had been at the time of Elizabeth's visit in 1564. After 1610 Green's old range along Milne Street, towards Silver Street, was extended into a second court of three sides, two stories high. Most of the money came from Sir John Claypole; who preferred, however, to send his son to Emmanuel. The extensions added six Chambers to the College accommodation. Later in Hill's reign, in 1622, work was begun on a third Court, behind the Chapel, towards Trumpington Street. The land was acquired by Thomas Buck, University Printer, a Jesus man who had become a Fellow of Catharine Hall in 1615, and then Bursar: the new court was usually known as Buck's Court. So when Hills died in 1626, Catharine Hall had its Old Court, its Second Court (sometimes known as Archers's Court) and Buck's Court (which had a bowling green). And the College had a mind to further expansion still. In 1626 the Fellows made a point of cultivating the Master of Caius, Dr John Gostlin (who was to die later in the year); they gave him two suppers in Hall, with wine, tobacco, and dessert apples — the first costing £1. 1s. od., the second £1. 4s. 3d. In his will, dated October 1626, Dr Gostlin gave to Catharine Hall the Bull Inn and its Yard, on the King's side of the College. Building did not begin on this site, however, until 1631, under Richard Sibbes.

Three distinguished names belong to the Catharine Hall of Hills.

James Shirley, the author of thirty surviving plays, friend of Charles I and Inigo Jones, entered the College in 1615; two years later than his Derbyshire friend Thomas Bancroft, who later invoked the 'precious years' the two spent together, feeling 'in our poetic brains' a 'whirling trick, then caught from Katherine's wheel'.

Thomas Goodwin of Christ's became a Fellow of Catharine Hall in 1620, and remained until the mid-1630s. He was to be connected with Trinity Church in Cambridge, the prominent evangelical pulpit, first as Lecturer (1628) and then as Vicar (1632). During the later 1630s, the decade of Laud, he almost went to New England, but lived in Holland instead, returning in the early 1640s to become a member of the Westminster Assembly of Divines, Chaplain to the Council of State after the execution of Charles I in 1649, and, in 1650, President of Magdalen, Oxford. His autobiography[42] is amongst the most detailed personal accounts of the Calvinist theology of conversion. He was apparently converted from 'the lusts and pleasures of sinning, but especially the ambition of glory and praise' in October 1620, the year following his move to Catharine Hall. 'I thought myself to be as one struck down by a mighty power'. While at Magdalen in the 1650s he was to interview an entrance candidate in a darkened room, wearing six night caps, asking the lad (who fled) whether he was 'of the number of the elect'. There is no memorial of similar techniques at Catharine Hall.

The third worthy was John Arrowsmith. A Johnian, he was Fellow of Catharine Hall from 1623 to 1631, and was to be a member of the Westminster Assembly. He was at ease in the period of the Civil War, Commonwealth, and Protectorate. Master of St John's, 1644; Regius Professor of Divinity, 1651; and Master of Trinity from 1653 until his death in 1659.

The fourteenth Master (1626 to 1635) was Richard Sibbes; as distinguished as Overall, more of a famous name, and of a puritanical, though not a schismatical, school of churchmanship. He was a Johnian, who matriculated in 1594, as the theological controversies which were to involve Overall were gathering momentum. He was elected a Fellow of his College in 1601; and when in 1602 the most noteworthy of the Cambridge Calvinists, William Perkins, died, Sibbes was chosen to succeed him as Lecturer at St Andrew's Church (opposite Christ's). In 1610 a subscription by townsfolk instituted a Lectureship at Holy Trinity Church: and Sibbes was their first choice. His function was to preach on Sunday at 1 p.m., the same time as the University Sermon in Great St Mary's. Gown went to Great St Mary's, Town to Holy Trinity (and then to their separate

---

[42] Goodwin, *Works*, Volume v, 1704.

parish churches). In theory — in fact, many students preferred to hear Sibbes, and for this reason, probably, he lost the Lectureship in 1615. (It was a well-paid position, with a stipend of £40, which in 1624 was to be raised to £80, ten times more than a Mastership — one man was to decline a Bishopric in favour of it.) In 1617 Sibbes went to London as preacher at Gray's Inn, one of the most intellectually influential London pulpits.[43] In spite of his slight stutter, Sibbes became all the rage, and in 1624 the chapel of Gray's Inn was enlarged, partly to cope with the crowds. Sibbes remained attached to Gray's Inn until 1635, and if he preached every Sunday, as he should have done, he must have spent three days a week away from Catharine Hall.

The London Puritan Lecturers of the 1620s and 1630s have been studied in our day, notably by William Haller and Christopher Hill.[44] By the late 1620s there were about 120 of them, nearly sixty being from Emmanuel (Christ's and St John's were also well represented); but there were eight from Catharine Hall.

In 1628 Sibbes earned the tribute of a rebuke from the new Bishop of London, William Laud. His fans at the Inns of Court included the young John Pym, and the Solicitor General, Henry Yelverton, who may have been influential in securing Sibbes's election at Catharine Hall.

During the 1630s about thirty Sibbes titles were published, most of them collections of sermons: an edition in the 1860s runs to seven volumes. Goodwin was one of the editors, after Sibbes's death. His most popular work was one of the first: sermons on Chapter 12 of Matthew, published in 1630 with the title *The Bruised Reede and Smoaking Flax*, which had run to five editions by 1635. His first published volume (apart from works by Cambridge colleagues which he edited) was *The Saints Cordials* in 1629. Another picturesquely titled volume was *Bowels opened: or, a discovery of the Neare and Deare Love, Union and*

---

[43] W. R. Prest, *The Inns of Court*, 1972, Chapter IX: 'Preachers, Puritans and the Religion of Lawyers'.
[44] Haller, *The Rise of Puritanism, 1938*; Hill, *Society and Puritanism in Pre-Revolutionary England*, 1964.

Communion betwixt Christ and the Church (1639). He was in the Cambridge tradition, pioneered by Perkins and Andrewes, of practical spiritual comfort and counsel. In 1637 Goodwin edited *The Spirituall-Mans Aime. Guiding a Christian in his Affections and Actions, through the sundry passages of this life.* Another work in the same vein was *A Consolatory Letter to an Affected Conscience, full of pious admonition and divine instruction.* Richard Baxter, Izaak Walton, John Cotton, and Hugh Peter were among those to pay tribute to Sibbes. The inclusion of the moderate anglican Walton — biographer of Richard Hooker, John Donne, George Herbert, and Nicholas Ferrar of Little Gidding — demonstrates that Sibbes was not a puritan 'party man'; indeed at Gray's Inn the extremer puritans thought him too timorous, and too respectful of authority — a Trimmer.

Cambridge men in the first half of the seventeenth century were very susceptible to sermons. In 1620 a rather typical undergraduate tells us of his Sunday.[45] A sermon in College Chapel, then the sermon in Great St Mary's, then a sermon in a parish church, followed, at five o'clock, by supper — after which he went through his notes on the three sermons. (In addition, he probably went to the afternoon 'catechising' in College, which was compulsory for undergraduates and B.A.s.) Official Cambridge piety was quite demanding. And it could be supplemented. A High-Churchman complained in 1636 that in Trinity College some sixty to eighty undergraduates gathered for extra prayers in their Tutors' rooms: prayers 'longer and louder by far at night than they are at chapel in the evening'. (We have seen John Bradford exercising a similar influence in 1550.) Godly Tutors were much in evidence in the first half of the seventeenth century: It is true that Robert Cecil complained in 1602 about 'the negligence, dissoluteness and boyishness of many Tutors', occasioning 'the undoing of many youths, both in learning and manners'. But it was possible to be pious and also fun. One of the complaints against an influential puritan Tutor at St John's in the 1560s was that (apart from making his pupils 'sing the Geneva psalms in tunes made for most

[45] Symonds D'Ewes of St John's; some of his diary published in 1851 by J. Marsden, *College Life in the Reign of James I.*

wanton and light ballads') he kept in his chamber 'conies, dogs, rats, birds, virginals: and useth to go a birding with his boys, to the great reproach of the ministry'.[46] It was the duty of a Tutor to see that his pupils were (1603) 'thoroughly instructed in points of religion', that they 'diligently frequent public service and sermons, and receive the holy communion' (four times a year at least: there was a celebration once a month). An undergraduate at Trinity in the late 1640s (a youth addicted to the printed sermons of Sibbes) paid tribute to his Tutor: [47] who was 'careful of me, inquired of me what company I was acquainted with, sometimes read lectures to us, prayed with us in his chamber every night, and had sometimes about thirty pupils, and was a generous savoury Christian'. That particular young man had been briefed by his father to pray every night and morning, to read the Bible, to keep a written record of his meditations, to take notes during sermons, and to 'maintain the just medium between too much solitariness and too much company'. Some undergraduates thought themselves holier than their Tutors. A sermon by a puritan don in 1628 advised the young men to boycott any 'carnal tutor': 'find out a man in whom the spirit of God dwells, one that is renewed by grace'. That was at Queens'. Presumably the undergraduates of Catharine Hall under Sibbes would found have their normal spiritual diet adequate.

And in the regime of Sibbes came the new building operations made possible by the land bequest of Dr Gostlin. A 'fair building of stone and brick', begun in 1631, ready for occupation in 1634, completed in 1637; Bull Court, or Gostlin's Court, or, later, Walnut Tree Court. Under Sibbes also funds were acquired for six scholarships (some of this from the Gostlin estate), and for the upkeep of four poor divinity students; and some land was left to the College in 1631 to provide for the sons of poor and godly men (this was a bequest shared with Emmanuel). It is true that there were quarrels in the College during Sibbes's reign (mainly about the auditing of the expansion finances).

[46] Quoted from State Papers Domestic Elizabethan Vol. xxxviii (Public Record Office) in Porter, *Reformation and Reaction*, 128.
[47] Heywood and Wright, *Transactions*, ii, 513–14.

But the tribute of Thomas Fuller remains valid. (In Sibbes's period at Catharine Hall Fuller was at Queens', and also, from 1630, curate of St Bene't's). Sibbes, Fuller wrote,[48]

'found the House in a mean condition, the wheel of St Catharine having stood still (not to say gone backwards) for some years together: he left it replenished with scholars, beautified with buildings, better endowed with revenues.'

There survives a report of 1636 on the condition of College Chapels in Cambridge. Its tone is anti-puritan; and it was probably prepared for Laud by John Cosin, Master of Peterhouse (who as a student had been an admirer of Overall). 'Of late', Cosin said of Catharine Hall, the Chapel was 'as irregular as any, and most like Emmanuel' (where the altar stood in the body of the Chapel, and where impromptu prayers supplemented or replaced the Book of Common Prayer). But in 1636 'there is some uncertainty what they do in the Chapel'. Ralph Brownrigg had succeeded Sibbes as Master in 1635, and his policy was not yet fully known. Canon David Lloyd, who wrote a biographical sketch of Brownrigg in the 1660s,[49] commended his 'particular great esteem' for the Prayer Book: Brownrigg honoured Cranmer and the compilers of the liturgy, admired its 'excellent *matter* and prudent *method*', and saw good in it for 'all sober Christians'. When in December 1643 the ageing Suffolk farmer William Dowsing reached Catharine Hall with his demolition men he recorded that Brownrigg had the odd opinion that there should be 'more reverence due to the place called the Church than any other place'. And Brownrigg had objected to Dowsing's smashing a window inscription ('Pray for the soul of him that made this window'), breaking a stained glass window of John the Baptist, and pulling down statues of St George and of 'the popish Katharine and Saint'. Dowsing was also alarmed by Brownrigg's respect for the communion plate. But by then Brownrigg was Bishop of Exeter as well as Master of Catharine Hall: consecrated May 1642. He had been of puritan sympathies, but was not a party man.

---

[48] Fuller, *Worthies*, ed. P. A. Nuttall, iii, 1840, p. 185.
[49] David Lloyd (1635–1692), *Memoires*, 1668, pp. 405–6.

Lloyd painted him as a hater of 'unquiet and pragmatick Spirits, which affect endless Controversies, Varieties, and Novelties in Religion to carry on a Party, and under that Skreen of Religion, to advance their private Interests in publick Designs'. There is a hint in Lloyd, as there is in Walton, that a moderate Anglican pattern agreeable to the author is imposed rather cavalierly on the subject of the essay; but it is no doubt true that while Brownrigg was sufficiently in the Sibbes tradition to appeal to Oliver Cromwell, he was devoid enough of puritan dogmatism to be supported by Charles I. He seems essentially to belong to that tradition of Cambridge liberal and reasonable Christianity which Overall and Andrewes had adorned, and which was developed from the early 1630s, mainly in Emmanuel, by the group later known as the Cambridge Platonists. Lloyd, at any rate, thus depicts him.

'He could endure *differences* among Learned and Godly men in Opinions, especially sublime and obscure, without distance in affection. He thought that *Scripture* itself in some points was left to us less clear and possitive, that Christians might have wherewith to exercise both *Humility* in themselves and *Charity* towards others.'

Looking back at the sixteenth-century Reformers, Brownrigg was 'not so addicted to any one Master, as not fully to use his own great and mature judgement'. He stood by '*Orthodox* Divinity and orderly *Conformity*'; and Brownrigg's definition of Orthodoxy would have been regarded as pernicious Novelty in the 1630s by old-style Cambridge puritans, who saw developing (under such as Cosin) a liturgical and non-Calvinist revival which was a great affront to the Godly. For Brownrigg 'kept to the Doctrine, Worship, Devotion, and Government in the Church of *England*: *which*, he would say, *he liked better and better, as he grew older*'.

Like Sibbes, Brownrigg was a Suffolk man, who went up to Pembroke as a Scholar in 1607. Andrewes had left that college in 1605, but his successor as Master, Samuel Harsnet, was in the Andrewes tradition. Brownrigg was elected a Fellow of Pembroke in 1611. (Does Brownrigg's association with Pembroke explain Evelyn's curious error about Andrewes being Master of Catharine Hall?)

There was some confusion about Brownrigg's election as Master of Catharine Hall in 1635.[50] When Sibbes died, the Senior Fellow was a Scot, John Lothian, who had been appointed Fellow in 1622 by royal mandate, as Woodlark's statutes required that Fellows must be English (before those Statutes, one Fellow had been a Scot, and one French), Lothian knew that the Master must be both English and a Doctor of Divinity. However, at 6 p.m. on the Sunday after Sibbes' death, Lothian sent for Robert Creighton, M.A., a Scot; friend of James Stuart, Duke of Lennox; Fellow of Trinity and Public Orator. The deadline for the election was Wednesday morning; and Lothian suggested that if Creighton wanted the Mastership he should ride immediately to Court (where he was known) and get a dispensation from Charles I from the provisions of the College Statutes. Creighton had a letter from the King by noon on Monday. Unfortunately for Lothian's plot, this took the form of a recommendation rather than an absolute command. Creighton arrived back in Cambridge on the Tuesday night. By then, the other five Fellows, including William Spurstowe — none of whom knew about the plot — had voted for Brownrigg; and Lothian, biding his time, had voted for Brownrigg too. Creighton was told of this vote when he visited Lothian at 10 p.m. on Tuesday. Lothian read the royal letter, saw that it was merely a recommendation, and urged Creighton to ride back and get a more definitive royal order — promising meanwhile to delay Brownrigg's admission. The existing royal letter was shown to no other Fellow; and Creighton felt himself entangled in 'a twisted and interfering business'. (Sir Charles Snow's *The Masters* is a splendid guide to the donnish mind.) On the Wednesday, Brownrigg was told at Pembroke that he had been elected at Catharine Hall; apparently the first he had heard about it! He was told the rumours about Charles's letter, and declined to go forward if the King were definitely to support Creighton. But the five Fellows had not actually seen the letter; they emphasized the 'rumour' angle; and Brownrigg allowed himself to be admitted

[50] Account based on the documents printed in 1856 by J. E. B. Mayor. *Cambridge in the 17th Century*: autobiography of Matthew Robinson, pp. 132–46.

as Master in the Chapel of Catharine Hall. When this news reached the Court, Charles was angry, and wrote to Cambridge suspending Brownrigg. The affair was thus in the open, and enquiries dragged on for many weeks. The Chancellor, Henry Rich, Earl of Holland, wrote to the Cambridge Heads of Houses ordering them to interview the Fellows of Catharine Hall and 'endeavour by all fitting and convenient means to inform yourselves rightly concerning the said election'. And a month later Cambridge gossip had it that Brownrigg would be confirmed in the Mastership. The crucial fact was that Creighton waived any claim; and by the autumn of 1635 Brownrigg (rather to the distress of Laud) was secure in the Lodge of Catharine Hall.

This initial situation must have been irritating to Brownrigg, with his dislike of intrigue. But time passes, and the College continued to flourish. Entries rose (while the entries at Trinity in the late 1630s, for example, declined). During Brownrigg's reign the members of the College included (1640) Oliver St John (not the famous puritan lawyer, later Chancellor of the University, but the son of Sir Rowland St John); Oliver Cromwell's second son Oliver, who entered the College early in 1642, when he was just nineteen — he was to die of smallpox at the age of twenty one; and John Ray the naturalist. Ray migrated to Catharine Hall in June 1644 after six weeks at Trinity; he remained at the College for two years and five months, and then returned to Trinity, of which College he became a Fellow in 1649.

Brownrigg was Vice-Chancellor for the two years 1637–9. William Spurstowe praised his policy in 1638: he 'hath much reformed the University. Not a scholar could I see at any tavern. Luxury is much restrained from walking the streets and roving openly, as it hath done.' Although Brownrigg had on occasion tactfully to deal with the interfering Laud, the Archbishop would have approved of such a reforming policy, which reminds one of his own rigorous attempts at University discipline in Oxford. In 1643 Brownrigg was to be Vice-Chancellor for a further two years. (Richard Holdsworth, Master of Emmanuel, who had held the office for three years, had been imprisoned in London.) But the Unquiet Spirits were waxing hot. Brownrigg was forced to retire from his Bishopric of Exeter. And in 1645 he was put in prison in London, allowed to return to Cambridge merely to wind up his affairs as Vice-Chancellor, and ejected from the Mastership — one of eleven Cambridge Heads of Houses to be deprived in the 1640s. Until his death in 1659 he lived privately in Berkshire. His true fame belatedly began in the 1660s, when over 130 of his sermons were printed, in eight volumes; and, with Sandys and Sibbes, he joins the list of the Masters of Catharine Hall to have contributed to the history of the English sermon. In 1668 he was included by David Lloyd in his *Memoires of the Lives, Actions, Sufferings, Deaths of those Noble, Reverend, and excellent Personages that suffered by Death, Sequestration, Decimation, or otherwise, for the Protestant Religion, and the Great Principle thereof, Allegiance to the Sovereign.*

And Lloyd's tribute to his reign at Catharine Hall (though Lloyd was an Oxford man) could hardly be bettered:

'it was wonderful to see, how the *Buildings*, the *Revenues*, the *Students*, and the *Studiousness* of that place increased by the Care, Counsel, Prudence, Diligence, and Fame of Dr *Brownrig*; who had such an eye to all, that he oversaw none; frequenting the Studies, and examining even younger Scholars, that they might be incouraged in Learning and Good Manners.'

Our period ends sadly. Charles I was executed in January 1649. (He had stayed near Cambridge in 1647; and one of the people he had wanted to see was Brownrigg.) In October 1649 all graduate members of the University, and all future takers of degrees, were to swear a new oath, the so-called 'Engagement': 'I do declare and promise that I will be true and faithful to the Commonwealth of England as the same is now established, without a King or House of Lords'. William Spurstowe, who had succeeded Brownrigg as Master, refused to take the oath, along with the six Fellows, and the seven left Cambridge. The College was in confusion. The accounts for 1648 were unsigned, those for 1649 signed by two Fellows only — and those for 1650 were not audited at all. There were only eight matriculations from the College in 1650, the lowest figure since the late

1590s. Spurstowe had held office in a melancholy college. He had been an undergraduate at Emmanuel, then a Fellow of Catharine Hall under Sibbes. He was more of a 'party' man than Brownrigg; and in 1641 had joined with four others to write a tract against Episcopacy, issued under the awkward name Smectymnuus, constructed by combining the initials of the authors (William Spurstowe became *UUS*). Milton published a defence of their tract in 1642. Two of the five were to send their sons — Stephen Newcomen, and Benjamin and James Calamy — to Catharine Hall. Benjamin and James were uncles of the non-conformist historian Dr Edmund Calamy, who mourned the fact that they were both 'carried away with the tide, and swam with the stream, which was the way to preferment, and became clergymen in the Established Church'.[51] Benjamin became a celebrated Tutor of the College.

The Masters of Clare and Trinity had been ejected in 1645, together with Brownrigg. And six Heads of Houses, including Cosin of Peterhouse, had been removed in 1644; in which year two hundred dons and students were said to have left the University. The Grand Remonstrance of December 1641 had affirmed that the House of Commons intended to 'reform and purge the two Universities, that the streams flowing from them may be clean and pure'. In 1642 some colleges — but not Catharine Hall — sent silver plate and cash to the King. In the summer of '42, Oliver Cromwell, M.P. for the Borough, made his presence locally felt, Cambridge became a garrison town, the atrocity stories began — and Town seemed at last to have triumphed over Gown. A complaint of 1643 mourned the 'sad, dejected state of Cambridge': 'our Schools daily grow desolate, mourning the absence of their professors and their wonted auditories'; 'numbers grow thin, and our revenues short'; 'frighted by the neighbour noise of war, our students either quit their gowns, or abandon their studies'. Early in 1644 a committee was set up in Cambridge with authority to call members of the University before it — and power to expel and replace them. This committee, which at that time consisted of

[51] Calamy, *An Historical Account of my own Life*, ed. J. T. Rutt, 1829, I, 57.

five townsmen, made it clear that all members of a college, including servants, must take the 'Covenant': which involved approval of the abolition of Episcopacy and a promise not to assist the King. Later in 1644 a Visitation of the University was made by Edward Montagu, Earl of Manchester, an *alumnus* (like Cromwell) of Sidney Sussex — and the expulsions began. But no Fellows of Catharine Hall were at that time expelled. Brownrigg was a good man to hold the fort in such times, with his appeal to most shades of opinion. Indeed, in the years 1640 to 1645 entries to the College were conspicuously high. Spurstowe was humble, meek, innocent and peaceable; and unable to cope with the tensions of the late 1640s. After leaving Catharine Hall in 1650, he lived privately, until after the Restoration he became a chaplain to Charles II, and continued — here at least he is in the great tradition of the Masters of Catharine Hall — to publish sermons. Two volumes had been printed before his election to the Mastership; three came in the 1650s; and three in the 1660s, including *The Spiritual Chymist*, which had three editions in two years. Spurstowe died in 1666.

The New Jerusalem in England was by 1650 beginning to seem an untidy affair. Indeed, for three decades many Cambridge men had been looking across the Atlantic to New England (as 'the north parts of Virginia' came to be called from the 1610s). One of the reasons given for emigration in 1629 by John Winthrop, who had been at Trinity, was that Oxford and Cambridge were 'so corrupted as (besides the unsupportable charge of their education) most children (even the best wits and of fairest hopes) are perverted, corrupted, and utterly overthrown by the multitude of evil examples and the licentious government' of the colleges.[52] In the 1630s about 65,000 people crossed the Atlantic from England: about 45,000 went to Virginia and the West Indies; and about 20,000 to New England, including 100 Cambridge M.A.s (as against thirty-two from Oxford). The known list includes seven Catharine Hall men.

The association of the College with America in the seventeenth century is traditionally limited to some mention of

[52] *Life and Letters of John Winthrop*, ed. R. L. Winthrop, 1869, I, 310.

8

Nathaniel Bacon, Fellow Commoner in 1660, who went to Virginia, a gentleman of quality with a fine farm, in 1674, and led in 1676 a rebellion against the Royal Governor of the Province; a revolt which came to be celebrated in the eighteenth century in colonial folklore as the first popular revolt in British America.[53] There is no denying the glamour of Nathaniel Bacon; who died of dysentry in October 1676. But the seven College puritan emigrants of the 1630s were really more reputable. And, arranging Cambridge colleges by the contribution of their alumni to that emigration, Catharine Hall ties with Magdalene for third place: being beaten by Trinity, with twelve names, and Emmanuel with thirty four.

Hanserd Knollys spent 1638 to 1641 at Dover, New Hampshire. He had gone up to Catharine Hall in 1629, under Sibbes, and became a parson and schoolmaster at Gainsborough, Lincolnshire, in the region known to American historians as 'the cradle of Massachusetts': because of the separatists from those parts in the early seventeenth century who eventually inspired in 1620 the voyage of 'The Mayflower' and the founding of Plymouth Colony. Knollys returned to Old England, hopefully, in 1641. (Indeed over sixty English emigrants to New England in the 1630s eventually came back.) Knollys, an independent thinker with a burning hatred of authority, eventually died in 1691 at the age of ninety-two. Also from 1638 to 1641, Robert Peck was minister of Hingham, Massachusetts, twelve miles from Boston. Peck had entered Catharine Hall under Hound, in 1595, and, after taking his B.A. in 1599, transferred to Magdalene, whence he proceeded M.A. in 1603. From 1605 to 1638 he was rector of Hingham, Norfolk — between Cambridge and Norwich. In 1635 some of his parishioners had emigrated and founded Hingham, Massachusetts; and eventually he persuaded himself to join them. Returning to England in the early 1640s, he went back to Hingham, Norfolk, where he died in 1656: a nicely symmetrical life.

[53] For Bacon's Rebellion see David Hawke, *The Colonial Experience*, 1966, pp. 244–9.

Two Catharine Hall men were particularly associated with Harvard College. John Knowles, by origin a Magdalene man, was elected to a Fellowship at Catharine Hall under Sibbes in 1627. He in the 1630s became a puritan lecturer in Colchester, until he left England for Boston in 1639. In 1640 he became assistant minister at Watertown — now a suburb of Boston. He remained in New England until 1651 (for some months indeed daring to tour Virginia as a missionary!), and returned to become a lecturer at Bristol. In 1659 the General Court of the Massachusetts Bay Colony appointed Knowles one of the Old England Trustees to raise funds for Harvard. At the Restoration Knowles had to leave Bristol, and he lived in London for the last twenty-five years of his life, a member of what Samuel Eliot Morison has called the first 'Harvard Club of London'. In 1672, on the death of Charles Chauncy, Knowles was offered the post of President of Harvard. He declined it: he was sixty-six. The second Harvard-orientated man was John Sherman. He matriculated from Catharine Hall in 1631, under Sibbes (again!), crossed the Atlantic in 1635, and, like Knowles, eventually settled in Watertown; he was minister there in 1647, and at the same time was appointed an Overseer of Harvard. Sherman remained in Massachusetts until his death in 1685. In the early 1670s he was on the Overseers's Committee which drew up the architectural plan for a new building, Harvard Hall. Admiral Morison has pointed out that Harvard Hall, complete by 1677 (and burnt in 1764) conspicuously resembled the Eachard buildings at Catharine Hall.[54] Sherman became a Fellow of Harvard in the 1670s; and one of his daughters married the Massachusetts-born Samuel Willard, a noteworthy Vice-President of the College in the early eighteenth century.

John Lightfoot, Master of Catharine Hall since 1650, notable Oriental and Hebrew scholar, died in 1675: the longest reign as Master thus far in the history of the college. In the eighteenth century some biographers of Lightfoot stated as a fact

[54] S. E. Morison, *Harvard College in the 17th Century*, 1936, p. 428. Morison has material on Knowles on pp. 367, 390, 393; Sherman, 351, 428, 440, 538; the Lightfoot 'bequest', p. 289.

that he bequeathed his library to Harvard. The Harvard Library was destroyed by fire in the 1760s. Admiral Morison, the historian of seventeenth century Harvard, has stressed that there is no mention of such a gift in Lightfoot's will (a copy of which is at Somerset House). And he concludes: 'there was no such bequest'. Dr Luckett is sceptical about Morison's guess-work. The evidence of the will is indeed negative. But Dr Luckett argues that late seventeenth century wills were notably unprecise; that book bequests are not necessarily mentioned in wills, now or then; and that the eighteenth century tradition of the bequest is too firm to make Morison's conclusion definitive.

A third Catharine Hall man, in addition to Knowles and Sherman, was associated with Watertown. This was Nathaniel Norcrosse, another product of the Sibbes period, who came up in 1632. Norcrosse went to Massachusetts in 1638, had settled in the port of Salem (fourteen miles from Boston) by 1641, and then moved to Watertown in 1642. He returned to England in 1650, and became vicar of Walsingham, Norfolk, from which he was evicted in 1660. He died in 1662.

Finally, we have two Catharine Hall men connected with Long Island; then under the jurisdiction of Connecticut. John Youngs was born at Southolt, in East Suffolk, went to Emmanuel in 1620, but took his B.A. in 1623 from the Catharine Hall of John Hills. He became a parson in Suffolk; and went to New England in 1637, first to Salem, but in 1641 to Long Island, as minister of a township he named Southold — he died there in 1672. A Yorkshireman, Robert Denton, was the other Long Islander. He became a student at Catharine Hall in 1621, again under Hills, and eventually became a parson in Halifax. He crossed the Atlantic in 1638, to Connecticut. Soon he moved to Hempstead, Long Island, where he remained until his return to England in 1659. He died in 1663. Denton was a tiny man, and blind in one eye. Cotton Mather wrote of him that his 'well accomplished mind in his lesser body was an Iliad in a nutshell'.

Those were the Catharine Hall men who fled 'from the Depravations of *Europe*, to the *American Strand*'. The words are

Cotton Mather's, from his *Ecclesiastical History of New England,* 1702.[55] Mather, like earlier New England historians, linked the Atlantic emigration of the 1630s with the example of the exiles to Germany and Switzerland in the reign of Mary: all were 'powerful brethren driven to seek a place for the exercise of the Protestant religion, according to their consciences'. The spirit of Sandys lived on in Sherman and Knowles. Catharine Hall men in the 1630s, as in the 1550s, were able to brave the ocean and the wilderness in search of the spiritual Utopia: the wilderness being a place at once of iniquity, of trial, and of redemption.

[55] Extract in Perry Miller and T. H. Johnson, (eds), *The Puritans,* 1938. Harper Torchbook edition, 1963, I, 163.

Church and College, 1660–1745

By RICHARD LUCKETT

Fellow of the College

ON 31 March 1717 Benjamin Hoadly, Bishop of Bangor, Chaplain to George I and formerly Fellow and tutor of St Catharine's Hall, preached before the King a sermon (which was soon afterwards published) entitled *The Nature of the Kingdom, or Church, of Christ*. The immediate consequence was a controversy without parallel in the annals of eighteenth-century England. By July of that year no less than seventy-four pamphlets had appeared — attacking, defending, or simply missing the point of Hoadly's argument. As the Bishop's son subsequently noted: 'The Distraction of Men's Minds, of different Sentiments and Parties, was so great on this Occasion . . . that for a Day or two the common Business of the City was at a Stand, little or nothing done on *The Exchange*, and even many Shops shut up'.[1] A further consequence of the sermon was that the Lower House of Convocation set up a committee which, after investigating Hoadly's views, declared that they tended to 'subvert all Government and Discipline in the Church of Christ and to reduce His Kingdom to a State of *Anarchy* and *Confusion*', as well as to 'impugn and impeach the Regal Supremacy in Causes Ecclesiastical' — in other words, that the Bishop's opinions were both heretical and treasonable. But before the report could be presented to the Upper House (the next stage in a process which, so Hoadly's opponents hoped, would lead to the censure and perhaps even the impeachment of the Bishop) the proceedings were brought to an abrupt halt. By royal command Convocation was prorogued; it was not to meet again to transact business for over a

---

[1] Benjamin Hoadly, D.D., *The Works* (ed. John Hoadly, LL.D., 3 vols, London, 1773), II, 429.

century. Hoadly received several earnests of the royal favour, and before long was rewarded for his fidelity to the Whig cause by accelerated promotion within the hierarchy which many of his listeners and readers understood his sermon to deplore. The chairman of the committee that had endeavoured to castigate him, on the other hand, was with some ostentation removed from the list of Royal Chaplains. The cleric thus reproved was no less a person than Thomas Sherlock, Hoadly's undergraduate contemporary at St Catharine's, now in plurality Dean of Chichester and Master of the College.[2]

The Bangorian Controversy, as it came to be called, was not merely a paper war, nor was it simply another skirmish between Whig and Tory, this time in an ecclesiastical context. Rather, it dealt with issues of principle, fundamental in their importance both to the church and state. In his sermon Hoadly urged that the basis of Christianity was the individual's communion with Christ, and that sincerity was the sole test of truth. The corollary of this contention was developed in another of his works, the *Preservative against the Principles and Practices of the Non-Jurors* (1716). There he argued the same case, but with the intention of defending the legitimacy of the Glorious Revolution and of asserting that the subject's loyalty was to the established civil power; in particular he endeavoured to play down the notion of church authority. By so doing he hoped to demolish the moral scruples which prevented the non-jurors (the high churchmen who had refused to swear allegiance to William III and his successors and who denied the validity of ordinations save those stemming from the Bishops who had refused to take this oath) from acquiescing in the *status quo*. All of this had an immediate bearing on a specific piece of legislation, the Test Act, and it was the contention of Hoadly's opponents, Sherlock amongst them, that the Bishop wished to see this abolished, thereby flooding the country with new Whig

---

[2] Even as undergraduates, according to an anecdote recorded both by Bishop Browne and by W. H. S. Jones in their histories of the College, Hoadly and Sherlock were rivals. For the correct version of the anecdote, and an account of its dubious origin, see Edward Carpenter's *Thomas Sherlock, 1678–1761* (London, 1936), p. 4, n.

voters, and entailing significant changes in the University and
its colleges. For each graduand and Fellow was required on his
admission to swear in 'Open Hall' that he would be faithful
to the King and abjure the Bishop of Rome (thus excluding
Roman Catholics), and he was, moreover, required to take
Holy Communion in public at least once a year (thus debarring
Dissenters). In fact the indignation created by Hoadly's
undermining of the Test Act was such as to distract attention
from his quite extraordinary rejection of the concept of a church
visible. It was sufficient that the Bishop was 'the embodiment of faction, rebellion, and profane Latitudinarianism'.[3]

When Jonathan Swift met Hoadly in 1710 he characterized
him as 'the Whig clergyman', the concatenation of party and
profession being so damning, in Swift's eyes, as to need no
further remark, beyond that he encountered him, as was
to be expected, in 'a deal of ill company'.[4] 'Ill', for Swift,
meant Whig, and for a clergyman to be a Whig at a time
when the Church of England truly represented the Tory
party at prayer was, indeed, remarkable. But there could
be no mistaking the politics of a man who, in 1709, had been
the subject of a formal vote in the House of Commons, a
vote by which the Whig majority presumed to recommend this
mere vicar to the Queen, on account of his writings 'tending
to the Advancement of natural and revealed Religion, and to
the Justification of the noblest Principles of Civil Liberty.'[5]

Hoadly, however, was never a conventional figure, even
in appearance. Heavily marked by smallpox, and so badly
crippled that he habitually walked with a stick, until his
mid-thirties he looked acutely consumptive. But the comparative wealth attendant on the happy coincidence of his
theological views with the political needs of ascendant Whig-
gery enabled him to take carriage exercise, and the consequent
combination of fresh air and inertia soon inclined him to

[3] M. Dorothy George, *English Political Caricature to 1792* (2 vols, Oxford, 1959),
I, 68.
[4] *Journal to Stella*, Letter III.
[5] Hoadly, *Works*, I, ix.

PLATE III

THOMAS SHERLOCK

Pensioner 16 . . . –98;   Fellow 1698–1714;   Master 1714–19

J-B. Vanloo p'nx't   *By Courtesy of Messrs Christie, Manson & Woods Ltd*

PLATE IV

BENJAMIN HOADLY
Pensioner 16 . . . –1696; Fellow 1697–1701

Wm. Hogarth p'nx't   *By Courtesy of the Trustees of the Tate Gallery*

corpulence. This his son endeavours in his memoir to qualify, but there is evidence enough in the surviving portraits. On these the Bishop must have cast an instructed eye, for his first wife, Sarah Curtis, was herself a painter: the alliance testifies once again to his unconventionality and, failing heiresses, to his business acumen. Whilst Bishop of Bangor Hoadly never once set foot in his diocese; a point surprisingly omitted by the wontedly acrimonious commentators on his absence is that this might well be construed as the practical expression of his own theological position. The general impression of Hoadly is unsympathetic, but when he was treacherously and persistently libelled by a former French Jesuit to whom he gave shelter and patronage, he behaved with exemplary patience and generosity.[6] It is arguable that there was more than party loyalty in Bishop Burnet's description of him as a 'pious and judicious Divine'.[7]

Thomas Sherlock was scarcely so extraordinary a figure, though his aspect and manner could both be formidable. Pope, probably with reference to an athletic reputation gained in his Eton days, dubbed him the 'plunging Prelate'; contemporaries describe his voice as gruff, but it proved effective and moving in the pulpit. He was a noted preacher whose style Dr Johnson affirmed to be 'very elegant, though he has not made it his principal study'; the great lexicographer also on occasion recommended his sermons as improving reading.[8] If he had little of Hoadly's originality of mind he was at least a better writer; Pope sneered at Hoadly for his 'periods of a mile', but the same charge could not be levelled against his antagonist. In his *Trial of the Witnesses of the Resurrection of Christ*, Sherlock produced a work which was a best-seller largely because of the vivid presentation. In this examination of Christian Evidences there are Counsel for the prosecution and the defence, and a judicial summing up precedes the jury's acquittal of the Apostles on a charge of fraud. Canon Charles

---

[6] Neville Williams, *Knaves and Fools* (London, 1959), pp. 61–7.
[7] Gilbert Burnet, *History of his Own Time* (2 vols, London, 1724–34), II, 538.
[8] James Boswell, *Life of Johnson* (2 vols, Oxford, 1904), II, 189, 564.

Smyth has aptly compared the appeal of this work with that of Frank Morison's *Who Moved the Stone?* in the thirties.[9]

Nevertheless, we should not allow the obvious differences between Sherlock and Hoadly to blind us to certain similarities. No less than Hoadly, Sherlock was ambitious, and his opponents were not slow to label him avaricious as well, though the charge has little foundation.[10] No less than Hoadly, Sherlock was a 'political' cleric, but with the advantage that his politics were readily interpretable as attempts to defend the status of his profession. And the two men had been both undergraduates and Fellows of the same society, Catharine Hall. Moreover, the Bangorian Controversy, which brought them into national prominence, was about issues which closely concerned the College. The relationship can best be expressed by a résumé of the history of the College in the half-century preceding the death of Queen Anne.

In a sermon preached in 1745, 'on the occasion of the Rebellion in Scotland', Sherlock, by that time Bishop of Salisbury, sketched out a spiritual history of England from the time of the Reformation onwards.[11] In it he described the restoration of Charles II as a divinely-ordained return to 'our happy constitution in Church and State' brought about 'not by force of arms, or the power of princes, but by overruling the passions of men; so that even *they* became instruments in restoring these blessings, who had been greatly concerned in destroying them'. His words are not inapt as a summary of the events of 1660 in St Catharine's.

John Lightfoot, who became Master in 1650, had been a loyal servant of the Parliament that appointed him. But he was also a traditionalist in ecclesiastical matters and, save on the point of episcopacy, an adherent of the doctrines of the Church of England. When he recorded the execution of Charles I in the register of his living at Great Munden, Hertfordshire, he

---

[9] Canon Smyth has kindly communicated his notes for a commemoration sermon preached in the College Chapel, 1963.

[10] See the comments by the Rev. T. S. Hughes in his introduction to Bishop Sherlock's *Works* (5 vols, London, 1830), i, lxviii–lxx.

[11] Printed as Discourse XIV in vol. iii of the *Works*. The MS. is in the muniment room of the college, press mark xvii/6.

added the bleak observation: 'murdered'. Thus it is not surprising that the experience of the decade 1650–60 seems to have convinced him, along with so many others, that bishops and a king were preferable to what Sherlock called 'an almost infinite number of disagreeing sects' and, in civil matters, the rule of the Major-Generals. Yet (and in this he was unusual) Lightfoot did not ignore the implications of the change of régime. He visited Spurstow — his predecessor as Master, ejected by Parliament in 1649 — to propose his reinstatement. But Spurstow, a man of independent means now living a sequestered life in the country, refused this offer on the grounds of old age.[12] Lightfoot thereupon applied to the King, who 'generously bestowed his Letters upon him to confirm and settle him in the mastership'. On his coming down to Cambridge he was greeted by the Fellows some miles from the city; they had ridden out in a body to welcome him. Bishop Browne, the first historian of the College, pronounced this to be 'creditable to all concerned', and his opinion is echoed by W. H. S. Jones. This is a view which is not entirely convincing; Spurstow had been put into the Mastership by the Assembly of Divines, and since he was not elected he had no more title to it than Lightfoot. The Fellows' action presupposes communication with Lightfoot during his visit to Spurstow (how else could they have known of his return?). Their welcome can hardly have been spontaneous and the whole episode suggests a certain

[12] W. H. S. Jones in his history of the College (Cambridge, 1936, p. 100) erroneously states that Lightfoot visited Brownrigge; the confusion derives from a less than lucid passage in Bishop G. F. Browne's history (London, 1902, p. 131). But Brownrigge died in 1659 (see D.N.B. and Bishop John Gauden's *A sermon preached in the Temple-Chappel at the Funeral of Dr Brounnrig, late Lord Bishop of Excester* . . . (London, 1660)); the episode is described by John Strype in his life of Lightfoot prefixed to the first English edition of Lightfoot's *Works* (ed. George Bright, D.D., 2 vols, London, 1684), I, xxvii–xxviii. It should also be noted that there appears to have been no question of Lightfoot's being 'elected' in 1660, though Browne and Jones suggest that this was so. He was simply 'confirmed and settled' in the Mastership. A letter written by Sir William Dawes on his resignation of the Mastership in 1714 (see below, p. 131, n. 39) suggests that the notion of a free election to the post was not even by that date taken for granted: Sherlock became Master because Dawes and Blackall (an ex-fellow and then Bishop of Exeter) decided he was the man for the job and instructed the Fellowship accordingly.

amount of premeditation. The outcome was thoroughly satisfactory, and Lightfoot deserves commendation for his tact, but
his action was probably less quixotically generous than Browne
implies.

Lightfoot hastened to put his house in order. In post-1660
issues of his *Harmony, Chronicle and Order of the New Testament*
the original dedication of that estimable work to Oliver
Cromwell was replaced by a eulogy of Charles II. From 1663
the number of admissions to St Catharine's began to rise, and
for ten years the College appears to have been working at a
level approaching that of the period shortly before the civil wars.
The increase in admissions is of interest, because in this respect
St Catharine's does not altogether reflect the general trend;
during the latter half of the seventeenth century the total of
undergraduates at both universities dropped, despite the fact
that the population remained constant or increased.[13] The
Restoration, and the comparative increase in political stability
attendant on it, might have been expected to bring about a
dramatic change, but its beneficial effects were at once negated
by the restrictions of the Clarendon Code and the exigencies of
the Act of Uniformity. The Code, by preventing dissenters
from pursuing careers in the established church or as teachers,
professions for which the universities acted as training institutions, necessarily reduced the number of men in the country at
large who had a practical motive for seeking a university
education. Furthermore, by debarring dissenters from teaching
within the universities it deprived the colleges of the services of
many scholars whose contributions would have been of the
utmost value, particularly since many dissenters had scientific
interests; for an example we need look no further than the
great botanist John Ray, a former Catharine man who in 1662
held a Fellowship at Trinity, from which he resigned rather
than sign the declaration required of him.

---

[13] For a general discussion see Hugh Kearney, *Scholars and Gentlemen: Universities
and Society in Pre-industrial England* (London, 1970). For the rise in admissions see
Jones (op. cit., p. 99) and Kearney's graph derived from the Venns' *Alumni
Cantabrigienses*.

The consequence of the Clarendon Code was to make the universities and the established church heavily dependent on each other, and to restrict a spirit of free enquiry within the universities. This was in part a reaction to the rôle played by university men in the long Parliament: indeed Christopher Wase, a Beadle-at-Law at Oxford, was moved to consider, in a book published in 1678, whether in fact the universities had not positively bred sedition; he opined that this was not so, but the view, as he acknowledged, was widely accepted.[14] Both Oxford and Cambridge became traditional and authoritarian in outlook; in 1683 the Oxford Convocation publicly condemned 'certain pernicious books' on the grounds that they asserted that civil authority derived from the people; amongst the proscribed works were those of Goodwin, Owen, Baxter, Buchanan, Milton, Hobbes and Cardinal Bellarmine — the two last being authors whose outlook has been castigated in the present century as totalitarian. It is not surprising, therefore, that in the Restoration period the universities became increasingly the preserve of the gentry and the clergy, institutions at best traditionalist and at worst reactionary.

Many people, including Anglicans, disapproved. 'If the noblesse have a mind to have their children put in the Clergie's pockets, much good may it do 'em' reflected John Aubrey, no puritan, as he set about his own plan for educational reform.[15] The existing alternatives, the Inns of Court, were much patronized, and the meetings of the Royal Society in London added a further attraction to the capital, which continued to increase in importance. A further alternative was the Grand Tour and a private tutor — a scheme which carried the imprimatur of John Locke, who himself never attempted to disguise his contempt for Oxford and Cambridge. But St Catharine's, at least temporarily, seems to have enjoyed an enhanced popularity. What explanation can be advanced for this?

The most satisfactory answer is that, whatever we may think of the restricted function of the universities in the post-

[14] Christopher Wase, *Considerations concerning Free Schools in England.*
[15] Anthony Powell, *John Aubrey and his Friends* (new and rev. ed., London, 1963), p. 231.

Restoration social order, the College fulfilled this function with considerable success. For this we may adduce a specific reason. In 1641 William Spurstow, a Fellow of the College and, as we have seen, subsequently Master, was one of the five divines who collaborated as 'Smectymnuus' (the name was compounded of their initials) in *An Humble Remonstrance*, the celebrated attack on the Arminianist assertion that episcopacy was inseparable from the Royal prerogative. This attack, however, stopped short of Sir Edward Dering's 'root and branch' position, which called for the extirpation of all bishops, for it admitted of a valid 'primitive' episcopacy. Spurstow's attitude reflected a view current in St Catharine's, since the then Master, Brownrigge, was known as a bitter enemy of Laud and a 'great Man for the anti-Arminianist Cause, yet as a mighty Champion for the Liturgy of the Church and Ordination by Bishops alone'.[16] In 1660 we find amongst those admitted to the College the name of Stephen Newcomen, and in 1663 that of Benjamin Calamy. As Browne noted, both of these were sons of Spurstow's co-authors; in both cases, moreover, the fathers were ejected from their benefices under the Act of Uniformity. But their sons continued at the College and in due course took orders. In other words, Lightfoot (himself described as 'not very scrupulous' in fulfilling the provisions of the Act) and the College had evidently arrived at an accommodation which permitted moderate puritans who could not renege on their past to the extent of submitting to the discipline of the Act to send their sons to the College notwithstanding.[17] Benjamin Hoadly's father, a schoolmaster of New England birth and non-conformist opinions, may have sent his son to St Catharine's with this in mind. Spurstow's views provide a clue as to how the accommodation became

[16] Laurence E[a]chard, *The History of England from the beginning of the Reign of King Charles the First to the Restoration of King Charles the Second* (Volume the Second, London, 1718), p. 870.
[17] This is not to suggest that the College circumvented the Clarendon Code; the essential point is that Lightfoot pointed the way to an *accomodation* which was acceptable to men whose inclinations were, broadly, puritan. Unfortunately the records of the oathing of Fellows, which might throw more light on the matter, are incomplete from 1618–89 (*Admissions of Fellows* ledger, muniment room, press mark XL/33). For Lightfoot and the Act of Uniformity see the article in D.N.B.

possible; the Fellows of the College, following Lightfoot, seem
to have been prepared to take a broad view of doctrinal issues
in order to create a clergy which exercised some real power in a
stable society, a power which found expression in the church
courts. Lightfoot himself was explicit in this attitude: he wished
to 'beat down Enthusiasm . . . To maintain the honour of
Learning and a Regular Clergy; and to shew the necessity of
keeping up publick Communion with the National Church'.[18]
The general intention is clear and decisive, but the need to
'shew the necessity of keeping up publick Communion'
indicates an interesting and illuminating ambivalence.

The aim is equally evident from the writings of John Eachard,
a Fellow since 1659 and, on the death of Lightfoot in 1675 his
successor in the Mastership. Eachard's *Grounds and Occasions
of the Contempt of the Clergy and Religion Enquired into* (1670) is a
lively satire written in a fluent and entertaining style, which had
a significant influence on the development of English prose,
and to which Jonathan Swift was considerably indebted.[19]
It was designed to expose the poverty and ignorance of many
of the clergy, and to encourage the improvement of this state of
affairs. Eachard was not, as he put it, 'any contriver of an
incorruptible and pure crystalline Church, or any expecter of a
reign of nothing but Saints and Worthies: but only an honest
and hearty Wisher that the best of our Clergy might, for ever,
continue as they are, rich and learned! and that the rest
might be very useful and well esteemed in their Profession!'.[20]
Several passages in *The Grounds and Occasions* relate to the
universities; Eachard ponders the advantages of a 'strict
examination' for entrance, with 'all that was sent up not fit for
their purpose' returned home 'by the next carrier', and he is

---

[18] Strype in Lightfoot, op. cit., I, xxxvi. Of Lightfoot in the Commonwealth
period Strype says that he 'was convinced how he had been Trepanned, and
saw his error'.

[19] The fullest and best account of Eachard and his writings is provided by Edite
Mason in her *Life and Works of John Eachard (1636–1697)* (unpublished Ph.D.
thesis, London, 1967).

[20] Quotations are from the reprint by Edward Arber in *An English Garner* (Pens-
hurst edition) (12 vols, London, 1909), VII, 241–312.

sceptical about the value of Sizars, representing them as the dupes of those who wish to save a servant's wages. The exploiters, he says, have their own rationalization of this: 'Bedmaking, chamber-sweeping, and water-fetching were doubtless great preservatives against too much vain philosophy'. But he goes on to point out, without irony, that 'it is ten times more happy, both for the lad and the Church, to be a corn-cutter or tooth-drawer, to make or mend shoes, or to be of any inferior profession; than to be invited to, and promised the conveniences of, a learned education, and to have his name only stand airing upon the College Table [i.e. notice-boards], and his chief business shall be, to buy eggs and butter'.

Contemporaries did not always appreciate the ironies of *The Grounds and Occasions* and several were swift to take exception to some of Eachard's more startling suggestions, such as that there was a need for some 'vent for our Learned Ones, beyond the sea', to which it would be possible to transport 'so many tons of Divines yearly'. Reading the work today we note Eachard's deep concern for the quality of the Church and its ministers, and his assumption that the principal duty of a university is to train such ministers.

Eachard's other writings include a witty and hard-hitting attack on Hobbes in which, according to Dryden, he 'baffled the philosopher of Malmesbury' with 'raillery and reason'.[21] He also published counter blasts to attacks on his *Grounds and Occasions*, but after 1673 he apparently ceased to write, and his entire literary production falls within the years 1670–3. Perhaps he would have written more had it not been for his increasing involvement in College affairs from 1673, the date when Lightfoot, encouraged by a former member of the College, Matthew Scrivener, Vicar of Hazlingfield, commenced rebuilding. In the person of John Lightfoot the College could boast a Hebraist of immense learning and international repute, so immersed in his subject as to be called the 'English

---

[21] John Dryden, preface to *The Works of Lucian* (London, 1740).

Rabbi'.[22] In John Eachard it had a controversialist whose works ran into numerous editions and attracted widespread attention. In John Strype, who was an undergraduate in the 1660s, it gave to the world an ecclesiastical historian whose biographies and collections of material remain essential sources to this day.[23] But the buildings of the College were neither worthy of its objects nor convenient for the attainment of them — the accommodation being, as Strype remarks, quite inadequate — and it fell to Eachard, who was responsible for the financial side of the project from the first, to carry through the long and laborious process of remedying this.

He did not live to see the project completed. But he did see the construction of the new Hall, Buttery, Combination Room and Library (1675–7) of the Lodge (now Old Lodge, built in 1676–8), and of D and C staircases (1679–87).[24] He arranged the finance of the building operations, served twice as Vice-Chancellor, and contrived both to run the College and to take pupils. His fund-raising activities were exceedingly involved, and when W. H. S. Jones came to describe them in his history of the College he accused Eachard of 'irregularity' in his transactions. The charge is unwarranted, and characteristic of Jones' tendentious account of Eachard.[25] At his death, it is true, Eachard left the College with a number of outstanding debts, and his personal indebtedness (for he was 'always ready to fling in' from his private purse) encumbered those of his relatives who found themselves his executors. The principal method used for raising money, the guaranteeing of annuities against a subvention, proved less successful than had been

[22] For Lightfoot see Strype's 'Life' cited above, and D. M. Welton, *John Lightfoot, the English Hebraist* (Leipzig, 1878). The slighting reference to Lightfoot by Dr Philpott, quoted by Browne (op. cit., p. 115) and repeated, though with qualifications, by Jones, is a gross misrepresentation based on supposition. None of the historians of the College have done justice to his scholarly achievements, which give him a claim to be a founder of Oriental Studies in the university.

[23] For Strype see his *Works* (19 vols, Oxford, 1812–24) and the index by R. F. Laurence (2 vols, Oxford, 1828).

[24] For the rebuilding see Dr Sydney Smith, 'The Seventeenth Century Rebuilding of St Catharine's (*St Catharine's College Society Magazine*, 1963).

[25] Dr Mason (op. cit., pp. 33–44) offers a valuable corrective.

anticipated, partly because of the unsettled political situation between 1685 and 1691.[26] In addition Eachard borrowed from the University Chest whilst Vice-Chancellor, and his executors and the College were left to repay this money, which had been used for the benefit of St Catharine's.

It remains for a future historian to disentangle the whole complex business of the finance of the building, an affair which throws much unexpected light on late seventeenth-century economic life, both institutional and private. For our purposes one observation will suffice. In his book of moral characters, *The Holy State* (1648), Thomas Fuller describes the qualities requisite for 'The Good Master of a College'. His recommendations are sound and practical: the learning of the Master, for instance, 'if beneath eminency is far above contempt. Sometimes ordinary Scholars make extraordinary good Masters. Everyone who can play well on *Apollo's* harp cannot skilfully drive his chariot'. The good Master 'winds up the tenants to make good Musick, but not to break them'. Yet Fuller goes on to say that the good Master 'counts it lawful to enrich himself, but in subordination to the Colledge good . . .'.[27] It is this last recommendation that bears on Eachard. It was taken for granted in the seventeenth century that Masters should do well out of their Masterships: Eachard entirely failed to fulfil this expectation: he impoverished himself during his period in office. That his relatives suffered also is a fact which cannot be denied, but it is largely attributable to political circumstances, the protracted and wasting illness that beset Eachard in his last years, and the failure of a number of guarantors (including Fellows) to meet their obligations. The value of his achievement, on the other hand, is incalculable; it pays dividends to this day.

---

[26] This reason was specifically given in a printed appeal for funds drawn up by the Fellows and the new Master, Sir William Dawes, after Eachard's death. A copy is preserved in the Muniment Room.

[27] Thomas Fuller, *The Holy State* (4th ed., London, 1663), pp. 92–4.

Whilst building progressed, the life of the College went on though bachelors' feasts were curtailed for reasons of economy, and from time to time plate was sold to raise money. However, the influence that the political upheavals of the period exercised on St Catharine's was not merely financial and, in the interplay of personalities, ideas and events, we can detect cross currents that had certainly not abated when the controversy of 1717 came to a head. Benjamin Calamy, son of Spurstow's collaborator in *An Humble Remonstrance*, was elected into a Fellowship in 1668, and left the College in 1674 to become perpetual curate of St Mary Aldermanbury, formerly his father's parish. He owed his appointment to Sir George Jefferies, then Recorder of London and in due course to become notorious as the Judge at the Bloody Assizes, a man whose reputation belies his devout Anglicanism. That Calamy was ardent for compromise in matters of religion is amply demonstrated by a sermon which he preached before the Lord Mayor and Aldermen of the City in July 1673, whilst he was still a Fellow of St Catharine's. This is an impassioned plea for the promotion of 'our Catholick Christianity' by exhortations to 'a greater care and study of those things, which have never yet bin made matter of controversie, about which all sides and parties are agreed'.[28] The sermon is remarkably ecumenical in tone, though the precise would probably have disapproved of Calamy's animadversions on the futility of overmuch attention to obscure passages of scripture — an attitude which he had in common with Eachard. It is, nevertheless, a profoundly Anglican work: Calamy is calling for dissenters to re-enter the fold of the established Church. After leaving the College Calamy pursued a successful career in London parishes, and in 1685 became a Prebendary of St Paul's. In that year Henry Cornish, a Sheriff of London, Calamy's parishioner and his close friend, was executed for alleged complicity in the Rye House plot. Calamy supported Cornish at his trial and shortly

---

[28] Benjamin Calamy, *A Sermon . . . at Guild-Hall Chappel* (London, 1673), p. 27.

afterwards died — principally, it is said, of grief.[29] His funeral
sermon was preached by William Sherlock, Master of the
Temple and also a Prebendary of St Paul's, but not, like his
son Thomas, a Catharine man. The incident, and the association of Calamy with a Whig and a rebel, mark both the revival
of that division within the Church which was an inevitable
result of the accession of the Roman Catholic James II, and the
first direct evidence of a connection between the Sherlock
family and the College.

In April of 1686 Eachard was personally involved in a
political issue, for together with other representatives of the
University, including Isaac Newton, he appeared before
Jefferies to show cause why they had refused to comply with
the Royal mandate to admit Alban Francis, a Benedictine
monk, to the degree of Master of Arts without administration of
oaths. For his involvement Eachard was censured by the
Ecclesiastical Commission, and Peachell, the Vice-Chancellor,
was ejected both from that office and from the Mastership of
Magdalene. This episode was but a minor consequence of
James' Declaration of Indulgence which, by its suspension
of the penal laws for failure to take the sacrament, immediately
broke the power of the ecclesiastical courts and undermined
that alliance of Church and State which, however tenuous,
provided the basis for the attempted revival of clerical status
after 1660 — a revival in which St Catharine's was deeply
involved. Lightfoot might have been reluctant in his recognition
of the dependence of church order on episcopacy and of
episcopacy on the king, but his actions show that, in practice,
he accepted such a dependence. A later generation of St
Catharine's scholars such as John Strype, his cousin James
Bonnell (author of a *Harmony of the Holy Gospels*, and Accountant-
General of Ireland), James Calamy (Benjamin's brother,
elected a Fellow of the College in 1678), Offspringe Blackall

[29] Browne (op. cit., p. 135) maintains that Jefferies himself sat on this case and
that Calamy 'withstood . . . his former patron'. But the trial was in fact before
Jones, Chief Justice of the Common Pleas (see G. W. Keeton, *Lord Chancellor
Jeffreys and the Stuart Cause* (London, 1965), p. 338. See further Calamy's *Works*
edited by his brother James (London, 1690) in which Sherlock's sermon is
reprinted.

(also elected Fellow in 1678) and John Leng (a notable classicist, subsequently Bishop of Norwich, elected Fellow in 1688) took this dependence for granted in their writings.[30] But the Declaration of Indulgence, with its recognition of the claims of bodies other than the established church, destroyed the relationship at a blow and threatened to resurrect the old anarchy; and the Glorious Revolution, however beneficial to laymen, brought the clergy but cold comfort. In 1689 it became necessary to swear new oaths, to William and Mary, and to do this meant abjuring the principles on which they had long argued the established church to be based — loyalty to the rightful monarch and the discountenancing of all rebels.

In the event the majority of clerics took the oath, but five bishops, headed by Sancroft (Archbishop of Canterbury), and four hundred clergy, refused and were ejected. This was no mean proportion. Two Fellows of St Catharine's (a third of the Fellowship) were amongst those who suffered, and they, together with the rest of the non-jurors, served as an uneasy reminder to their former brethren of the latter's apostacy: they seemed, it has been well said, 'a ghost of the past, confessors who stood in the ancient ways, devout, logical, and insistent'.[31] For a time the non-jurors counted William Sherlock amongst their number — a surprising recruit, for his background, if Dr South is to be believed, was non-conformist. In fact his adherence did not last long, since in 1690 he published *The Case of Allegiance due to Soveraign Powers Stated and Resolved*, in which he gave his reasons for submitting to the oath. The circumstances that had brought about his change of attitude were somewhat extraordinary. Archbishop Sancroft, shortly before he was deprived of office, had ordered the publication of a book by Bishop John Overall (Master of St Catharine's 1598–1607) in which it was argued that Government

---

[30] Bishop Browne (op. cit., p. 150) refers to Bonnell as the author of *Pious Meditations*, the implication being that he wrote a book of that title. The only work by Bonnell that ever appeared in print was the posthumous *Harmony of the Holy Gospels* (London, 1705). But Bonnell's saintliness is not in question, and it occasioned contemporary comment: see William Hamilton's *Life and Character of J. Bonnell* (London, 1703).

[31] G. V. Bennett, 'Conflict in the Church', in Geoffrey Holmes (ed.), *Britain after the Glorious Revolution 1689–1714* (London, 1969), p. 160.

was of divine institution. This work had been suppressed by James I, who resented ecclesiastical interference in politics, for the rather odd reason that Overall was expounding the opinion of Convocation, which could not be allowed to have views on such matters. Sancroft had brought the book to light again in order to support his opinion of the illegitimacy of the Revolution, but he had evidently failed to observe that Overall asserted, with reference to the United Provinces, that 'when a change of Government was brought to a thorough settlement, it was then to be owned and submitted to, as a work of the Providence of God'.[32]

It was this passage that convinced Sherlock, and it is unlikely that his views went by without notice in St Catharine's. Not only was Overall a former Master; Sherlock had been a friend of Benjamin Calamy whose brother James, a Fellow of the College, was in 1690 preparing an edition of Benjamin's sermons in which he reprinted Sherlock's eulogy. At the Temple Sherlock held the post which had been filled with conspicuous success by Richard Sibbes (Master of the College, 1626–35) and which had been occupied informally by Ralph Brownrigge during the last years of the Interregnum. A further association with the College is indicated by the arrival of Sherlock's son Thomas as an undergraduate in 1693.

The Glorious Revolution did not prevent St Catharine's from continuing to function as a place of scholarship and teaching, but it shook its finances and undermined the principles which had guided it since the Restoration. This is not to say that St Catharine's was disloyal to the new order; it never became, as certain Oxford colleges did, a nest of Jacobitism. When Queen Mary died in 1694 both John Leng and Thomas Sherlock contributed poems to *Lacrymae Cantabrigiensis*, a volume of elegies by members of the University. The difficulty facing the College was a long-term one, the question of its rôle in society at large, and this, of course, was equally a difficulty for every other college in the two universities. But in St Catharine's the problem was exacerbated by limitations in size and in

---

[32] Burnet, op. cit., II, 212–13; William Sherlock, *The Case of the Allegiance*, 3rd ed., 1691, pp. 4–5.

resources; it could never be as comprehensive in its objects as a larger institution, and the will of its Fellows counted for a great deal.

It was the College's good fortune, however, that John Eachard was succeeded on his death in 1697 by a man uniquely qualified to pilot it into the next century. This qualification was not a matter of age but of character, reputation and connections; at the time of his election as Master, Sir William Dawes was no more than twenty-five and, since the minimum age at which the requisite Doctor's degree might be conferred was thirty, a special dispensation had to be obtained for this to be carried through. He came of a family which had suffered greatly for its royalism, though his father, created a baronet in recognition of his services to the Crown, redeemed the family's fortunes by a well-judged marriage. William was the youngest of three sons, and intended for the church from an early age; he was also something of a prodigy.[33] At the age of fifteen he had mastered Hebrew; at eighteen he composed a poem in heroic couplets entitled *The Anatomy of Atheism* — though this, as he admitted, fell short of his original intention of 'putting all the articles of our christian faith' into verse.[34] His original university was Oxford, where he became a Fellow of St John's within two years of his admission; he came to St Catharine's after the sudden death from a fever of his eldest brother, Sir Robert, a Nobleman at the College, the news of whose demise arrived simultaneously with similar tidings of his other brother, a naval lieutenant. At twenty-one, whilst a member of the College, he wrote a full-length prose work, *The Duties of the Closet, being an earnest Exhortation to private Devotion*, and this achieved considerable success.

At the age of twenty-two Dawes married Frances D'Arcy; in the next year, so soon as he was of an age to do so, he took

---

[33] Dawes, however, scarcely compares with William Wotton, who entered St Catharine's in 1676 aged nine years eight and a half months, and was admitted B.A. at the age of twelve years and five months (see C. R. Haines, *St Catharine's Society Magazine* for 1934).

[34] Sir William Dawes, *The Whole Works* (3 vols, London, 1733), III, 299. I am indebted to John Wilford's 'Preface' for much valuable information.

orders and shortly afterwards, having attracted the favourable notice of Archbishop Tenison, became Dean of the Peculiar of Bocking in Essex. 1697 saw his election to the Mastership at St Catharine's, and in 1698 he served as Vice-Chancellor. It might well be supposed that such rapid advancement was inconsistent with excellence of character and attainment, but for this view there is no evidence. The preface to *The Anatomy of Atheism* strikes, it is true, a priggish note, but by the time he penned *The Duties of the Closet* Dawes had achieved his ambition of writing 'with all the plainness and simplicity imaginable, and with as much brevity as a discourse of this nature would bear'. As Master he brought a lustre to the name of St Catharine's, and during his time in office the College's material position improved substantially. On 1 September 1704 the chapel, a 'bare *case*' on Dawes' accession, was at last ready for its dedication by Symon Patrick, Bishop of Ely, the sermon being preached by John Leng and afterwards printed by the University Press. In October 1710 the first elections were made to the Conduct Fellowship (effectively a chaplaincy) established by Moses Holwey, and to the Frankland Fellowship (a form of senior scholarship).

During this time Dawes continued to receive preferment; soon after Anne's succession he was made a Royal Chaplain, and in 1707 he was advanced to the see of Chester. Undoubtedly his political views helped to hasten his promotion, as the circumstances of his appointment make clear. According to Bishop Burnet the Queen took matters into her own hands, and disregarding a promise by the Lord Treasurer that 'Preferments should be bestowed on Men well principled, with relation to the present Constitution [Burnet is here endeavouring to express the sense of Whig without actually using the word] . . . did secretly engage himself to Dr *Blackall* for *Exeter*; and Chester . . . to Sir *William Dawes* . . . These Divines were in themselves Men of Value and Worth, but their Notions were all on the other side; They had submitted to the *Government*, but they, at least *Blackall*, seemed to condemn the Revolution, and all that had been done pursuant to it. *Dawes* also was looked on as an aspiring Man who would set himself at the head of the Tory Party: so this Nomination gave a great disgust'.[35] The great disgust, however, can scarcely have afflicted St Catharine's, who thus had their Master and a prominent former Fellow and Tutor consecrated Bishops on the same day.

Burnet was opposed to the politics of both men, particularly those of Blackall, so we should not necessarily expect fairness from him, but his view of the two Bishops was fundamentally just. Dawes was an opponent of Jacobitism, a loyal supporter of William III and of the Protestant succession.[36] At the same time his theological outlook did not seem entirely consistent with such loyalties, and his tendencies were undeniably authoritarian. The difficulty can be illustrated from the writings of Dawes' intimate friend Blackall, which he subsequently edited. In 1708 Blackall asserted, in a sermon preached before Queen Anne (the very platform that Hoadly was later to utilize), that rulers are God's ministers on earth, whom no man can question or resist. It was an opinion shared by Dawes. Both Bishops were loyal and neither had any truck with the Jacobites. But the tendency of their arguments smacked of St Germains.

Dawes and Blackall were diligent in the pursuit of their calling. Their ideal is suggested by Dawes in his memoir of Blackall, when he describes the latter's 'primitive simplicity and integrity, constant evenness of mind and uniform conduct of behaviour, unaffected and yet most ardent *piety* towards God, orthodox and steadfast faith in Christ, disinterested and servent *Charity* to all Mankind and exact discharge of all relative duties'. Their concept of their task was paternalistic, and they were associated with Leng in the work of the various Societies for Promoting Christian Morals and the Society for the Propagation of Christian Knowledge. The manner in which Dawes exercised his influence in the college is indicated by his choice of the chapel as the burial place of his wife, who died, aged only twenty-nine, in 1705. The elaborate memorial tablet reads (to quote a contemporary translation): 'She was a Woman who (if ever any did) deserv'd to be buried within the

[35] Burnet, op. cit., ii, 487–8.
[36] Dawes, op. cit., i, xlii.

sacred Walls of this Chapel; as being, while she lived, the
Glory and Ornament of the College, and the Example, as well
as the Delight, of the learn'd Members thereof'. Both Dawes
and Blackall endeavoured to carry over their pastoral attitude
into politics: their aim was the restoration of the clergy to
something like the status they had enjoyed before James brought
in the Declaration of Indulgence, with an active church freed
from political manipulation (though they intended it to be a
political force in its own right) and the ecclesiastical courts
once more a power in the land.[37]

The most brilliant proponent of the views of the 'Church'
party was Francis Atterbury, who was largely responsible for
the establishment of Convocation as a semi-autonomous body,
and who evolved the splendid doctrine of the 'Providential
Revolution' in order to reconcile the absolutist notions in
which many churchmen fervently believed with the embarass-
ing events of 1688. It was Atterbury who stage-managed the
Sacheverell trial, and made 'High Churchman' a phrase in
everyday use. He hoped for a unified Tory ministry and a
unified Tory church, and it was his aim to achieve this before
the death of Anne brought in the House of Hanover and the
Whigs. The Whigs, in their turn, alleged that Atterbury
wanted to subvert the Hanoverian succession, but this does not
seem to have yet been the case: his object was a Protestant
King and a high church régime.

In these circumstances Dawes emerged as the leader of the
moderates; he held that Atterbury was dangerously high-flying,
and he was inclined to attend to Whig suspicions of Atterbury's
Jacobitism. Atterbury's answer was to introduce the Schism
Bill which, through its prescriptions for the strict licensing of
teachers by the bishops, promised to restore to the church much
of the power it had lost. The Bill was violently assailed by the
Whigs, and the Tories, as Atterbury had anticipated, were
forced to unite. When the Bill passed into the Lords, Dawes,
in this year appointed Archbishop of York, gave it his support,

[37] My indebtedness in what follows to Norman Sykes's *Church and State in England
in the Eighteenth Century* (Cambridge, 1934) is, inevitably, considerable. I have also
consulted Bro. George Every, *The High Church Party 1688–1718* (London, 1956).

thereby assuring the solidarity of the party. It was due to become law on 1 August 1714. But Atterbury's efforts were in vain. On that day the Queen died and Dawes, who was visiting his province, was the first to proclaim the accession of George I to the citizens of York.[38]

Dawes, on his elevation, was succeeded as Master by Thomas Sherlock, the appointment being proposed by Dawes after consultation with Blackall.[39] Dawes took advantage of the high favour in which he stood with the Ministry to obtain an Act of Parliament annexing a Canonry of Norwich to the Mastership, thereby greatly enhancing its value. The Dean and Chapter of Norwich, as may well be imagined, treated the project with hostility, and it was not until 1719 that Sherlock finally took his stall in the cathedral. When he did so he for a short time combined that office with the Mastership of St Catharine's, the Mastership of the Temple, the Deanery of Chichester and a Canonry at St Paul's. It can scarcely be supposed that he contrived to fill all of these posts adequately, but there is no evidence that he was negligent in his conduct of College affairs. Theologically he continued the tradition of Dawes and Blackall — Tory, high church and authoritarian — though in his sermons there is less emphasis on private devotions, and this might be seen as tending to vitiate his position.

The tradition was under attack before 1714, and by no less a personage than Hoadly, whose ungainly, limping figure, once familiar within the courts of the College, now seemed to threaten it from outside. Three years after vacating his Fellowship on his marriage he was inducted into the London living of St Peter Poor, 'in a great Measure' we are told, 'by the Recommendation of the Reverend Dr William Sherlock' — the father, that is, of Hoadly's rival, Thomas.[40] Sherlock, since the publication of *The Case of Allegiance*, had moved increasingly close to the Whig position, and obviously he and

---

[38] See Lady Mary Wortley Montagu's *Letters* (ed. Robert Halsband, 3 vols, Oxford, 1965–7), I, 213.
[39] See the letter printed in Browne (op. cit., pp. 173–4).
[40] Hoadly, op. cit., I, viii.

Hoadly found each other's views congenial. Both men denied the divine origins of kingship and asserted, though with qualifications, the sovereign power of the people. In so doing they were in flat opposition to the views of Dawes, Blackall, and of Thomas Sherlock. Hoadly's outlook had much more in common with William Sherlock's than did that of the latter's own son, though the succession of Thomas to his father's office as Master of the Temple suggests that there was no personal rift between them. In 1705 Hoadly was reproved by the Lower House of Convocation for advancing views which were considered 'dishonourable to the Church', and from that time onwards he became progressively outspoken, perhaps in proportion to the extent to which his future depended on the success of the Whig cause. Soon he was pouring scorn on Blackall, albeit with scrupulous (and effectively ironic) expressions of esteem for the Bishop's integrity and '*Episcopal Character*'. He had his reward for his consistency and fidelity to the Whig leaders when he was offered the Bishopric of Bangor in 1715.

In that year Thomas Sherlock, as Vice-Chancellor, carried to George I a letter of thanks for the King's gift to Cambridge of a valuable collection of books, an acknowledgement of the University's loyalty during the recent Jacobite rebellion. Neither Sherlock nor any other Fellow of St Catharine's was a Jacobite, and College and University remained staunch adherents of the Protestant Succession. But those who wished to see the Church restored to its former status can have had little hope that, whilst men such as Hoadly — 'a Dissenter and Socinian in lawn' — monopolized the preferments, there was any real possibility of attaining this end. It had vanished with the death of Anne.

The Bangorian Controversy was, in fact, a forlorn hope, a last and outraged attempt by Tory divines to draw the attention of the nation to what they considered to be the pernicious absurdity of latitudinarian doctrines. Hoadly's standing as a bishop gave them the opportunity to present the extent of the scandal in lurid tones. Convocation, the creation of Francis Atterbury, headed the attack, with Sherlock, Master of a college whose most illustrious sons had, for over fifty years worked for the furtherance of a learned and powerful clergy, in the van. The nation stopped and wondered, the funds fluctuated, the Tories rallied somewhat, and the printers prospered. But the endeavour, however gallant and (given certain premises) logical, failed. The failure did not prevent the moderate Tories from making an eventual return to power, nor Thomas Sherlock from obtaining advancement and even, in due course, the offer of the Primacy, which he refused.[41] But it marked the end of the 'Church' party as a political force, an end sealed when in 1721 Atterbury (appointed Bishop of Rochester just before Anne's death) was impeached in the Lords for treason and fled the country. Hoadly, needless to say, played more than a small part in the inevitable pamphlet war that accompanied these proceedings.

The failure of the 'Church' party also had moral consequences. In his sermon on the '45 rebellion (quoted earlier) Sherlock painted a sombre picture of 'the ruin of vertue and religion' in his age, and in his later works he repeatedly revealed that the contemporary scene filled him with dismay. 'The unruly passions of men must be governed,' he wrote, 'either by force or by religion.' But the professors of religion lacked conviction and, observing London street life, the Bishop was inclined to believe that the civil power was equally unwilling to attempt to exercise authority. If a leading and successful churchman could be so openly pessimistic, it is not surprising that lesser men repined. In 1719 Sherlock had been succeeded as Master of St Catharine's by Thomas Crosse, whom he disliked and who was said to have been elected 'for no other reason but that a senior might be removed out of the way'.[42] Consequently Sherlock did not use his ecclesiastical patronage to further the interests of the College, though in due course he did make generous benefactions in its favour. Without the support of the one former member who both possessed real influence in public life and also adhered to the principles that had guided it in the past, the College lacked direction.

---

[41] Sherlock, op. cit., I, lvi.
[42] Sherlock, op. cit., I, lxx.

Between 1660 and 1719 the College produced more than its quota of eminent men. They are not on the whole remembered today, because their achievements, though great, were ephemeral. Lightfoot's 'Talmudical and Rabbinical Learning', Eachard's satires, the serried and voluminous histories of Strype, the devotional works of Bonnell and Dawes, the sermons of Calamy, Blackall and Eachard, all were written in the service of the Church, and it was assumed that the College's task was to further that service. But when the Church became subordinate to the civil government and no longer possessed power of its own, and the civil government, by its use of patronage as an appendix to politics, sapped the Church of its vitality and conviction, the College faltered. This happened throughout Oxford and Cambridge, but colleges less exclusively clerical in their tendencies had other resources.

It is noteworthy in this respect that, since the Restoration, St Catharine's had produced only one writer — John Eachard — whose works retain today any interest for the student of literature; and even Eachard's writings are, in fact, an offshoot of the polemics of church politics. Whilst it is probably the case that Trinity Dublin was the characteristic college of the Restoration *littérateur*, there is significance in the absence in St Catharine's of any poet or playwright save the excruciating Sir John Cutts (a soldier-versifier, of whom Swift made a laughing-stock). The interests and achievements of the Fellows were limited, as perhaps Edward Capell, the mid-eighteenth-century Shakespearian editor recognized when he presented his magnificent library of English poetry and drama to Trinity (Cambridge) rather than to St Catharine's, his own College. In the early years of the century a visitor to St Catharine's library remarked on the poverty of its holdings; this was partially remedied by bequests and gifts from Thomas Neale of Bramfield (1705), Thomas Crosse (who gave two hundred volumes in 1728) and Bishop Sherlock, whose books arrived from Fulham Palace in 1761.[43] Sherlock had previously given six hundred pounds for the alteration and refitting of the

[43] For the poverty of the library see J. E. B. Mayor (ed.) *Cambridge under Queen Anne* (Cambridge, 1911), p. 179.

College library, and he also left lands to pay the stipend of a scholar-librarian. The gift was munificent, but in terms of the College's needs it came too late.

If St Catharine's failed to be literary it was equally unproductive in the field of the natural sciences or mathematics. There was certainly no hostility to such studies, for J. F. Vigani, who settled in Cambridge about 1683 and twenty years later became the first Professor of Chemistry in the University (a non-stipendiary, titular post) lived for a time in the College, and Jones hazards that Eachard had an interest in his work.[44] Of more significance was the arrival in December 1697 of John Addenbrooke, whose uncle had previously been a member. Addenbrooke was elected Fellow in 1704, and in 1709 was admitted an extra-licentiate of the Royal College of Physicians.[45] He vacated his Fellowship in 1711, shortly after taking a doctorate in medicine. As Jones points out, it was not strictly within the terms of the statutes for a Fellow to study medicine, and this may account for Addenbrooke's resignation, but it is more likely to have been a consequence of his marriage to a Miss Fisher, a connection of Sir William Dawes. Addenbrooke's association with the College was clearly very close; his nephew also became a member and subsequently served as Chaplain to Thomas Sherlock when the latter was Bishop of Salisbury. To the College Addenbrooke gave his medicine chest, and he was buried in the ante-chapel. It would be wrong, however, to think of him as in any sense a medical pioneer: his gift to the library of money for the purchase of Gassendus' *Works* argues a conservative approach to his calling, and his only publication was an *Essay on Freethinking* (1714) which controverts agnostics with assertions that would not have come amiss from Blackall, and is, furthermore, positively alembical in its style. Addenbrooke is memorable for his charity rather than for any eminence as a scholar, and he certainly did not initiate any tradition of natural science in the College.

---

[44] D. A. Winstanley, *Unreformed Cambridge, a Study of certain aspects of the University in the eighteenth century* (Cambridge, 1935), p. 143; Jones, op. cit., p. 103.
[45] For Addenbrooke see the three articles by A. W. Langford in the *St Catharine's Society Magazine* for 1935, 1936 and 1937.

In 1745, the same year in which Sherlock meditated on the ruin of society, the death of Mrs Mary Ramsden brought the College the bequest of the residue of her very considerable wealth.[46] Her generosity stayed the College against inflation and allowed for a major expansion of the Fellowship. In her 'Rules and Orders' for the administration of the benefaction she specifically willed that 'the Fellows of this foundation be not confined, but be at liberty to apply themselves to and follow the studies of any of the learned professions of Divinity, civil and canon Law, or the common Law of England, or Physics, or any other of the liberal arts and sciences, without any obligation upon them to go into orders . . .'.[47] Superficially this seems to have been just the opportunity that the College needed, but the situation was in fact far from straightforward. The Ramsden Foundation Fellows (properly the Skerne Fellows) were in effect Bye-Fellows, with no power in the government of the College and no teaching duties. The first elections were to be made by the Master and Fellows of the Old Foundation, and though the Skerne Fellows were to vote on equal terms in subsequent elections this virtually ensured that they would continue the existing tradition of the College. And like Sherlock's gift of books the benefaction came at the wrong moment, when the impetus of the Restoration tradition had died and no new object was adequately in view. The real benefits of the foundation would be felt much later.

Benjamin Hoadly has from his own day to the present been the subject of bitterly critical comment.[48] Bishop Browne, in his history, echoes the general opinion. We should not too readily take these criticisms for granted. Hoadly was avaricious, yet the same could be said of Sherlock; Hoadly's faults were those of the contemporary ecclesiastic, of whatever persuasion. But his opinions, for all that they challenged the assumptions on which his church and his former college had run, were of the utmost importance. Their influence in liberal circles was vast,

---

[46] The estate, however, was not conveyed to the College until 1767.
[47] Jones, op. cit., p. 118.
[48] Notably by Sir Leslie Stephen in his *History of English Thought in the Eighteenth Century* (2 vols, London, 1876).

and extended to America, where his writings have been attributed a significant rôle in the 'growth of a Revolutionary frame of mind'.[49] They belonged, in short, to a democratic, not an authoritarian age. It would be incorrect to suppose them to be original: the denial that Christ left behind him any 'visible human authority' was at least as old as Erastus, and it is not unjust to apply to the respective positions of Hoadly and Sherlock in the Bangorian Controversy the terminology of the early seventeenth century, and to call them Erastian and Arminian. But Hoadly, for all his prolixity, and perhaps because of it, spoke to his age, and the age — indeed the century — listened. It was, appropriately enough, one of the precursors of the Romantic poets, Mark Akenside, who in an ode addressed to the Bishop caught the essence of this. 'Who is this' he makes the assembled Houses of Parliament ask, 'who:

> Could a whole Nation disengage
> From the dread Bonds of many an Age,
> And to new Habits mould the public Mind?

The history of the Bangorian Controversy is not the history of the College, nor is the history of the College in this period the history of the Bangorian Controversy. The day-to-day life, which in a sense mattered much more, cannot so easily be recovered. But an examination of the Controversy and of the College's associations with it does suggest why the qualities that made St Catharine's remarkable in the post-Restoration period did not avail in the century that followed. It may also suggest something of the nature of these qualities, and of the concomitant weaknesses. And in conclusion we may permit ourselves a futile but attractive speculation; what if Hoadly, no less than Sherlock a product of the College, had been elected Master in the latter's stead?

[49] See Bernard Bailyn, *The Ideological Origins of the American Revolution* (Cambridge, Mass., 1967), p. 38, n. I am indebted to Dr J. M. Thompson for this reference. It is worth observing that Nathaniel Bacon, the seventeenth-century Virginian rebel, had been a member of the college. Cf. pp. 105–6 *supra*.

10

Fellow Commoners and the
College Plate, 1473–1875

By DR SYDNEY SMITH

Fellow and Tutor; quondam President and Steward

LIKE the buildings, or the books in the Library, the College's silver or its pictures can serve as a guide to much that went on within the College at various periods in its history; and the evidence can be illuminating even when (as is so often the case) it is not complete. The silver of St Catharine's throws special light on the place of the Fellow Commoners in the College at various periods, since there are very few pieces of plate recorded as belonging to the College that did not originate as gifts from Fellow Commoner members. Even when the plate bears no name or arms to identify the donor there is strong evidence that such pieces were often acquired by exchange for damaged or unfashionable plate which had been given by a Fellow Commoner.

Since pieces of plate have, from time to time, been sold, re-made, lost or borrowed, it is not possible to work simply from the pieces themselves. To identify the pieces, and the Fellow Commoners with whom most of them are associated, has called for extensive (and at times tedious) checking through several sources; and a record has been compiled on cards of each man, with the identity of the piece of plate, its appearance in the plate audits, its disappearance from the audits, whether this was because of exchange or of sale, if this is on record. If, as sometimes happened, money or a gift in kind was recorded instead of a gift of plate, this also has been indexed. Much biographical information from Venn's *Alumni Cantabrigiensis* has gone into the record, and several Fellow Commoners are identifiable who do not appear in Venn, especially during the seventeenth century.

The College records which proved of most value in the search were:

1. The Audit Books from 1622, with a few gaps, to the present day. Men entering the College are named, and whether they were Fellow Commoners (sometimes Noblemen), Pensioners or Sizars, is indicated. College fees would be affected since a Nobleman paid 7s. 6d., Fellow Commoners 5s., Pensioners 2s. 6d. and Sizars 1s. on admission; and although Fellow Commoners were identified as such in most years, the fee paid indicates their status on the occasions when they were merely called 'Mr'. Equally, if a Pensioner transferred to the status of Fellow Commoner, the event and the fee are recorded in the Audit Book.

2. The University Matriculation Lists provided valuable information although they do not always tally with the Audit Books. The explanation lies in the fact that not all men who were admitted were matriculated. In the early seventeenth century matriculation took at least one year, and many never got that far. Oliver Cromwell, for example, was admitted as a Fellow Commoner at Sidney Sussex in April 1616; but he resided for one year only and did not matriculate and, in consequence, never graduated. The University therefore has no record whatever of his residence although the College records are unequivocal. In the seventeenth and eighteenth centuries many young men of good family, with landed estates, did not seek a degree but wanted a legal qualification from the Inns of Court so that they might in later life act as magistrates on their estates. An analysis of the members of the Long Parliament reveals that 'Far more numerous than practising lawyers were the gentlemen who had been to one of the Inns of Court with no intention of being called to the Bar. Opinions differ on the quantity of law most of them imbibed; but the general verdict is probably, as so often with students, a harsh one'.[1] St Catharine's was certainly the preliminary training-ground of several

---

[1] D. Brunton and D. H. Pennington, 1954, *Members of The Long Parliament*, p. 6.

members of the Long Parliament, and study of the entry of
Fellow Commoners reveals that some who can now be identified
escaped the historical analysis. No doubt a similar enquiry into
Pensioner admissions would reveal that some Pensioners like-
wise escaped scrutiny; but, lacking the confirmation of Audit
and Plate Lists, the enquiry would be less reliable.

3. The College Admission Book contains only minimal
information when it was begun in 1642, but this was later to
include the name of the man's Tutor; and the College Register,
running from 1623 to 1736 affords much supplementary
information.

4. The College Audits are confirmed and extended by the
numerous entries recorded from time to time in the Conclusion
(Order) Book, and later audits appear from time to time on odd
scraps of paper.

From these various sources coverage is good for the period
from 1637 to 1650. On this last date a careful inventory was
made by the newly-intruded Master (Lightfoot) and by six
Fellows who were considered politically reliable.[2] Then there
is a gap in the records until 1684, when growing indebtedness
for rebuilding made a careful count of realizable possessions
necessary. From then up to about 1710 the Audits mark a
relatively high number of pieces as suitable for sale or exchange,
but from about 1710 onwards the financial position of the
College became more secure and sales or exchanges of plate
figure less frequently.

Through this mass of information it is normally possible to
tell which pieces were the gift of Fellow Commoners since the
piece — specified as a Beaker, Bowl, Can (often a Kann) or
other utensil — would be denoted in the list along with the
name of the donor. Normally the piece would carry the arms of
the College and those of the donor. So much was this the
normal practice that absence of the donor's arms seems in-
variably to have been noted. Though some pieces carried only
the College's arms, they were probably obtained in exchange

---

[2] See p. 103, *supra*.

for worn-out pieces presented by Fellow Commoners, the identity and arms of the original donor being lost sight of in the process.

The Fellow Commoners, who played so important a part in the creation of the College's plate, figure from the first records of the College. The first two were recorded as being in residence when the College was opened on 25 November 1473;[3] James Wylleborde (a Scot) and Edmond Bacton then soon became Fellows of the small post-graduate foundation. It is still not easy to define a Fellow Commoner concisely and without ambiguity but it is clear that in the fifteenth century they were often men of some standing as senior graduates who shared the amenities of the Fellows' table, and throughout the period covered by this essay there are occasional records of the admission as Fellow Commoners of senior men who were candidates for higher degrees in Theology, Law or Medicine. Some of these men made gifts of plate, but this does not seem to have been obligatory, as it became for undergraduates who were admitted as Fellow Commoners.

This usage, of admitting undergraduates as Fellow Commoners, seems to have arisen in the sixteenth century, developing from the custom of serving separate Commons to Fellows and to Scholars. A Pensioner could therefore (presumably at his option, if he could afford the cost) be at Fellows' Commons or at Scholars' Commons. The distinction emerges when Queen Elizabeth visited Cambridge in August 1564 and a list of the numbers of residents in each college was compiled for her information. St Catharine's, with only twenty-one men in residence at that time, had thirteen in Fellows' Commons. There were seven scholars of the College, and the Master brought the total up to twenty-one; so none of the Pensioners was in Scholars' Commons.

That the College was small, and to that extent intimate, may be judged from the fact that although the Earl of Sussex was

[3] See pp. 18–20, *supra*.

lodged there during Elizabeth's visitation the College was unable to accommodate his retinue, who had to find lodgings in the town. But it was a retinue of more than a hundred men! All the evidence available would emphasize the small numbers of St Catharine's men at that time. The only college of anything like comparable smallness was Corpus Christi, with thirty-two members.[4] From Venn's analysis of numbers of matriculations from 1544 onwards it appears, making allowances for those who came into residence but who did not matriculate, that St Catharine's averaged from two to three admissions in each year; and according to the figures for 1570 in John Caius' *Historiae Cantabrigiensis Academiae* St Catharine's then had only twenty-one Pensioners as against Queens' with seventy-seven and Christ's with fifty-one Pensioners in addition to fifty-three Scholars and thirty-nine Sizars. Consumption of bread[5] was consistent with quite a small society, and the consumption of beer also tallied with a small size. But the College drank a notably high proportion of double beer, which would fit in well with a high proportion of senior members.

Undergraduate numbers at St Catharine's were, in short, few until the beginning of the seventeenth century; and when numbers of undergraduates rose, numbers of undergraduate Fellow Commoners, with their gifts of plate, rose in proportion. Undergraduates, moreover, brought an increasing complexity in college life, and with it increasing evidence of administrative practices, including an annual audit of accounts. The increase in the number of undergraduates can be correlated with the development of the tutorial system, which had been started by Richard Sibbes (elected Master in 1626) and had been continued and improved under his successor, Ralph Brownrigg. The result was that when the College was assessed for Poll Tax in 1641 St Catharine's returned 102 members as against 124 at Queens' and 163 at Christ's. The change in relative size from the Elizabethan figures is notable and indicates a comparable growth in public esteem. It also fits in with

---

[4] Cooper, *Annals*, II, 206–8.
[5] For a table of consumption of bread and beer; see Jones, *History*, p. 400.

the audit evidence, which survives with minor lacunae from 1623 onwards.

Once such accounts begin to be available the number of Fellow Commoners can be reckoned with fair accuracy. The record for 1623 shows that six Pensioners and eight Sizars were admitted. There are no records for 1624–6, but in 1627 the entry was twenty-four, of whom three were Fellow Commoners. Annual numbers matriculating increase to a plateau from 1637 to 1641, followed by a steady decline to 1649. These, of course, were years of great political strife and civil war. For the whole period two hundred and ninety-one Pensioner admissions are recorded, a hundred and twenty Sizars, and ninety-one Fellow Commoners, a little over eighteen per cent of the whole. The size of the entry indicates that the tutorial system was working well; for the Tutor was the great attraction who drew youths to a college. The quality of the entry confirms this view and shows that the power wielded by the Tutor was exercised with knowledge and judgement. From the beginnings of the tutorial system in 1627 until 1635 the Tutor was John Knowles, a divine who became famous for his extreme Puritanism. He emigrated to the New England settlements,[6] but even there he incurred censure for his refusal to use a prayer book and to wear a surplice. But when he returned to England (but not to St Catharine's) in 1651 it was reckoned that no less than forty-seven of his former pupils were either Members of Parliament or of the Assembly of Divines.[7]

Amid the increasing numbers of junior members of the College, the various classes were distinguished by their gowns, which denoted their status as Fellow Commoners, Pensioners or Sizars. The Fellow Commoners were distinguished in other ways also. Though most Pensioners and almost all of the Sizars proceeded to their degrees, normally after three years in residence, many Fellow Commoners, having taken about a year to matriculate, spent only one further year in residence before proceeding to an Inn of Court. Perhaps wisely, with this in view, they were required to make a gift of plate for their

[6] See p. 107, *supra*.
[7] Browne, *St Catharine's*, p. 120.

personal use, or of money in lieu, at or shortly after their admission. The gift, engraved with the College's arms as well as with those of the Fellow Commoner, appeared in audit lists even while the donor was still in residence, and when tutors were slow in paying the money to the Bursar the debt of 'Plate Money due from the Tutor' would be entered in the accounts. The transaction was an important part of the College's financial arrangements, and indeed of the finances of all colleges.

In the first surviving record of plate, the audit for 1623, is the record 'for Mr. Alston's plate £2. 10s. od.'. This purchased a Can, put into the Treasury and so audited until 1647; the gift of a Fellow Commoner, Peter Alston, who graduated B.A. in 1627, was admitted to Gray's Inn in 1628 and died in 1632. His younger brother, Thomas, also from Bramford, Suffolk, matriculated as a Pensioner in 1631. But the value of the cash-contribution varied with the price of silver, and this was rising steeply. The £2. 10s. od. contributed by Peter Alston probably bought a Can weighing between fifteen and twenty ounces troy, but by 1637 the value of an acceptable piece had risen to £3. 10s. od., as may be judged from the entry (which also casts some light on the habits of Knowles), 'Plate due to the Colledge: from Mr. Knowles, 1 Peece for Mr. Piggott, in lue of this £3. 10s. od.'.

Evidence of a comparable system, and of a fixed contribution, comes from St John's College, where the Master and Fellows decreed as early as 1569 that 'every fellow-commoner should give on admission a silver potte or goblette . . . in weight X ounces'. This must be engraved with the man's name and arms. Then, in 1576 a payment of 33s. 4d. within a month of admission was demanded, to 'buy plate or books', and in 1638 St John's reverted to a system of actual gifts of plate, specifying 'in valew worth fooure pounds' instead of a weight of ten ounces.[8] Fellow Commoners of St Catharine's were also required to make a contribution of £2 for the purchase of books in addition to their contributions of plate, but it is not

[8] Victoria County History, Cambridge 1959, III, 448.

LEGENDS TO PLATES OVERLEAF

PLATE V

Candlesticks reading from the left:

(1) Maker: Wm Cafe, London 1766. Donor, Wm Cecil Grave Fell. Comm. 1773.

(2) Maker: Robert Makepiece and Richard Carter, London 1777.

(3) Maker: Edw. Feline, London 1737. Given Francis Whichcote 1764.

(4) Candlestick with snuffer tray en suite. Maker: James Gould, London 1732. Donor, Strelly Pegge of Beauchief, Derbyshire. Admitted Pensioner 1726, later Fellow Commoner.

(5) Maker: Wm Cafe, London 1759. Donor, Robinson Morley, Fellow Commoner 1751 (see text).

PLATE VI

upper left, Rose water ewer. Maker: William Fawdery, London 1703. (see text)

upper right, two-handled cup. Maker: Robert Cooper, London 1713. Donor, Francis Winnington, Stanford, Warwickshire. Admitted Fellow Commoner 2 November 1710.

lower left, Cruet. Maker: R. Peaston, London 1769. Donor, Henry William Bunbury. Admitted Fellow Commoner 30 January 1768.

lower right, Base of Henry Bunbury Cruet with inscription and engraved weight showing assessment for plate tax. (59 oz. 6 dwt.)

PLATE V

PLATE VI

clear at what stage of their careers this was expected of them. Towards the end of the seventeenth century they had to meet a charge of £1 levied at about the time of their graduation. The Fellow Commoner was then called a 'Midsummarian'.

Though the Fellow Commoner was assessed at a common figure for his contribution of plate it was not always easy to turn the cash into silver. Goldsmiths and silversmiths were sorely tried to get the metal for their craft as the Thirty Years' War in Germany, Huguenot troubles in France, Spain's failure to overcome the Dutch, and the unsettled conditions in England presaging the Civil War, meant that plate was being melted down for currency and there was little silver available for new fabrication. Some cash contributions never bought plate therefore; Piggot, for example, who entered the College in 1631 and whose payment Knowles was late in transferring, never had an entry in the plate list against his name, and the general state of the silver market meant that, so far from the purchase of plate being a normal habit, the tendency was to melt it down, especially in times of financial stringency. 'Plate had always been regarded, both by individuals and by public bodies, as a reserve of capital which could be realized in an emergency.'[9] But the need to sacrifice plate came as a shock, and it was doubtful whether plate which might soon have to be melted down was worth the cost of elaborate finishing, or perhaps even of fabrication at all. So, although plate above the common run was occasionally bought, the early Fellow Commoner pieces were simple cans and beakers for use at table. They weighed about fifteen ounces troy and were good for reasonably careful use but were liable to damage. Pewter therefore was widely used, and there are constant notes of the repair of pewter in the audits.

The College's plate suffered not only from the general conditions which made the purchase of plate costly and the melting down of pieces common in the seventeenth century. There was also a need for ready cash to pay for the buildings which were being erected. Some money paid in to purchase plate was

[9] C. Oman, *Caroline Silver*, 1970, p. 2.

diverted in the mid-thirties to help pay for the building of the old E Staircase, the kitchens and buttery, begun in 1630 and finished in 1637. The likelihood of a piece of plate being sold would seem to have varied with its location in the College. The early audits list the location of the pieces — in the Master's Lodging, in the custody of individual Fellows or in the Treasury. Pieces in the Treasury seem to have been particularly vulnerable to sale or exchange, though there are cases where a piece formerly in the Treasury, and then apparently disposed of, turns up again in service. The vulnerability of plate which was not in daily use but was stored in the Treasury as a capital asset should, perhaps, cause little remark; and the needs of the College were pressing, while new contributions played a smaller part than might have been hoped. Plate for use in the Buttery or in the Combination Room would be signed for by the Butler (who can thus be identified); and there was also plate for use at Holy Communion.

The first silver-audit, of 1623 (on the cover of the audit book) was taken at a time of financial disputes between the Master (John Hills) and the Fellows.[10] It fitted in with an audit of the furniture in the Master's Lodging, and allows some information to be recovered from the earlier period. The College at that time possessed sixteen pieces of plate, and since some of these pieces survived to the reasonably complete audit of 1637, where they were recorded with the name of the donor, it is possible to identify the donor from Venn's *Alumni*. Of these the earliest to emerge is William Foster, who matriculated as a Sizar at Lent, 1589. He gave a gilt Cup with Cover, in all probability to mark his proceeding D.D. in 1618, when he was appointed Prebendary of Chester. His later appointment as Bishop of Sodor and Man in 1633, not long before his death in February 1635, was not marked by a further gift. But his Cup was audited, variously described as a Bowl or a Wine Cup, up to 1650. Peter Alstone's Can, as has been seen, reveals the practice of payment of a specified sum in cash as early as 1623, and the Beaker of Philip Hodgson, who matriculated as a

[10] Jones, *History*, p. 88 *et seq.*

Fellow Commoner in 1616, also survives in the audit from the earlier period.

But the sixteen pieces audited in 1623, together with the nine pieces contributed by Fellow Commoners up to 1639, make a meagre total although every Fellow Commoner admitted between 1623 and 1639 gave a Can or a Beaker. They were added to from other sources. In 1624 it was recorded that eighteen silver spoons, marked 'KH Butteries' (the engraving being done by Peter Muser for one shilling) were bought from payments made by newly-admitted Fellows. Mr Lothian, Mr Meeres and Mr Arrowsmith each paid £1 on his admission and 'the surplus of the plate which was bought and exchanged' made up the sum of £3 16s. od. The purchase of the spoons was accompanied by the purchase of 'rough towels' for rubbing the plate, and perhaps this is an indication of the sort of treatment to which plate was subjected, explaining both the need for frequent repair and the use of earthenware and pewter. The eighteen spoons, however, had survived intact up to the audit of 1637, for that audit lists as College Silver:

Communion Challice	1 College Bowl
3 wine cups	1 College Beaker
1 College Pot	5 salts — whereof 2 trencher salts
18 spoons	2 College cans

In addition there were listed thirty-seven named Fellow Commoner pieces — thirty-one cans under the names of their donors, three bowls and three pots. One of the trencher salts had been bought as recently as 1636; for 9s. 6d.

The list as audited at 1637 was soon to be upset for reasons of state rather than for internal financial reasons.

Archbishop Laud had threatened to visit Cambridge in 1635, and in 1636 his inspectors made a report on the religious practices of the University and the colleges. They took especial objection to the practices of Emmanuel College; but they found St Catharine's almost as bad. At Catharine Hall 'of late they were as irregular as any and most like Emmanuel'. The result of the ecclesiastical visitation is apparent in the silver audit. In 1636 a 'Taffaty Carpet for the Table', identified in the audit

as the Communion Table, was bought for £1 1s. 0d., and on
27 July 1637, four Fellow Commoner pieces and the College
Cap Can were exchanged for two silver flagons for the Communion Table; the College Bowl was exchanged for a patten on
20 November 1639.

The plate holdings seem to have settled down to a short
period of relative stability after these changes, though only
thirteen of the eighteen spoons could be found at the audit of
1638. Additions were forthcoming; of ten Fellow Commoners
admitted in 1640 nine gave a piece of plate. But plate was
scarce by 1642, so that of the twenty-three Fellow Commoner
admissions between 1643 and 1646 only eleven gave plate and
only three pieces of plate were recorded from the six Fellow
Commoners admitted between 1647 and 1650. The audit of
1650 therefore records a decline in plate holdings. In itself this
audit has an interest, for it was held by the new Master,
Lightfoot, and six Fellows, following hard after the expulsion
of Spurstow and the existing six Fellows at the end of 1649.
The spoons continued to disappear; the 1647 audit had
recorded only twelve, 'and one lost', while in 1650 only eleven
were to be found. Since twelve such spoons, marked KH, were
sold in 1811 it seems that at least one of the missing ones must
have been found. More significant than the spoons, however,
was the fact that whereas in 1647 sixty-two cans were audited,
of which forty-four were put into the Treasury, the new Master
and Fellows, in 1650, could only account for twenty-nine.
Thirty-three cans and two beakers which had figured in 1647
received no mention. They could have been sold to meet
College indebtedness; or they could have been disposed of to
assist either King or Parliament. There is complete silence; no
guide to conjecture.

Some notion of the value and weight of plate at this time can
be got from the list of plate surrendered to King Charles at
York in 1642 by Queens' College.[11] The list notes the weight of
each piece and shows that a pot or tankard averaged sixteen to
nineteen ounces and a beaker twelve to thirteen ounces. A

<hr />

[11] Cambridge Antiquarian Society, Communications, 1857, Vol. 1, no. 7.

payment of £2 10s. od. in the 1620s in lieu of a can of about sixteen to nineteen ounces weight would show that silver then cost roughly three shillings the ounce, and a comparable payment of £3 10s. od. in the mid-thirties would give a price for the silver of about four shillings the ounce. Another estimate of the cost of plate arises from the circumstance that in 1626 Thomas Buck was paid £4 0s. 6d. for a silver gilt standing salt acquired by him for the College. This salt was always identifiable in subsequent listings until it was sold in 1688 and was weighed with the rest of the College plate. The weight was 41 ounces, which means that in 1626, even when fashioning and gilding are included in the price, Mr Buck paid only 2/– the ounce troy. But in all respects Mr Buck was an excellent man of business, who did the College many services.

It is interesting to note that the most splendid piece surrendered to the King and listed by Queens' College was a bowl and cover weighing 109 ounces, the gift of Theophilus Fiennes (or Fines). He entered at Queens' as Lord Clinton, in 1616, and two years later succeeded to the Earldom of Lincoln. Though his silver went to the royal cause, Lincoln supported Parliament, and this may account for the fact that his son and heir, Lord Clinton, entered St Catharine's in the third quarter of 1642. His payment for entry as a nobleman (7/6d.) is entered in the Audit, but times were unpropitious and he did not emulate his father's generous gift of plate. In fact no gift of plate is recorded from him although the audits from 1643 to 1647 carry against his Tutor, Daniel Duckfield, 'plate not given in Ld Clynton and booke'.

The inroads into the holdings of plate which are revealed by the 1650 audit were not made good in the subsequent years. Only thirteen Fellow Commoners were admitted during the eleven years from 1650 to 1660, as against sixty Pensioners and forty-four Sizars. Few of these Fellow Commoners were able to contribute plate, and it may be surmised that such few pieces as were given had not been newly fashioned but were older family pieces used for the purpose. Out of three Fellow Commoners admitted in 1653, one made a gift, a twenty-four ounce tankard whose weight would seem to indicate that it came from some household store. Out of three admitted in 1654, one made a gift of £12; this appeared later in the records as a tankard but it was not recorded when the purchase was effected, and the cost of £12 for a tankard as against the cost of £2 10s. od. a generation earlier is significant. Four more Fellow Commoners were admitted in 1659, of whom one died before payment and none of the other three is recorded as having given either money or a piece of plate. The correlation between the events of the Great Rebellion, the execution of Charles I in 1649, and the austerities of life under the Commonwealth could hardly be better, and the general picture is borne out by the internal history of the College. After 1648 income from room rents fell drastically while substantial bills had to be met for maintenance of the buildings. In 1657/58 repairs amounted to £60 6s. 7d. and the Bursar, John Slader, had to be reimbursed £61 od. od. from the Treasury. It was in the Treasury that silver not required for daily use was lodged as a form of capital investment, and the College in this period would be profiting from the increase in the value of its plate. But to meet the Bursar's requirements would have needed the sale of about twenty cans.

Not all audits survive for the Commonwealth period. But there are deficits in the annual accounts from 1648 to 1664, and the College's position was worsened when in 1650 it was called on to pay twelve guineas annually for local tax, from which it had previously been exempt. This was a considerable burden to carry with an annual income of only about £160. Nevertheless, out of the thirty-five Fellow Commoner pieces which were noted at the audit of 1650, some survived to finance, at least in part, the re-fabrication of the grander types of plate which is recorded when plate audits were resumed in 1684.

The changes which are then apparent are that contributions in plate were significantly heavier in weight. Silversmiths after the Restoration of the Monarchy had sufficient quantities of silver available and, in the face of competition from immigrant French Huguenot silversmiths, a noble weight and an attractive simplicity of design became usual in the work of the London makers. Ostentation seems to have flourished after the Restoration, but it must also be remembered that before the late 1680s, when the City, and banking and stock-holding techniques, made it more easy for surplus money to be used as capital in commercial expansion, plate was a relatively safe and a very common investment. The significant part played by plate as an investment can be seen from the fact that the fortune of many banking houses was founded on firms dealing in plate which had been supplied to their order by craftsmen. Hoare's early trading books, for example, record sales of silver to clients, and loans of money advanced to clients on the security of plate:[12] and it is interesting to note that the receipts for contributions towards the cost of rebuilding the College include an item, 'Mr. Richard Hoare Goldsmith £1 1s. 6d.'.

None of the pieces which the College owned, or came to own, during the period from 1660 to 1700 survive today. They were sold to meet the costs of the rebuilding. But the records enable us to reconstruct something of an inventory, and to make it evident that the College had to some extent recovered its connection with the social class which produced Fellow Commoners. It has always been accepted that John Eachard, an active Fellow from 1658 till his death in 1697, was outstanding in rousing interest in the College among potential benefactors to the building schemes to which he devoted so much of his time. It is evident also that his recruiting power, as Tutor and later as Master and Tutor, among the higher gentry was equally important for the general finances of the College. Under him the proportion of Fellow Commoners rose significantly because he maintained admissions in that class in a time of general decline in Pensioner and Sizar entry; and the Fellow Commoners and their families rallied to pay contributions for building or reducing College indebtedness while the capital realized on their gifts of plate gave relief at a time of financial stringency.

The figures for admissions to the College for the period from 1650 to 1730 show considerable variations. In ten-year groupings they are:

[12] C. Oman, *Apollo*, 1957, 65, 173–6.

	Fellow Commoner	Pensioner	Sizar	% Fellow Commoner
1650–60	13	60	44	11.1
1661–70	25	141	53	11.4
1671–80	11	93	72	5.9
1681–90	20	39	35	21.3
1691–99	10	47	37	10.6
1700–10	12	35	33	15.0
1711–20	6	35	45	7.0
1721–30	7	37	37	8.6

The remaining decades to 1790 had respectively 8, 0, 4, 3, and 4 Fellow Commoner entries.

Among the men of good family and substantial fortune who began to be entered under Eachard were several sons of former members of the College and, in contrast to the previous period, of twenty-five Fellow Commoner entries recorded up to 1670 twenty-three made contributions of plate. But once the rebuilding of the College had begun contributions in cash or in kind were preferred, so that between 1671 and 1680 only seven pieces of plate were recorded from twenty-one Fellow Commoners. The voluminous Eachard correspondence[13] yields ample evidence of the needs of the College at this time, and the reactions on the plate may be seen from a typical entry dated 24 July 1680. Roger Wilbraham of Nantwich writes of his son Randle, who entered as a Fellow Commoner in 1680: 'I understand by my son that Mr Moyle hath acquitted me of my promise of the xth which was in lieu of a Plate, that is expected of course from Fellow-Commoners at their leaveing the Colledge. I thought in the posture the Colledge stands Money might be as acceptable as Plate: And finding it was so, I am glad I had the good happ to gratify you in any thing who have so highly oblig'd yo'r very humble servant.'

A side-light on the education of the Fellow Commoner is given in a further letter from Roger Wilbraham, dated 1 January 1680/81: 'You are pleased to intimate in yo'r letter that you Designe when the Holy-daies were over he should learne French and after that Musick, the latter (as lesse

---

[13] Muniments, XL/13/63 and 98.

pertinent) I could wish might be deferred for one halfe year at least, till he bee better acquainted with Aristotle; And if it may be with your approbation, I would have him immediately to enter himselfe for a month or six weeks to learn to dance, both to better his carriage, and to exercise his limbs in hopes it may be a means to shake off that lazy distemper of the Jaundice which stole upon him unawares.'

The high proportion of gifts of plate recorded in the decade 1660–70 did not last. Of the twenty Fellow Commoners admitted between 1681 and 1690 only seven gave plate; and only one piece is recorded from the ten entries of the next decade — a tankard weighing 27 oz. 18 dw., given by James Sotheby and disposed of in part exchange for two sauce boats in 1740. But it is clear that many contributed cash, varying from £5 upwards. The average was £10, and some gifts greatly exceeded the average, for Eachard was a good persuader. Sir Francis Willoughby, for example, who entered as a Fellow Commoner in 1682, gave a tankard weighing 69 oz. 10 dw. and probably worth at least £20 at then current prices.

Within the general picture of gifts of plate or of cash, and the needs of the College for money in hand, it is clear that the simple use of plate as an amenity of life played its part, and that the College's holdings of plate had been substantially refashioned after the Restoration, in the fashion dictated by the mode of heavy weight and simple design of the period. The mode prevailed until about 1725, and although no examples survive in the College of the pieces made up to 1700 there are still numerous pieces dated from between 1700 and 1725. The refashioning of even older pieces is made clear by the inventory of 1684, which was no doubt made with the necessity of sale in mind. The pieces were weighed before sale and were indentifiable up to sale, so that it is possible to give some idea of their weight and quality. Of earlier plate this inventory lists Mr Buck's large standing salt, seventeen spoons, a beaker and the trencher salt, with a frosted tankard bearing only the donor's arms. The Communion plate still included one of the 1637 flagons and a chalice with cover. The new pieces (with weights added from other lists) are listed as:

11

Large two eared plate called the Combination Plate (30 oz.)
Cup KH
8 salts mark'd Cath. Wheel
2 Porringers marked KH "E Sumpt. Coll" (each 14 oz.)
2 Pint Plates Cath. Wheel (19 oz. 10 dw. and 22 oz.)
Quart 2 eared plate new markt with Kath Wheel (22 oz.)
A Trenchard Plate new markd (11 oz. 10 dw.)
eleven beakers Cath Wheel (each 15 oz. 10 dw.)

There was a large demand for salts, and six were bought for
Christmas, 1688, of total weight fifteen ounces. The porringers
graced the Master's Lodging. The two-eared plates were
double-handled cups; pint plates were in all probability
tankards.

These pieces showed a significant increase in their silver-
content over comparable pieces made in the earlier part of the
seventeenth century. But the weight of silver was less indicative
of value than it would have been at the earlier period. Samuel
Pepys' Diary for 19 October 1664, reads: 'Coming home,
weighed my two silver flaggons at Steven's. They weigh
212 oz. 27 dwt., which is about £50 at 5s. per oz., and then
they judge the fashion to be worth above 5s. per oz. more —
nay, some say 10s. an ounce the fashion. But I do not believe,
but yet am sorry to see that the fashion is worth so much, and
the silver come to no more.' Pepys seems to have been unduly
gloomy; his flagons were very probably highly decorated and
gilded, but the value of a silver can of 26 oz. 15 dw. in 1674,
with 'labour' was £10 — something slightly less than 8/– the
ounce.

The heavier pieces in fashion in the early eighteenth century
were less liable to wear, and less in need of refashioning, than
the earlier lighter pieces. But the College got little satisfaction
from these merits. The recently-acquired pieces had to be sold,
often in an almost brand-new condition. The Order Book
carries, among others, the entry that 'On May 3d. 1687 it was
agreed and voted by the Master and Fellows of St Catherine's
Hall, that the plates given by Sir Tho. Barnardiston, Mr John
Owen, Mr Robt. Spurstowe, Mr Francis Gerrard, Mr John
Knyvett, Mr Augustus Brograve, and Mr Edward Partherick
should be sold and the money applyed to the rebuilding of the

College'. Eachard, who signed the order along with three Fellows, added the note:

3 severall parcels viz.
1) 76—0 0
2) 44—6-3
3) 76-19-9
196—6-0

Eachard's note continues, 'Then 402 oz. misc. tankards and pieces of plate to Sir Charles Caesar 22 Nov. 1688'. The list of pieces[14] so sold includes two weighty pieces, Sir John Rouse's tankard of 50 oz. 10 dw., and Mr Peter Hussey's tankard of 45 oz. 10 dw. But they could not have been taken by Sir Charles because they were listed in the inventory taken at Christmas, 1688, and again on 16 February 1698. Here a later mark described the two pieces as 'sold', and Hussey's tankard was indeed part of a sale made on 20 February 1691. Sir John Rouse's tankard, however, was still in the possession of the College on 26 September 1704, when it was one of the pieces exchanged for a Rosewater Bowl and Ewer. Two things emerge clearly from these records. The silver was an important means for dealing with the problems of capital accumulation and realization; and Sir Charles Caesar did not take possession of these two valuable pieces. In the standard accounts of the rebuilding he is depicted as a man who drove a hard bargain. But the reverse is true. He was a considerable benefactor who gave £250 outright for the buildings, and in discharge of a debt of £100 he got 307 ounces of silver, not 402 ounces. This meant that he was paying 6s. 6d. the ounce at a time when the London price for plate melted down (boyled) was 5.8/– the ounce and the Cambridge price was 5.1/– the ounce. Sir Charles Caesar's generous treatment of the College involved a minor payment, to Mr Desborough of 5/– for weighing the plate and listing the pieces at Christmas, 1688.

In February 1691 the silver was looked over and it was then shown that plate was not only being used as a capital holding. It was also being exchanged and refashioned and brought into current fashion. The 1690/91 audit records an item of 'Exchange

14 The list of pieces is printed in Jones, *History*, p. 386.

of Plate £2–17–5' and explains that 'The drum salt, the old round salt, the Kettle Drum salt, two cups markt KH one, the other Coll Arms exchanged AD 1691 for six new salt sellers and two pint tankards which was more than these was allowed by the College'. The two processes, of selling for cash and of exchanging and refashioning, went on side by side, and Eachard's successor as Master in 1697, Sir William Dawes, set about clearing the College's debts by sales of silver.

Early in the Dawes period, therefore, on 23 August 1697, 'It was agreed and voted by the Master and Fellows of St. Katharine's Hall that the Plates given by Mr Hatcher, Mr Goodwin, Mr Beddingfield, Mr Knivet, Mr Jenny, Hatton Rich, Mr Bence, Sr Francis Willoughby, Mr Hussey, together with a great salt seller and Frosted tankard should be sold and the mony apply'd to the paymt of the Colledge debts . . . Memorandum. All the Plate above mentioned except Mr Hatcher's Tankard was sold at London for £101–6–6, Mr Hatcher's Tankard was sold at Cambridge for £7–3–8. In all £108–10–2'.

The contribution towards the College's finances may seem to us slight, and we may regret the disposal of so many pieces which would have been both interesting and valuable if they had survived. But the College was treating its plate according to the conventions of the period, and it must be remembered that not all of the disposals were for financial reasons, and that the pieces were often worn out and unserviceable. After the inventory of 1698 had listed the plate again, the Conclusion Book records that on 26 September 1704 'It was then agreed by the unanimous consent of the Master and Fellows that the Tankards given by Sir John Rouse, Sir Charles Caesar and Mr Kemp should be exchanged for a new Bason and Ewer, and that the ten old Beakers commonly used in the Hall being much bruised and broken should be exchanged for eight new ones of a more convenient size and the overplus of money (if any be) should be applied towards new Communion plate. That the Monteith given by Mr Middleton should be exchanged for a new gilt Patten for the use of the Communion and that the old Communion plate, viz. a flagon and cup and cover and small trencher plate weighing in all seventyeight ounces should be exchanged for a gilt Basin and two new cups and covers now provided for the use of the new Chappell, and that the money wanting to compleat this new plate should be raised out of the money given at the Communion'.

The maker of the new ewer and basin was **William Fawdery**, who received 153 ounces of sterling silver (925 parts in 1,000) and returned 99 ounces at the new Britannia standard (958.3 parts in 1,000). The fashion therefore cost about 3/– the ounce, which compares favourably with other evidence available. A large order of sterling plate for the Devonshire family in 1687, for example, cost between six and seven shillings the ounce, and Paul de Lamerie was paid 6/2 the ounce for Britannia standard metal and 5/– the ounce for fashioning in 1724, when making the Treby toilet service now in the Victoria and Albert Museum. The workmanship of this service is both elaborate and superb, and was no doubt considered worth the money.

The price paid by the College for ordinary pieces was comparable to that paid for special weight and workmanship. The audit for 1734/5 mentions the sale of a two-eared Buttery Plate weighing 20 oz. 14 dw. for 5/2d. per ounce; but a similar piece newly-fashioned bought from Sam Urlin Jr, cost 6/8 the ounce and weighed 31 oz. 10 dw.

In the changes, sales and refashioning, the donor's name was often lost sight of; but not always. Sometimes the donor's name was carried on the newly-fabricated piece, and sometimes the documentation recorded the continuity. The two-eared cup given by Mr Darnal, who entered as a Fellow Commoner in 1661, is, for example, particularly well-documented. By 1698 it had been exchanged for a pint tankard weighing 17 oz. 10 dw., and his name survives to this day on a pair of candlesticks, acquired by 1800. Similarly, Mr Dove entered as a Fellow Commoner on 12 June 1708, and gave a three-pint tankard soon after coming into residence, the cost for carriage (one shilling) being recorded in the 1708/9 audit. The donor's arms and those of the College were not engraved, or at least the work was not paid for (four shillings) until 1716/17. About half a century later Dove's tankard also seems to have been exchanged for candlesticks, since two bedroom candlesticks of London date-mark for 1775 bear the inscription 'Caroli Dove Generosi'. Survivals are not confined to candlesticks however. Two much-rubbed sauce-boats with the London date-mark for 1744 are still in daily use. The maker's mark is illegible but they bear the name of John Sambrooke and they derive from a College Order of 16 November 1774, by which John Sambrook's large two-eared cup of 40 oz. was to be sold and 'the money laid out by the Bursar in the Purchase of new and useful plate'. A worn-out tankard of 27 oz. 18 dw., the gift of James Sotheby, was also to be disposed of for this purpose, but no piece of plate seems to have been engraved to carry on the memory of Sotheby's gift.

Silver forks and silver-hafted knives were bought. They were ground and engraved at a cost of 13/3d., as the audit for 1749–50 records. But candlesticks were clearly much in demand in the second half of the eighteenth century, possibly because of the acceptance of the custom of serving the college dinner late in the day. Mr Robinson Morley of Selby, Yorkshire, found his plate-money used for this purpose. He entered as a Fellow Commoner in May 1751 and was reported to have given £12 for a gift of plate by the audit of 1753/4. But his money was not spent, on a pair of candlesticks from Mr York, silversmith, until the 1758/9 audit. Morley's candlesticks actually cost £14–19–5; they were made by William Cafe, a specialist with a considerable reputation, and within a year the College received a matching pair. These were the gift of Sir Thomas Charles Bunbury, a Fellow Commoner who entered on 17 April 1756. Later, he was to be the winner of the first Derby, in 1780, with his horse Diomed. Cafe also made for the College four more candlesticks with square bases. The pattern was clearly popular with the College, for four such dated 1773 were made by John Carter, and a further eight, dated 1835, were made by Jos. Taylor. All are of fine quality and heavily cast, and they get, and stand up to, regular use, as does the other plate from this period. The list would include four silver salts, still in daily use, with a London date-mark for 1737, made by David Hennell and bought from Mr York for £6–19–3 in 1774/5.

Unlike John Wesley — who, when he was required to make a return of his plate in 1776, replied, 'Sir, — I have *two* spoons in London, and *two* spoons at Bristol. This is all the plate I have at present; and I shall not buy any more while so many around me want bread' — the College was accumulating plate, and fortunately it was doing so in a good period. Wesley's retort arose from a tax imposed by Newcastle in 1756 'on persons, including bodies politic or corporate, having in their possession silver plate to a certain quantity'. Owners of plate were required to 'deliver at an excise office, annually, an account of the number of ounces of plate for which they were chargeable' and owners of plate in pledge were to be liable for tax, not the persons holding it unless they brought it into use. The tax was 5s. for persons having between 100 and 200 ounces and 5s. for each further 100 oz. up to 4,000 ounces. The tax was in force for twenty years, until it was repealed by Lord North in 1777, and it proved 'very vexatious and troublesome in the levying and collecting the same, and of small advantage to the public'. Church plate, and the stock in trade of goldsmiths, silversmiths, manufacturers and dealers, was exempted, but not the plate of colleges. St Catharine's therefore paid 10s. 6d. in 1756 to have its plate weighed — and several pieces still have their weight engraved underneath. The tax payable amounted to £2–10s. paid in alternate years, and this indicates a holding of some six hundred ounces, excluding Communion Plate, which was not liable for tax.

At the end of the eighteenth century and the start of the nineteenth, money was piling up in the College's plate fund. Since 1786 a uniform capitation fee of £6 had been imposed on Fellow Commoners. Thomas Lloyd was the first to pay, in that year, and subsequent Fellow Commoners up to the early 1840s seem to have made their contributions under this rule. Admissions of Fellow Commoners were variable and unpredictable; but in accumulated effect they were not negligible. By decades, starting from 1801, Fellow Commoner admissions totalled 6; 13; 31; 21; 14; 7; and 8. This takes the story up to 1870; and C. P. Boyd, in 1874, was the last entry in that category. Their capitation payments up to 1840 amounted to £444, and this served as a basis for a policy of energetic replacement and renewal of the College's plate.

Of several lots of spoons, teaspoons, and forks which were owned when the plate was audited in 1800 only a single tea-spoon now survives. But it served a purpose in the process of renewal and replacement as a prototype for the numerous Victorian copies which were made and which are still in daily use. Other, and more impressive, purchases of table-silver were made from time to time. In 1810/11 Mr Parker supplied two large parcels of plate, receiving considerable amounts of old plate in exchange; he was also paid £137–18–3 in cash. Equally important purchases were made from the firms of Lambert and Rawlings and from Rundell and Bridge, who were famous as the employers of Paul Storr and as goldsmiths to George IV. Rundell and Bridge received a payment of £156–9–7, and between 1825 and 1844 these two firms supplied plate worth £422–14–1. These were not only cash transactions; a punch ladle, a pepper box, mustard pot, two salt cellars and several knives were no doubt disposed of as no longer fashion-able or serviceable; and Colman's tankard and Mr Bracken-bury's Cup with lid surmounted with a pineapple, dated 1775, were exchanged. The dozen spoons marked KH, survivors from the eighteen bought in 1624, together with four marked with a Griffin Head, were sacrificed. But the new plate was extremely heavy, serviceable and solid. It is used daily and shows little sign of wear; and it includes twelve new silver pint beakers bought on 4 December 1800. They have been added to since, but they serve the Fellows and their guests regularly at High Table.

The new silver of the period 1825–44 was engraved with donors' names in 1843, by Peters, for a payment of £7–10–0. Not a single piece of the pre-1825 purchases was marked with the donor's name; indeed the capitation system would have made it difficult to identify donors with pieces though the list of the donors of the Capitations up to 1825 is in the muniments. But the earlier unnamed silver can still be distinguished from the pieces which derive from Fellow Commoners' gifts because the Fellow Commoner pieces carry the Catharine Wheel enclosed in a shield while the earlier unnamed silver carries a plain Catharine Wheel.

Much of the stability of the College in the first half of the nineteenth century can be directly ascribed to the humanity and to the efficiency of George Elwes Corrie, who began to be a tutor in 1817, and who held continuous office in the College until he became Master of Jesus College in 1847. Admissions of undergraduates greatly increased under his care, and those of Fellow Commoners, with their capitation fees for the silver fund, kept pace, rising to thirty-one admissions in the decade from 1820 to 1830 and to twenty-one in the next decade. It is quite probable that family influence played some part in this, for Corrie's brother Daniel, sixteen years his senior, stayed in the College as Archdeacon of Calcutta in the summer of 1835. He was then entered as a senior member, but left the College to return to Madras as Bishop, and to die there in 1837. It is interesting to note that at that time several Fellow Commoners were entered as having served with the armies of the East India Company. The Bentinck reforms were then ushering in a more enlightened approach to the social problems of India, and the connection between the College and the Bishop, and the fact that all the ex-East India Company Fellow Commoners became ordained, cannot be overlooked.

While the connection between the armies of the East India Company and the College would seem to have substance, there seems to be no evidence to support the tradition that 'After the battle of Waterloo a large number of officers left the army, so many of whom came to St Catharine's that it was known as the *Church Militant*'.[15] The suggestion that 'the College silver with its spoons and forks' was 'presented in gratitude by Officers of Wellington's Army' at least cannot be substantiated. Only two Fellow Commoners would fall into this category: C. Maitland, a former artillery captain, came up in 1819 as a Pensioner candidate for ordination at the age of thirty-four and later became a Fellow Commoner; and F. Byers, also an

[15] G. F. Browne, St Catharine's College, 1902, p. 32; H. P. Stokes, *The Cambridge Scene*, 1921, p. 69; St Catharine's Society Magazine, 1951, p. 8.

artillery captain, entered as a Pensioner in 1821, aged thirty-three, and also became a Fellow Commoner while in residence. For the rest, the spoons and forks in daily use are indeed the gifts of Fellow Commoners, mostly of the Corrie period, and are inscribed with the names of those whose composition payments were put to this use. But they were Fellow Commoners attracted by the tone given to the College by its senior members, largely by Corrie; men like Maitland who, seeking ordination, chose 'Catharine Hall, as the College best suited to my views and feelings'.[16]

After about 1840 big changes took place. The general system of capitation charges from which silver might be bought often dropped out of use, with the result that bulk engraving of the silver ceased. Personal and individual gifts became more common, and they were engraved with the donor's name; but not with his arms, for many of the donors did not bear arms. At the same time, public taste showed a growing feeling for antiquarianism, so that many of these gifts were not of contemporary fabrication. The result was to add some notable pieces to the College's holdings. Such are the four Paul Storr entrée dishes with covers which were presented by James Spurrell, who entered as a Fellow Commoner in 1843, aged twenty-seven. His gift bears the London date-letter for 1803. The silver Coffee Pot, London made by William Williams in 1755, did not come into possession of the College until 1853, the joint gift of T. W. Christie and J. B. Curtis. Both were admitted as Fellow Commoners in that year, Christie being then forty-one years old.

The custom of presenting a choice piece, of antiquarian interest, has continued alongside the purchase of new-fashioned pieces, and is still a feature in the numerous gifts (largely from Fellows but sometimes from former members of the College) which continue from the end-date of this essay up to the present day. The silver fund was kept going, and from 1860 onwards capitation charges, when levied, were paid in to a specific account. Fellow Commoners continued to be admitted

[16] Jones, *Story of St Catharine's*, p. 106.

until reform took a grip on Cambridge in the 1860s and the 1870s; and the last admission was in 1874. But they came in decreasing numbers, sometimes seeking higher degrees in medicine or law after graduation elsewhere, some seeking a B.D. Degree under Elizabethan statutes which dubbed them 'Ten Year Men'. Sometimes such men were already priests, who combined parish duties with their studies. Many of them must have been older than the Fellows with whom they dined on High Table, and few of them were undergraduates drawn from the landed families, who had composed the bulk of the former Fellow Commoners. Their numbers, in any case, mean that they contributed little, and it is difficult to reconcile the fact that only seven Fellow Commoners, of all types, were admitted in the decade from 1850 to 1860 with Bishop Browne's statement that after the Crimean War 'the officers of the army and navy who resided at St. Catharine's formed a very agreeable addition to the social life of the place'.[17] Few as they were, when the Fellow Commoners paid their capitation it went to the silver fund; and by 1898 that fund was able to afford to buy a pair of silver gilt candlesticks for the Chapel — which they still adorn. They were bought from Messrs Barkerton for £86–11–0, and the purchase almost extinguished the silver fund. But no mass disposal of plate has been needed since 1810 either to finance College costs or to get new-fashioned pieces. The massive elegance of the early eighteenth-century pieces and of those acquired during the nineteenth century is now much esteemed, and is in evidence in daily use, since such plate does not wear out. The silver fund, moreover, was not completely extinguished by the purchase of the Chapel candlesticks. It survived into 1917 with a cash balance of about £22, and it has since been reanimated by personal gifts of money and by grants from corporate income. So the need for particular articles can, in a modest measure, be met although Fellow Commoners are no longer there to finance purchases; and the workmanship and the taste of the twentieth century will be on record.

[17] G. F. Browne, *St Catharine's College*, p. 32.

The Nineteenth Century

By PROFESSOR E. E. RICH

Master

THE election of the Reverend Charles Kirkby Robinson as Master in succession to Henry Philpott on 16 October 1861, has probably attracted more, and more adverse, comment than any other event in the history of the College. For Jones, Robinson's tenure of office 'can only be regarded as a tragedy'.[1] The 'Robinson Vote' takes up the opening chapter of Winstanley's classic history of Victorian Cambridge,[2] and the space allotted to the episode is merely a reflection of the attention which the election aroused at the time.

The actual election in Chapel has been fully chronicled and there is nothing of importance which can be added to the story. Philpott, who had been elected in 1845, and who had proved a powerful and well-esteemed Head of the House, had been nominated for appointment as Bishop of Worcester in January 1861. But he did not resign the Mastership until the end of September; and this gave the small body of Fellows only too much time to arrange the election of a successor. But in the event the election was mis-managed; that at least is quite clear. Philpott's resignation having been received, the senior Fellow, Joseph Milner, summoned the Fellows to meet in Chapel on 16 October. This was according to the College's statutes; but according to a new set of statutes which had been framed only in 1860. The old statutes, set by the Founder and left largely unchanged in the only revision, that of 1549, would have allowed only three days between the declaration of a vacancy and a meeting to elect a new Master; the 1860

---

[1] W. H. S. Jones, *A History of St Catharine's College*, C.U.P., 1936, p. 191.
[2] D. A. Winstanley, *Later Victorian Cambridge*, C.U.P., 1947, pp. 1–19.

The College in 1688. The buildings recently set up, as well as those which, today only planned, in a short time will be actually constructed. By David Loggan

PLATE VIII

The College in mid-nineteenth century

code allowed between fourteen and thirty days, with special terms if the vacancy occurred in the Long Vacation.[3] In taking the extra time for their meeting, when they had so much warning of the election that they could surely have met earlier if they had wished, the Fellows were clearly making the election under the new statutes; and in electing Robinson they confirmed this, for he was merely an M.A.; he did not hold the degree of Bachelor of Divinity, as he would have been required to do under the old statutes.

When the election is examined in the light of the 1860 statutes, however, serious anomalies appear. Five Fellows met to make the election, and the subsequent scandal arose directly from the difficulty of making a decision within so small a body. But according to the 1860 statutes there should have been nine Fellows, and although provision was made for the Fellows to remain under the old statutes if they wished and for the financial provisions of the new statutes to be implemented gradually while the interests of existing Fellows were preserved, there was no reason why this clause should not have been implemented and there is no record (as yet discoverable after long search) to indicate why, or how, any decision was made not immediately to increase the number of Fellows to nine. Rather, everything points in the opposite direction; for the intention of the new statutes was that the four new Fellows should be the four Skerne Fellows, who were already members of the College on Mrs Ramsden's foundation although, under the old statutes, they were not full members of the governing body.

The old statutes had provided for six Fellows, or more or less according to the circumstances of the College; in practice, five was the rule. In addition, since 1776 there had been six 'Skerne Fellows', elected under separate rules as set out in Mrs Ramsden's will. In effect the Skerne Fellows were a separate foundation within the same College and the difficulties arising from the situation had led to a long-drawn Chancery case, lasting from 1813 to 1820. In the knowledge that a revision

[3] There are many copies of the statutes in the muniments. For a comparison of the codes see Jones, *History*, pp. 339–74.

of statutes was imminent, and that such fellowships were under review, the College had been given permission not to fill Skerne Fellowships which had fallen vacant in 1859 and in 1860, so that when the new statutes came into force there were five Fellows on the 'Old Foundation' and four on Mrs Ramsden's foundation. The new statutes dealing with the Skerne Fellows had been enacted in advance of the other statutes, in January 1860, giving ample time for their implementation before the election of October 1861; and they ordered that in future the number of Skerne Fellows should always be held at four instead of at six, and that these four should be in every way equal to Fellows on the Old Foundation, 'with regard to the amount of stipend, the right of sharing in the administration of college business, the right of succession to the ecclesiastical preferment of the College . . . and all other matters whatever'.[4]

The intention, clearly, was that the Skerne Fellows should take place alongside the Fellows of the Old Foundation, and although the clauses allowing for slow implementation of the new statutes and for due regard to personal considerations should not be overlooked, there seems no reason why this should not have been done in time for the election. The Skerne Fellows under consideration were not recent appointees, ignorant of College affairs; indeed they would seem to have had more experience and to carry more weight than the official Fellows who exercised the right to vote. Of the latter, two, Crabtree and Hurst, had been Fellows for only one year; they were elected in September and November 1860, respectively. By contrast, the oldest of the four Skerne Fellows, Edmund Yorke, had been elected in 1810 and had held his appointment for over fifty years; John Glendall had been a Fellow since 1822, William Parr since 1844, and even the most recent of them, George Morley, had held his Fellowship for six years.

While the new statute for Skerne Fellows had been promulgated as far back as January 1860, the main body of the new code had been sealed and delivered on 10 May. Officially these statutes were imposed on the College by the external

[4] For the 1860 Statutes cf. Muniments, xix/1.

authority of a Royal Commission, and there is no record that they were approved or accepted by the Fellows although, except for the rules on the number of Fellows, they obviously were so accepted, and were in operation by the time of the election. Indeed, the College Memorandum Book,[5] which carries the record of all resolutions, elections, and official actions at that time, has only one reference to the new statutes — to implement the new statute on scholarships and to turn them into Open Awards, to be given for merit only, without regard to schools or to locality. For the rest, the new statutes apparently came into force automatically and, barring any resolution to the contrary, they should have been fully implemented before the 'Robinson vote' took place.

No explanation can safely be hazarded for the failure to put the new statute on Fellowships into effect. Perhaps an explanatory record may one day be found — for it is still difficult to use the College's muniments in confidence that all the evidence has been discovered. But the fact which must be accepted is that the comparatively long-term Skerne Fellows were not given a vote while almost half of the voting Fellows were new to College business. The further fact which must be accepted is that there can have been nothing underhand or controversial about this flouting of the intention of the new statutes. It was accepted on all sides, without comment, even at the height of the controversy over the election — so much so that subsequent writers have also passed over the anomaly in silence.

This strange episode must rouse speculation as to the possible results if the vote had been made by a society of nine Fellows instead of by a mere five, of whom two were candidates. At least the increase in numbers must have minimized the importance of the vote of one of the candidates. But the anomaly is the more remarkable because, in the event, this particular clause in the new statutes of 1860 never was implemented. Some parts were accepted, so that when in 1874 J. R. Lumby was elected into the Skerne Fellowship vacated by the death of Yorke it was agreed that he must enjoy the same rights and

[5] Muniments, L/83.

privileges as a Fellow of the Old Foundation 'by the statutes confirmed on 10 May 1860'.[6] But the Skerne Fellows who existed in 1860 remained separate, Morley holding on until 1877, Glendall till 1882 and Parr till 1889; and the number of Fellowships was never brought up to nine. Even when the 1860 code of statutes was itself superseded in 1882 the number of Fellowships was fixed at six, or more if the revenues sufficed; not at nine.

The further remarkable aspect of the non-fulfilment of the Fellowship clause of the 1860 statutes arises from the consideration that this was one of the most important reforms which the Commissioners sought, both for the Cambridge colleges in general and for St Catharine's in particular. They devoted a whole section of their Report to the issue of Bye-Fellows, who enjoyed their amenities without any duties and without responsibility for college administration; and they cited St Catharine's as a college which would obviously benefit from absorbing the Bye-Fellows into the general fellowship of the College.[7] This was a part, and a vitally important part, of the general approach to the Universities of Oxford and Cambridge. Colleges and Fellowships were under fire. In particular 'sinecure' or 'absentee' Fellowships were targets for reformers; and, as Vice-Chancellor and an important public figure, Philpott was aligned with the critics — which makes the continuance of the Skerne Fellowships all the more odd.

University reform had been a political issue for more than a generation by 1860. Mistrust of the colleges as seed-beds of Anglican authoritarianism, and emphasis on education as a problem of national importance, had been revealed in a bill sponsored by the Earl of Radnor in 1837; and though the bill was defeated it revealed widespread uneasiness. The colleges petitioned against the bill, stressing their own powers to introduce such changes as were necessary. But they were obviously disinclined to use the powers which they claimed. New codes of statutes at St John's and at Christ's achieved little and the other colleges, including St Catharine's, did

[6] Muniments, L/83.20.iii.74.
[7] *Report of Her Majesty's Commissioners*, 1852, p. 168.

nothing. In the University, supporters of the bill were un-
popular, and a petition that religious tests should be abolished
got few signatures.

But the colleges could not hold their positions, if only because
many who were conservative within their own college were
aware of the need for reform at the level of the University.
Philpott was one such.

In University administration the *Caput*[8] placed great power
in the hands of the Heads of Houses, and their dominance
came under strong criticism. As the disciplines of academic
study expanded from the concentration on theology, law,
mathematics and the classics, moreover, there followed a
stream of proposals for diverting some college revenues to the
University so that the costs of the new curricula could be met
from University sources.

In 1849 the Senate had appointed a syndicate to revise the
University's statutes. The ensuing report was chiefly notable
for its proposal to abolish the *Caput* and to replace it by a more
democratic *Council of the Senate* — a proposal which won
approval both from academics and from external critics. But
external criticism was consolidated when in 1850 a Royal
Commission was appointed to report on the state, discipline,
studies and revenues of the Colleges and the Universities of
Oxford and Cambridge. Thirteen colleges petitioned against
the appointment of the Commission and three of them, Jesus,
Clare and St Catharine's, declared their right to refuse to
answer enquiries.

At St Catharine's two of the five Fellows wanted to ignore the
commissioners altogether; but the Master and the remaining
three Fellows contented themselves by protesting formally that
'No power, other than the Visitor of the College, acting in the
manner appointed by law, has authority to require answers to
questions respecting the affairs of the College', asserting 'That
the College itself is competent to decide upon the desireableness
or necessity of introducing changes or modifications into its
system of administration'.[9]

---

[8] For the *Caput Senatus* cf. 1852 *Report*, p. 13.
[9] Muniments, L/83.22.xi.51.

12

It fell to Philpott to make this declaration of college autonomy, and in so doing he showed the ambivalence of his attitude towards reforms, for he had strongly approved the report
of the Senate's syndicate of 1849 on reforms in the University's
statutes. But perhaps his declaration of college rights should be
taken largely as a formality; for two days after he had rejected
the commissioners' powers to compel the College to give
evidence he was himself putting his very considerable knowledge
of the College and of its history at the commissioners' disposal,
as an act of grace. Philpott did not publish his volume of
*Documents relating to St Catharine's College in the University of
Cambridge* until 1861; but his evidence before the commissioners
of 1851 shows that he had already done a great deal of the work
for which all subsequent writers on the College must be in his
debt.

His knowledge of the past of the College, however, did not
prevent Philpott from facing new issues. Though he saw grave
defects in the system, he believed that private tuition could not
well be abolished, as did Whewell, reforming Master of Trinity.
But he strongly favoured opening up to undergraduates a
greater number of courses leading to an honours degree,
trusting that this would lead to the free and independent
development of their minds.[10] In such forward-looking attitudes
Philpott was in tune with the commissioners; and in his wish to
preserve collegiate values they were in tune with him. Their
Report, delivered in 1852, dealt very gently with the colleges,
recommending revisions of their statutes, suggesting that their
Visitors should take their responsibilities seriously, and pro-
posing that a Parliamentary Board should be appointed with
power to bring about necessary changes on lines which would
be laid down in Parliament.

Following on the Report, government policy was blocked
out in a speech by Russell. The main points were to be the
creation of a democratic system for University administration,
admission of non-collegiate students, Fellowships open to
competition and subject to renewal of tenure, and allocation of

[10] *Evidence*, p. 258 et seq.

more of the revenues of colleges to tuition. This policy was to be forced on the colleges if they did not put their own houses in order. Philpott would have been in favour of all of these proposals. But the University was hanging back as Russell outlined plans for a Royal Commission which would leave the University until Michaelmas 1855 to work out its own remedies and would then apply compulsion.

At this juncture, in January 1854, St Catharine's sought royal approval for an amended code of college statutes.[11] To Philpott it must have seemed increasingly inept to try to administer a nineteenth-century college, largely devoted to the preparation of undergraduates for a widening range of Tripos examinations, according to statutes devised in the fifteenth century for a handful of post-graduate theologians; for the revision of 1549 had brought no significant changes from the Founder's Statutes of 1475 (or thereabouts). Nothing is on record of the discussions which must have preceded this petition of 1854, but it obviously indicates the triumph within the College of the reformist views of Philpott, and it was accompanied by a resolution that any answer sent to the commissioners should be sent in the name of the Master and the Fellows — which indicated a considerable change of front.

But though the College was in a less intransigent mood in 1854 than it had been in 1850 there was no sign of a positive move for reform coming from within the College, even though it was but a college of five Fellows headed by a Master known in the University and outside 'as the person, who from his moderate views, business habits and knowledge of the University, is best qualified to give the most valuable assistance and advice'[12] — an encomium from the Prime Minister as Philpott tried to draft a bill for Cambridge which would satisfy both the politicians and the academics. His draft bill foundered at Westminster because it did not sufficiently curb the powers of the Heads of Houses, and his move for a new code of statutes for the College also sinks out of sight. Nothing further is heard of the 1854 petition for new statutes.

[11] Muniments, L/83.11.i.1854.
[12] Winstanley, op. cit., p. 283.

But Philpott was made Vice-Chancellor for the second time in 1856, and his stature was such that he was even elected for a third tour of duty in 1857.[13] He was at the very heart of the matter as his own proposals were withdrawn, amendments based on petitions for open election of the Regent House and of the Non-Regent House for the University were put forward, and in March 1856 a new bill was proposed, with support from Palmerston and from Prince Albert as Chancellor of the University and from Philpott as Vice-Chancellor.

The Cambridge University Act of 1856, which resulted, set up the *Council of the Senate* to replace the *Caput* as the inner cabinet of the University and had so far met the demands of the 'great movement of liberal progress' for removal of the barriers which 'long excluded so many of our fellow subjects from the enjoyment of civil rights on account of differences in religious opinions' (to quote the Report of the Commissioners in 1852)[14] as to allow all degrees except in divinity to be taken without a declaration of support for the Thirty-nine Articles. Membership of the Senate and tenure of University posts were still restricted to members of the established church, and college statutes remained untouched; but it was clear that administrative and educational reform was on the move, and that it was strongly tinged with anti-clericalism.

So much had already emerged from the tussles of the past decade and from the Report of the Commissioners in 1852. But whereas the 1852 report largely left the colleges alone with recommendations for reform, the Commission appointed by the Cambridge Act of 1856 was to supervise and advise the colleges and the University as they set about revisions of their statutes — and if by 1858 the colleges had not come forward with acceptable proposals the Commission was to have power to enforce changes. The colleges were given the right to protest against any statutes so made by the Commissioners, and new statutes were then to be devised. But the re-drafts were to be 'for the same purpose' and the assumption would be that the views of

---

[13] His first appointment as Vice-Chancellor was in 1846, the first year of his Mastership.
[14] *Report*, p. 44.

the Commissioners would be forced along; disagreement could be on detail, not on principle.

In broad terms the principles of the 1856 Commissioners were never in doubt. The political background to the Act, the endless discussions and petitions which had preceded their appointment, their own knowledge of Cambridge and their participation in the 1852 report, had all contributed to the outline. They aimed to secure a large measure of secularization, to modify statutes which required Fellows to take Holy Orders and to increase the proportion of lay Fellows in colleges, to replace oaths of religious orthodoxy on admission to fellowships by solemn declarations, to modify insistence on celibacy at least to the extent of exempting professors. They also sought to divert to the University some college revenue, so that the costs of change and development (in particular the costs of increases in the stipends of professors and of building laboratories for scientific teaching and experiment) could be accepted and the maximum educational value could be got from the wealth available. Coupled with this went a desire to free both fellowships and scholarships from local and other non-academic conditions.

In the statutes which emerged in 1860 for St Catharine's little of this is to be seen except for the creation of Open Scholarships and the largely still-born statutes for the absorption of the Skerne Fellowships.

To explain Philpott's actions as Vice-Chancellor the historian has the memoranda of other university officials and his correspondence with General Grey, private secretary to Prince Albert. For his dealings within the College there is very little to go upon, and much of the story must be read backwards, judging views and motives from what was accomplished. Taken in this way, the statutes of 1860 would show a man who was deeply immersed in the history of the College and who could give detailed accounts of the problems which had arisen to trouble its past, but who accepted the College as in a fair way to manage its own affairs and who desired no major changes at College level. This, indeed, may well be the explanation for the non-effectiveness of the Fellowships statute. For

Philpott was completely the master of the Chancery case which had run on from 1813 to 1820 because the Skerne Fellows had filed an information with the Attorney General asking that they should be active members of the governing body of the College when the revenues from the Ramsden Estate were under discussion, and that more of those revenues should be allocated to themselves; and he had apparently emerged from his study of the case with so little respect for the Skerne Fellows that, although he had accepted the Commissioners' ruling in principle, he had rendered it ineffective in practice.

The whole Chancery case had arisen because of the dogmatic detail of Mrs Ramsden's will. Taking a high line with any possibility of inflation in prices or depreciation in currency, she had laid it down that she wished the rents of her estates to remain as they stood in 1745, with 'no attempts, if possible, made to raise them'. Assuming that this would be done, she had balanced her budget for maintaining the local charities which she supported, erecting the Ramsden Building, and meeting the costs of the six Skerne Fellows and ten Skerne Scholars whom she endowed. Fellows and scholars alike were to get their rooms free, and the Fellows were to have a stipend of £52 a year if they kept six months in residence, the scholars £15 each. On these figures it was to be assumed that from rents of between £600 and £700 there would be a small annual surplus, and this Mrs Ramsden directed to be paid into the common stock of the college, for repairs, improvements or other general uses.[15]

But even before the Ramsden Building was completed, the 'advancement' of the Adlingfleet property had led to more generous treatment of the scholars than the will had ordered.[16] The first Skerne Fellows were not elected until 1776, and in 1795 the Lord Chancellor had ruled that the clause forbidding increases in rents was untenable in law; the College as trustee must make the best use of the property,[17] and quite substantial

[15] For Mrs Ramsden's Will see Muniments, xi/1, xi/2, xi/5, xl/43. Cf. Jones *History*, pp. 114–25.
[16] L/83.9.ii.70.
[17] L/83.14.iii.95.

surpluses began to be available. The Fellows of the Old Foundation had not been ungenerous in their use of the wealth which came under their control from this source. They voted additional income to the Skerne Fellows as well as to themselves,[18] and in 1807 a further revision was made, so that a Skerne Fellow might then get £52 from the Ramsden Estate and a further total of £68 a year from 'College Stock' without restriction as to residence.[19] So the Skerne Fellows, apart from their accommodation, might expect more than twice the stipend which Mrs Ramsden had bequeathed to them.

Officially the increase came from the College Stock. But the real source of the money was the Ramsden Estate, which by 1813 was producing an annual revenue of about £2,400.[20] The surplus went, according to the will, into the common stock and thereby fell under the control of the Fellows of the Old Foundation; for Mrs Ramsden had made it quite clear that she wanted the Skerne Fellows to be Bye-Fellows without a vote in the government of the College. They attended the Audit Meetings and knew the sums involved, but they had no control. If they had been given any powers they would have given a larger allocation to themselves, but they would also have shown their disapproval of the major use to which the Ramsden surpluses were currently allocated; this was the Patronage Fund, whose history deserves separate treatment.

The case of the Skerne Fellows (officially the case of the Attorney General v. the Master and Fellows), dragging on from 1813 to 1820, must have left its mark still on the College when Philpott came up as a freshman in 1825. It was by any reckoning a remarkable case, in which the Lord Chancellor confessed both that he knew little of Cambridge and its conventions (for he was an Oxford man) and that his initial feeling was that the verdict would go to the Skerne Fellows. But he ultimately ruled that the surplus Ramsden revenues must go to the common stock of the College and that only the Fellows of the Old Foundation were entitled to decide on the uses to which it

[18] L/83.10.iii.90.
[19] L/83.21.iii.07.
[20] xxvi/1. L/83.4.iii.15.

should then be put. He emphasized that he was sitting as Lord Chancellor *in curia*, not as Visitor of the College *in camera*, for Mrs Ramsden had deliberately refused to appoint any Visitor for her foundation; and he pronounced that 'The King is the Visitor of this College, the King is the Visitor of the Old Foundation'.[21]

The effect of the verdict was to confirm that the Skerne Fellows were a separate foundation within the College, clearly separable from, and in some respects subordinate to, the Fellows of the Old Foundation. This was exactly the sort of situation which the Royal Commissioners found undesirable, and with so clear a declaration of the situation available it is all the more astonishing that Philpott should have departed from his general support for the Commissioners' principles on this point, and that they should have accepted the departure. But, of course, in theory the change to a single foundation would seem to have been accepted in 1860. It was only in practice that the Fellows of the Old Foundation retained all the power.

It is not at all easy to discover what part, if any, the Skerne Fellows played in the life and work of the College. They were forbidden to marry and were given free rooms, so they might be expected to be in fairly constant residence; and they would normally be younger, at least on appointment, than Foundation Fellows. But, to judge from their college bills and their payments, they were habitually out of residence for long periods. This may well have been due to the fact that whereas a Foundation Fellow was only allowed to accept a benefice outside the College if it did not involve a cure of souls, did not involve residence, and was not worth more than ten marcs a year, a Skerne Fellow was allowed to hold a living up to the value of £20 a year so long as it was not more than twenty miles distant from Cambridge.

Whatever effects the Chancery case may have had on Philpott and the other Foundation Fellows, it did not estrange the Skerne Fellows although it left them out in the cold. They

[21] xxvi/1/11.

could hold their fellowships for years on end, with no special duties to perform, and some of them seem hardly to have been academic in their outlook. There was one 'Yorkshire Fellow of Catharine Hall' known as 'Captain' Clapham, whose appearance was so military as to cause him to be remarked as a 'd – – – – d gentlemanly unacademic-looking fellow'; and the best of them were intermittent in their attendance although from time to time they may be found taking office as Prelector or Steward, or even as Proctor, when Foundation Fellows declined. Notable among them was Edmund Yorke, who had migrated from St John's in 1809. He was elected a Skerne Fellow in 1810 and held the Fellowship until his death in 1871. On his death-bed (in lodgings in Chelsea) he told his solicitor that he had received much pecuniary benefit from the College, the Master having advised him not to resign his Fellowship. He wished the College to benefit in return, but his will proved difficult, partly because he had made more bequests than his estate of about £23,000 would cover, partly because he had endowed a University Prize for an essay on Primogeniture with his holding in Consols. At the time of drafting his will that holding was worth about £800, but at his death it stood at over £4,000 and everyone, including the University authorities, realized that this was an absurdly large bequest for such a purpose. Against his better judgement, the Master of the Rolls had no choice but to award the whole amount in Consols to the University, and the College refused to appeal against this judgement. But the bequest to the College proved to be worth about £7,000, and the Yorke Fund was called upon in 1893 and again in 1913 to finance the purchase of the college playing field, the freehold of which is ascribed to that fund.

What can be gleaned about the Skerne Fellows makes a picture of reasonable friendliness and sense. In 1835, for example, Joseph Romilly, the Registrary, dined with Philpott in hall, and noted in his diary: — 'no wines & no cheese in hall: no young man goes out of hall till the scholar has said grace: & all the youths remain standing while the fellows march out. — In the Comb. room they wisely have no fruit: there were 2 little round tables (one on each side of the fire) each provided

with its bottle of port.'[22] Of the six diners that night two were
Skerne Fellows. It is a pleasant picture; but a 'period picture',
for the Skerne Fellowships were sinecures. If the vision in 1860
was forward to a new impulse in teaching they should clearly
have been absorbed. Only if the vision was backward, to the
litigation and to personalities, can the non-implementation
of the new statute be understood.

But, save for the creation of Open Scholarships, the statutes
of 1860 do seem obsessed with the past rather than with the
future. It would be fair to say that they may be judged from
the simple fact that they were drafted in Latin (though in
fairness it should also be recognized that the Supplemental
Statutes were in English).

The other serious law-suit of the period had come in the early
days of Philpott's mastership. His election had reduced the
number of Fellows in Holy Orders to two whereas the existing
statutes ruled that there must always be three, of whom two
must be priests and one might be a deacon. When numbers fell
below this quota the senior lay Fellow must either take Holy
Orders within a year or resign his Fellowship, unless one of the
junior Fellows volunteered to bring the number of clerics up
to the requirement by taking orders.

The problem arose in November 1846, since the man elected
in Philpott's place, J. P. Pine, was a layman who, although he
soon took Deacon's Orders, died in April 1847. One of the
Fellows in Priest's Orders, Francis Proctor, had in the meantime
resigned his Fellowship to get married. The College was therefore short of a priest, and after Pine's death of a deacon too.
Rather perversely, as it would seem, another layman was
elected to fill the vacancy caused by Pine's death and the
senior layman, C. W. Goodwin, was required either to take
Orders or to forfeit his Fellowship. Goodwin had been a Fellow
since 1840. He was, says G. F. Browne, a Hebraist, a botanist, a
geologist, a Coptic scholar, an accomplished Anglo-Saxon
scholar and a good German scholar; he turned to the law
and finished his career as a judge at Shanghai and then at

[22] Romilly *Diary*, C.U. Library, Cam.b.860.1.

Yokohama. But he was not a theologian and he did not wish to take Holy Orders. He accepted the situation until the quota had been filled by the election of a new layman (Purton) who took Deacon's Orders, and the election of a deacon (Bonner Hopkins) who took Priest's Orders. Then Goodwin appealed to the Chancellor, claiming that by the statutes he should indeed be deprived of *the emoluments* of his Fellowship while the statutory number of clerics was not available, but that he should not be deprived of the Fellowship itself, and that when the numbers had been righted he should be restored to the emoluments once more, merely losing the emoluments for the period of default. The ingenuity of Goodwin's plea attracted the Lord Chancellor; but he ruled against him, much influenced by evidence that there were similar rules at other colleges[23] — at Pembroke, St John's and Christ's, for example — and St Catharine's faced the Royal Commissions with no doubt about this aspect of the statutes. Of the five (or perhaps six) Fellows, three must be in Holy Orders.

In their dealings with other Cambridge colleges the Commissioners pressed hard for revision of statutes which required Fellows to take Holy Orders. At St John's, proposals to abandon the rule that Fellows must be ordained and celibate were defeated, but college officers were no longer obliged to be in Orders and Professors and University lecturers could be elected to Fellowships without taking Orders.[24] At Corpus the Commissioners refused to give up 'the principles by which they have been guided in the case of other colleges' and insisted on the exemption of at least four Fellows from the obligation to take Orders.[25] It might have been expected that, with Philpott in control, St Catharine's would gladly have abandoned the rule for clerical Fellowships. But once more Philpott looked back over his shoulder in college affairs, and the new statutes neatly prevented any recurrence of the sort of trouble which Goodwin had caused, while confirming the system of

---

[23] xxxi/1/6.

[24] E. Miller, *History of St John's College*, p. 86.

[25] P. Bury, *The College of Corpus Christi and of the Blessed Virgin Mary, a history from 1822 to 1952*, C.U.P., 1952, pp. 52–4.

clerical Fellows. The new statutes confirmed that at least three Fellows must be in Holy Orders, but they brought change by ruling that if one of the priests vacated he must either be replaced by a priest or else that the replacement must take Orders within a year unless a *senior* Fellow offered to make up the quota of priests. Emphasis now was on the newly-elected Fellow, not on the senior lay Fellow; and if the number of priests was not duly filled it was the new Fellow who was to be deprived of his Fellowship. In phrasing the new statute the lessons of the Goodwin case were taken to heart, for the wording was precise and full, making it clear that the recalcitrant layman was to be deprived not only of the emoluments but of the Fellowship itself — *et pro non socio habeatur*. This was a neat and effective remedy; but it amounted to a clarification of old principles rather than an enunciation of new ideas. It was clean against the principles of the Commissioners, with whom Philpott was normally in agreement. But perhaps it would be asking too much to expect a potential bishop to play ducks and drakes with the clerical rules of his own College.

The influence with the Commissioners which Philpott undoubtedly enjoyed was, in fact, exercised to shield St Catharine's from the full impact of the reforming ideas which he would have supported where other colleges were concerned. The reforms which the statutes of 1860 brought were not of great significance for St Catharine's. The rule of celibacy was maintained but was modified to the extent that a Professor might retain a Fellowship with a wife so long as his stipend did not exceed £500 a year, and provided he did not want rooms in College. But open apostacy from the Church would entail forfeiture, and although a Fellow was allowed to make a solemn affirmation instead of an oath of acceptance of the doctrines of the Church of England, this was but a slight indulgence which would not have allowed a convinced nonconformist to be admitted to a Fellowship. Fellowships were, however, made something more attractive in that stipends might run up to £300 a year; and they were made something less of a nomination in that any vacancy (presumably up to the new total of nine, though in practice only up to the agreed total of five) must be filled within a year unless financial stringency forbade it.

In these rules the new statutes were, once more, confirming existing practice. The object in view was to make Fellowships attractive on the one hand, but yet to ensure a flow of talent on the other. In a society of only five fellows such a balance was extremely difficult to achieve, and Philpott had inherited a situation marked by tenures which were excessively long by any standards. But he had been fortunate enough to achieve an empirical solution in the early days of his mastership. Within four years of his election all the Fellows who had held office in 1845 had gone; Corrie was the last to go, as Turton appointed him to the Mastership of Jesus. Whether Philpott made good use of the power which fell into his hands must be judged from the conduct of the Fellows when his control was withdrawn; but he had undoubted authority, since in 1807 the Lord Chancellor had ruled that the Master's assent was necessary for the election of every Fellow.[26]

The authority of Masters of colleges emerged in other ways, and was one of the points on which the Commissioners did not entirely agree with the internal reformers. The Commissioners tried to stabilize the rewards and amenities of Masters while diminishing their burden of administrative responsibility. For St Catharine's they decided that, whereas under the old statutes the Fellows enjoyed five-sixths as much dividend as the Master, in future they should only get half of the Master's dividend. They did not always manage to force their views on colleges. Corpus, for example, succeeded in getting the statute 'De Vice-Magistro' withdrawn in draft; but the office of President caused no problems at St Catharine's. The Founder's statutes had included such an officer, and he had been given a stipend in the revision of 1549. His position and his duties were perhaps slightly emphasized in 1860, but he was still not given power to use the college seal, and although he was given precedence over other Fellows and was to exercise the authority of the Master during the Master's absence, there was no

[26] xxi/7/20.

significant change here — certainly nothing which would in any way derogate from the authority of the Master. The new statute may perhaps reflect Philpott's experience during the times when the University made heavy demands upon him, but it would have left him unchallenged within the College.

Much of the authority which Philpott so obviously wielded derived from his knowledge, his experience, his personal character and his external relationships in the University and at Westminster. Like Jowett, he could have been described as a man who, all his life, had a weakness for getting and keeping authority in his own hands, or in the hands of those whom he could influence. As they protested against the readiness of the Commissioners to leave excessive power in the hands of Heads of Houses, the ordinary members of the Cambridge Senate alleged that all Masters either controlled the decisions of their Fellows or else knew how to manipulate and to evade them. There is no reason to believe that Philpott was an exception to this generalization. Reforming Masters, such as Jowett, or Whewell of Trinity, or Adrian of Pembroke, were not hard to find (Corrie being a notable exception); but within their own colleges they were often conservative. Philpott's mastery over this College was unquestionable, his pre-eminence clear. He had enjoyed something between a free hand and a controlling influence in the choice of the Fellows who stood with him as the College faced the Commissioners, who accepted (and evaded) the statutes of 1860, and who then met to elect his successor. He left behind him men who proved unable to face the challenges or to grasp the opportunities.

Within St Catharine's Philpott's oustanding achievement as Master would seem to have been his success in entertaining to dinner in hall Queen Victoria and Prince Albert, shortly after the Prince had been elected Chancellor of the University. The duty fell upon him in 1847, during his first tenure of the Vice-Chancellorship. There is a tradition in the College that his greatest moment was when he succeeded in walking backwards across the uneven cobbles of the court, before Her Majesty and the guests, all the way from Old Lodge (then in use by the Masters) to the hall. But that is only hearsay; what

is certain is that the Duke of Wellington slept in comfort in
the Lodge and that he was commanded by the Queen to tell
Philpott that in no commoner's house had Her Majesty ever
been made to feel so completely at ease.[27] Philpott's later
relations with the Prince were always cordial and understanding.

For the rest, evidence about the internal state of the college
during Philpott's time is scanty. His testimony before the
Commissioners gave no analysis of the college's finances, but
the fees were set out and they support his contention that 'the
necessary expenses of residence in College being small, persons of
limited means are enabled to join upon almost equal terms in
all common pursuits of University study and in the competition
for honours with the sons of persons of a higher class of society
and of more abundant means'.[28] He was strongly in favour
of the existing system, which by his time had reached a point
at which it could be said that 'students of different classes of
society and of different means and circumstances are brought
to associate together during their residence at the University';
and at his own College fees were so graded that this was
obviously true. Annual payments were indeed moderate, even
for a nobleman (of whom there were none in residence). The
nobleman had to pay £40 a year for tuition, the Fellow
Commoner £20, the pensioner £10 and the sizar £3. Quarterly
payments, paving tax and library tax, between them, came to
less than a pound a year even for a nobleman, room-rents
varied between £5 and £10 a year, dinner in hall was charged
at 14/– a week, and a charge for 'detrimenta' in kitchen and
buttery was levied at 8/4d. a year. Other costs, for food other
than hall dinners, for books, coals and service, and probably for
private tuition, had also to be met. But the basic charges for
residence were certainly moderate and would justify the claim
that a special college or hostel for poor students was not
needed in Cambridge since colleges such as St Catharine's lay
within the means of poor men and conferred considerable
benefits on them.

[27] Compare G. F. Browne, *St Catharine's College*, London, 1902, pp. 214–15.
[28] *Report*, 1852, Evidence, pp. 179–85.

That the College had a recognizable character and unity can be gathered alike from the evidence to the Commissioners and from the less formal reminiscences of an undergraduate of those days, George Forrest Browne, later a Fellow and later still Bishop of Bristol. Philpott, for example, reported that all five of the Fellows of the College were engaged in giving lectures and that this was adequate to prepare men for their college and University examinations in the Arts and to prepare men who were reading law or medicine for attendance at the lectures of their professors. If he thought such provision inadequate, he said he would either hire resident graduates or fellows of other colleges to give the necessary college lectures.[29] In short, he believed in college teaching and the tutorial system as it then existed, and he thought that St Catharine's measured up to these concepts.

From the *Recollections* of G. F. Browne comes more personal evidence of the character of the College as he knew it in his undergraduate days. Browne came up to St Catharine's from St Peter's, York, in 1852, enjoying the preferences which a Yorkshireman could still claim. He later wrote, perhaps in a vein of episcopal righteousness, that 'We were an exceedingly idle set of young men, not unstrenuous, or vicious, or indolent, but very idle in regard of study'. As an undergraduate Browne quickly attracted attention, and Philpott promised him a Fellowship if he would follow up the Mathematical Tripos with the Classical Tripos — a course which the College favoured, three of the Fellows having taken double Firsts in the first six years of the Classical Tripos. Ill-health prevented Browne from complying with the suggestion, and since two of the Skerne Fellowships were being held vacant pending revision of the statutes, he withdrew to teach at Trinity College, Glenalmond. But he remained deeply attached to the College, to which he returned later. 'We were proud of our little College', he wrote, 'and of its importance not many years before, when Dr Corrie was its trusted Tutor.' In Corrie's time the college

[29] Loc. cit., pp. 180–3.

had boasted some seventy undergraduates instead of the thirty-six who were members under Philpott as Master.[30]

Whether the College could properly be described as small, by the standards of the mid-nineteenth century, is open to doubt. The University Registrary, in his evidence to the Commissioners, gave figures for admissions to the various colleges over ten-year periods — an exercise which reduced him to the statistician's absurdity of quoting fractions of a man. For the ten years prior to 1850 St Catharine's had admitted, on average, 18 men a year as against $3\frac{1}{4}$ at King's, $12\frac{1}{2}$ at Clare, $7\frac{5}{8}$ at Pembroke and $7\frac{3}{8}$ at Sidney Sussex.[31] In 1851 St Catharine's had 69 undergraduates in residence. Peterhouse had 42, Clare 45, Magdalene 50, Trinity Hall 59, Pembroke 27, Sidney Sussex 26, King's 14 and Downing 13. Though obviously not a large college, St Catharine's was diminutive in an affectionate sense rather than in any critical sense, at least by comparison with other colleges. The size of the College, and the type of undergraduate would, however, explain the success of the Boat Club in those days; for it is recorded that in three years, 1854, 1855 and 1856, the boat went up twenty-one places, making its bump on every night save one and making two bumps on one of the nights.[32]

This was a close and friendly society over which the somewhat austere Philpott and his five undistinguished Fellows presided. But undergraduate numbers did not improve; only nine freshmen were admitted in 1857–8, only six in the next year, and only ten in 1859–60. At midsummer 1860 there were only forty men in residence — six Fellow-Commoners, seven Bachelors of Arts, twenty-four pensioners and three sizars.[33]

This, as Browne noted, was a recession from the numbers attracted to the College by Corrie; and in other ways the College was in a weaker state on Philpott's resignation than

---

[30] G. F. Browne, *The Recollections of a Bishop*, London, 1915, p. 46. L/83.4.xi.59; 21.ii.60.
[31] *Report*, 1852, Evidence, pp. 66–7.
[32] Browne, *St Catharine's*, pp. 250–1.
[33] XL/32; L/16.

13

it had been at his election. The immediate comparison, of course, is that the College which Philpott left behind proved unequal to the strains of a disputed election to the Mastership, complicated by knowledge that the successful candidate had voted for himself. But this was precisely the situation as Philpott had taken office; indeed, not only had Philpott secured election by his own vote but his predecessor, Joseph Proctor, had virtually done the same, and Proctor's predecessor, Lowther Yates, had most certainly done so.

It may seem odd that such a man as Philpott should not have been the unanimous choice of so small a society as St Catharine's was in 1845, for he had shown his ability early in his career, gaining the great distinction of Senior Wrangler in mathematics in 1829 and then turning to the newly-established Classical Tripos to gain another First Class. Elected a Fellow forthwith, he soon revealed that capacity for management which marked his career throughout, his knowledge of college and University business growing rapidly as he held office as Bursar, as Proctor, as lecturer and as examiner. As Bursar he had done much to bring the College into line with the changes which had taken place in the social and economic life of the country, spending money on enclosures, drainage, and tithe-redemption for the College's estates and drawing up new scales of fees for those in residence and those who wanted to keep their names on the 'boards' of the College.

Nevertheless the small society of 1845 contained a scholar and an administrator who could challenge comparison. George Elwes Corrie, a Lincolnshire man, had come up as a pensioner in 1813, and was unanimously elected a Fellow in 1817, as soon as he had taken his degree. He had held office continuously as Dean since 1818, managing admissions with such conspicuous success that he won the admiration of later generations. From 1838 onwards he had been Norrisian Professor of Divinity, but this did not prevent him from continuing as Dean or even from accepting office as Steward in addition.[34] He had been Tutor when Philpott was admitted

---

[34] L/83, passim.

in 1825, and he certainly thought that his own claims were superior to those of his former pupil. University gossip, as recorded in the diary of the Registrary, held that when Philpott had voted for himself and it was evident that this would give him the Mastership 'Corrie gave no vote but said "I agree" (or "I acquiesce")'. He then (the Registrary continued) behaved as well as possible under his disappointment; he accompanied Philpott to the Vice-Chancellor, and on the following Sunday he preached in Chapel on brotherly love. He was, however, the sort of man about whom legends gather and Browne, who knew him personally and admired him immensely, records in his History of St Catharine's that, when it came to his turn to vote, coming after the others as Senior Fellow, he 'delivered himself thus, "Nevertheless, gentlemen, I record my vote for George Elwes Corrie".[35]

No aspersions were cast at either Philpott or Corrie for voting in their own favour; it was quite acceptable in such a small society that a good man should vote for himself. No question of propriety or of loyalty arose, and until Turton, acting as Visitor to Jesus College, conferred the Mastership there on Corrie in 1849 he continued to serve St Catharine's loyally and industriously. As Philpott gave up the Bursarship the Professor took on that office and acted as President, Bursar and Dean. His career at Jesus leaves no doubt that he would have conferred great distinction on St Catharine's, and he would have held office through until 1885 — a long period during which the 'remarkable steadiness' and industry for which he was noted, and the personal sensitivity which marked him, would have been invaluable, as would his utterly uncompromising honesty.

That a college of only five fellows should contain two men of the stature of Philpott and Corrie is a great tribute to Philpott's predecessor, Joseph Proctor: all the more so in view of the miserably weak and unsatisfactory state of both

---

[35] The unpublished *Diary* of Rev. J. Romilly, University Registrary, is in the University Library, Cam.b.860.1. Corrie's journal runs from 1836 to 1843 and throws no light on the incident. See M. Holroyd (ed.), *Memorials of the Life of G. E. Corrie, D.D.*, Cambridge, 1890.

College and University when Proctor assumed office. He had been elected a Fellow in 1783, became Master in 1798, and died in office in 1845 — an almost indefensibly long tenure by modern standards, but one in which much was accomplished.

In Europe, as the nineteenth century opened, the humanitarianism of the revolutionary movement was buried; military authoritarianism held sway under the French Consulate. In England laws against freedom of the press and against workmen's combinations emphasized the uneasy autocracy of a government which had failed to meet the challenge of the industrial and agricultural changes of the period. The Gag Acts still held, the Test and Corporation Acts debarred Roman Catholic and Protestant dissenters from equal civil rights and even from University degrees. For, although a man could come into residence without a religious test if his college allowed it, he could not take his degree without making the Oath of Supremacy. If he could not declare himself a member of the Church of England he must at least accept the King as Governor of the Church and must declare that no foreign prince or prelate had any authority within the realm, and that the Prayer Book and the Thirty-Nine Articles were in accordance with the word of God. There was no latitude possible, and the College Register of St Catharine's records a long succession of Masters and Fellows who on their admission took their oaths and made their declarations in the 'Open Hall' of the College.

With such tests, the Universities were bound to the Church, as the Church was bound to the State. The Church's ministry to the people had been thrown out of gear by movements of population which made nonsense of old parish and diocesan boundaries, while the clergy had often lost contact with parishioners to whom they represented nothing but a high Toryism in conflict with all movements for reform. Static in a changing world, the Church stood much as it had stood in 1689; and it controlled the universities to such an extent that Edward Gibbon, utterly frustrated by his experience at Oxford, could declare that the failure of the Universities was due to the fact that their government still lay in the hands of clerks.

The limited numbers of undergraduates and the high proportion who did not read for honours underline the defects of the universities and of the colleges. At St Catharine's the number of men who proceeded to any kind of degree as the century opened was negligible — in 1798 only four men took their B.A.; in 1799 a further three. Two were presented for their degree in 1800, a solitary Bachelor of Physic in 1801, two B.A.'s in 1802, one in 1803 and one more in 1804. In 1800, 1801 and 1802, no freshmen were admitted to the College, which clearly shared to the full the defects of the University.

The failure to attract undergraduates, even with the Ramsden Foundation to offer great advantages to boys from Yorkshire and Lincolnshire, was ascribed to a dispute between the Master and the Senior Fellow. With good reason the Master explained to the Visitor that 'Young men are deterred from becoming members of a Society which is considered as still engaged in Litigation, and the Rights and Interests of whose members are considered as yet remaining to be decided upon'. If proof of this statement were needed the career of Thomas Turton would provide it. As a Yorkshireman he would have liked to come to St Catharine's. But the open dispute between the Master and the Tutor, who conducted admissions, deterred him and he went up to Queen's in 1801. He migrated to St Catharine's in 1803, was Senior Wrangler in 1805, and became in turn a Skerne Fellow, a Foundation Fellow, Tutor, Lucasian Professor of Mathematics, Regius Professor of Divinity, Dean of Peterborough, Dean of Westminster, and then Bishop of Ely. A fine judge of wines, pictures, and people, he brought to St Catharine's many men who migrated from other colleges, as he had done himself.[36]

The dispute which prevented Turton from beginning his Cambridge career as a St Catharine's man arose from the election of a successor to Lowther Yates. Yates had been Master for twenty years when he died in 1798 — an undistinguished

---

[36] Professor Sedgwick, also, told Corrie that he would have followed his father to St Catharine's but that 'owing to the disputes in the College at that time the Master would not allow any admissions', Holroyd, *Memorials of the Life of G. E. Corrie*, p. 222.

and slightly ludicrous character, but vigorous and forthright. His election had seen three of the five Fellows (including Yates) each voting for himself on the first count; sanity then prevailed, Yates secured a majority, and no contention followed although some of his actions as Master were denounced as 'arbitrary, unstatutable and illegal'. But he never won the complete loyalty of the Fellows, and he did nothing to change the ways of the College although he was able to lend a fair sum of money (some £4,000) to provide cash in hand. His Tutor, Joseph Thorpe, known as 'Cardinal' Thorpe, was said to have illustrated a lecture on the Law of Extreme Necessity by telling his class (who would all have been members of the College) that 'Suppose I and Lowther Yates were struggling in the water for a plank which would not hold two, and that he got possession of it, I should be justified in knocking him off', adding with great vehemence 'D – – – n him, and I would do it too, without the slightest hesitation'.

Yates' successor in office, Joseph Proctor, was not elected but was appointed by the Lord Chancellor as Visitor. Whereas when Yates had been elected the Fellows had composed their first differences, on his death they proved obstinate. According to what must almost be regarded as an established custom, the senior Fellow, the Reverend Joshua Waterhouse, voted for himself. The next senior, the Reverend Joshua Wood, also voted for himself. Only one of the five Fellows voted for Waterhouse, but with his own vote this left him with two votes which, though not a majority, was more than anyone else could muster. Waterhouse therefore declared himself elected, made the declarations and took the oaths with all solemnity, and installed himself in office. The three Fellows who had not supported him thereupon appealed to the Visitor, for by statute a majority of votes was needed. At this juncture two of the Fellows, Proctor and Burrell, were pushing the claims of Philip Gardner, a former Fellow who had resigned to take a college living; but Proctor, with a well-timed opportunism which would surely not have been unnoticed by the Visitor, qualified himself for consideration by taking the degree of Bachelor of Divinity (which by statute the Master must hold, unless he held a doctorate in Divinity) five days before he appealed against Waterhouse's assumption of authority. The Visitor declared that no valid election had taken place since no Fellow had got a majority of the votes, and that the lapse of time since Yates' death gave him the right to nominate. He nominated Proctor, and an admirable choice it proved to be.

Physically vigorous, a good judge of horses and of men, Proctor twice held office as Vice-Chancellor, and it was reported of him that he was nominated yet again at a time when he was in residence at Norwich. Though then almost seventy, he mounted his horse, rode the sixty-odd miles to Cambridge, 'pleaded his infirmity' as a sexagenarian was entitled to do, and rode back to Norwich again.[37]

In an age when the Master of Peterhouse had assumed office by virtue of a *Writ of Mandamus* although the majority of the Fellows had supported another candidate and the Visitor of that College had declared for yet a third man,[38] when the Master of St John's had been elected by a majority of a single vote, with the junior Fellows holding out against a strong pressure-group of peers and prelates, the Archbishop of Canterbury and Lord North,[39] the circumstances of Proctor's appointment called for little remark. Waterhouse retired from the Lodge with good grace and, as President, admitted Proctor to office, while the Fellows voted the considerable sum of £600 for repairs and improvements to the Lodge (that is, Old Lodge as it now stands).

But the appointment was bound to leave some bitterness, and William Atkinson, the Fellow who had voted for Waterhouse, showed less magnanimity than his principal. Despite orders from the Visitor that differences and disputes should be entirely forgotten, he carried on a long and bitter feud with the Master and with the Master's strong supporter Charles Burrell. It was a feud characterized by 'a Free use of very unbecoming language' and 'Acrimonious Effusions of Bile'; at

---

[37] Browne, *St Catharine's*, p. 209.
[38] H. Gunning, *Reminiscences of the University, Town, and County of Cambridge,* 2nd ed., London, 1855, I, pp. 107–9.
[39] Miller.

one stage Burrell openly called Atkinson a perjurer, and Atkinson continued to rumble and to spit even when he had withdrawn from the College to Stapleford. He still held his Fellowship in 1808, and at that time he protested bitterly against deprivation although he had then been elected a Fellow of Christ's![40]

Throughout this unsavoury affair the Visitor supported Proctor, whom he adjudged to be 'exceedingly reputable'. He went further and attempted to bolster up the authority and the income of the Master as against the Fellows, holding that by current practice the revenues were used 'in such a manner as not to benefit the Master in so great a Degree as the Dignity and Superiority of his station over that of the Fellows necessarily required'. The Visitor was greatly concerned to make the Mastership attractive to good men, and to ensure that able Fellows should stay on in Cambridge in the hope of ending their careers in the Lodge. But a financial enquiry which the Visitor instituted leaves the impression that the Master was already well provided for, by comparison with the Fellows; and that the notion of maintaining Fellows in office was not acceptable to the Master, who, on the contrary, thought that a great object of college policy should be to achieve a flow of talent among the Fellows by encouraging them to resign and to take themselves away from Cambridge. For this he was prepared to see college revenues used, if necessary at the cost of the Master's emoluments.

But the Master was in fact not badly provided for. Officially his dividend from Fellowships Estates was, and remained, in proportion to that of a Fellow as six is to five, and his 'Commons and butters' exceeded those of a Fellow by only £2.12s. a year. In addition he received a meagre allowance of £1.14s.8d. a year for a servant — and this the Visitor increased to £45. But the Master also received the rent from the rectory of Guilden Morden, some £215 a year; and he held the canonry at Norwich which was attached to his office, the income

---

[40] For the Proctor–Atkinson correspondence see extracts in Jones, *History*, pp. 325–32. The appeals to the Visitor, and the formal documents, are in xxi/7/20; xxi/7/22–3; xxi/7/34; L/83/passim.

from which varied with the price of corn but averaged £550.12.7d. for the first six years of Proctor's mastership. So the Master could count on an income in the region of £900 a year as against a Fellow's expectation of about £140 or less. They all had their accommodation and amenities, the Master in the Lodge undoubtedly better housed but the Fellows able to receive payment for holding college office. Such payments, however, bore no relation to the value of the Mastership; the Bursar got £42 a year, the Steward £20, and the Tutor £25.

The Master, therefore, was comparatively affluent; and his authority was vindicated also. At the time of Proctor's appointment the Fellows had kept two fellowships vacant from 1799 to 1801 and had divided up the revenue among themselves. They had also decided to pay rates and taxes on their rooms from corporate income instead of from their own pockets. Without the Master's consent they had renewed the appointment of Joshua Wood as Bursar, and with Atkinson in the lead they had put and carried motions at a College Meeting in defiance of the Master's claim that he alone had the right to put a motion forward for voting. Proctor contested all of these actions, and in one issue after another the Visitor supported Proctor. He ruled that the Master must have consented to the election of every Fellow, that he alone (or the President in the Master's absence) could put a motion to a College Meeting, that he alone could appoint the Tutor, that his concurrence was necessary for the appointment of the Dean, the Bursar and the Lecturers, and that it was his clear duty to prevent non-residence by Fellows and to see to it that they dined together in hall.

This was a thorough vindication; and the Visitor gave Proctor his head also in the matter of tenure of Fellowships. Here the bone of contention was the Patronage Fund. The accepted way of getting Fellows to resign was to offer them a college living — and with only Ridgewell and Trunch and Gimingham (united as a single living in 1751 but separated again in 1793) and the Founder's gift at Coton, St Catharine's was ill-provided, especially since the livings were not wealthy. It had been one of Proctor's first acts when he became Bursar, in 1791, to attempt a remedy by setting up the Patronage Fund; for he held strongly that college livings should be made 'a sufficient Object for men of Character and Learning'. As the benefits of the Ramsden Bequest began to accrue the College had found itself with annual surpluses to invest. Fellowship dividends were increased in 1784 on the ground that 'the College Stock is very considerable and yearly increasing', and in succeeding years balances were invested in Consols, so that by 1790 almost £4,500 was so invested. It was at that juncture that it was agreed that this accumulating stock should be called the Patronage Fund and should be used to augment the ecclesiastical patronage of the College.

The first uses to which the fund was put were designed to make the existing livings more attractive. The Rector of Coton was to get £120 a year from the fund and the Vicar of Ridgewell £150. Then livings were to be bought for the use of the Skerne Fellows, no living to cost more than £2,500 and all of them to be at least twenty miles from Cambridge — a distance which would ensure that the appointed Skerne Fellow resigned his Fellowship. This, however, was not permitted by the Visitor or by the Master in Chancery to whom the enquiry into the College's finances had been entrusted. By 1805 the holding in Consols stood at £10,787 and it was accepted that it would be proper to use this money to augment the incomes from livings; but, although the source of wealth was the Ramsden Estate, it was held that it would be contrary to Mrs Ramsden's will to spend the money on buying livings for the benefit of 'her' Fellows.[41]

The Patronage Fund therefore survived notwithstanding the views of two successive Lords Chancellor, Loughborough and Eldon, that 'Good men must not be drawn from the College', and that 'It looks like a bad arrangement if the Master's Income is not to be increased, and if the Fellows are to apply the Income to increase College Livings'. 'The Mastership must be such that the best men may stay for it'. The Visitor's anxiety was not only to preserve the status and emoluments of

[41] For the Patronage Fund cf. L/83.16.XII.1791; XXI/7/22; XXI/7/23; P/1/1.

the Master; he also felt that, as a matter of policy, it was better to have good Fellows and to keep them than to push along a succession of indifferent scholars; better to spend money on residence than on college livings.

But the Visitor's powers were limited to matters in which an interpretation of statutes was involved, or on which an appeal had been made to him. The Patronage Fund having been accepted as within the statutes and within the terms of the Ramsden will, it was for the Master and Fellows to run it. This, in view of the misgivings which had been expressed, they did with some caution although both Proctor and his sturdy supporter, Burrell, never modified their view that this was the best way of ensuring that new ideas and comparative youth should not be overborne by set ways, elderly complacency, comfortable habits and the frustrations of compulsory celibacy. But the income from the holdings in Consols was no longer primarily devoted to this purpose; it was used for the general needs of the college and the comparatively easy flow of Fellows, which was the object in view, was certainly not achieved.

It is a fair generalization that in the early years of the nineteenth century the average tenure of a Fellowship at a Cambridge college was about ten years and that fellows were 'mostly men of well under fifty who were waiting their turn for a college living'. But although Browne wrote that 'Fellowships used to be vacated in sufficient numbers by the acceptance of college livings', this was never true of St Catharine's. Of those in office at the time of Proctor's appointment Waterhouse held his Fellowship for forty years, from 1774 to 1814, Wood for thirty-seven, from appointment in 1779 till death in 1816, Atkinson for twenty-seven, from election in 1781 till deprivation in 1808, and Burrell for fifty-five years, from 1787 till his death in 1842. Proctor himself had been elected a Fellow in 1783, and he died in office as Master in 1845, a period of service of sixty-two years! Atkinson was for once right when he maintained that it would require very considerable augmentations to make the College's livings fit for a man with a family, and in 1813 the Visitor was informed that in the past sixty-two years only one Fellowship had been vacated by a presentation to a college living.[42] Even when Burrell had left his private fortune to augment the fund, and extra livings had been bought at Newent and at Marnhull, Fellows still preferred to stay in Cambridge, and a succession of non-fellows was called upon to fill the livings. Only Little Shelford, purchased in 1879, proved attractive, and that was near enough to Cambridge for a college officer or a bye-fellow to hold it, although a Fellow on the Old Foundation (if such a term can be used for the period after 1879) should have been debarred by statute from accepting a cure of souls or a stipend of the size involved.

The college statutes demanded the resignation of any Fellow who held an appointment or patrimony of more than ten marcs a year in value, and this had been put forward as one possible way of securing resignations. But although the Visitor was asked in 1799 for a ruling on the 'Ten Marcs Statute' in view of the changes in the value of money since the fifteenth century, he does not seem to have made any reply and in practice the rule seems to have been ignored. In 1791 a writ was issued by the Court of King's Bench requiring that the Fellowship of Joshua Wood should be declared vacant since he had been appointed Vicar of Madingley, which was worth more than the maximum of ten marcs. But the Lord Chief Justice declined to act in what he described as a domestic dispute, within the province of the Visitor. This decision was of considerable importance in legal history; it did nothing to help the College, where Wood continued to hold his Fellowship although proof of his non-residence was added to the fact that he was in breach of the 'Ten Marcs Statute', and it meant that unless the other Fellows appealed to the Visitor, a Fellow could accept a living which allowed him to remain ostensibly in residence — as Wood did, and as later Fellows did.

This conclusion was emphasized by the fact that the oldest of the three livings which the College possessed, that of Coton, could certainly not be used to secure a resignation. This had

[42] xxvi/1/2, p. 7.

been ascertained in 1795, when the resignation of Waterhouse was demanded on the ground that he was Rector of Coton. But the Lord Chancellor then ruled that the College itself was Rector of that parish, Waterhouse was merely a chaplain or curate appointed by the College; since the very foundation of the College a Fellow had been Rector. Whatever money the Patronage Fund spent to improve the living at Coton would, therefore, have no effect in securing the flow of talent which Proctor and Burrell had at heart, and the complete change in the Fellowship which was achieved within the first four years of Philpott's Mastership must be regarded as fortuitous and exceptional.

The interminable litigation of the period, and the financial report of 1807–8 required by the Lord Chancellor, make it possible to reconstruct the administrative system then in use. Year by year the Bursar borrowed from the accounts of estates with special purposes (such as the Therfield Estate for the maintenance of the Sherlock Library, the Histon Estate devoted to Frankland scholars from Coventry, Guilden Morden Rectory rents for supplementing the Master's stipend, or the Ramsden Estate for Skerne Fellows or Scholars) and lent the money to the Steward for the general running costs of the College. As college bills were paid, and the Steward was in funds, the Bursar recovered his loans and reimbursed the named endowments. On occasions he might borrow from an affluent Fellow (as the College had borrowed from Lowther Yates) but such transactions would normally be for a particular purpose and would run for a period of years whereas transactions between the internal accounts of the College would be squared off, at least on paper, at each audit. The account into which such loans were paid, and from which the Steward paid the day-to-day running costs of the College, was called the Audit Account or the Audit Book Account, and the actual assets of that account were called the General Stock of the College. For example, the surpluses of the Ramsden Estate revenue were paid into the Audit Account to swell the General Stock of the College, and allocations from the General Stock were made to the Patronage Fund or to other purposes.

The system was simple, and it worked well. It left the allocation of surpluses from named funds to the Master and Fellows
and enabled a Bursar such as Burrell to achieve an unostenta-
tious prosperity and comfort. Under Burrell the leases of the
College's estates were revised, rents were increased, and
improvements were undertaken. Strongly though he supported
the Patronage Fund, as Bursar he secured a ruling that the
revenues from the College's holding in Consols should be used
for the general purposes of the College, and he and Proctor
went to work to gain possession of the land along the boundaries
of Silver Street and Queens' Lane.

First the narrow strip of 'void ground' fronting on to Queens'
Lane was leased from the Corporation for 999 years in 1808;
then it was purchased outright in 1839. This was little more
than a pavement, but in 1813 a more important move was
made when three pieces of ground in St Botolph's Parish (in
effect the Fellows' Garden) were bought from Queens' College;
the procedure required legal validation of the right of such a
corporation as Queens' College to dispose of land, and the
price was proportionate to the situation of the land, £1,372.
The same considerations applied when, in 1836, an even more
important purchase from Queens' was made, the Old Printing
Office and the adjoining Anatomical Schools and Almshouses
in Silver Street. For this the price was £7,700, and the Master
and Burrell each gave £1,000 towards the purchase.[43] The
College therefore got possession at this time of the south-west
block of the Island Site which it occupies, and was prepared
for expansion when the time should come. For the moment no
new building was put in hand; but in the next generation this
area was used for a new Master's Lodge, making Old Lodge
available, first for a Fellows' Building and then for undergraduate use.

This was a period when much of Cambridge was being
rebuilt, in part to accommodate more undergraduates and to
accommodate them better, in part to satisfy that re-awakened
sense of the past which produced the so-called 'Gothic Revival'.

[43] vii/2/a; l/83, 2.iii.1810; 2.vi.1813; 24.iii.1836; 1.vi.1839.

As yet St Catharine's took no part in this; the changes in the windows of hall and library lay a generation ahead. But the Bull Hotel was rebuilt, and its severely classical front provoked adverse comment. Much of the re-fashioning of Cambridge lay in the hands of William Wilkins, a Fellow of Caius who had begun his architectural career by designing the simple classical buildings of Downing College but who then became a complete convert to an ornate Gothic style. To him are due the dining hall and the Wilkins Screen of King's College, and he even secured the consent of the Provost and Fellows to his proposals to Gothicize Gibbs' Guilding! At Corpus he demolished the old Master's Lodge and the Elizabethan chapel and built the new court, fronting on Trumpington Street, with a new chapel, lodge and dining hall.[44] No false modesty prevented him from airing his views on the plans for rebuilding the Bull.

In an open letter to a local paper he wrote, 'if the plan for the Bull Inn be carried into effect, it will be the severest visitation that ever Vandalism conceived or Barbarism inflicted upon the University at large. And when the mercenary spirit in which such a building is planned (for mercenary it must ever be considered where the evil is attributable to the desire of obtaining a higher rent from an increased accommodation) is contrasted by the liberal and princely outlay made by the neighbouring colleges in the genuine spirit of improvement, it must ever be regarded as a monument of bad feeling and worse taste'. As 'the Architect upon whom the good fortune has fallen of being the designer of some of the most prominent buildings of the University' he refused to be 'a silent spectator of measures calculated to render his studies abortive'.[45]

With the passage of years, the Bull has stood up well to comparisons with Wilkins' work. But he was right in stating that the motive for rebuilding was financial, the creation of a property which would let at a good rent. It was an investment which the College did not find it easy to undertake for, although the Audit was reasonably balanced, a new parsonage was in

---

[44] For Wilkins see R. Willis and J. W. Clark, *The Architectural History of the University of Cambridge*, C.U.P., 1886, passim, especially I, pp. 297, 302–4; 564–5.
[45] Charteris, Manea, Upwell Thorney *Advertiser*, 28 March 1828.

hand at Coton, an Enclosure Act had been obtained there and required to be implemented, and enclosures were being financed on many of the other estates — at Brinkley, Norton, Chesterton, Barton, Fockerby, Adlingfleet and Nether Whitacre. These enclosures were accepted as investments which would bring improved income; but in the meantime they meant that it was not easy to find capital for building. So, to put through the Bull project, the College had to sell £6,000 of its Consols in March 1828, a further £1,000 in October, and £4,439.12s.6d. 'being the amount of our stock' in March 1831. This should have meant the end of the holding in Consols, and perhaps even of the Patronage Fund; but dividends continued to come in, and a further £4,800 was sold in March 1836.[46]

This last sale, however, was not due to the Bull but to the purchase of the Silver Street land from Queens', a purchase for which the generous gifts from Proctor and Burrell were insufficient, so that the College had to borrow £2,000 from the Reverend Dr French, Master of Jesus.[47] But these were capital transactions, distinct from the day-to-day running of the College.

Perhaps as good an indication of the 'running account' situation as could be got may be seen in the way in which the porter's wages were increased by £20 a year in 1810, and the cook's by a like amount in 1811. The Bursar and the Steward had their stipends increased by £30 and £20 respectively in 1810, and though the Steward was reduced again in 1815 the Bursar continued on until 1842, when he was increased to £120 a year. In the same mood, in 1826 the Master and Fellows 'fully sensible of the many services which the Rev. C. W. Burrell, the President, has rendered to the College . . . unanimously agreed to add to the President's stipend Twenty-nine pounds thirteen shillings and fourpence, as long as Mr. Burrell shall hold the office'.[48]

---

[46] L/83, 28.vi.28; 26.iii.33; 24.iii.36.
[47] L/83/24.iii.1836.
[48] L/83, 21.iii.1810; 11.xii.1810; 16.xii.1811; 13.xii.1826; 15.xii.1841.

The financial stability of which these increases and transactions were signs was, of course, largely due to the increased
rentals from the Ramsden Estate, and the Skerne Fellows
understandably protested at the uses to which the revenues
were put, especially at the increases in stipends for college
officers. But the Ramsden rents were not the sole cause of
solvency, nor must the balanced budgets be post-dated.
Already by Trafalgar year (1805, the year by which, at last, it
was possible to answer the Visitor's request for a financial
statement) the College was reasonably prosperous. Debts then
amounted to £1,062, of which the late Master's executors
claimed £420; but there was a balance of over £999 in the
Fellowships Estates account, the Ramsden account showed a
surplus of £543 for the year 1804, payments to scholars were
less than the income of the scholarships account, the Patronage
Account had been built up to a holding of over £10,000 in
Consols, and over £1,000 had been spent on an enclosure at
Coton which would result in greater rents being paid.[49] This
was a stable background for development even if the Fellows
protested, as part of the continuing dissension which centred
round Atkinson, that they were less well rewarded than fellows
of other colleges.

Although Proctor and Burrell were riding high, their troubles
were not all overcome easily or quickly. In particular they
failed to establish that turn-over in the small fellowship by
which they both set so much store. In the immediate context
of Proctor's election one of the disputes had arisen from
failure to elect to two vacant fellowships of which the income
was divided among the remaining three. The Visitor ruled
that elections up to the statutory number of six (in fact, there
were only five) should be resumed as soon as finances allowed,
and ordered that the revenues from the vacancies should be
returned to the general stock of the College. Elections were
resumed in 1803, and the failure to achieve brief tenures
among the new Fellows must be read as a sign of undoubted
success in choosing reputable men.

[49] xxi/7/24; Report to Visitor, 9 November 1805.

14

These were men of character and stature, not mere aspirants to a college living but candidates for high academic distinction. It did not matter that Turton held his Fellowship for twenty years, Corrie for thirty-two, or Burrell himself for more than half a century. Starkie, elected in 1803, became Downing Professor of Law, Turton became Lucasian Professor of Mathematics and then Regius Professor of Divinity, and Corrie became Norrisian Professor of Divinity. Nothing but good came from long service by such men, and their tenure of Fellowship was terminated, not by the amenities of country parsonages but by the intellectual challenges of other appointments; or by the calls of matrimony.

Following after the first group of 'Proctor Fellows' came Temple Chevallier, formerly a Fellow of Pembroke, second Wrangler in the year in which Corrie had been eighteenth. He came to St Catharine's in 1820 and proved a notably able tutor. He was a distinguished classic as well as a mathematician and was in turn Hulsean Lecturer and then (having resigned his Fellowship in 1826 in order to get married) Professor of Mathematics and then Professor of Astronomy at the newly-founded Durham University. His contemporary, Thomas Durham, though not so distinguished, was another who terminated because of the celibacy rule, and the list could easily be multiplied.

As yet, in Proctor's time, celibacy was not a matter of hot dispute either within the College or within the University. The general acquiescence, reflected in the 1852 Report of the Royal Commissioners[50] that the practice of celibacy was inseparable from the college system and that any revision of statutes should continue the rule, was the more extraordinary because it accepted that Fellows of Colleges alone in the kingdom should be subjected to this limitation by statute. The Commissioners remarked that the statutes of some colleges were silent on this point, and St Catharine's was an example of this. Neither in the Founder's Statutes nor in the revision of 1549, which was operative in 1860, was celibacy enjoined. But

[50] *Report*, 1852, p. 172.

the omission was made good by University Statute, since in the Elizabethan code for the University it was decreed that 'Socios Collegiorum maritos esse non permittemus, sed statim postquam quis uxorem duxerit, socius Collegii desinat esse'. Before the Reformation (as the Commissioners pointed out) no statute was needed on this account since Holy Orders entailed celibacy and the colleges were in effect clerical foundations. But from 1549 onwards the College's statutes had ruled that there might be as many as six Fellows, of whom at least three must be in Orders; so there could be, and there often were, two or three laymen among the Fellows, and those who were priests could also marry as far as the Church was concerned. But priest and layman alike would have to relinquish fellowship for wife. Fellows were forbidden to enjoy a status which was permitted for all other priests, and which even Masters of Colleges might share.

Inevitably such a situation caused comment, and the Royal Commission of 1850–2, while accepting the rule, tried to modify its effects in driving away good men by exempting Professors and University Lecturers from the ban. There does not seem to have been very strong feeling among University reformers on this problem, and a movement in the middle years of the eighteenth century to allow a man to have 'a wife and a fellowship with her' had died although a certain amount of pamphleteering continued.[51] Perhaps the explanation lies in the fact that the resident Fellows had come to terms with the system.

Celibacy remained the rule, with some slight modifications, until the University Statute was altered in 1871; indeed at St Catharine's it was made more explicitly compulsory since the Statutes of 1860 for the first time stated that marriage was one of the reasons for which a Fellow should be deprived. This would seem to be yet another example of the way in which the 1860 statutes (and Philpott, their sponsor) were looking backwards rather than forwards; and the result proved disastrous. One of the major results of the celibacy rule was to

[51] e.g. University Library, Cam.c.500.29. *Reflections on the celibacy of Fellows.*

mark out a clear distinction between the Master and the Fellows, and to make contests for Masterships doubly difficult. The possibilities were shown when, for example, Whewell resigned his Fellowship at Trinity in order to get married, only to be recalled as Master within the year. At a different level, Gunning tells how his tutor at Christ's, a worthy man disappointed of the Mastership, gradually lost his interest and his value when the lady whom he had expected to take to the Lodge as his bride rejected the 'rectory house' which was all he could offer if he took a college living in order to marry. A noticeable feature was the verve with which celibate Fellow after celibate Fellow throughout the University was able to 'lay his hands on' a suitable wife as he came to be elected to a Mastership. But able men were certainly driven away from their colleges by the system, and a frustrated candidate for a Mastership who was also condemned to celibacy or resignation had a double reconciliation to make.

It was this issue of celibacy which, according to G. F. Browne, lay at the heart of the outcry over Robinson's election. For Jameson seems to have accepted the outcome, including the fact that Robinson had voted for himself, until he was informed that Robinson was engaged to be married and would shortly have resigned his Fellowship for that reason. There seems to have been no secrecy about Robinson's engagement, but Jameson apparently had not heard of it — perhaps because Robinson was Vicar of Christ Church, Barnwell[52] and not constantly in residence in College. The affair may indeed have even more point than would at first appear, for Jameson accepted the Rectory at Coton within a year of Robinson's election, and vacated his Fellowship by marriage within eighteen months of his failure to win the Mastership.

When gossip got to work the University indulged its sanctimonious condemnation to the full. However much it may be evident that within the small Fellowship of St Catharine's serious candidates for the Mastership had consistently voted

[52] His obituary notice in *The Times*, 14 July 1909, says he was Vicar of St Andrew the Less from 1859 to 1862. But Browne (*St Catharine's*, p. 233) is correct in stating that he was at Barnwell.

for themselves, Victorian Cambridge could not be expected to forego such an opportunity for censoriousness. Heads of Houses were in a quandary, for if they made a courtesy call they would seem to condone the vote; if not, they would be offending against their own social code. For the most part they did not call on Robinson or his wife; and when they did so they brought little comfort if, like Whewell of Trinity, they issued an invitation to dinner and then behaved so rudely as to embarrass everyone present. Even Corrie, looking back to the election of 1845 and pronouncing that 'It is the purest election that has taken place at St Catharine's for two centuries' nevertheless added, 'But I shall not call on Dr Robinson'. The extract comes from the Diary of the Registrary of the University, Joseph Romilly, but there is something slightly apocryphal about it since Robinson at the time of the election was not yet a Doctor, and an intimate friendship between Corrie and Robinson lasted up to Corrie's death.[53]

It must be confessed that the Fellows of the College were as much at fault as any other members of the University, if not more so. They supplied the basic gossip on which all else was founded; and the initial mistrust of Robinson's character. Francis Proctor, for example (a nephew of the former Master), wrote shortly after the election that 'Jameson was weak in declining to vote for himself. Robinson, with a sharpness worthy of a Yankee, taking advantage of the amiable weakness, and Joe Milner weakly sanctioning a clear piece of roguery.'[54] But the problem did not arise from the fact that Robinson had voted for himself, though that was the aspect of the incident on which gossip fastened. Initially, it was not unacceptable that he should have done that, and Jameson was blamed by Proctor for not having done the same — as Robinson always maintained that he had advised his rival to do. The unacceptable act was held to be that Robinson had broken an agreement that neither he nor Jameson would so vote; and

---

[53] One of Corrie's last acts was to send Robinson a nosegay of snowdrops, and to receive a touching acknowledgement. Holroyd, p. 320.

[54] Letter of 31 December 1861, in Willis Clark Collection, University Library, Cam.b.861.1.

Robinson always denied that such an agreement had ever been made or that Jameson had any reason for assuming such an agreement. Philpott, writing from Worcester to Ralph Blakelock, a former Fellow, and openly regretting that the Fellows had not chosen to recall Blakelock to be their Master, said 'Common report tells me that Robinson and Jameson agreed, as old friends, to vote for each other, but that Robinson, voting after Jameson had voted for him, voted for himself in breach of the understanding and so secured the Election. I fear that the story is too true'.[55]

Robinson was not aware that anything was amiss until he had been away for his honeymoon and had returned with his bride. In the brief time before he left for Scotland he had found Jameson friendly and co-operative. Jameson had gone with him to the Vice-Chancellor to present his credentials and had accepted office as President (an office in the Master's gift) and as Dean. According to one account, Jameson's attitude completely changed when he learned, for the first time, that Robinson was to get married.[56]

Certainly a palpable mistrust pervaded the College by the time Robinson got back from his honeymoon to Cambridge. But within a year or so the heavy blight seemed to have been dispersed. In December 1861 Philpott intervened to get Jameson and Robinson to issue a joint statement, 'much derided' but yet incontrovertible, that they accepted the possibility of 'a misapprehension in the mind of each of us as to the intention of the other'. As far as the issue of a broken agreement was concerned that should have been the end of the matter; and in fact the hubbub died down.

Jameson accepted the living at Coton, whose income was augmented by the College (perhaps as a gesture of goodwill), in June 1862. He then withdrew from the College, and resigned his Fellowship in June 1863. So far had trust been restored that G. F. Browne, who had refused a Fellowship under the notion that the Master had been guilty of a dishonourable action,

[55] Loc. cit., 5 November 1861.
[56] Jones, *History*, pp. 139–48.

now accepted, and was elected into the vacancy which Jameson had created by his marriage and resignation. Browne only held his Fellowship for two years before he also vacated because of marriage. But he continued in residence and continued to hold college office, as Dean and Prelector, Chaplain and Tutor, to serve as Proctor on the College's nomination and to play so large a part in the administration of the University that (as he said of himself) he was even pointed out to strangers as the embodiment of the University. Within the College he was appointed the Conduct Fellow from 1866 onwards — a Bye Fellowship which, like the Skerne Fellowships, had survived the 1860 statutes and which conferred dignity and amenities on the Chaplain without involving him in the government of the College.

Browne's return to Cambridge is a curious episode since he was already contemplating marriage and cannot have envisaged a long tenure as a Fellow. But his talents were such that he stayed until 1891, when he went to be a Canon of St Paul's, subsequently to become Bishop of Stepney and then Bishop of Bristol. In the University he became the first Secretary of the Local Examinations Syndicate and the first Editor of the University Reporter, and he was appointed one of the two secretaries to the Royal Commission of 1877. He was an outstanding Proctor, and his position was such that he was asked to accept the University living of Ashley with Silverley with a licence for non-residence 'to keep out an undesirable candidate'. Within the College he continued active and dominant despite his lack of Fellowship in its fullest sense. He continued to lecture, both on the Old Testament and on Mathematics, and though he had to pay rent for his rooms and was in other ways clearly not considered as of equal status with the Fellows, that a non-Fellow should be appointed Tutor (as Browne was in 1883)[57] was at once a commentary on his own abilities and on the defects of the Fellows.

Of those who had mismanaged the Robinson election only one, Crabtree (also from St Peter's, York) remained when

[57] M/2/1, 29.x.1883; 11.xii.1883; Browne, *Recollections*, pp. 90, 114; *St Catharine's College*, pp. 236–8.

Browne came back to Cambridge in 1863. The College might seem to be running smoothly. But damage had been done. Robinson was passed over for the Vice-Chancellorship (an extraordinary slight in those days) and the new Fellows who were elected were not of Browne's stature although some of them lasted longer — indeed, up to the 1914–18 war. For the moment, however, it seemed as though the joint statement of Robinson and Jameson had achieved its purpose. True, no Fellow was ready to take on the Bursarship and Robinson himself was forced to act in that capacity. He had previous experience both as Steward and as Bursar and was conscientious and fair in his office; but, as in his Mastership, he lacked the purposefulness to make hard decisions and to carry them out.

A sign of the stability which had been reached, and of the weakness which underlay the conduct of College business, may be seen from the financial situation. In May 1853 it had been agreed that at the Audit in each year 10% of the gross revenues from Fellowships Estates should be set aside for an Improvements Fund before a dividend was declared. This was sound policy, both progressive and conservative, and the rate for the earmarked fund was increased to 15% in 1860. Then, under Robinson, it was reduced to 10% in 1864, to 5% in 1866 and to $2\frac{1}{2}$% in 1867.[58] This, by comparison with earlier practice, was mortgaging the future for increased dividends.

If the quality of the new Fellows was not such as to make up for the weaknesses of the Master, the undergraduates admitted under Robinson also contributed little. Under Philpott admissions of freshmen had run at about ten to twelve a year; in 1872 fifteen men were admitted, in 1873 sixteen. In view of the great national interest in university education and of the demand for admissions, this was a negligible increase, certainly not enough to indicate any great vitality in the undergraduate body. With Browne preaching in Chapel about the former greatness of the College, when with Corrie as a real Tutor the College had been full, the undergraduates were fully aware of the situation and felt the 'inferiority complex of that time'[59] acutely.

---

[58] L/83, 4.v.1853; 21.ii.1860; 7.xii.1864; 11.xii.1866; 5.xii.1867.
[59] Compare letter from H. B. Luard, printed in Jones, *History*, p. 336.

A blight had certainly descended on the College. Other colleges had their troubles too, and peace might well have continued at St Catharine's, but the fires were raked over, and flames burst forth again in 1867–8. For this Browne was responsible; indeed, in his *Recollections* he states with some complacency that he advised Robinson to re-open the election story and to demand explanations as opportunity offered.[60] This was advice entirely in keeping with Browne's forceful personality, but disastrous in view of the bruised withdrawal which had been Robinson's reaction hitherto, a withdrawal entirely in keeping with his character. It was this second outburst of criticism, renewed after some six years of acquiescence, which turned the Robinson vote into the *cause célèbre* which it became, and which did such lasting damage to the College.

The first move in the revival of the strife came when Robinson put in a *supplicat* for the degree of Doctor of Divinity. In those days, and until recent times, all Heads of Houses could safely assume that a Doctor's Degree was theirs for the asking. But Robinson's grace was *non-placeted*. Voting went in his favour and the degree was awarded by eighty-two votes to twenty-six, figures which revealed that a hard core of residents, when challenged, found him quite unacceptable, that there was a substantial number who wished to make the best of the situation, and that he had the strong support of the College in the face of external criticism. It was reported that the gallery of the Senate House was packed with St Catharine's men and that many of the voters had been brought up from the country for the occasion.[61]

Robinson had apparently won a round; or Browne and his supporters had won a round for him. But the vote had stirred up the whole controversy, copies of lampoons and skits first published in 1861 were re-issued with a caricature of a grace for a doctor's degree. The fat was in the fire again and Browne was delighted since, as he maintained, his purpose was to get the controversy into print, so that Robinson and the College

[60] Browne, *Recollections*, p. 117.
[61] Willis Clark Collection, Cam.b.861.1, University Library.

could be vindicated and the scandal could be nailed down. His course took him into a head-on collision with R. Shilleto, a Trinity classic who had become a Fellow of Peterhouse only in 1867, after a long career as a coach and a schoolmaster, a reputable scholar who seems to have felt some genuine indignation but who became engaged largely because the opportunity to write Greek verse lampoons was not to be missed. But if Shilleto was slow to take up a moral attitude he refused to be pushed around by Browne and he thought what he called 'the Cat-hole situation' a proper object for derision. The two men clashed after a dinner in King's at which Shilleto, apparently with no very serious undertones, indulged his sense of humour with an indifferent pun, linking Robinson's name with 'robbing'. It was neither a new nor a very funny play on words, and it certainly was bad manners to have uttered it in the presence of a senior member of the College, present as a guest. Browne took Shilleto up with enthusiasm, setting on foot a long and sententious correspondence which he then published, and breaking off relationships with Shilleto and with his family.[62]

Browne was well content. He had brought the controversy once more into the daylight and had stirred up such feeling that he and the Fellows, not one of whom had been a participant in 1861, published in June 1868 a Flysheet recounting the circumstances of the election. The Flysheet is printed in Jones's *History of St Catharine's*[63] but the heading of 'Flysheet issued after the Robinson election' obscures the fact that seven years had elapsed since the events narrated. The purpose of the statement was to make it clear that the Fellows did not believe that Robinson had broken any agreement with Jameson. There was no questioning the fact that he had voted for himself, and the statement opened by declaring (with justice) that 'it is the recognised custom in the College that Candidates for the Mastership vote for themselves'.

Whatever truth there may have been in the account given in the flysheet, Jameson regarded it as a dishonest breach of the

---

[62] The full Browne–Shilleto correspondence is in xxxiii/7.
[63] Loc. cit., pp. 334–6.

truce which Philpott had arranged between Robinson and himself, and from his semi-retirement on the south coast (for he had put in a curate to do duty at Coton and was in ailing health) he came out with his own version. This, while still leaving open the possibility that Robinson might have been genuinely mistaken in 1861, was forthright in declaring that Robinson and the Fellows were acting in bad faith as they re-opened a discussion which had been closed by mutual agreement.[64] Browne had blown the dying embers into a fire once more, and had so mis-managed the affair as to turn the heat of the controversy on to the whole body of the Fellows as well as on the Master.

The moment was singularly unfortunate, for in the summer of 1868 the College made itself ridiculous in the affair of Norman Moore, a promising undergraduate with a wide and reputable circle of friends in the University. Moore in 1868 was in his third year, reading Natural Sciences and having won a scholarship by his performance in the Mathematical Tripos. He turned to medicine and subsequently distinguished himself by selection as Harveian Orator, Physician to St Bartholomew's Hospital and other offices. He became a great authority on many aspects of medicine and was in 1920 awarded an honorary doctorate by the University. His interests were not exclusively medical however; he had strong literary leanings and in addition to over four hundred contributions to the Dictionary of National Biography he wrote a *History of Medicine as illustrated in English Literature*; and he did much to recover the grammar and literature of ancient Ireland from oblivion. In 1909 he was made an Honorary Fellow of the College and accepted that honour.[65] But in 1868 he was sent down for 'conduct inconsistent with the due maintenance of discipline'. He was allowed to return to take his degree examinations only 'under certain restrictions'.

Moore had been in residence during the Long Vacation of 1868 when one evening in Hall another undergraduate took

[64] xxxiii/7.
[65] Compare W. H. S. Jones, *The Story of St Catharine's College*, Cambridge (W. Heffer), 1951, pp. 165–6.

exception to something he had said and threw a salt-cellar at him.[66] Two days later, misunderstanding a remark made by Moore, the same man struck him on the head. Curbing a naturally turbulent temper, Moore went to the Tutor to ask for redress.

The Tutor (actually the Junior Tutor at that time) was A. W. Spratt, a St Catharine's man who had come up from Norwich, had won his first class in the Classical Tripos of 1864 and had been elected a Fellow in 1865. Spratt served the College in a variety of offices until 1918, and he set his mark upon it during the half-century for which he held his Fellowship. Normally, reported G. G. Coulton, he dressed like a gamekeeper in defiant untidiness. With a character as strong as Browne's, Spratt was outspoken, vitriolic, and violent as a matter of habit. He was the best scholar in the College and had a great reputation throughout the University and among the schools. To a few of his pupils he revealed himself as a man of warm sympathy and generous understanding, atoning for the isolation in which the College involved them by binding them together in a closely-involved college life. But to most men he was 'something worse than a giant Grim'; 'so formidable and aweinspiring to the ordinary man that most of his pupils' energies were absorbed in their anxiety not to rouse the potential wrath of their tutor'.[67]

Obviously antipathetic to a man who would not return blow for blow, Spratt barred Moore from attendance in Hall, suggested that the affair should end in mutual apologies and, when Moore had said he had not wished to turn the Hall into a scene of uproar and that he would not apologize because he did not think he had committed any offence, referred the affair to the Master, who was at that time in residence at Norwich. To Norwich Moore took himself, and there found the Master most sympathetic. At first Robinson also suggested mutual apologies; failing that, he asked that the matter might be dropped since the other man would soon be out of the College.

---

[66] *A Narrative of the case of Mr Moore of St Catharine's College, Cambridge, by Whitwell Elwin, Rector of Boston,* 1868.
[67] Compare R. Conway in *St Catharine's Society Magazine,* 1932.

But he said that no blame could attach to Moore and that the conduct of the other man had been disgraceful. Satisfied with this sympathy, Moore called on some friends near at hand and gave them an account of the interview; and in the following October came once more into residence for the Michaelmas Term.

It was not until about a month of term had passed that Moore was called before the Senior Tutor, Carr, and was gated for misconduct; he immediately appealed to the Master and was appalled to learn that Robinson now claimed that he had expressed sympathy in the summer only 'as a friend', not in an official capacity. The gating was confirmed and Moore served out his punishment. But his friends were indignant and one of them, the country rector on whom he had called after seeing Robinson at Norwich, warned the Master that he intended to publish an account of the affair. For, said the Reverend Whitwell Elwen, 'No man was safe, there could no longer be any trust if an undergraduate could solemnly be absolved by the Master of his College in August, and without a fragment of fresh evidence be condemned in November'. Carr warned Moore that he would be in danger of severe punishment if any account of the affair were published, and when his friends had nevertheless gone into print Moore was called before a tribunal of the Master, Carr and Spratt, and was sent down.

This was a most unedifying story; and though Moore had not yet attained real distinction he was obviously able, obviously in the right (if somewhat obstinate) and obviously victimized. The College could not stand this kind of adverse publicity on top of the renewal of the Robinson pamphleteering and the way in which Browne had contrived to put the whole body of the Fellows in the pillory.

The situation was set to produce the sort of college which G. G. Coulton[68] found when he came up as a classical scholar

---

[68] For Coulton see Jones, *Story of St Catharine's*, pp. 167–8. Coulton's reminiscences are in *St Catharine's Society Magazine*, 1937. Coulton was awarded a scholarship on 13 June 1877. He was registered in the Admissions Book as a pensioner on 16 June, but since he received payments as a Frankland Scholar this was certainly an error. The Frankland Bye-Fellowship had been turned into a scholarship, and divorced from its affiliations with Coventry, by the statutes of 1860.

from Felsted in 1877 — a small college of fifty-two men, closely bound in a strong *camaraderie*. But small as numbers were, there was no accommodation in College for freshmen, not even for scholars, and 'the Governing Body did not take us undergraduates very seriously, nor we them'. To undergraduates the Master was 'an ineffectual and pathetic figure' about whom the main knowledge was that he was ostracized by many of the senior members of the University. The Senior Tutor, the Reverend Edwin Trevor Septimus Carr, was a better classic than Coulton realized, and he had a critical wit. But he also had a pathetic tremor in his voice, a large mulberry birth-mark on his face, and an easy-going idleness of character which made him 'hopelessly unbusiness-like, not to say negligent'. One of his more perceptive pupils wrote of him that he was a man wholly devoid of ambition for himself and, by an easy and fatal transition, for the College. But most of the classical tuition went to Spratt, who also held office at that time as Junior Tutor; and there was yet a third distinguished classic in this small body of Fellows, Alfred Pretor, elected in 1871, but seldom in residence. Absenteeism was a charge levelled by Coulton also against W. T. Southward, yet another classic, elected in 1876 but whose services were so little required that he taught the Sixth Form at Dulwich.

The Fellowship had, in fact, become almost completely a classical preserve — and that at a time when the extension of University curricula was a major concern. The one partial exception was J. R. Lumby; and even he had begun his career with a First in the Classical Tripos. He had been a Fellow of Magdalene, and he continued to live in Cambridge as a coach after he had forfeited his Magdalene Fellowship by marriage. St Catharine's elected him as a widower in 1874, after he had developed an interest in theology and been Vice-Principal of Leeds Theological College; and in his election the Fellows at last put into partial practice the 1860 statutes on Fellowships, for Lumby was elected a 'Ramsden Fellow' in the vacancy created by Yorke's death, but with the same rights as a Foundation Fellow, according to the statutes of 1860. He was a candidate for the new Chair of Anglo-Saxon in 1878, and in

1879 became Norrisian Professor of Divinity. His vast fund of odd knowledge, his great physical strength, his total lack of humour, and his assertive character made him a difficult companion for the equally assertive Spratt, and Lumby made no mark upon the College, dominated by its classical coterie, save as a source of stories and satires. He could bend pokers round his arm, he knew the price of wooden legs, with or without brass ferrules — and he lacked the finer instincts.

> I heard the voice of Lumby say
> 'My height is six foot one;
> I'm forty inches round the chest,
> My weight is twenty stun.'

> I heard the voice of Lumby say
> 'I know six hundred creeds;
> I don't believe in one of them
> (We never did at Leeds).'

> I heard the voice of Lumby say
> 'Sense I postpone to sound;
> Let others argue to the point,
> I argue round and round.'

The author of the parody was reputed to be Spratt; whoever he may have been, the conclusion is clear; with Lumby as their only exception to inbred classical interests, this was an unbalanced Governing Body. To Coulton, even in the comparatively mellow retrospect of 1937, they were the 'Old Gang', determined to guarantee themselves against criticism by electing only nonentities and absentees when vacancies occurred.

But vacancies now were seldom available. The singular misfortune, for the College, was that this group of men, so markedly unqualified to carry the College into the new era, was equally markedly long-lived. Even with Lumby dying at the comparatively early age of fifty-nine, this group of Fellows averaged seventy-nine years of life. Moreover, the earlier vacancies in Fellowships had been due to insistence on celibacy, not to the attractions of the College's livings; and by a new set of statutes, accepted in 1882, marriage was no longer forbidden to a Fellow. The arguments against celibacy were sound enough. But the outcome was not altogether admirable. Not only did men, who would otherwise have made way for fresh blood, soldier on to the end of their days, but they now had other interests than their men and their studies and their colleges. The 'Don-forsaken undergraduate' began to figure in University literature. But the trouble at St Catharine's stemmed less from the active competition of other interests than from indifference and from failure of understanding and purpose.

But however indifferent or arbitrary the Tutor may have been, however remiss in the keeping of accounts the Bursar or the Steward ultimately proved, as yet there was no failure in ordinary administrative competence. By Michaelmas 1873 there was a balance of over £6,000 available for building, and the Fellows also sold their holding in Consols of over £28,000. In December 1873 (perhaps thinking to commemorate the four-hundredth anniversary of the founding of the College, although there is no evidence to support such an assumption) they approached W. M. Fawcett, an architect, with proposals for a new college building. This was to be on the Queens' Lane–Silver Street site, 'on the condition that those buildings be an exact reproduction of some ancient building to be chosen for this purpose'.[69] In 1868, as the Robinson dispute was again awakened, Fawcett had been responsible for building a bay on to the eastern end of the Hall and for gothicizing the windows of Hall and Library and panelling the Hall. The panelling, at least, is a fine example of Victorian craftsmanship. But, though again the muniments contain no evidence on the point, the Fellows would seem to have been so uneasy that, mercifully, they went no further with plans to gothicize the rest of the main court. They were, however, so convinced by Fawcett that they briefed him for other building projects.

The original suggestion was that a building on the Queens' Lane site should be used for a library, a muniments room or treasury, and a few college rooms; and the Fellows had several ancient buildings under consideration, with the idea that they

[69] M/2/1, passim.

should build an exact reproduction of the external features of one of them but should modify the internal arrangements and adapt them to college use.[70]

That was the notion in January 1874. But by mid-March of the same year the Fellows had agreed to build a new Master's Lodge on the site, the house to be a reproduction of the front of Sawston Hall. Before the end of April the plans had been explained by the architect, modifications to his ideas had been accepted, the external plans had been approved and it had been agreed that the panelling from the buttery should be removed to the new Lodge and that more old oak panelling should be bought. Final plans were approved in May 1874, a tender for £7,147 was accepted in June, work went on through 1875 and the final touches were added early in 1876 with decisions to build an eight-foot wall along Silver Street, to order wrought-iron railings for Queens' Lane and to build a carriage-house on the site of an old dwelling-house and stables on Silver Street. The final cost was over £9,000.

The Lodge so constructed was one of a series of mid-Victorian creations in the Cambridge colleges; Emmanuel, Pembroke, St John's, King's, and St Catharine's all built lodges at about this time and in much the same vein. Opinion has varied considerably as to the merits and demerits of the St Catharine's venture, but at least it has proved possible to adapt it to modern conditions. That would not have been a recognizably good feature in 1876, and one of its early critics, G. F. Browne, voiced an opinion which has been repeated many times and which is still true. The new Lodge had been so placed that it precluded all chance of building a new court on the site which had been so providently acquired by Proctor and Burrell.

There was a noticeable air of haste in the building of the Lodge, and rumours have been current that the lavish and ill-considered use of money was accepted as a means of tucking away surplus funds in bricks and mortar, where they could not be impounded by critics of the College. In particular, it has been suggested that the building was undertaken as the abrupt

[70] Loc. cit., 12.i.1874. L/83, 29.x.1873.

15

ending of discussions for an amalgamation with King's College under the terms of the Oxford and Cambridge Act of 1877 made some enquiry into the administration of the College likely. Consideration of the dates makes this impossible, for the Lodge was planned in 1874 and built in 1875 while the Oxford and Cambridge Act was not passed until 1877 and the discussions with King's did not begin until 1880. Nevertheless, some desire to 'Salt down' balances must not be ruled out, nor indeed should it be deprecated. The Royal Commission of 1850 had been forced to abandon its proposals that colleges should pay part of their revenues to the University, but the desire persisted and was part of a strong move to equip the University for the teaching responsibilities which were insistently demanded. In January 1872 a fresh Royal Commission had been appointed especially to enquire into the revenues of the colleges and of the universities, and the Report, delivered in 1874, left no doubt that the Commissioners were directing national policy towards statutes which would compel colleges to allocate some of their wealth to the needs of the universities. A further Report, on University teaching in the Natural Sciences, set the generosity of college endowments, and their support of non-resident Fellows, against the universities' need to increase Professorial stipends and to provide for university Lecturers. St Catharine's was vulnerable as such reports circulated. The opportunity to put the balances safely out of reach while at the same time proclaiming faith in the Master was not to be missed. Although Browne disapproved of the siting of the new Lodge, the decision to devote the resources of the College to this purpose was in line with the policy which he so strongly advocated. The new Lodge under-wrote the Master.

That St Catharine's should try to discount in advance a proposal that college revenue should be taxed for university needs may seem to call for remark since the Royal Commission which at last secured enforcement of this proposal, in 1882, was presided over by Philpott and was administered, as one of its two secretaries, by G. F. Browne. The Commission was appointed under the terms of the Universities of Oxford and Cambridge Act of 1877 — an Act resulting from debates in which the 'idle Fellowships' of the colleges were contrasted with Professorial stipends running as low as £100 a year, with the need to encourage research and to maintain libraries, laboratories and museums. The colleges were not without their champions, and St Catharine's was not alone in its vulnerability. Sir Charles Dilke, a Trinity Hall man, had fair support even from liberal opinion, as he protested against proposals for plundering the colleges, 'the noblest foundations in the world', in order to set up 'a couple of bad copies of a German University'[71] and Thomas Thornely, looking back with kindly eyes to the Trinity Hall which he had entered in 1873, wrote that the Master of those days had the reputation of being a kindly and hospitable old gentleman who kept an excellent cellar and was a discriminating judge of wine. 'Doubtless he was all this,' wrote Thornely, 'but we had no opportunity of finding out any part of it for ourselves, since neither his wisdom nor his wine ever came our way. We caught an occasional glimpse of him as he was led or pushed by his wife, with seeming reluctance, into his seat in chapel. Beyond this we saw nothing of him, and were only dimly conscious that something which had no meaning for us was lurking in the background of our College life.'[72] It is easy to understand Lord Edmund Fitzmaurice's proposal to abolish the 'comparatively useless position of Heads of Houses'.

Such radical proposals came to nothing; but the Oxford and Cambridge Act of 1877 was passed with three major objects in view: to provide revenue for better instruction, by the Universities, in Arts, Science and other branches of learning, by compelling the colleges to contribute for this purpose; to set aside some Fellowships in the colleges for Professors and other University officers; and to regulate the conditions and tenure of Fellowships so as to make them more valuable as adjuncts to teaching and to research. Commissioners were appointed for each university, and when Lord Chief Justice Cockburn died Philpott succeeded to the Chairmanship of the Cambridge

[71] Compare A. I. Tillyard, *A History of University Reform*, Cambridge (W. Heffer, 1913), pp. 217–18. Winstanley, *Later Victorian Cambridge*, ch. VII.
[72] T. Thornely, *Cambridge Memories*, London, 1936, p. 39.

Commission. The Commissioners were given power to make new statutes for the colleges and to abolish old ones, to modify conditions for tenure of Fellowships or of college office, to regulate fees and charges, and to alter the terms of trusts under which colleges received revenue or held property. They could also make provision for the union of any two Cambridge colleges if two-thirds of the Fellows present and voting at a college meeting so desired; at Oxford the consent of the Colleges' Visitors was also required. The Commissioners' powers were limited by the setting up of a Committee of the Privy Council to hear appeals from colleges and by a clause which allowed the Universities and the colleges until the end of 1878 to propose amendments to their own statutes. But such amendments would need approval from the Commissioners, who in effect were given overriding powers subject to the general consideration that the needs of the colleges for educational and other collegiate purposes must be safeguarded.

The chief change introduced into the statutes of the University (which, typically, Philpott is said to have written out in his own hand, translating them from the Latin) was the taxation of college revenues for University purposes. In principle Philpott had supported this notion throughout his career; in practice he had allowed his college responsibilities to predominate in 1857; and in 1881, Browne says, he was only in favour of modest contributions and was overborne by the majority of his fellow-commissioners, whose assessments of about 10% of corporate revenue plunged the colleges into deep gloom. St Catharine's, with a gross corporate income of £6,861, was assessable for University Tax on £4,363 of that sum in 1878 and would be required to find £436 a year for tax.[73] This was the lowest income of any college except Magdalene, and the lowest assessment of all except Magdalene and Downing.[74] The Fellows proposed to find their contribution by raiding the Scholarship Fund for ten per cent of its income, £176, and by suppressing one Fellowship, estimated to be worth £260. The mystery of the 1860 statutes comes into view

[73] M/2/1. 3.iv.78.
[74] Tillyard, op. cit., pp. 274–5.

once more, for the Fellows assumed that there were nine Fellowships (as there should have been, according to the statutes, although there never were more than five), and they proposed that five should continue to be filled, one should be suppressed, and three should be transferred to a General Fund which would make up any short-fall in the University payment, would pay for a Prize Fellowship, and would subsidize the educational work of the College.

These suggestions for meeting the assessment, however, did not find their way into the statutes which the Commissioners made for the College, nor did many of the suggestions embodied in draft statutes which the Fellows drew up in November 1878.[75] The Commissioners came to their conclusions and sealed their findings on 21 March 1881,[76] and though the Fellows went on 'considering' the new code into May 1882, no changes were made after the Commissioners had reached their decision. But whereas there is no evidence that the Governing Body shared in the framing of the 1860 statutes (though Philpott's voice was undoubtedly listened to), the 1881 code was certainly discussed and agreed between the Commissioners and the Fellows. A sealed copy of the existing statutes and a revised copy of the old statutes were provided for the Commissioners, the Master and the Fellows met once a week over a fair period in 1877 to revise their statutes and to prepare suggestions for the Commissioners, the Master, Carr, and Spratt, were named as the College's representatives to discuss with the Commissioners in 1879, and in 1880 the first draft from the Commissioners was discussed at length and several amendments were put forward.[77] The amendments were in part concerned with the college livings, in part they were concerned with revision of the assessment for University Tax. No concession was secured which was out of line with the treatment of other colleges. The one significant exception made for the College was that it continued to be required that the Master must be

[75] M/2/1, 22.x.1877, et passim; L/83, 11.xii.1878. The draft proposed in 1878 is in s/1/1.

[76] *Parliamentary Papers*, 1881, vol. LXXIII, pp. 66–83. Jones, *History*, pp. 341 et seq., prints from a copy dated 3 May 1882.

[77] M/2/passim.

in Holy Orders. This was against the general policy of the Commissioners, but it permitted the Norwich canonry to continue attached to the Mastership.

But the rule that at least two of the Fellows must be in Priest's Orders and at least one in Deacon's Orders was abandoned, as was insistence on celibacy[78] — though no wives or families were to reside in college except by special permission. There were now to be six Fellows, or more if finances permitted; but even with consent from the Visitor the number was not to be reduced below six although a delay of up to a year in electing might be allowed in special cases. Fellows' dividends might run up to £250 a year, and the Skerne Fellowships, of which two were still in existence, were at last definitely abandoned, three-quarters of the Ramsden revenue going to the general income of the College and one quarter to the Scholarship Fund. Further, the College was to find room for one Professor as a Fellow, and it was empowered to elect Honorary Fellows, to elect eminent men who had not graduated at any university as Fellows, and to create Supernumerary Fellowships which would entitle their holder to all the rights of a Fellow except dividend. This would permit College or University Lecturers, whose income derived from their teaching, to be elected Fellows without giving them the right to share in (and so to diminish) the dividend.

In all of this the Commissioners were imposing on St Catharine's a formula which they applied to all colleges. It was a formula which derived largely from proposals which had been put forward by the reformers at Trinity and which aimed at tying Fellowships to residence, to scholarship, and to teaching duties. Celibacy having been abandoned, and clerical predominance, and the probability that any Fellow (at least in the larger colleges) might have a living for the asking, it was feared that much of the value of the reforms would be jeopardized if married Fellows took the chance to remain, idle

---

[78] But W. T. Southward forfeited by marriage in 1890, perhaps because he had chosen to remain under the old statutes. He was then elected afresh on condition of his becoming Chaplain; this must have been an election to the Conduct Fellowship, which survived the reforms of 1860 and of 1882.

and uxorious, for the rest of their days. The colleges, including St Catharine's, were therefore given statutes which required that the maximum tenure of a Fellowship should be for six years, re-election being only possible if a man held college office and resignation being compulsory if he accepted a Chair, a Fellowship or a Headship elsewhere, or a living of £400 a year or more. For most colleges such a statute would have the desired effect of preventing long tenures of 'idle Fellows'. But at St Catharine's the clause allowing re-election of college officers made the major condition valueless; and when it was added that twenty years' tenure as a college officer conferred the right to a life-fellowship, the Six-Years' Rule was rendered completely abortive. In so small a society college office spread to all Fellows.[79]

In effect, therefore, the Fellows as they stood in 1882 were guaranteed life tenures if they wished. In 1886 they reported that they had six Fellowships, of which five were filled and one was in abeyance to meet the University Tax if required. There were then no Professors, no Readers and no University Lecturers among them, and only three were directly employed in the educational work of the College. No Fellowship had been awarded as a result of open competition, and no changes had been made since 1882. But none of the Fellows was, as yet, married.[80]

The new statutes had made but little difference in the ways of the Fellows, and little in the lives of the undergraduates. Numbers remained pretty constant, at about twenty admissions a year. But as the great and wealthy colleges, like the smaller ones, reorganized their scholarships on an open system, under pressure from the Commissioners, they had far more to offer both in awards and in teaching, as well as in reputation at schools where a generation of masters who had been in residence at the time of the 1861 election was now in power. So the better men went elsewhere. As one of that generation has written 'Since the College was not much sought after at that

---

[79] The draft statutes proposed by the Fellows in 1878 had proposed a seven-years' initial tenure and twenty-five years' service for a life-fellowship.
[80] *Parliamentary Papers*, 1886, LI, p. 582d.

time a proportion of us had attempted without success to obtain scholarships at the larger colleges; that is, we were on the edge of scholarship standard. This meant that we were all reading for honours whereas up and down the University at that time a large proportion were content to read for an Ordinary Degree'. He concludes, 'It must be admitted however that we got very few Firsts',[81] and the figures reveal that during the ten years from 1898 to 1907 the College gained only one First Class, in Mathematics, where Trinity gained 255, St John's 160 and King's 117.[82] The dice were heavily loaded against the smaller colleges, and St Catharine's suffered particularly severely; one man who came up in 1881 and took a First Class in Natural Sciences recorded his memories of what he felt, 'must have been the lowest ebb of the life of the College, overshadowed by the Master's long ostracism'.[83]

But to his own men the Master was a very gentle, harmless old man, and though there was 'no intercourse between Dons and undergraduates except in the lecture room' the undergraduates, most of them, enjoyed a happy time, and they felt involved in maintaining the reputation of the College in the face of so much external criticism.

The new statutes of 1881–2 saw the College through until revisions were undertaken in 1921 and again in 1926, the 1921 revision a voluntary one while that of 1926 was a compulsory adjustment to the requirements of yet another Royal Commission, appointed in 1924. The 1882 statutes made it possible for Lumby to be elected a Professorial Fellow in 1886 — an election carried through after some difficulty arising from 'the printing, with a view of circulating, some private letters, assumed to bear upon the election, without the permission of the writer'.[84] They permitted also the election of the College's first Honorary Fellows, in 1887; Bishop Philpott of Worcester, Bishop Boyd Carpenter of Ripon, and G. F. Browne, newly elected Disney Professor of Art and Archeology.[85] The statutes

[81] Memo by H. P. Trist, freshman in 1902.
[82] Tillyard, op. cit., p. 303.
[83] Jones, *History*, p. 336.
[84] M/2/1, 18.vi.1886.
[85] L/83, 3.vi.1887; M/2/1, 3.vi.1887.

served a purpose perhaps; but they did nothing to break the College out from the slough into which it had fallen. Rather, by perpetuating in office, and permitting marriage to, the limited body of existing Fellows, they made it inevitable that the College should remain static in an age of progress.

That much was amiss may be gathered from the negotiations which had taken place with King's College while the Commissioners were still sitting. First came attempts to buy the Bull Hotel, with discussion continuing from March 1878 to April 1879.[86] Spratt, to his credit, was always against the very idea, maintaining that St Catharine's needed room to expand and should never sell the freehold. But the Master and the Bursar were instructed to negotiate on the basis of land or money which would produce a revenue of £400 a year up to 1882 and £600 a year thereafter, since the lease of the Bull produced £400 a year then and was due for renewal in 1882. King's offered farms at Alderbury or at Coton in exchange, and required that St Catharine's would not oppose a move to close King's Lane. Eventually a price was agreed at £18,300, though Spratt held that at least £20,000 should be asked. But the Bursar of King's felt that this price so far exceeded the value of the property that the Copyhold Commissioners would not permit his college to make the deal.[87] So, apparently, it proved, for the deal fell through, the College spent money on improvements, and the Bull brought in a satisfactory rent while offers to buy it for £30,000 were being made before the end of the century.[88] Ultimately, the Bull proved essential to the building developments of 1966–7.

King's had not at that time a large number of undergraduates, and they did not feel themselves to be wealthy. In 1882 they admitted only twelve freshmen, in 1883 and again in 1884 twenty-four. But 90% of their men read for honours during the half-century from 1851 to 1906,[89] and they had a

[86] xxxvii/1/1–2.
[87] M/2/1, passim, up to 25.iv.1879.
[88] Loc. cit., 25.xi.1889.
[89] Reports of the Council, 17 November 1883; 15 November 1884, University Library, Cam.b.500.8.[25]

gross income of over £38,000 as against the £5,000–£6,000 of St Catharine's,[90] despite the effect of the agricultural recession of the period on their revenues. With so many assets, in land, wealth and talent, it may seem odd that King's should have been anxious to develop by absorption rather than by growth; but so they undoubtedly were. The reasons must be a matter for the historian of King's College; for St Catharine's the interesting thing is the light which is thrown on the standing of this College, and on the response which the Fellows made to external challenges.

As soon as the negotiations for purchase of the Bull had reached their conclusion, in November 1879, the Fellows of King's turned to Clause 22 of the Oxford and Cambridge Act, and set up a committee to consider the possible advantages of amalgamating the two colleges under the terms there laid down. Pooling of resources, both for teaching and for administration, was a common topic of discussion. The financial commission of 1872, reporting in 1874, had made it clear that although the smaller colleges had to spread their basic costs over fewer men, yet they were less expensive than the bigger colleges; on the other hand, the arguments for larger units stood out, especially in face of the impossibility of finding teaching resources in a small college for the rapidly expanding academic disciplines of the period. Over five times the cash was available for each undergraduate at King's, compared with his contemporary at St Catharine's,[91] and the discrepancy in the number of Fellows in proportion to undergraduates was even more striking. The reason for this was that the two colleges admitted substantially the same number of men, but that there were so many more Fellows at King's. As against the King's admissions of about twenty-four, St Catharine's admitted twenty freshmen in 1879, for example, and sixteen in 1880. But, as Browne ruefully noted,[92] there were only five Fellows at St Catharine's as against forty-six at King's. 'The lack of

[90] Tillyard, op. cit., pp. 274–5, 300.
[91] Tillyard, op. cit., p. 298.
[92] Browne, Recollections, pp. 228–30.

Fellowships looms larger and larger at St Catharine's.' This was true even though the proportion of men reading for honours was high, St Catharine's ranking third in the whole University in this respect, next after King's and Sidney Sussex, with 54.9% of the men reading for a Tripos.[93] Much reliance must have been placed on coaching and on external teaching, for with only three Fellows actively engaged within the College it was impossible to cover a wide range of subjects, and college lectures were, in any case, almost universally despised. An insight into the situation may be got from the fact that Browne, resigning from the Chaplaincy and appointed a Tutor under the new statutes, was detailed to lecture in the Lent Term on Old Testament subjects and in the Easter Term on general mathematical subjects.[94] 'College lectures,' wrote Thornely, 'were indisputably poor, and regarded more as a form of discipline than as a means of advancing knowledge. University Lecturers had not yet been created (in 1873), and intercollegiate lectures were rare, while professors catered only for the more advanced students, if indeed they condescended to lecture at all'.[95]

The current arguments against the costly management of small units and the incompetence of small societies in the face of the new Triposes were very much à propos, and in November 1879 the Fellows of King's appointed a committee from among themselves to put the idea of a merger to the Fellows of St Catharine's. There the idea was not scorned; a general meeting was appointed, and when it took place, in February 1880, it was agreed 'That provided satisfactory arrangements can be made, it is desirable to effect the complete union of King's College and St Catharine's College'. The Master and three Fellows approved the resolution, Spratt and Southward voted against.[96] Browne would have given his support to the merger, but although he was Secretary to the Commission he was not a

[93] Tillyard, op. cit., p. 298.
[94] M/2/1. 29.x.83; 11.xii.83.
[95] Thornely, *Cambridge Memories*, pp. 38–9.
[96] L/83, 23.x.1876; M/2/1–4 December 1879 to 20 April 1880, University Library, Cam.b.500.8.[18]

Fellow and had no vote. The majority was, in any case, adequate.

St Catharine's had been ready (despite Spratt) to sell the Bull. The required majority was now in support of proposals which would have effectively ended the life of the College. The Provost of King's was to be Provost of the united college, and in discussion which lasted over three consecutive days the two colleges agreed that the position and rights of existing Fellows of both colleges should be safeguarded, that Robinson should retain the Norwich canonry and his title of Master, should take precedence next after the Provost, and should receive fair compensation if he should vacate the Lodge. It was also agreed that the two colleges should seek an Act of Parliament which would attach the Norwich canonry to the Norrisian Chair of Divinity when Robinson vacated it. Except for the Skerne Fellows (of whom two still existed) the Fellows of both colleges were to rank in seniority in order of their election within their own colleges, and the only point of difference of any substance arose over the name of the united college. St Catharine's objected to a proposal that the title be 'King's College of our Lady and St Nicholas and St Catharine'; but even here agreement was reached at a joint meeting on 19 February 1880. The title was to be 'King's College of the Blessed Virgin Mary, St Katharine (*sic*) and St Nicholas, commonly called King's and St Katharine's College'.

All was complete, but for formal ratification by the two colleges. On 13 April 1880, therefore, thirty-two of the Fellows of King's met and agreed by twenty-three votes to five, with three abstentions (the Vice-Provost, in the Chair, not being counted), that a complete union was desirable. A suggestion that the vested interests of the Fellows of St Catharine's should be commuted for money payments was heavily defeated, and King's agreed to apply to the Commissioners for the complete union of the two colleges, subject to the agreed conditions. But, almost overnight, and without record as to the underlying reasons, opinion had changed at St Catharine's. The inherent difficulty, as Browne saw it, had always been that Robinson was in disfavour in many quarters and had no prominence in the University. It was scarcely to be expected that he would ever succeed to the Provostship,[97] and his future role had been forecast in the provision which had been made for him if he should vacate the Lodge or if he should accept a living in the gift of either of the colleges. From initial support of the merger he turned to opposition, and a week after King's had agreed to apply to the Commissioners for complete union St Catharine's recorded that 'The Master and Fellows of St Catharine's College having carefully considered the proposed scheme for the complete union of King's College and St Catharine's College, are unwilling to consent to the amalgamation of the two Colleges'. The voting on this occasion was four against amalgamation and only two in favour, for Lumby had changed sides as well as the Master. Although he had the same rights as if he were a Fellow on the Old Foundation (as had been ordered in the 1860 statutes) he was nevertheless technically a Skerne Fellow and would have been discriminated against in the terms of the merger. It is not altogether fanciful to see, here again, the results which followed from the peculiar implementation, or non-implementation, of this clause of the 1860 statutes.

But even without Lumby the voting against the merger would have been decisive, since the Act of 1877 required that any merger should be supported by the votes of two-thirds of those voting. The Master's change of mind, with Spratt and Southward standing firm, made this impossible. Although, at Oxford, Balliol absorbed New Inn Hall, Merton took in St Alban Hall and Oriel merged with St Mary Hall, no amalgamation took place in Cambridge under the 1877 Act. For St Catharine's the project of union was dead; the College negotiated its own new statutes and faced its future under them. The society which thus survived was, however, not only unfitted to face the future because of its small numbers and its academic limitations; it was also unhappy and divided.

The negotiations with King's alone would leave no doubt about this; but the difficulties which arose from rendering the College's accounts in the form demanded by the Com-

[97] Browne, *Recollections*, p. 230. Robinson's change of mind was probably due to a strong letter against the proposed merger which Philpott sent him.

missioners cast yet further shadows. Robinson had done
a further tour of duty as Bursar in 1866 and 1867 (the years
in which the new Lodge was built), and then Carr took over, to
give way to Spratt in 1874. These were not unprosperous years;
the 'improvements' in Hall and Library, and the new Lodge,
bear witness to the annual surpluses available. The agricultural
recession which hit King's, John's and other large land-
holding colleges, seems to have passed St Catharine's by. As
against the value of £250 set on a Fellowship by the Commissioners and the new statutes, the dividend was £281.12s.6d.
in 1877 and £257.3s.9d. in 1880. The College was able to afford
some remissions in rents, and money was available for repairs
to cottages in Coton and Barton, for repairs to the church at
Newent, for the purchase of the advowson of Little Shelford
and for acquiring yet another house on Trumpington Street.
But Spratt was as unbiddable in his bursaring as in most
things which he undertook. Re-elected Bursar in October 1882,
he absented himself from the audit meeting and was duly fined
and required to make up his accounts in the form now specified.
Then, in December, the Master brought to the notice of the
Fellows certain 'serious matters' in the accounts of the 'late
Bursar' — for Carr had replaced Spratt in office — and the
college solicitor was called in.

Obviously Spratt had been obstructive, and probably idle,
but had done nothing criminal or even seriously wrong, for the
audit was successfully concluded in March 1883 and Spratt
was continued as Praelector and Tutor, and was appointed
Steward also in 1884.[98] At that time it was solemnly resolved
that no Fellow should hold the office of Bursar for more than
five years in succession — but the rule was never observed.
The inner history of this dispute cannot now be unravelled,
but it would seem to have been a matter of temperament
rather than of principle; and to have shown, as the negotiations
over the Bull and over amalgamation with King's had also
shown, that whatever offices Spratt might hold or might not
hold, he dominated the College as the new statutes came into
force.

[98] M/2/1, 27.x.1882 to 27.x.1884.

This may be to read history backwards, but so the event proved. For the thirty years between the end of negotiations with King's, acceptance of the new statutes and reconciliation over the Bursar's accounts, and the outbreak of the 1914 war, Spratt in effect ruled. During this period, right up to the election of Rushmore as a Fellow in 1907, and the death of Robinson in 1909, only one new ordinary Fellow was elected. He, it is true, was a mathematician, not a classic — C. J. Lay, elected in 1890. Another election indeed brought to the College H. C. G. Moule, but he came as a Professorial Fellow, holding the Norrisian Chair of Divinity. Moule had been in the First Class of the Classical Tripos in 1865, along with Spratt and Pretor, but he had then turned to theology, had taught at Marlborough and had served a country living between turns of duty as Fellow and Dean of Trinity, and had come back to Cambridge as Principal of Ridley Hall in 1880. Moule was undoubtedly a man of charm and of distinction; but Professorial Fellows were a class apart, his election did not come until 1899, and he remained a Fellow only for two years, until he was appointed Bishop of Durham in 1901. Moule made little difference; and Lay also made no impact on the College. He was a mathematician and nothing else, and even so his thoughts were so far from the lectures which he was required to give that he was capable of turning over two pages of his notes at a time, attaching the end of one mathematical problem to the beginning of another.[99]

While the financial situation of the College gave no cause for alarm within the contexts of a small college, the relationships of Dons and undergraduates and the ability of the College to fulfil a teaching commitment were far from satisfactory. The University was in transition, with University lectures and University Lecturers replacing the colleges, and with supervision of a man's work accepted as the college's role, rather than instruction by way of college lectures. Thornely was one of the first University Lecturers to be appointed as the recommendations of the Commissioners began to be implemented,

[99] Memo. by H. P. Trist.

and his evidence is that 'College lectures were indisputably poor, and regarded more as a form of discipline than as a means of advancing knowledge'. But college lectures persisted, to some extent modified by arrangements for exchanges between colleges; and St Catharine's was badly equipped to make the system work.

One bright light shone in the obscurity. John Neville Figgis came up from Brighton College in 1885 as senior mathematical scholar.[100] But at the end of his first year he came last of the four scholars to be examined in the May examination and his scholarship was reduced. 'Without any conspicuous enthusiasm for the study', to quote his room-mate R. R. Conway, he managed to achieve a good second class in the Tripos and then came up for a fourth year to read History. Here he found his true bent and was the only man to be awarded a First Class (bracketed with a Girtonian). He stayed on in Cambridge, winning a succession of university prizes and achieving a rare distinction by winning the Prince Consort Prize with his *Divine Right of King's* in 1892 — a work still unsurpassed, for which the College awarded him a prize of £15! But it was not as a writer that Figgis most excelled, distinguished though his work was in knowledge, perception and style. His strength lay in his teaching ability and in the friendly relationships which he maintained with his pupils and with a wide cross-section of men, graduates and undergraduates, members of St Catharine's or members of any other college. He was never elected a Fellow although he was appointed Chaplain in 1899; and he did not enjoy the privilege of rooms in College.

Figgis's genius for friendship was his great contribution to the College; his rooms in Tennis Court Road swarmed with men of every stamp and pursuit, and Figgis had great talents as a host. For a dozen years he played an important and active part in the life of the College, offering warm understanding and good humour where the Fellows offered only indifference, irascibility, or pained withdrawal. He accepted a college living at Marnhull, in the Diocese of Salisbury, in 1902 but held it for

[100] For Figgis cf. Jones, *Story*, pp. 166–7. R. R. Conway, *St Catharine's Society Magazine* 1937, M. G. Tucker, *John Neville Figgis*, London, 1950.

only five years until, feeling that he was not doing his best work in 'the most attractive parsonage in Dorset', he joined the Mirfield Community and devoted the rest of his life to the community and to the intellectual side of clerical work.

Figgis was elected an Honorary Fellow of the College in 1909 (together with Norman Moore). This was one of the first acts of the Master and Fellows after the death of Robinson and the election of Johns to the Mastership. The election of these two sons of the house marks both a new outlook and some sense of remorse for the way in which they had been treated, the one in his being sent down, the other in his non-election at a time when the Fellows were constantly keeping a Fellowship vacant even to the extent that they held that the consent of the Visitor would be needed if they wished to elect up to the full statutory minimum of six.[101]

Figgis, therefore, represents at the same time a living criticism of the existing Fellows and a great mitigation of their defects. Intellectually of the highest rank, and moving in the most exalted circles, he was 'at home' to undergraduates and at home with them. They were comparatively few in numbers but not desperately few, and they shared 'an intense College patriotism' and intimacy which involved them in all college activities. This fitted in well with their simple domestic life, a life which centred round dinner in Hall and service in Chapel, the two correlated by an order of 1873 which decreed that evening Chapel should be held at 5.00 p.m., dinner in Hall being at 5.30. Lack of gas or electric lighting, or of running water, went far to explain what to modern eyes would seem to be a Spartan existence — only Chapel and Hall were lit by gas — and of thirty-three sets of rooms in College six were occupied by seniors. About half of the men were lodging in rooms; but the rooms were close to College, and that was as well since the bicycle was only just becoming acceptable in Cambridge.

Admirable though Figgis was as a foil to the rest of the High Table, he did not affect the bases of the establishment. It was Spratt who increasingly dominated the College, and the

[101] M/2/1, 22.x.1877; 29.xi.1905; 23.xi.1906.

16

situation was relieved by developments which appealed to Spratt — music, especially music in Chapel; athletic activity; and the nurturing of a self-reliance among the men which went far to offset the condition of the College. Thus the various athletic clubs were united into the Amalgamated Clubs in 1888, with Figgis, of all people, who 'never played a game in his life, unless we count subsequent efforts to ride a bicycle', playing an active part in reconciling differences. Then in 1893 money was diverted from the Yorke Fund for the purchase of the first five acres of the College ground at Newnham, later grants being derived from the same source. It was plausibly urged that this saved payments for games on Parker's Piece, and few of later generations will question the wisdom of the allocation of funds though it aroused adverse comment at the time.

Less open to criticism was the expenditure on music and on Junior Combination Room. The undergraduates had asked for assignment of a reading room in 1886 (and for a lavatory) and one of the two rooms formerly occupied by Browne was set aside for this purpose; gas lighting was to be laid on, a grant of £10 was made towards purchase of books, the College was to pay for coals and the undergraduates were to pay for service. The room was to be closed by ten o'clock each night. The early venture ran into debt (not seriously) and the College met the liability (only £5) and continued official support for the development. It was a development which, taken with the support of the men's games, reveals an interest in the men's activities which had a real value in binding the College together.[102]

Equally, the development of the Music Society brought senior and junior members together. One member of the College at that time writes that 'St Catharine's had a reputation in the Music world and we normally held an annual concert in May Week. Our chapel choir was also of a high standard, consisting chiefly of choral scholars with a contingent of boys and a couple of professional altos from outside the College.

---

[102] M/2/1, 4.vi.1886; 25.x.1886; 27.iv.1888.

Southward was the Choir Master and Spratt the organist and the latter's sense of discipline would lead him to adjure Southward publicly and vehemently to turn up in time, a scene which would cause vast amusement to the assembled company'.[103] Another writes, 'Being in the Choir, I found real pleasure in Mr Southward's unfailing energy in training us — even if Dr Spratt at the organ on a few occasions loudly disagreed. That worthy Don also stopped the custom of year's sing-song evenings — two in the first term and the 1st year's men giving the last in the Lent Term. It was a good way of us meeting together, so I was chosen to approach him. Expecting any kind of reception I was surprised at his insisting that we had one good Concert instead, and at his offer to help finance the expense. And this he did. So the Music Society soon came into existence'.[104]

It was in the Chapel, and in the building of the organ and the gallery, that what Jones has called 'the apotheosis of Spratt' was achieved. The costs of Chapel and of Chaplain had been accepted as legitimate charges on college revenues in the 1882 statutes,[105] at a time when the anti-clerical bias of some reformers was clear. Some ten years were, however, to pass before there seemed to be adequate funds for serious re-appraisal of the Chapel itself. It was then, in 1892, agreed to appeal to former members of the College for a Chapel Restoration Fund and to spend £1,000 on the Chapel itself and £1,000 on a new organ.[106] The first step would be to erect a gallery for the organ, and estimates were accepted for the gallery and staircase, for removing the monuments and for panelling the ante-chapel. The total estimates came to £3,094; they included six 'figures' and six frames for the figures, the frames costing more than the figures. Fortunately the figures were given up, and the Chapel was left attractive in its simplicity and balance. The specifications for the organ were left to Spratt, Southward and the Master,[107] the old organ was sold for £75 to Messrs

[103] Memo from Trist.
[104] Memo from F. E. Smith, freshman, 1897.
[105] M/2/1, 3.iv.1878.
[106] M/2/1, 1892–6.
[107] See Browne, St Catharine's College, pp. 260–2 for the specification.

Norman, who contracted to build the new one for a further £925. Donations came to £1,300, and with an interest-free loan from the Caution Money Fund to help the building of a vestry, the costs were covered.

This was something much more, and more meaningful, than an indulgence of the musical interests of a couple of the Fellows. Spratt and Southward, and the other Fellows, contributed generously towards the costs, and the whole Chapel and ante-Chapel were transformed in the operation. Browne gives a detailed account of the result and of the opening ceremony, in 1895, in his *History of St Catharine's*, and concludes that, 'It was difficult for any one who had not seen the Chapel since the old times to realize that it was the same building'.[108] There was a feast in the evening of the dedication, and a clear light is cast on the College by the memories of one of Spratt's pupils: 'At Spratt's table he collected a band of his old friends and pupils: during the subsequent oratory much was said about everyone but him: we could not stand that, but got up and drank his health with most emphatic musical honours.'[109]

Fitting as the tribute certainly was on that occasion, it was a sign of a society troubled even in the midst of its jubilation. There was no acute financial problem; the audits were satisfactory and balances were available for purposes which met with approval. But the Fellowships were too few, and were held, apparently for ever, by the same elderly men. Change and adjustment could not begin until, in 1908, Pretor died. His place was filled by F. M. Rushmore, who since 1907 had held an additional Fellowship on condition that he undertook the duties of Lecturer in History. As a historian Rushmore was a poor substitute for Figgis. College numbers had been maintained by acceptance of non-collegiate students from Cavendish Hall, Fitzwilliam Hall and elsewhere, and Rushmore had come to Cambridge as the Chapel was re-opened in 1895, with a Teacher's Certificate from St Luke's College, Exeter, where he had shown considerable character in leading student protests against the poor teaching, and against the indifferent

[108] Op. cit., pp. 244 et seq.
[109] *St Catharine's Society Magazine*, 1932.

amenities.[110] He fell easily and naturally into the ways of a college where the undergraduates were convinced that they alone made their College respectable in the eyes of the outside world. He was a Choral Exhibitioner, and he became second Boat Captain; but he took an indifferent second class in the Historical Tripos of 1898 and went to teach at the Perse School.

Something of a new spirit was already stirring in the Governing Body, and Rushmore's return was a sign of change. In 1905 the living at Newent fell vacant, and the Master privately wondered 'Will Mr Carr or Mr Southward accept it?'.[111] Neither of them did, and a discussion generated as to the power of creating a sixth Fellowship, with a note in Robinson's book in April 1906: 'Rushmore, 2nd Master of the Perse School; good Bass singer; Captain of U. Volunteers; good business man.' Then, in December, with Robinson noting that 'There must be six fellows or more if the revenues allow it', it was agreed to elect Rushmore to an additional Fellowship, to appoint him Lecturer in History for one year and Assistant Tutor for one year, with the usual allowances of rooms and commons and with a stipend of £100 a year from the Yorke Fund, and £120 a year from the Tutorial Fund;[112] the Fellowship dividend was at that time about £220 a year.

Rushmore was followed within a year by another master from the Perse School, W. H. S. Jones, a distinguished classic, with a formidable array of publications already behind him, and with practical interests which belied his unworldly air. The very fact of Jones's appointment not only emphasizes the weight which already attached to Rushmore's opinions but also underlines the withdrawal of the old classical Fellows from direction of the College. Jones was elected in 1908. Then, in 1909, Robinson died. He had long been in failing health and his notes on college business fall off so much that (perhaps significantly) the last note made by him in his 'clasped vellum book',[113] as he called it, was of the election of Rushmore; he

---

[110] From Rev. F. Fuller, Tutor at St Luke's College.
[111] M/2/1, 29.xi.1905; ND. 1906.
[112] M/2/1A, 30.iv.1906; 19.iii.1907. M/2/1, 7.xii.1906.
[113] M/2/1A.

never copied out the letter to be sent to Rushmore though he left space for it.

The Fellows, at whose instigation is not clear, turned to a distinguished Assyriologist, the Reverend Claude Hermann Walter Johns, a Fellow of Jesus, and unanimously elected him Master on 5 October 1909. There can have been no secret about the needs of the College; one of the Fellows of those days has recorded that the other colleges were dissatisfied with the part which St Catharine's played in organizing inter-collegiate lectures, the senior and the junior tutor were in open disagreement, and it could not be overlooked that Spratt, notwithstanding the rule to the contrary, occupied the whole of Old Lodge with his wife while he also kept a set of rooms on 'B' Staircase for his work, at a time when there was an acute shortage of rooms for men in College. The first note made by Johns was, in March 1910, 'College accounts gone into and much discussed'.[114] There seems to have been little doubt in his mind that the three senior Fellows, Spratt, Carr, and Southward, would have to go. But Johns did nothing precipitately, perhaps because he was on personally friendly terms with them and thought that they were so near the end of their careers that they should be allowed to conclude with compassion.

In the meantime, the financial situation was fair and a dividend of £225 was declared for 1910[115] while agreement was reached that a proper sinking fund should be set up to meet extraordinary expenses and that the Trust Funds should be investigated. The quality of the undergraduate members was also under scrutiny, and in 1911 the Fellows agreed (after complaints from the Censor of Fitzwilliam) that no non-collegiate student should be accepted as a migrant after his third term. They agreed that no migrant from any other college be accepted unless all three tutors favoured him, while they also decided that membership of the Amalgamated Clubs should be compulsory and that the Tutor should collect the subscriptions and that 'unless in exceptional circumstances

[114] M/2/1A, 2.iii.1910.
[115] Loc. cit., 20.vi.1911.

no student be admitted who will not enter into the common life of the College sufficiently to mark him as a college man'. At the same meeting a benefaction of £1,000 was thankfully received from Mr Phillips for a Crabtree Scholarship — an award for which character (as far as it could be judged from a boy's career at school) and non-academic merits were taken into account.[116] The cleaning and lighting of the Hall were also under discussion, and the question of action over the coal which was being worked on the Ramsden Estate was taking up much time.

It was not until the middle of 1912 that anything clear emerged, and then it took two forms. First, in June, 'The College decided to take preliminary steps to enlarge the accommodation for students with a view to building additional rooms on the adjoining College property'.[117] In December it was ordered that an offer made by a donor, whose name was known to the Master, for the erection of a detached building on the site of 'the Grove' be accepted. Early in the new year, plans were considered and it was agreed that the scheme was financially possible. The plans would have resulted in the building of a library and other rooms across the front of the court,[118] facing Trumpington Street, and although most St Catharine's men would insist that a court so closed off would be undesirable, the plans had considerable merits[119] — and we should probably have got used to a four-sided court by now! The Phillips benefaction was to be used for the purchase of the house at 65 Trumpington Street, to enlarge the site, the Building Fund paying interest to Crabtree Scholarships, and the Master was asked to manage a building appeal, since the anonymous donor offered £10,000 and the estimated cost of the building was £16,500.[120]

---

[116] Loc. cit., 3.v.1911. This benefaction for a Crabtree *Scholarship* seems to have been lost sight of. The Crabtree *Exhibitions* begun in 1914 (cf. pp. 289–90 *infra*) were partly financed from the Tutorial and Caution Money Funds.

[117] Loc. cit., 14.iii.1912.

[118] Loc. cit., 29.i.1913; XXXVI/7.

[119] For a copy of the appeal and of the proposed elevation of the building, see Jones, *History of St Catharine's*, pp. 37–8.

[120] M/2/1A, 3.ii.1913.

Then misgivings began. The identity of the donor has never been clearly established although suggestions have been made. It is reported that he was a local landowner who had made a similar offer to another college with the undisguised intention of depriving his son of his patrimony, and that the offer had there been refused. Whatever the reasons, having 'gladly accepted' the offer in February 1913, the Fellows in March decided that the estimates were beyond the College's powers, and in April they decided unanimously to refuse to accept the still anonymous gift. It must remain possible that the objections were not all personal or moral but that some reluctance to close off the court was voiced, for in talks with the donor's solicitors the point was made that no fresh offer on the lines of a fresh site should be offered by the College although any such proposal by the donor would be considered.[121]

Rushmore was busy for a further year drafting letters which left no doubt about the College's attitude while stating that in declining the offer the College had no intention to show any discourtesy to the donor and regretted that he should have received any such impression.

For Johns, as the intermediary, the whole episode must have been embarrassing and frustrating, and it revealed to him, if he did not already know it, that he had in his Governing Body a group of men who were arbitrary and irresponsible in their reactions. Other incidents would in any case have left him in no doubt on this. In October 1912 time was taken up as the Fellows 'Discussed Southward's Tutorial Fund balance sheet', and Johns' Diary is largely filled with unidentified lists of figures which reveal him as wrestling with the financial statements while his annotated copy of the statutes shows that he was wondering whether he could force on resignations. Once more, there seems to have been no alarm as to the actual financial position; the College was ready to undertake its share of the cost of the projected new building, money was available for keeping farms and property in repair, and the dividend for 1912 was £249, which was as close to the permitted maximum of £250 as could be got.

[121] Loc. cit., 8.iii.1913; M/2/3, p. 5.

But the Yorkshire coal issue was looming large, and in October 1913, Rushmore was appointed Junior Bursar with a special view to the coal property. He was able immediately to report that the College was involved in two separate disputes arising from Mrs Ramsden's Norton property. The surface owners were challenging the College's title to the minerals under the common lands; and the Askern Colliery Company was seeking an injunction which would enable it to cease paying any further rents or royalties to the surface owners. Counsel's Opinion was taken and an arrangement was agreed with the great surface owners, G. B. Cooke-Yarborough and the Dowager Countess of Rosse.[122] The College's claim was based on the fact that it was Lord of the Manor of Norton and so owned the mineral rights for the common and waste lands of the Manor; and a series of small legal actions, culminating in a decision of the Court of Appeal, in October 1915, confirmed this view. But the smaller surface owners, and the Askern Colliery Company, were not satisfied. The College's right to sink pits, or to grant the right to do so, was contested through the lower courts and in 1918 was denied by a verdict in the Court of Appeal and in 1919 in the House of Lords. Here also it was decreed that the earlier verdict, that the mineral rights on the common and waste lands belonged to the Lords of the Manor, was bad law. The Lords' verdict, however, only applied to those who had fought the College so far, and not all the landowners had done so, so that the earlier verdict on this subject stood for those who had not been involved at the last stand. The College had been engaged in a complicated legal tussle for something like seven years and had accepted costs of over £10,000 in difficult times. It had emerged with some part of the wealth which at one time had seemed to be within its grasp, and it faced the costs and difficulties of the post-war period with a heavy debt to be settled.

In January 1919 it had been agreed that the College should borrow from its own trust funds, as far as possible, to settle the costs of litigation. But while the Bursar was instructed to sell

[122] M/2/3, passim.

the remaining capital in the Burrell and Yorke Funds and to lend the money to the Norton Coal Account, it was necessary to run an overdraft of over £8,000 on this account and the outlook was uncertain,[123] brightened only by the zest with which the immediately post-war generation of undergraduates was determined to enjoy a collegiate life in Cambridge. The mood was evident in the changes on High Table also, for 1919 saw both the end of Johns' Mastership and the end of the tenure of the three senior Fellows who had held power for so long.

Authority had, in many ways, slipped out of their grasp before the crisis of 1919. Rushmore had been made Assistant Bursar in 1913; he was also Prelector, Tutor, and Secretary to the Governing Body. Carr was President and Bursar, Spratt was Tutor, Steward and Dean, and Southward was Chaplain and Tutor. It was Southward, notoriously unbusinesslike, who was responsible for Tutorial Accounts while Carr, in defiance of the order of 1883 which limited tenure of the Bursarship to five years, had held office continuously since 1884 although he had accepted the living at Little Shelford in 1892. The roles of the Senior and Junior Bursars were, however, clearly defined in 1913, and Carr was restricted to the function of receiving and disbursing college moneys and the keeping of Bursarial accounts;[124] the real work of running the administrative side of the College lay in Rushmore's hands, and as the need for emergency statutes to tide over the 1914–18 war period, the frustration of the coal dispute and the decline in revenue, made their impact on the College he carried more and more responsibility.

Fees, of course, dwindled to a trickle during the war of 1914–18. But the period was marked by the selling off of some properties and investment in War Loan and other more remunerative stocks (a movement which had been anticipated by small sales of land during the 1880s as railway companies sought land for track-laying), and though tutorial and lecturing stipends suffered, and had to be supplemented, the Fellows'

[123] M/2/3, 3.iv.1919; 2.x.1919.
[124] M/2/3, p. 1.

dividends were maintained. But confidence was lacking and book-keeping was slip-shod. At the audit period of 1915 a proposal was made that the College accounts should be audited by a professional auditor; Spratt thought such a move unnecessary and it was ultimately agreed that Fellows should first audit and that then the accounts should be submitted to professionals.[125] A dividend of £243 was declared for the year and no further problem arose at that time, possibly because the strain of office was beginning to tell on Johns, who was absent from duty for the Michaelmas Term of 1916 and was unable to act as an auditor. At that juncture it was the Bursarial accounts which were chiefly under discussion, and Carr, the Bursar, was in the Chair as President.

But the Bursarial accounts were cleared, the same procedure for audit was accepted for the following year, and in March 1917 a dividend of £238 was accepted while in March 1918 the auditors announced that they had examined the Bursar's books and found them correct and that the Bank pass-book and the Bursar's statement of balances were approximately in agreement. But, they said, the Steward's account was overdrawn to the extent of £2,600, so that although the Bursar had a balance of about £3,500 the two accounts were set against each other by the Bank and there was no money available for payment of dividends. This was regarded (rightly) as most unsatisfactory, the Steward was asked to furnish an explanation within ten days, and the accountancy firm of Price, Waterhouse and Co. was called in to examine the accounts and to advise on a simpler and more modern method of accountancy.[126] When he gave his explanation of his deficits, Spratt, as Steward, added to the uneasiness by revealing that a further £900 was owed to the College cook, and he was asked to provide more detailed information within a month. At the same time it was revealed that the Caution Money had been used to buy furniture for college rooms and that the rent paid by undergraduates for their furniture had been absorbed into the Tutorial Fund.

[125] Loc. cit., 25.x.1915; 1.xii.1915.
[126] Loc. cit., 11.iii.1918 et seq.

Within four days the Master announced to the Fellows that he had appealed to the Visitor to investigate the past financial management of the College. He had also arranged for a representative of Price, Waterhouse and Co. to come to Cambridge, and it was agreed that the Steward's Fund, the Tutorial Fund, the Caution Fund, the Wine Fund and the Tutorial Accounts should all be submitted to his scrutiny. This was happening just at the time that the College was having to make up its mind to carry its coal dispute up to the House of Lords and to pledge itself to cover the costs involved. The strain on the Master must have been severe, and he had the added embarrassment of difficult personal relationships to overcome. He had, however, decided that tolerance could go no further. The Steward (Spratt) having claimed that part of his overdraft was due to moneys which the Tutor (Southward) and the Bursar (Carr) had not paid into his account, Johns ruled that such debts must be proved and then should be honoured, that payments which had been made from the Steward's account for the Chapel organ must be authenticated, that the cook must be paid, and that the Steward's salary must be paid into the Steward's account until his overdraft was paid off. He held up payments to the tutors until the liabilities of the Tutorial Fund had been met, and he ruled that Southward's share of the money made available to the Tutorial Fund under the emergency statutes should be left in that fund. These rulings the Master also submitted to the Visitor; but the answer which he got has not been put on record.

Within the College, with sales of outlying farms and the investment of the moneys under discussion, and with 3/5ths of the salaries and dividends due at the end of September 1917 voted only on 13 May 1918, the Master brought under discussion the legality of the way in which Barclay's Bank had granted overdrafts against the signatures of the three college officers involved — Carr as Bursar, Spratt as Steward and Southward as Tutor. With the Furniture Fund, the Caution Money and the Wine Account also under discussion, and with the Master making rulings which made responsibility for debts personal to the officers, it is not surprising that a committee should have been set up to consider a complete revision of the Statutes or that Jones should have moved for 'a complete change of College Officials'. That was in June 1918, and the Master promised to give his views at the next meeting.

But the summer months passed in internal transfers between the different funds, transfers which reveal to how great an extent the College and its statutes and trusts had been treated with casual non-attention to detail, with nothing which could be called dishonesty but with a sort of free-handed arrogance which it was impossible to defend. It was early in September before Rushmore was appointed sole Tutor and 'The Master announced that it was felt by the majority of the Fellows, that changes should be made in the appointment of Bursar, Dean and Steward'. In October the Master himself took over as Bursar, with Jones as Steward;[127] the accounts were not yet squared off however, and the three deposed officers were still being pressed to furnish information and to meet their responsibilities as the war came to an end in November 1918.

Peace brought not only new enthusiasms but new problems. The transference of responsibility for teaching from the Colleges to the University was a process which was not ended until the Report of the 1924 Royal Commission had been implemented — indeed, it is a process which in all probability has still not reached its term — but the first signs that this was to be a point of departure for the post-war University may be seen when the Tutor was instructed to report to a committee to consider a scheme suggested by the General Board of the University for the pooling of lectures. St Catharine's would welcome a proposal to throw all lectures open without fee and would make a contribution for this purpose. But the fee suggested would be 'impossibly high' and some of the proposals

---

[127] The Minutes [M/2/3] are clear on these events. Jones gives the impression that the clash culminated in 1917, that the Master acted without consulting the Fellows, and that he (Jones) had serious misgivings. Of the three significant episodes, the decision to call in professional auditors was first made in December 1915 and was repeated on 11 March 1918; the removal of existing officers was proposed by Jones himself on 14 June 1918 and was accepted on 3 September 1918; and the new officers (including the Master as Bursar) were *elected* on 28 October 1918.

would deprive the College of its powers to elect its own Fellows and Lecturers. The scheme must be opposed for that reason.[128]

But new problems had to be met, and new men had to meet them. The struggle over the accounts was virtually over; Price, Waterhouse, were told that their services would not be needed further. Caution Money, the Tutorial Account, and even the Steward's account were rectified when, after Spratt and Southward had been told to settle their disputes, on 30 April, 1919, Southward agreed to pay £321 into 'the old Steward's Account' and this extinguished the last of the overdraft. At the same meeting it was resolved 'that one or two Supplementary Fellows be elected next Term if financial arrangements can be made to render such a step possible', and to indicate that this was a realistic proposal, at the next meeting, in June, both Spratt and Southward were allowed to get the tutorial stipends which had been withheld from them.

The end of the road was in sight, but Johns did not attend a meeting after 28 October 1918. His health was failing, and on 2 October 1919 he wrote to say that he wished to resign the Mastership. Southward had died that summer and it had been agreed to elect to a Fellowship the Headmaster of Plymouth and Mannamead College, the Reverend H. J. Chaytor, who was forthwith appointed Dean and Chaplain. He later became Master, and he certainly left his mark upon the College. Then in October D. Portway and L. F. Newman were elected into two supernumerary Fellowships which were created. The Master's resignation was accepted on 5 December 1919 and forthwith the Fellows adjourned to Chapel to elect his successor. They were two of the old regime, Spratt and Carr; two of the pre-war reformers, Rushmore and Jones; three new men, Chaytor, Newman and Portway; and a Professorial Fellow who enjoyed a European reputation as an agricultural botanist and who had played a yeoman's part in supporting Johns throughout his troubled Mastership, Professor R. H. Biffen. There and then, unanimously, they elected the Right Reverend Thomas Wortley Drury, Doctor of Divinity, Lord Bishop of Ripon.

[128] M/2/3, 21.xi.1918.

Drury was seventy-three when he took office in 1920, but he did not lack vigour, humanity or perception. He showed high courage in accepting an office which had taken such a toll of Johns — for Johns was dead within the year, as was Spratt. But the mood of the College was not to be mistaken; Drury and his team were to reap where Johns had sown. New statutes were in the making, new men were in command; above all, new ideas were being accepted. The nineteenth century was over. It ended for St Catharine's in 1919.

The Nineteenth-Century College :
Rise, Decline and Resurgence

By OLIVER MacDONAGH, M.A., PH.D.

*Former Fellow, Professor-Elect of History, Institute of Advanced Studies,
Australian National University, Canberra*

HISTORIANS, especially if they are Anglo-Saxons, un-
wearyingly remind each other of the uniqueness of
historical phenomena. They might profitably remember
the converse truths, that every particular phenomenon contains
or reflects something universal, that none is fatherless, heirless
and cousinless in the world, and that each is linked backwards
and forwards and laterally with innumerable fellows. The
affaire Robinson is unhappily, and unfairly, the best remembered
phenomenon in the history of the nineteenth-century College.
The episode is bandied about amongst the half-informed as the
simple cause of St Catharine's temporary decay in the mid-
Victorian era. But (in the view of the present author) Robinson
was more a symptom than a cause of the decline; the episode
was more a product than a shaper of circumstances; and
St Catharine's was, over the entire spread of the nineteenth
century, as representative of the smaller colleges of Cambridge
as a whole as it was peculiarly fortunate in the first fifty years
and peculiarly ill-starred in the second.

The 'disputed' Mastership election of 1861 has been analyzed,
in all its elements, elsewhere.[1] Suffice it to say that the balance
of probability lies heavily against Robinson's having behaved
improperly. The imputation that he lied directly scarcely
deserves attention; it rests solely on the assertion of the
disappointed candidate, and is contradicted not only by
Robinson himself but by all that we know of his character

---

[1] W. H. S. Jones, *A History of St Catharine's College* (Cambridge, 1936), pp. 139–48.

and by every other piece of surrounding evidence. For what it is worth, the real charge against him seems to consist, not in his having voted for himself, but in his failure to disclose his impending marriage — and with it the loss of his Fellowship — to his rival, Jameson. It was then commonplace to vote for oneself in such elections; in fact, some argued that it was a necessary corollary to being a candidate. The outgoing Master, Philpott, had voted for himself in a very similar situation to that of 1861: it was Philpott's own vote which had secured him the Headship of the College in 1847 against a most distinguished senior, Corrie. But failure to disclose a relevant fact might be a different matter. Was Robinson's engagement, however, a relevant fact? It is difficult to see why it should have been. The utmost that might be said in favour of such a view is that Jameson might have felt that the Mastership in a college without his senior and original patron, Robinson, would be a much more attractive proposition than a Mastership won by the odd vote in five over a rival who remained in College and perhaps also in college office; and that to this extent he had been misled as to the future. But if it was this which moved Jameson to protest, it was not a grievance which could be publicly paraded. After all, the great Whewell had forfeited his Fellowship at Trinity by marriage in October 1841, only to be appointed to the Mastership before the month was out. In fact, Jameson never made Robinson's failure to communicate the fact of his engagement a ground of complaint, or even alluded publicly to Robinson's engagement.

The essence of the matter seems to be that Jameson could quite properly have secured the election by voting for himself, that he therefore brought his defeat upon himself and that, as often happens in such cases, he directed his later chagrin, not against himself, but against the victor. Jameson appears soon to have regretted his 'quixotic' action. It is important to note that he did not show this regret immediately, for his apparent acceptance of Robinson's vote with equanimity undermines his later claims that Robinson had promised to support him. But he could not proclaim that he would have acted differently had he known in time either that Robinson would soon be married or

17

that his own vote would decide the issue. The world at large would simply have smiled at his folly and self interest, and said with Lady MacBeth —

> What thou wouldst highly,
> That wouldst thou holily.

Hence, consciously or unconsciously, or half-in-half, Jameson came to falsify his discussions with Robinson before the election: apparently both men were awkward, tangled in various hypotheses and embarrassed, anyhow. Not only does all this seem to be much the most plausible explanation of the imbroglio today. It should also have been apparent, if not on the very morrow of the public dispute, at least by 1868 when the entire Fellowship of the College issued a fly-sheet setting out the salient facts of the election — excepting of course all mention of Robinson's bethrothal.

If this is correct, the problem was, almost from the start, not what had actually happened, but why Jameson's charges had such a powerful and unwarranted effect. Of course, mid-Victorian mawkishness and punctilio were factors: it is difficult to imagine late Georgians or even early Victorians adopting the 'noble' stances or expecting the Arnoldian 'disinterestedness' which appear to have contributed much to the trouble. Robinson's cold, narrow, and unprepossessing personality was doubtless a factor, too. But all this goes only a very little way towards explaining the vast disproportion between the event and the consequence. We are still left with the problem of the power of Jameson's accusations. And to appreciate the magnitude of this problem, to appreciate the curiosity of the Robinson 'scandal' to the full, we need only recall the Mastership election of Robinson's predecessor next but one.

After all, as recently as 1798, the candidate who received most votes, but not an absolute majority, failed ultimately to win the Mastership of the College. This went to a junior Fellow, Proctor, who was not even eligible as a candidate at the time of the election — or indeed until six days before the Lord Chancellor appointed him against the wishes of the majority of the Fellows. An entry in the College Memorandum

Book[2] for 14 December 1798 tells the somewhat unedifying tale of how Proctor rendered himself eligible for appointment by obtaining a Divinity degree: 'We the undersigned Fellows are content that Joseph Proctor should proceed to his B.D. degree, J. Proctor, C. W. Burrell' — Burrell being Proctor's sole ally in the Fellowship. Proctor's petition to have the election of Waterhouse declared void came up in the Court of Chancery on the 20th; and on the same day he himself was elevated to the Mastership by the Chancellor. Over the next eight years, the feud between Proctor and Burrell, on the one hand, and the dissident majority of the Fellows, on the other, landed up before Eldon as Lord Chancellor on no less than three occasions, Eldon's decision in every case favouring the new Master and his solitary supporter. A naked, embittered and well-publicized struggle for power within the College raged for more than a decade. Yet so far from this inauspicious — not to say discreditable — beginning casting a cloud upon St Catharine's and ushering in a season of decline, it was the prelude to a mildly golden age.

The contrast, therefore, between the disputed elections of Proctor and of Robinson could hardly be more marked. The first was almost exuberantly scandalous; the second a mere matter of — at most — gentility and 'words of honour'. Even if interpreted with the utmost rigour, Robinson's self-assertion pales to nothing against Proctor's. Robinson was immediately accepted, even by Jameson, as rightful Head, and neither challenged nor thwarted by the Fellowship. Yet the election of 1861 is generally accepted as both launching and sustaining the blackest period in the history of the College. So we return with added puzzlement to the question: why was the Robinson election so significant? But was it? It is the conclusion of the present author that the election *per se* was of only minor significance in the College's decline, and that the decline itself was the product of quite other and much larger factors. Robinson became a scapegoat, and the election of 1861 a myth or badge of failure, which apparently explained a phenomenon but in reality merely provided a sufficient outward symbol to

[2] L/83. College Muniments.

satisfy lazy minds. The true answer lay deep in the institutional structure of mid- and late Victorian Cambridge.

II

Broadly speaking, the history of nineteenth-century Cambridge divides in two, appropriately enough, about 1850. The foundations of the first phase were laid in, though only obliquely affected by, the Revolutionary and Napoleonic era. Between 1790 and 1810 the numbers of matriculated students increased very rapidly; the Mathematical Tripos became firmly established and the ground was being laid for the addition of the Classical Tripos in 1824; academic excellence was being pursued by a substantial minority of undergraduates and in more and more appointments to College Fellowships; and, all round, the reforms pioneered in St John's and Trinity were spreading throughout the University. From 1810 to 1850 Cambridge was more or less stabilized in the new pattern, with the total number of men in residence at about 1500. The majority read, for a pass degree, a smattering of Mathematics, Classics, Divinity and Reformation History. But the gold standard which backed the entire academic system was the Mathematical Tripos, and to a much lesser extent, the Classical. Fellowships were generally awarded on the results of the Triposes, and teaching for the Triposes was generally provided by Fellows either as College Lecturers or perhaps more commonly as private coaches. College teaching was indispensible but insufficient for honours, and even, in most cases, for a pass degree; University teaching existed only in a handful of outlying regions such as Law;[3] coaching had to fill the chasm. The *primum mobile* of the entire system was the Tutor. It was he who attracted undergraduates to a college; it was he who taught them or arranged their teaching; it was he who dominated in the Fellowship. This first era of reform restored Cambridge (and of course the other ancient university) more or

---

[3] The 'Civil Law Classes', the examinations admitting to the degree of LL.B., began in 1815. They were succeeded by the Law Tripos in 1858, which became the Law and History Tripos in 1870 and reverted to the unmixed Law Tripos in 1875.

less to the national importance which she had enjoyed in Tudor and Stuart England.

St Catharine's was poorly placed in the new situation. She started the nineteenth century with a minute undergraduate body (perhaps half a dozen), a small effective Fellowship of four or five, impoverished, short of space for any material increase in numbers and racked by internal quarrels. Yet she responded magnificently to the challenge. In a stable situation where undergraduate numbers were a real measure of a college's fortunes, St Catharine's success is readily apparent in the subjoined table:

TABLE I

Numbers Matriculating:

	St Catharine's	Trinity & St John's	University
1800	0	45	129
1810	6	122	213
1820	18	201	427
1840	23	210	459

From 1815 to 1850 St Catharine's accounted for almost five per cent of the total undergraduate body in the University, and almost five per cent of the degrees. If Trinity and St John's are excluded, the proportions would be nearly ten per cent in each case. Out of seventeen colleges, St Catharine's stood ninth on both counts, or seventh if we omit Trinity and St John's from consideration. To put it another way, half the colleges in the University were smaller and less distinguished. For in this period, St Catharine's enjoyed more than her proportionate share of University honours; and for its size, the Fellowship was probably unrivalled in intellectual calibre. Turton and Philpott were both Senior Wranglers and Smith's Prizemen, Temple Chevallier Second Wrangler and Proctor himself Third Wrangler and Second Smith's Prizeman; and Jarrett and Goodwin were amongst the finest scholars of their day. To appreciate this achievement to the full, we must bear in mind the poverty of the College. Money mattered because it governed, partially at least, the number of awards, sizarships and Fellowships, and of livings to provide for those Fellows who could not, or would not, or should not, remain long in Cambridge; and in an academically competitive age the abler undergraduates took these things into account in choosing their college, and in deciding later whether or not to migrate. Money mattered, too, for new buildings to accommodate the new level of undergraduate residents; and St Catharine's is amongst the few colleges which did not erect new buildings in the first half of the nineteenth century. By the 1840s she had a considerably larger proportion of her undergraduates in lodgings than any other college. In the context, then, of scarce resources, her relative success appears all the more remarkable.

'Reformed Cambridge', however, was gradually overtaken and denounced by a new generation of reformers. By 1835 the new system was in turn embattled by the latest radicals. Part of the assault was of course provoked by religious exclusiveness and Anglican monopoly. But part was academic in purpose. Sir William Hamilton set out the radical case in 1836 as follows:

... the University of Cambridge stands alone in *now* making mathematical science the principal object of the whole liberal education it affords; and mathematical skill the sole condition of the one tripos of its honours and the necessary passport to the other: thus restricting to the narrowest proficiency all places of distinction and emolument in University and College, to which such honours constitute a claim: thus also leaving the immense majority of its alumni without incitement, and the most arduous and important studies void of encouragement and reward ... The private interest [which has superseded the public long ago] is that of the Colleges and of their Tutors; and in Cambridge there has for generations been taught, not what the ends of education, not what the ends of science prescribe, but only *what*, and that what *how*, the College Tutors are capable of teaching ... whatever are the subjects comprised in the tutorial mechanism of the time, will be clamorously asserted in the collegial interest; while all beyond it, especially that which cannot be reduced to a cathecetical routine, will be as clamorously decried.

Lord Radnor's University Reform Bills in 1835 and 1837, and motions for enquiries by Select Committees or Royal Commissions in 1837, 1844 and 1845, were beaten off, with the argument that the Universities would reform themselves.[4] And so the Universities did, however slowly, reluctantly and partially. The first major change which concerns us was the marked increase in severity in examinations in the 1840s; this was accompanied by compulsory attendance at lectures and an intensification of private tuition. The second was the extension of the honours schools beginning with the formation of the Natural Sciences and Moral Sciences Triposes[5] (the latter originally embracing, in modern terminology, History, Law, Philosophy and Economics) and the establishment of a Board of Mathematical Studies to standardize the teaching for and examinations in the Mathematical Tripos. The threat of a Royal Commission, which was eventually agreed to by Parliament in 1850, was the spur to these developments.

III

The second age of reform, which these changes ushered in, was, unlike the first, a period of constant growth and innovation. Total undergraduate numbers climbed steadily from some 1,600 in 1850, to 2,400 by 1880 and 3,200 by 1900. Moreover, both absolutely and relatively the numbers of men taking honours increased rapidly. In 1878, for example, 216 (or nearly half) of the 484 graduates were honours men, and in 1885, 327 (or just over half) out of 653. Again, by 1885 not much above one-third of the honours degrees were in Mathematics; in fact the number of degrees in the new Triposes together already exceeded the number in the Mathematical.

TABLE II

Honours Degrees:

	Math.	Clas-sical	Moral Sc.	Natural Sc.	Law	History	Theology	Or. L.
1878	93	57	6	17	16	12	14	1
1885	118	86	7	36	34	25	21	–

[4] *Hansard*, 3rd series, xxxviii, 509–30, 978–9; lxxiv, 1459, 1465–8; lxxix, 393, 453. In 1845, a solid phalanx of Tory votes, as well as assurances of rapid change, were needed to beat off the 'reformers'.

[5] Both Triposes were first examined in 1851. The Theology Tripos followed in 1857, the Law Tripos in 1858, the Law and History Tripos in 1870, the Historical Tripos in 1875 and the Semitic Languages Tripos in 1878.

The above table also indicates the rapid increase in the number of honours schools by 1880. Before the end of the century two more, the Modern Languages and the Mechanical Sciences, were to be added, and in 1905 the Economics Tripos. By 1900 the total number of honours degrees awarded easily exceeded both the total number of pass degrees conferred in that year, and the total number of degrees of all kinds of 1850.

This second phase of reform presented the smaller and poorer colleges with far more pressing and intractable difficulties than the first. As we have seen, St Catharine's provides a shining example of how the earlier challenges might be met. So long as the range of subjects taught was extremely narrow and one in which the Fellows themselves had been trained, and so long as the number of undergraduates remained small enough to be taught by two or three College Lecturers and housed, for the most part, in buildings designed for a modest student population, a small college might prosper — provided, but only provided, its handful of Fellows was first-rate in quality. This was precisely St Catharine's condition in the first half of the nineteenth century. Proctor was an unusually able man, as well as distinguished academically, and he was succeeded as Master by Philpott, perhaps the most outstanding man, all round, in the Cambridge of his day. Beginning with Turton in 1806, including Chevallier and Philpott, and continuing until the resignation of Corrie in 1849, the tutorial side was one of unbroken strength. Corrie, who was largely responsible for the College entry in the 1830s and 1840s, was recognized as one of the greatest of contemporary Tutors — with the additional advantage of being a sound Low Churchman in the days of Tractarian peril. All this changed in the second half of the nineteenth century. On the one hand, the demands on the Fellowship escalated; on the other, the quality of the Fellowship fell catastrophically. Herein, I think, lies the essential answer to the problem of the College's decline.

Ironically enough, the initial blame would seem to belong to Robinson and Jameson — not for their electoral scandal, but for their failure as Tutors. Robinson, who had been 22nd Wrangler, succeeded Corrie in 1850. In his five years of office the College entry fell steadily, from eighteen to ten. Evidently in an attempt to stop the rot, he persuaded Jameson to move from Caius to St Catharine's, and take over the Tutorship, in 1855; he himself turned to the Bursarship for office. Jameson was no more successful. The entry of 1855 was six, that of 1858 one less. Over Jameson's seven years as Tutor the average annual entry was but a fraction over nine. Thus the College numbers fell to less than half the level of the 1840s during a period of rapid growth in the total numbers in the university. In the next thirty years 1862–92, under Carr's Tutorship, the numbers gradually crept back to the level of the 1840s. In the 1870s the average annual intake was over sixteen, and by the end of his regime it had exceeded twenty once again. But this must be set against the background of a near-doubling of the university population, and also of immigration from the new non-Collegiate establishments and Halls of Residence, Fitzwilliam, Ayerst's, Cavendish and the rest. Not only did St Catharine's fall to supplying only some 2 per cent of the total undergraduate body; the quality of its men was diluted by the ease of entry. Again, it must be emphasized that the personal abilities of the Tutor were still crucial to a college's success; and poor Carr, for all his other merits, was a lamentable failure in the office. R. R. Conway, who was up in the early 1880s, throws an interesting light upon the reasons for his failure;

... an easy nature always led him along the line of least resistance, and ... he was a man wholly devoid of ambition for himself, and, by an easy and fatal transition, for the College. He found it small and it did not worry him that it grew less: migrants, a few of them I am bound to say very decent people, sought admission and he had neither the energy nor the heart to refuse them: he sought no honours, no promotion for himself, then why worry about the College? He lived in a century too late; he would have been far more at home in eighteenth-century Cambridge than he was in his own day, for he had little sympathy with modern manners...[6]

Spratt was fifty years of age and Southward forty-one when they succeeded Carr as a duumvirate in 1892. Perhaps the most charitable comment is that the years of waiting in the wings had

---

[6] St Catharine's Society Magazine, 1932.

sapped their energies and dulled their judgements. At any rate, it was not until Rushmore arrived upon the scene that competence and effectiveness returned to the Tutorship of St Catharine's. For more than half a century, the College had been weak in the decisive office; and of course the second-rate, just like the first-rate, breeds its own momentum — and for the great majority of this time Robinson had presided, lonely and listless, over the dissolution of St Catharine's reputation.

To turn from the personal to the more objective factors in the College's decline, we might look first at St Catharine's return to the parliamentary inquiry of 1886.[7] The College reported that it had had six Fellowships (one of them vacant because of 'present and expected diminished income'), three Fellows engaged in College teaching, none holders of University appointments, none elected in recent years and none elected by direct competition. Under almost every one of these headings, St Catharine's compares adversely with every other college in the University. Although the College's finances had gradually improved between 1810 and 1850, she was still amongst the poorest colleges at the mid-century, and thereafter her position worsened. St Catharine's had the second lowest gross income in 1883, at £5,500; only Magdalene was lower at £5,200. Twenty years later even this marginal distinction had been lost; St Catharine's at £5,700 was below Magdalene's £6,100.

In terms of yearly income per undergraduate, St. Catharine's was lowest of all at the latter date, and perhaps also at the former; and quite possibly the same is true for the number of awards and scholarships open to undergraduates. In this phase, the Fellowship contained in effect only two college teachers in its own ranks, and both of them were Classicists. As Conway observes, Carr and Spratt constituted the entire society so far as the undergraduates were concerned: 'the Master was a gentle recluse, Proctor and Turnbull were absentees, Lumby, our Professorial Fellow, was among us, but not of us, Southwood had not yet returned from the North'.[8] Thus at a stage when the range of University studies was being rapidly enlarged, when

---

[7] *Returns from the universities of Oxford and Cambridge* . . . , 1886, LI (214 – Sess. 1).
[8] St Catharine's Society Magazine, 1932.

the number of undergraduates, and in particular of honours men, was at its fastest rate of growth and when the University was beginning to emerge as a rival to colleges in many matters, St Catharine's was locked into obscurity by her poverty, her lack of breadth in teaching, her want of University teaching officers and, of course, her consequent failure to attract her fair proportion of the able men.

It must not be supposed that St Catharine's was alone in her plight. The weakness in her Fellowship may have been unmatched in any other college; but in her other misfortunes she differed from half-a-dozen others in degree rather than kind, and was in fact superior to most in the ratio of her entrants who graduated. Broadly speaking, as the nineteenth century drew to its close, the colleges divided increasingly into 'haves' and 'have-nots'. Ten colleges possessed between them 70 per cent of collegiate resources; the remaining seven had but 30 per cent of the whole. The ten colleges, divided into two groups, held their scholarship examinations in December, and creamed off both the talent and the numbers amongst the Cambridge aspirants. Then the other colleges 'come straggling in one by one, and glean the scanty ears which their richer rivals have left untouched'.[9] Nor was St Catharine's by any means alone in suffering a sudden reverse of fortune. When Jesus went Head of the River for 1875, and held that honour for eleven years, 'the inflow of freshmen became phenomenal; in 1878 they numbered eighty-seven, in the next year seventy-four . . . [But] After 1890, Jesus lost its athletic predominance and since then has suffered a decline'.[10] Corpus, the third largest college in 1865–8, was the second smallest in 1913. Pembroke had only one freshman on its books in 1862; and, according to legend, he escaped to Caius. But if St Catharine's belonged to a group of 'have-nots', she was also anchored firmly to the bottom of the group. Over the fifty-five years 1851–1906 St Catharine's had the second lowest total of honours degrees in the University; relative to numbers in each college, her total was the lowest. In the decade 1898–1907, when she was twelfth in size, she was last in

[9] A. W. Tillyard, *History of University Reform* (1913), p. 299.
[10] A. Gray, *Jesus College*, p. 166.

the number of 1st classes achieved. St Catharine's crop was but one 1st class in these ten years; the next worst performances were those of Corpus with five, Magdalene with eight and Downing with sixteen — all of them smaller colleges than St Catharine's — while yet another smaller college, Sidney Sussex, secured 54. St Catharine's was one of the most vigorous opponents in the early twentieth century of an entrance examination to the University, though the other 'have-not' colleges also resisted this as a threat to their numbers in residence. On the motion of 1912 to throw D.D. degrees open to persons who were not members of the Church of England, St Catharine's was the college which voted most heavily against, in the ratio of more than seven to one.

But when we discuss the years 1890–1914, we are discussing a phase when, as we shall see, the tide had turned in favour of the poorer colleges, including St Catharine's, and when factors making for their resurgence were slowly taking shape and effect. The nadir for the poorer colleges was probably the decade 1875–85; and here St Catharine's provides an epitome of 'the nadir of the nadir'. By any of the tests of college numbers, gross income, income per undergraduate, size of Fellowship or academic success or distinction, St Catharine's ranked lowest or lowest but one in the University. 'I well remember', wrote H. B. Luard who was up in the early 1880s, 'the inferiority complex of the time, which must have been the lowest ebb of the life of the College, overshadowed by the Master's long ostracism. There were only about 40 men in residence, half of them scholars, the rest non-descripts and leavings from other colleges'.[11] Whereas in the first fifty years of the nineteenth century, St Catharine's provided examiners or moderators for the Mathematical Tripos in fifteen of the annual examinations, in the second fifty years she provided none, despite a large increase in the numbers appointed. Whereas St Catharine's men won thirty 1st classes in the thirty years 1821–50, they won only nineteen in the vastly enlarged honours lists of the next thirty, 1851–80. The neighbouring college, King's, stood in

[11] Jones, *History of St Catharine's*, 336–7.

several respects at the opposite end of the scale. In the early years of the century, her undergraduate population was negligible; but gradually, and particularly after 1850, this changed. By 1880, undergraduate numbers had risen to fifty, and King's was thoroughly launched upon an expansionist career. But the Fellowship of King's was also almost fifty, and twelve of these Fellows were College Lecturers, teaching not only Mathematics and Classics, but also History, Divinity, Natural Sciences and medical subjects. Relative to undergraduate numbers, King's was both much the richest college in the University, and much the most distinguished in performance in the various Triposes. It was, in short, a classic 'take-over' situation, all the more so because of the convenient nature of the colleges' physical contiguity, and the fact that St Catharine's was, in a sense, a King's foundation. By 1879 the Governing Body of King's was wholeheartedly committed to a 'merger', in which the St Catharine's Fellows would receive King's Fellowships, and the Master and College officers of St Catharine's the nearest practicable equivalents to their posts and honours within the King's establishment. It seemed as if the logic of the era of 'free trade' and the 'competitive principle' in Cambridge was about to be realized in the creation of fewer, larger and more powerful 'units of production'. For, had the King's – St Catharine's merger been consummated, other amalgamations might well have followed in its train.

After initial indications of agreement, St Catharine's finally rejected the proposal by a single vote. Two of the Fellows felt so strongly that a grievous error had been made that they asked that their disagreement with the decision be recorded.[12] What is really interesting in the affair is that it was, apparently, Robinson who furnished the decisive opposition to the merger. However his inadequacies may have injured the College, at least he maintained it in existence. As if in contrapuntal irony, however, Robinson was also mainly responsible for the College building programme of these years, the only significant expenditure on the College fabric in the nineteenth century.

[12] Muniments, L/83. 20 April, 1880.

The erection of the Master's Lodge and the orielization of the main Hall window did almost as little to solve the College's fundamental problems of accommodation as they did (in the opinion of the present author, at any rate) to enhance its beauty.

It has been suggested earlier that the tide began to turn in favour of the embattled smaller colleges around 1885, although decades were still to pass before the full effects of this became apparent. Essentially, the interest of the smaller colleges was bound up with the rise of the University as against the collegiate system in general. To pursue our analogy with contemporary social and political developments, the era of 'free trade' and the 'competitive principle' at Cambridge, as well as in the country at large, was followed by a period of growing 'state power' and moderate 'state control'. The advance of the University, as against the colleges, had been faintly discernible since 1800. But in the closing years of the century it became rapid, palpable and decisive. The most critical single change was the introduction of College taxation for University purposes by the Universities' Act of 1877,[13] which in turn derived from the enlargement of the number of Triposes and in particular from the advance of the Natural Sciences. The Natural Sciences broke the back of college autonomy. Increasingly, their demands developed beyond the power of individual colleges to satisfy. Only St John's, Caius and Sidney ever set up their own laboratories, and these soon proved inadequate in the face of what A. W. Tillyard called in his admirable *History of University Reform* (1913), 'the demands of a subject always hungry and aggressive for more. There was nothing for it but to take toll of Collegiate riches. The outstanding fact . . . of academical history during the last sixty years is the growing power of the University. It had always retained the right of examining and giving degrees, of public discipline and a portion of the teaching. It has gained a larger proportion of the teaching and the right of taxation'.[14]

---

[13] 40 & 41 *Vic.*, c, xlviii.
[14] Tillyard, op. cit., pp. 296–7.

The process was gradual. In 1883, for example, the net colleges contribution to the University was only £4,600, less than the annual income of the poorest college. But thirty years later it was £22,500, four times as great as the lowest college income. In 1870 there were less than fifty University Teaching Officers, the majority of them being Professors. Forty years later there were more than one hundred and fifty, of whom less than one-third held Chairs. By 1914, the number of University Teaching Officers almost equalled the number of College Lecturers, and would soon surpass it.

All this steadily reduced the predominance of the wealthier colleges. Insofar as the University acted, the poorer ones stood on, or at least much closer to, an equal footing. Only the University's attempt to establish a common entrance standard for undergraduates struck at their immediate interest by threatening to cut their numbers in residence to a dangerously low level — and this 'reform' was successfully resisted for the time. Even in the areas of teaching where the University advanced least and slowest, the non-laboratory subjects such as Classics, Mathematics, History and Divinity, the new systems which evolved after 1880 tended to redress the balance in favour of the smaller colleges. Inter-collegiate lecturing re-placed the traditional college teaching in which every college, large or small, lectured to its own students and to none other. Although, in the new scheme, each college continued to arrange its own lectures, these were now thrown open to members of other colleges, and some measure of rationalization was achieved by periodic Conferences of Lecturers in the various Triposes. Thus, even in the area not directly invaded by University instruction, a levelling process was under way and the grievous disadvantages of the smaller colleges were further diminished. Moreover, two other factors in the general transformation of the University helped them further on the road towards parity. First, the great increase in total under-graduate numbers in the very late nineteenth and early twentieth centuries meant that the demand for places in the more powerful colleges quickly outran their capacity to supply them. Colleges would not or could not expand indefinitely although the University in general might. The inevitable consequence was a secular growth in the numbers, and improvement in the quality, of those entering the less fashionable places. Secondly, the proliferation of subjects studied at the University provided the smaller colleges with opportunities — if they were shrewd enough to perceive them in time — to make themselves centres of excellence in new or rising academic fields. Distinction and even pre-eminence in a frontier region of research and study was open to even the smallest and poorest college, and, once achieved, might serve as the nodal point for a general advance in academic standard and reputation.

V

Broadly speaking, then, the pattern of Cambridge development had changed yet again by the end of the nineteenth century, this time in favour of St Catharine's and her like. It needed only a supplementary change in the character of its Fellowship for the College to set forth upon a second course of resurgence and, finally, distinction. The history of the nineteenth-century College, beneath the confused surface of conflict and consensus, achievement and failure, spasmodic glory and creeping gloom, is basically simple. It corresponds with the grand movements of academic change — and, behind them perhaps, with still larger shifts in social and political arrangements in Great Britain. Our Ariadne's thread is University reform in its three main modern phases, the first born at the beginning of the nineteenth century, the second in its middle decades and the last at its very close. The first presented St Catharine's, and all other lesser colleges, with considerable new problems but also considerable opportunities, and herein the quality of a college's Fellowship was of much more critical importance than before. In this situation, no comparable college excelled, and perhaps no comparable college equalled, St Catharine's achievement. In the second phase, the problems of the smaller colleges became progressively more acute, and their opportunities progressively more restricted. In an obvious sense, this made more demands upon the Fellowship: now the smaller college had to run twice as fast to stay in the same place.

It is even arguable that, in the second phase, a minute and static Fellowship was doomed, more or less, to failure. The numbers and diversity of a college's lecturers and the size of a college's resources may by now have been too important to be offset by individual calibre, however high. And, of course, the peculiar tragedy of St Catharine's after 1850 was the fall in the calibre of its Fellows. However, as with Sieyes and the 1790s, it was something — in a sense it was everything — that the College could say of the mid- and late Victorian adversities, that it had survived them. By 1900 a new day for the poorer — no longer necessarily the smaller — colleges was at hand. It is very curious — but history teems with such curiosities — that Robinson, at once, as Tutor, the initial cause and, as Master, the enduring symbol of the College's decay, should also, by his intransigence in 1880, have rendered possible her ultimate salvation.

STATISTICAL NOTE

Most of the statistical data used in this essay and especially that relating to graduations, academic performance, college teaching and Tripos examinations generally, has been gathered from the successive annual *Cambridge University Calendars*. Additional statistical matter was drawn from the following parliamentary papers: *Numbers of students entered annually on the books of each college or hall within the universities of Oxford, Cambridge and Dublin . . .*, 1850, XLII (7); *Correspondence respecting proposed measures of improvement in the universities and colleges of Oxford and Cambridge*, 1854, I (123); *Select committee on Oxford and Cambridge university education bill*, 1867, XIII; *Returns from the universities of Oxford and Cambridge . . .* 1886, LI (214 – Sess. 1). J. A. Venn's *Oxford and Cambridge matriculations . . .* was also of use.

Many of the calculations are my own; but since they almost all involve no more than simple addition and subtraction, and the making up of percentages, even a semi-numerate sets them forward with some confidence.

18

The College, 1919–70

By T. R. HENN

Fellow, Senior Tutor, President, Reader in the Faculty of English

I

A PERSPECTIVE OF THE PERIOD

THE period 1919–70 seems, in retrospect, to divide itself naturally in time. The first phase was, perhaps, 1919–26, covering the Mastership of Bishop Drury and the Senior Tutorship of Rushmore. During it the College absorbed (with many makeshifts and expedients) the suddenly-increased numbers after the First War, and began to adjust itself to the many implications of that expansion. A society of five Fellows and sixty undergraduates seems to have been a viable proposition in 1914; it was clearly inadequate (with no increase in the Fellowship) for some two hundred and twenty men. By 1926 it was apparent that the rise in numbers was not a temporary post-war phenomenon, and that the multiplication of subjects in the University could no longer be met, even partially, by teaching within the walls.[1] The College, with its straitened finances and inadequate buildings, could do little more in this phase than temporize with the problem. Many of the double rooms were partitioned off; baths and electric light were installed. But the proportion of men in College was small, less than a third of the total; lodgings were difficult to obtain, and often remote, sometimes as far out as Romsey Town. Obviously the College would have to confront, sooner or later, the interlocking problems of the whole Island Site, the teaching provided by the Fellows, the increasingly costly maintenance of the

[1] There was, for example, no teaching by Fellows in Law, Mathematics, English, Geography: that for all the Sciences was clearly inadequate.

seventeenth- and eighteenth-century buildings, and the extent to which the results of financial mismanagement and misfortunes in the 'dark period'[2] could gradually be countered.

But there was another important event which made 1926 a landmark. The Royal Commission of 1923-5 had proposed radical alterations in teaching and administration throughout the University, as well as in many matters that affected profoundly the relationships between the Colleges and the University. Those involved, for most colleges, a drastic revision of their Statutes. Fellowships ceased, in the main, to be life appointments; those who chose to remain under the old system could do so, those who transferred to the new could claim compensation for loss of their rights. One effect was to ensure the gradual retirement of the elderly Fellows, whose functions in our history had hardly offset, by their experience and eccentricities, the problems and anomalies they had created in college life. At the same time there was an important gain from the new Statutes, for colleges were now compelled by the University to elect a number of Professorial Fellows, on a quota determined by wealth and size. Another consequence, not wholly foreseen at the time, was a most important modification to the whole principle on which Fellows had previously been elected. For it was now apparent that no college, except the very wealthiest, could afford to pay its Fellows a living wage without taking cognizance of whether they held, in addition, a University teaching post, or were likely to do so in the immediate future. Henceforward the salary of a teacher in Cambridge was to be determined substantially by the University.

But the most important effects were not fully apparent until after the Second War. The University Stipends Ordinances of 1946-7 set out the principle of the 'prime stipend', by which a University Teaching Officer was paid by the University a sum which had regard to his emoluments from his college: so that the University made certain deductions if the officer were in receipt of payments from a college, whether as fellowship

[2] Perhaps 1861–1909: or the Mastership of the much-maligned Robinson.

dividends or as stipends for certain major college offices, above a prescribed figure. It was therefore open to colleges to lower their dividends to a figure which did not attract deductions from the University payments, with the eventual result that more money could be made available for new Fellowships to meet the vastly expanding subjects for which provision had to be made. Among the consequences for St Catharine's was a steady increase in the number of Fellows, and a proliferation of the subjects taught 'within the walls'. Above all, it was clear that the claims of the University on the time and energy of Fellows were now in most serious competition with the needs of college administration, particularly as regards the important traditional offices of Tutor and Bursar. Nor was the situation made easier by the knowledge that, with the growth of the new Universities, promotion to their major posts was more likely to be earned by concentration on scholarship than by devotion to college work.

The next phase, covering the Masterships of Rushmore and Chaytor, may be thought of as 1926–39, extending over the war period until Chaytor's retirement in 1946. Rushmore's election was the result of an important historical event, the dissociation of the Canonry at Norwich from the Mastership which it had long augmented. Complicated legal processes were furthered by Sir John Withers, an eminent solicitor, benefactor and Supernumerary Fellow; as a result the choice of the Fellows was no longer restricted to those in Orders. But Rushmore did not live long to enjoy his Mastership, and Chaytor, who was then appointed,[3] could — ironically — have held the Canonry.

There followed a period of consolidation in various directions. The rate of election of new Fellows increased a little; there were now Rich and Waddams (1930), Sydney Smith (1939), Aston (1943), in addition to two Professors, Hutton (1937) and Winton Thomas (1943). F. S. Dainton came in 1945 to take charge of certain of the Sciences. There was a steady growth in scholarship and in athletic successes: the characteristic ethos of the 'twenties seemed to be maintained, stabilized, expanded.

[3] Appointed, that is, by the Visitor: the right of the Fellows to elect having lapsed through delay.

1939–45 is perhaps best seen as a 'holding period'. A number of Fellows, including the Senior Tutor (Portway) left for service. Those who remained faced the inevitable difficulties and hazards of war-time Cambridge. The College became host to two bodies from London, the Bartlett School of Architecture and the London Hospital School of Medicine. Both they and their staffs brought benefits as well as problems. Among the benefactors we remember Sir Albert Richardson, afterwards President of the Royal Academy, for his indefatigable energy and advice on matters concerning our buildings. Yet much of the traditional life continued; elections of Scholars and Exhibitioners were held, and these men resided for limited periods; a number of cadets spent six months as temporary members of the College. Some of them were to return after the war.

The next period might be thought of as from the end of the war to 1957, covering the Mastership of Portway.[4] The return of the ex-servicemen was marked by comparatively little dislocation, a profound sense of purpose, and none of the discontents that had been apparent in the corresponding 1919–22 generation, or which were to grow from 1964 onwards. At this stage the pressure of applications was excessive, and complicated by the claims of the backlog of award-holders, the obligations of National Service, and the inevitable limitations of lodgings and dining-space. For a time the Bull Hotel, taken over by American troops during the war, served as a miniature sub-College, and was finally incorporated within the walls. The ex-service undergraduate, having seen much of cities and men, provided a special and most welcome contribution of their own. In retrospect, two of the most fruitful periods may have been those from 1932 to 1939 and from 1946 to 1956.

At the same time the College as a Society took on a more homogeneous and logical shape, partly as a result of the pressure on admissions and the ever-increasing demands for teaching in old and new subjects. Up to 1939 (and 1945) the College was never completely filled; it was always possible to

[4] Fellow, 1919: subsequently Senior Tutor and Bursar.

squeeze in a few more. Now the number of undergraduates was stabilized at three hundred and sixty, an annual intake of about a hundred and twenty freshmen, selected from many times that number. A plan was made for the proportions of undergraduates between the various subjects read, since the old reputations of individual colleges for particular subjects had now been virtually submerged, and it was felt that we should, in this matter, represent a cross-section of Cambridge scholarship and life. Allied to this was a wholly new phenomenon: a sudden increase in the number of post-graduate students of many kinds, but particularly of those reading for the now almost indispensable doctorates. This demanded new administrative and tutorial arrangements, and had many bearings on the traditional life of the College.

The last phase, from 1957, covers Rich's Mastership, and changes both in the College and the University, on a scale and of a complexity that is without example in our previous history. The New Buildings, completed in 1967, amounted to a second (or third) refounding of the College. A steady increase in the number of Fellows, and in the diversity of their interests and habits, has combined with political and social changes of which the full impact cannot yet be assessed. Perhaps it is best seen as a time of consolidation, of projection, of decentralization of the problems that seemed so pressing between the wars, but which in retrospect were relatively simple. But the central event of this period was, beyond all doubt, the solution of the problems of the Island Site.

II

BUILDINGS

Much thought, discussion and planning went — as perhaps with all colleges — into the problem of the site. Our plot of land is erratic in its geometry, fortuitous in its northern boundary, and rigidly constricted by three roads. It has suffered (yet gained much aesthetically) by the accidental redirection of Milne Street, now Queens' Lane; which left the College back to front, to become the only three-sided court in the University. The temptation, on such a limited site, to close the Main Court by a fourth block (as in the Loggan print) has never been absent from the minds of successive Governing Bodies. This would have provided a new Hall, many rooms, perhaps a noble entrance gateway. Such a plan was advanced in 1914; it was fortunately postponed, then and on at least two subsequent occasions, on grounds of expense.

By 1930 the slow building up of reserves, some substantial legacies, both present and in prospect, and the repair of damage done to College resources by inefficient management (and some ill-fortune) in the past, made it possible to contemplate a phased rebuilding plan; to take advantage of what property could be re-possessed with relatively little loss, and to relate it to the then numerical strength of some two hundred and sixty undergraduates. The initial 'strategy' proposed by Kennedy, who had recently worked for King's, was to leave the front open and to frame the two great 'dominants' of the Chapel and Ramsden Buildings with more deferential North and South blocks, uniting them visually by means of architectural features and scale, and by pavilions which were intended to echo, when seen from Corpus, the features of the Queens' Lane Gateway. The first block, the present Hobson's Building (later to be 'tied' with some difficulty into the Bull Hotel complex) was completed in 1930, with the intention that it should later be balanced by a similar block on the south side. But in 1935 a serious and irremediable mistake was made, comparable in its effects to the misplacing of the Master's Lodge in 1875–6. The Johns Building, made possible by gifts from Mrs Johns[5] and named in memory of the Master who did so much to repair the fortunes of the College, was placed in exactly the wrong position; and the opportunity to lay out a new and spacious South Court, with perhaps a new Master's Lodge, was lost for ever. To make room for it the College demolished a pleasant two-storey building, long familiar as housing the J.C.R.;

[5] Widow of C. W. H. Johns, Master 1909–19.

and, to the south of it, a small swimming bath. The building itself, massive, unimaginative and aesthetically deplorable, remains an efficient eyesore. But such mistakes, and lack of vision, are not uncommon in the histories of colleges.

After the Second War it was found possible to continue, though with a different architect, the basic strategy. The present Woodlark Building rose on the site of the old Porter's Lodge. It is perhaps the most satisfactory building of the period as regards its architecture, and for the variety of its rooms furnished with exotic Empire woods, the gift of firms and individuals associated with the Timber Development Association.[6] It was completed in 1951 and opened by the Chancellor, Lord Tedder. At about the same time many of the rooms to the south of it, along Trumpington Street and Silver Street, were drawn into the College, as the Bull Hotel had been. For a time a temporary hut, built in the Bull Yard by its American tenants, served as an overflow Dining Hall and for other purposes such as concerts, meetings and plays.

But the central problem at this stage was that of the Hall and Kitchens. The Hall had been adequate, and much loved by many generations, for a College of sixty or seventy men; with the Gallery formed out of the Old Combination Room it would seat, perhaps, a hundred and forty, including the High Table. The Kitchens, which in the period between the wars had encroached out of sheer necessity on the two neighbouring staircases, had long been condemned as insanitary and inefficient, though generations of cooks had worked miracles there, particularly when three Halls each night became an inconvenient necessity. In the late 1950s our oldest building, 'E' Staircase, began to give cause for anxiety; ominous cracks appeared, widened under the stress of heavy traffic, and finally its undergraduates had to be evacuated. Trial excavations showed that, in the seventeenth-century fashion, its foundations were no more than notional. To preserve it would have meant complete rebuilding, perhaps encasing it in a 'skin' of masonry.

---

[6] This impressive benefaction arose out of a Dinner of the Association at the College: and was due in large part to the vision and energy of their Technical Director, E. H. B. Boulton.

Its fate probably accelerated the need of the Governing Body for immediate action. There were various possibilities.

A relatively new Senior Combination Room, connected with the Old Hall, had been built in Walnut Tree Court, with the intention at that stage that it would serve (as well as the old one) a new Hall to be built at the end of 'E' Staircase and roughly where the gateway to the Bull Yard used to stand. But the boundary with King's in this 'slum' area had always been obscure, and sufficient room for such a building depended on exchange or purchase of land on our behalf by that College. For a time it seemed possible that St Catharine's could sell sufficient land to King's to enable us to purchase a stretch of river frontage between Silver Street Bridge and the King's Mill, and outline plans were made for a new and wholly separate River Court; with all the amenities of rooms on the River, and all the administrative and social disadvantages of a relatively distant building.

Other alternatives were canvassed, and planned in outline; a lateral extension of the existing Hall to the north; three 'sky-scraper' blocks, in conjunction with King's, on land to be cleared between the end of the Chapel and the Bull Hotel. This, after the model stage, was finally abandoned because of interference with the King's Parade skyline and because of the various disadvantages of four-roomed 'flats' for undergraduate living.

The final plan was one of unexampled magnitude. It depended on the common-sense solution — one that had been thought unattainable — of clearing the whole available site and pooling it with King's; who had, indeed, made a take-over bid for the College when its finances and reputation were probably at their lowest. King's had long wished to build a Keynes Memorial Court, to remodel their inadequate buildings, and to bring order to the mean complex of buildings on either side of the 'dog-legs' formed by the north-eastern end of King's Lane. It was recognized that such a course would involve extensive destruction of the old landmarks, a loss perhaps more serious to St Catharine's than to King's; for in the clearance, not only 'E' Staircase (1633) but the noble brick tower of the Library, the new Combination Room and Walnut Tree Court itself would have to be sacrificed.

That the plan was carried through is due mainly to three people. There was the architect, Fello Atkinson, who worked for both Colleges with extreme tact and intelligence, and whose ingenuity was adequate to meet the difficult and varied demands set out by them. Secondly there was Kenneth Berrill,[7] Bursar of St Catharine's until 1962, who rendered important services to the College finances during the previous decade, and who then became Bursar of King's. The two Colleges were able to work together with a rare co-operation and a mutual understanding of each other's problems. Finally, the succeeding Bursar of St Catharine's, S. C. Aston, brought to the scheme his characteristic energy in surmounting the Shakespearean 'checks and disasters' implicit in such a vast undertaking; organizing the immensely intricate temporary arrangements which involved the building of a kitchen hut in the Front Court; and, above all, directing the complicated financial operations which were unique in the history of any college.

III

THE LIBRARIES

Hall, Chapel and Library, with some kind of accommodation for Fellows and Scholars, were the three indispensable components of a sixteenth-century College. But in 1919 the Library was in large part a museum, accessible only to Fellows; its noble stacks filled with books bound with a faith in their enduring quality, and concerned largely with theology and philosophy; reminders that Woodlark had founded the College for the study of Canon Law, and that many of its most distinguished alumni for three centuries had been clerics and theologians. At one end, over the Ante-Chapel, was John Addenbrooke's Medicine Chest, the subject of a Doctoral Dissertation;[8] sundry globes; some first editions, Shirley and

---

[7] Now Chairman of the University Grants Committee: K.C.B. 1971.
[8] An account of it by A. W. Langford is in the Society Magazine for 1927.

others; and other books, including a Caxton of great value. But as far as the undergraduate was concerned it was wholly dead, save when the Fellow who acted as Librarian exhibited it to visitors or to College Societies.

Perhaps a digression is indicated regarding the reading habits of the undergraduate. From 1919 to 1939 a man reading Arts would find it possible, on an initial expenditure of perhaps £10 in his first term and £5 each term afterwards, to build up a very fair private library in his subject; and this enabled him to do much of his reading and essay-work in his own rooms. Again, he could bring some of his books away in the vacation and, in accordance with the rhythm of the short crowded terms and long vacations, do much of his reading at home. To a certain extent he could rely on the different departmental and faculty libraries, and the more industrious could use (in proper academical dress) the University Library, which moved to its present site in 1934.

The changes after the Second War were considerable. Books were scarce and expensive, the numbers using them excessive. None of the 'outside' libraries was open at night. To meet the new conditions the Governing Body decided on some fundamental changes.

The Old Library, now rechristened for Bishop Sherlock, was gutted and completely reorganized as an undergraduate working library. The 'dead' books — of all kinds, but mainly theological — were for a time placed in glass-fronted cases on the staircase (they have since been put into storage), and the Library was planned as a 'living' organism for the use of undergraduates.

A first step was to make it a Memorial to those who were killed in the Second War. To that end the new chairs and tables were architect-designed to harmonize with the room and to afford the greatest possible comfort as working accessories. On each piece of furniture is carved the name of the men whom it commemorates; for the larger pieces, several names together. The next innovation was to throw the Library open all night without restrictions, and to accept the consequent risks of fire, and of some loss of books. At the same time the traditional

Library Fund was heavily overspent each year, on recommendations from the various Directors of Studies, and this policy has been continued. Accessions have been augmented by the substantial number of works published each year by Fellows and by former members of the College.

All libraries suffer from constricted space: the great libraries grow at a terrifying rate. A most welcome addition occurred when the New Buildings were completed in 1967. The ceiling of the Old Hall was lowered to give the new Senior Combination Room more satisfactory proportions, and the space thus made available was turned into a second Library, now known as the Armitage Library after the most liberal of recent benefactors.[9] This, in spite of certain inconveniences of control, is of great value and has made possible a complete regrouping of subjects. One day, perhaps, our finances will allow for more ample assistance: to the Librarian-Fellow, to the post-graduate Librarian Scholar who is now elected on a short-term basis, and to the present Secretary. The re-cataloguing, now in progress, is a major problem.

The modern undergraduate has thus at his disposal three main libraries; that of the Faculty or Department, the College, and the University Library. The first two allow limited borrowing during the vacations. With increased numbers of men their work-demands are not for one copy of a text but for several; even so it is a common complaint that they have to wait for a particular book. There have been some notable private accessions: especially the Modern Languages library of H. J. Chaytor, and that of T. R. Henn for English. Several Directors of Studies also maintain private 'lending libraries' for the use of their pupils.

All this goes some way to meet the changed reading habits of the men; more work, particularly on essays and papers, is being done at night in the library and less in rooms. For in addition to the availability of the necessary books, which is growing steadily in scope and comprehensiveness, men working in the library are assured of relative peace; and, in winter,

[9] R. C. D. Armitage was a former Scholar of the College. It is pleasant to record that he lived to see his most generous benefaction employed exactly as he wished.

warmth. Thus, while the College can show to the outside world few manuscripts or rare books, it does provide a gracious working environment which is in constant use.

IV
MEN

It is a truism that any college is a Society, self-governing and self-perpetuating. Through its methods of electing Fellows and College Officers it determines its reputation for scholarship, and the many parts which it should play in University administration. Through its elections of Scholars and Exhibitioners, and even more significantly by its commoner admissions, it determines its living quality as a Society. Over all, there is the problem of its characteristic ethos, and the extent to which leadership and tradition give rise to a living and organic community. It is proper first to consider some of the dons.

There is little doubt that the resurgent period — the word is from Rushmore's memorial brass in the Chapel[10] — was initiated by Rushmore and owed much to him. He himself had no pretentions to scholarship, but was an excellent administrator and a shrewd judge of men. In this last gift he was supported by Chaytor, who, as an ex-Headmaster, had contacts with many schools. Their work was complemented by Bishop Drury who came to St Catharine's from Ripon, and, previously, from the See of Sodor and Man. For seven years he served as Master and, in the words of the Commemoration Service, did much for the beautifying of the Chapel. Above all he was a man who radiated a love of the College and of his men : one in whose presence no evil could exist. W. H. S. Jones was for long the Bursar, and looked after the Classics : L. F. Newman exercised a general supervision over the Natural Sciences, and specifically over Agriculture. Donald Portway, afterwards to be Master, was brought in from Dartmouth to look after the engineering, to become in succession Proctor and Motor

[10] 'Huic collegio resurgenti
Operam curam vitam dedit.'

Proctor, and, incidentally, to supervise the installation of electric lighting. It is probable that in 1920 the number of Fellows — five — was the smallest Governing Body in the University, and certainly the College was the worst in its staff–student ratio; about 1:40. Of those five Fellows three were destined to become Masters.

The Tutorial system, always of immense importance in the life of a college, developed gradually. At first there were two Tutors, Rushmore and Chaytor, with 'sides' of about a hundred and ten each. On Rushmore's election as Master, Portway was added to the Tutors and became Senior Tutor at Chaytor's appointment in 1933, with Henn and Steers as assistants. L. F. Newman was a Tutor 1927–33, when he was appointed Bursar and Steward. In the absence of Portway, Henn and Rich, Steers became Senior Tutor during the difficult war years. Subsequently the position was, for a time, stabilized: with a Senior Tutor (who also looked after Admissions) and three Assistant Tutors, each in charge of 'sides' (representing rough subject-groupings) ranging from ninety to a hundred and twenty each. Experience suggests that the ideal 'side' is one of not more than seventy-five, to enable a Tutor to attain the most intimate possible knowledge of his men, both academically and socially.

It seems probable that the College system in general reached its apogee in the inter-war years. Because of problems of staffing, the number of Tutors has, at the time of writing, risen to seven, of whom one is wholly responsible for the Research Students in all subjects. Those who have had experience on various selection bodies — in particular the Civil, Foreign, and Armed Services — will understand the enormous importance of the Tutors' ability to write full and perceptive testimonials. This in turn necessitates the keeping of confidential records and comments, a matter that is sometimes misunderstood.

The planned expansion of the body of Fellows to cover the largest number of subjects inevitably resulted, under the system of appointing University Teaching Officers, in the election of many Fellows from other Colleges and Universities.

In 1948 it was remarked that no less than six members of the High Table had taken their degrees at Oxford. Today there is a high proportion of Fellows who are not, by 'breeding', St Catharine's men.

At the same time it is pertinent to note certain important changes in the work, perhaps even the *mores*, of the Fellows themselves. Between the wars the sets allotted to them were of generous proportions, and designed for living. It was laid down — I do not know whether by statute or legend — that the fire insurance on the buildings was not valid unless three Fellows slept in each night. During the period 1919–39 there were a number of bachelor Fellows,[11] and four others who 'slept in' three or four nights a week. It was considered normal for the married Fellows to sleep in, perhaps on two or three occasions: the more junior ones co-ordinating that pernoctation — a pompous but traditional word — with those more senior. This in turn meant that each of the major staircases or buildings had one Fellow in each night, but each staircase had still a number of men in the rooms. (It was not until the Fellowship increased greatly that most of the big eighteenth-century rooms became Fellows' sets, single or shared.)

It was then a tradition of college life that much visiting should go on late at night between the men themselves. It was customary, in the days of coal fires, to have a kettle on the hob, or ready in the gyp-room, for tea or coffee; with biscuits and tobacco. Wine and even beer were scarce because of the cost. If a Fellow were working late at night he not infrequently had late-night visitors from among his men; they might come to borrow a book, or ask a question, and stay to talk. This was one method of achieving the often-discussed 'Communication'. On empirical grounds it seems probable that those who have troubles and difficulties talk about them much more freely at night; so that a resident don who is well-seen and of a friendly disposition can do much good. If we go further back in time, before the first war, we are aware from biographies and novels

---

[11] L. F. Newman, J. A. Steers (until 1942), Christopher Waddams, E. E. Rich (until 1934), Sydney Smith.

how frequent was that visiting, and various forms of entertainment in small groups. When kitchen service was available many of the dons did their entertaining in this way, often for breakfast on Sunday mornings after Chapel, and such parties might last for several hours. The College has in recent times been helpful about enabling the Fellows to entertain; but it is doubtful whether the sherry-parties — now the commonest form of mutual entertainment — contribute as much as did the older and more intimate practices. Over the last two decades of our period the situation has changed perceptibly. The younger don, who will later develop unquestioned loyalty to the College that has adopted him, may have little interior knowledge of its tradition. He is appointed for life tenure at a comparatively young age.[12] He tends to marry young. In an overcrowded and ever-spreading Cambridge he finds it difficult to obtain a house within a reasonable distance of the College. The car has brought the villages all round Cambridge into a reasonable radius, and house-rent. But with a young wife and family, and without domestic help, there is the temptation or necessity to follow the practice of many civic universities. His College rooms may become, with his laboratory, a workshop rather than a second home. He will tend to leave College in the early evening, to return to his family in time for a supper, and to help with various domestic tasks. The old convention, by which all Fellows dined at least four nights a week, has long gone by the board. Luncheon is a more convenient substitute. The week-end habit has spread to some extent to Cambridge, and the 'College Act' of keeping Chapel has also fallen into desuetude, for many reasons. And because of the desire of so many to get home early (the traffic jams in the evening rush-hour are formidable), far more teaching than ever before is done in the afternoons and early evenings. The circle closes; many men cannot because of this teaching play games or row

[12] University Assistant Lecturers are subject to a probationary period of five years after which there is life tenure. Research Fellowships at the College are for three years; ordinary Fellows are appointed in the first instance for three years, and are thereafter subject to re-election at seven-year intervals. But the right of the Governing Body not to re-elect is rarely exercised.

to the extent they once could, and the six-hour day, five days a week, is gradually taking over. Again there is emulation of the practices of the civic universities; the week-end habit is now considered normal, together with vacations that tend, for the undergraduate, to be regarded as holidays in which extra cash can be earned.

There has been a healthy exchange of St Catharine's men with other colleges; a number of factors have now made such migrations so normal as to excite no comment, for it may well happen that a man of eminence in some particular subject finds that a college other than his own has a vacancy at a given moment when his own foundation has adequate teaching resources in that subject. Among the more notable of such migrations in the post-war years were R. T. H. Redpath to become a Tutor at Trinity, D. A. Davie to Caius, C. L. Wayper to Fitzwilliam and C. F. Kolbert to Magdalene: where S. C. Aston was a Bye Fellow in 1938. (He returned after the war to direct studies in Modern Languages, and became in succession Dean, Tutor and Bursar.) Aubrey Silberston, originally of Jesus, went to St John's after a time as a Research Fellow of St Catharine's; these Research Fellowships, of limited tenure, are now a feature of most colleges. John Vaizey, who held the Kenward Fellowship 1953–6, is now Professor of Economics at Brunel University. Sir Ivor Jennings returned to Cambridge, as Master of Trinity Hall, after a distinguished career as Vice-Chancellor of the University of Ceylon, and was one of the most eminent constitutional lawyers of his time. H. C. Darby succeeded J. A. Steers as Professor of Geography but remained at King's; R. F. E. W. Peel held the Chair of Geography first at Leeds and then at Bristol. A. T. Phillipson occupies a Professorial Fellowship at Churchill, R. S. Sayers, perhaps the most distinguished of our many Economists, has recently retired from his Chair at London. S. A. de Smith is a Professorial Fellow of Fitzwilliam, and D. T. Piper, Director of the Fitzwilliam Museum, is a Fellow of Christ's. O. H. K. Spate, another distinguished geographer, has held Chairs at Rangoon and at Canberra; Oliver MacDonagh, the historian, returned from a Chair at Adelaide to one at Cork; J. B. Segal, a Boxing Blue of distinction, is Professor of Oriental Languages at London. L. M. Harvey, now First Assistant Registrary, is a Fellow of Churchill, and T. G. P. Spear was for many years Bursar of Selwyn. W. K. Lacey, formerly Director of Studies in Classics, is now Professor of that subject in the University of Auckland. The latest addition to the list of Honorary Fellows is Sir E. I. Goulding. All in all, some twenty-five Fellows of the College have migrated within Cambridge, or left the University on promotion.

Among the Honorary Fellows the College numbers two Archbishops; the former Prime Minister of Malaysia; Lord Soper; and Sir Irving Goulding; as well as the Provost of Worcester College, a foundation with which we have long had a *concordia amicabilis*,

It may be said, in general, that a body such as a college expects its *alumni* to achieve distinction in their various callings at about the age of fifty. The sudden increase in our numbers after the First War, and their progressive increase[13] until 1960, could not have been expected to show results of this kind before the early 1950s. Nor could the pre-1914 College, with a large proportion of men reading for Orders, have produced many who attained eminence in what is now known as 'the public sector'. But the Second War found many who achieved distinction in the Service, and many ('numbered among our Benefactors') by their deaths. One of the most promising and colourful careers was that of Rupert Brabner, D.S.O., D.F.C.; M.P. (at the age of 28) for Hythe and subsequently Parliamentary Under-Secretary for Air, lost in an air accident in 1945 at the early age of 33. Another, happily surviving and now Professor of Education at Nairobi, is F. C. A. Cammaerts, sometime a leader of the French Resistance, who won a host of other decorations in addition to his D.S.O.

The range of service in all walks of life has been wide. Among them Air Marshal Sir Augustus Walker,[14] Sir Frank

---

[13] As a sample of these increases: 1920–1, 200 undergraduates and two research students: 1938–9, 289 undergraduates and 24 research students, and 1960–1, 366 undergraduates and 72 research students.

[14] K.C.B., C.B.E., D.S.O., D.F.C.

Bower, Sir George Elliston[15] and Sir Norman Elliott,[16] all of whom have been Presidents of the St Catharine's Society. There is a Permanent Under-Secretary in W. D. Pile,[17] once a Rugger player of note. There are many distinguished Head-masters; one of them, J. S. Woodhouse, was appointed to Rugby at an unusually early age, and C. R. Allison presided over the meteoric rise in the fame and fortunes of Brentwood.

The College has been less prominent, perhaps, in politics than in the Services, the Church, and the world of business. F. W. Mulley held ministerial office in two Labour governments. At the time of writing there are five M.P.'s: J. R. Horam, F. W. Mulley and N. J. Spearing (Labour); W. I. Percival and D. M. Walters (Conservative). The early connection of the College with the Welsh Schools was in part due to the interest of Daniel Hopkin[18] and, later, to that of W. E. Evans.

Among the Arts the most notable names are the actors, L. J. Genn and Ian McKellen: and especially Peter Hall for his work with The Royal Shakespeare Company. As regards literature, it would be invidious to attempt a catalogue; but we may notice among others the poets Patric Dickinson, J. C. Bayliss, Peter Champkin, Francis Warner,[19] the versatility in many fields of Jon Manchip White, and the European reputation of W. J. Strachan as a translator and art collector.

V

THE SERVANTS

No college could exist without its staff of servants, a fact which is sometimes overlooked by the more democratically-minded but less intelligent among the students. For social and economic reasons the older type of gyps and bedmakers of the pre-war

---

[15] Unionist M.P. for Blackburn, 1948–50: C.B.E.
[16] Now Chairman of the Electricity Council: C.B.E.
[17] K.C.M.G., 1971.
[18] Labour M.P. for Carmarthen, 1929–31 and 1935–41.
[19] Now Fellow of St Peter's College, Oxford.

period began to disappear after the Second War. For similar reasons there has been an accelerated turn-over rate in many departments of staff and office workers, as well as in the kitchens. Waiter-service at night is maintained with difficulty by bringing in schoolboys; at some colleges, whose belief in ceremonial is not conspicuous, it has been abandoned altogether.

It is perhaps well to record the circumstances of the change. From 1919–39 the average undergraduate had breakfast, lunch and tea in his own rooms; there was, of course, dinner in Hall, but in the mornings this was used for lectures.[20] An undergraduate of the period, living in an attic room on one of the major staircases, could expect in the morning to find his coal fire lighted, a kettle on the hob, and his breakfast-table laid. If he so chose, and could afford it, a message on his table would bring the breakfast of his choice, for any number, carried up by the kitchen porters. Coal was carried up to his gyproom on the backs of colliers, at the cost of some damage to the winding stairs, as well as to human dignity. The gyp saw that the sitting-room was kept clean and tidy: the bedmakers made the beds and saw to the laundry. One washed and shaved in one's room. Gyp and bedmaker left in the early forenoon, to return in the evening to set things to rights again, and probably to wait in Hall. The traditional commons; milk, butter and a small loaf of bread, appeared at intervals; unused, they became the perquisites of the gyp, with much else. If the gyp was a good one — and most of them were — he took a keen interest in his 'gentlemen', and in various subtle ways, including the free borrowing of assets of all kinds, made his staircase into a social unit. Moreover, practically all the sets in College had separate bedrooms and living rooms, even with the larger 'shared' rooms; this fact produced, in the undergraduate, a sense of domestic self-sufficiency and made his entertaining more genuine. In comparison, the modern bed-sitter, the product of economies in space, cost and upkeep, is apt to be as

[20] Only the Boat Club, while in training, had their breakfasts in Hall, often by the generosity of individual Fellows.

characterless as the corridor off which it opens. Again imperceptibly, the gyp set a standard of conduct: condoning such traditional activities as dinners and bump-suppers (and their consequences), but setting his face against anything that was likely (in his opinion) to 'bring the College into disrepute'. He was often a keen spectator at football matches, and followed the fortunes of the Boats; there was a little betting with his opposite numbers in other colleges, both on the games and (it was rumoured) on men who had been 'tipped' for Firsts.

The gyp, as a race, began to vanish about 1964. In the course of more than forty years the College had been served, on the staircases and elsewhere, by a number of men and women whose loyalty and strength of character had secured their position in the affection of many generations; the more eccentric among them becoming subjects for good-humoured *mimesis* at College concerts and the like. Their records of service are impressive. They frequently became, in that vivid Shakespearian phrase:

'the weather-beaten conduit of many kings' reigns'.

Among them (one can do no more than select from a long roll of names) are Charles Porter, who with his wife and son counted 110 years in the service of the College; Sid Alderton, who after retirement continued in part-time work, reckoning in all 62 years. George Simpkin, a remarkable character,[21] who served from 1899 to 1943; Johnson with nearly half a century; Sidney Brett who retired after 30 years, and — finally, after part-time work, in 1972. Many generations will remember with gratitude the groundsmen, the Lamberts, father and son: the father after 41 years (1919–60) still advising his son on the care of what must be one of the most perfect grounds in Cambridge. In the kitchens there is Rooke, now approaching 40 years of service since his apprentice days: the office staff, coping so valiantly with the ever-increasing flood of paperwork, and perhaps most remarkable among them, Mrs Nina Smith, the Senior Tutor's secretary, to whom the present writer

[21] Author of illuminating articles 'From a Gyp-Room Window' in the 1947 and 1948 Society Magazines.

wishes to record a special debt of gratitude. Another most
familiar figure is Jack Nixon, also with more than 40 years of
service, an indispensable figure of many qualities and functions.
Any college is now a many-faceted organism of great complexity and many officers; it is certain that those undergraduates
who mistakenly demand a measure of self-government have no
conception of the work 'behind the scenes' that makes possible
their academic life. Above all, there is the debt of the College
to J. F. A. Ablett, who has served so long and so faithfully, not
only in the administration, but in all the affairs of the St
Catharine's Society, and whom the Governing Body have
(without precedent) honoured by election to a Fellow-
Commonership. Without his assistance this essay would have
been the poorer.

One remembers with gratitude a number of Head Porters in
the Lodge, once imposing figures in frock-coat and top-hat, and
almost as powerful as the Dean on occasions of riotous assembly.
Much the same civilizing functions of gyps, bedmakers and
porters were performed by the older type of men and women
who let lodgings, usually 'tied' to a particular college and who,
at their best, did much to help the freshman to settle in during
the first few critical weeks of his residence. If, as so often, the
husband also worked in the College, there was a double tie;
and the fortunes of his men when they subsequently moved
into College rooms were followed with interest. Some of the
lodgings were in fact so comfortable that it was not unknown
for men to ask to remain in them for the whole of their three
years; certain of these highly-prized lodgings were within a
few minutes' walk of the College.

All this was changed after the Second War, and for a
variety of reasons. Work in factories or elsewhere became more
profitable than lodgers, and the influx of civil servants into
Cambridge meant that lodgings could now be let all the year
round rather than on a terminal basis. Some landlords resented
as tedious College regulations regarding gate-bills, keys, the
need to sit up late; others found that the 'new men' were often
ill-at-ease in this particular relationship. In the spate of post-war
building most colleges set themselves the target of sufficient

rooms in College to enable two out of the three years to be 'in': in addition to the traditional rooms for Scholars and Captains and Secretaries of Games.

At the same time the Catering and Wages Act of 1943 produced significant changes in this type of service. In the 'old days' many of the gyps, waiters, cooks, went to east-coast hotels for the Long Vacation, being technically 'dismissed' from the college roll, to return in late September after a change of scene and some profit to themselves. But the new law, and the steadily rising costs of keeping a college running beyond the relatively short academical terms, made it necessary for the colleges to devise continuous employment. This was done in two ways: by training some of the staircase staffs to carry out decorations and renovations in the rooms, and by letting out part of the college during the vacations to business firms and sometimes to academical bodies who wished to hold all kinds of conferences[22] under a single roof that provided facilities for meals, lecture rooms, a bar, and a College office and Porter's Lodge to assist with administration. The New Buildings were designed with this object in view, the rooms being self-contained with all facilities, and, in general, up to modern hotel standards. Thus the College has been associated with various bodies who return year after year, and have frequently become benefactors to the College through gifts and sometimes by foundations of various kinds.[23] One of the most generous and welcome gifts (made at a time when our resources for Fellowships were especially low) are the Permutit Fellowships, provided by the 'interest' of R. T. Pemberton. There is, perhaps, some slight effect from these conferences on undergraduate habits of residence and reading.

The Long Vacation, once an important and valuable feature of university life, has grown less popular; partly because of greater enterprise in travel (and more money for that purpose), partly because of the ease with which the undergraduate

---

[22] At the time of writing there are six such conferences scheduled for the academic year.

[23] Among them are the gifts and benefactions of The Timber Development Association, The Cost and Works Accountants, The Institute of Brewing.

obtains temporary and lucrative employment. There has been, arguably, much loss to the social life of the College. For Long Vacation residence all were in rooms in College, and men of widely-differing disciplines and interests had a chance to meet each other. The undergraduates and the college servants were drawn into closer contact, mainly through a cricket match with a team of undergraduates and dons, followed by a party for the wives and children. That this should have passed is more regrettable than the desuetude of the annual services in Chapel for the servants before the opening of the Michaelmas Term. The sense of unity, of comity in the College, was materially greater when these practices brought out its essential character as a House, a living organism.

VI

SCHOLARSHIP

A list of distinctions during the past fifty years would be tedious, and perhaps less than enlightening; but the changes and modifications in policy that have helped to determine these lists are of historical interest. In the period between the wars, and for a short time after, there was significant difference in practice between St Catharine's and the majority of the other colleges. These conducted their entrance scholarship examinations in December, and, in a competition which has always been noted for its severity, prided themselves on skimming the intellectual cream of the schools. St Catharine's, usually in collaboration with one other 'smaller' college, examined at some period of the Lent Term, usually towards the end. A number of Oxford Colleges held their examinations in January. For a considerable time we worked in partnership with Selwyn.

There were losses and gains in this system. The 'March Colleges' tended to acquire the reputation of being something like poor relations, at which candidates might have their last despairing chance to win some sort of an award. On the positive side it is certain that the examination frequently picked up excellent candidates who had escaped the December 'net' of the big groups; through illness, perhaps through bad or unlucky examining, or simply because the candidates had had an extra four months' intellectual maturity behind them. And for a time the St Catharine's–Selwyn combination was unique in that it alone offered awards, as the main subjects, for Geography and English,[24] and thus had a virtual monopoly in these Triposes until other colleges followed suit. The strength in these subjects perhaps offset the relatively small numbers of candidates in Classics, which by the end of the Second War was, throughout the University, a wasting subject.

There were two further features of the St Catharine's system. The first was that of awarding a number of places to those who did not gain awards: the second was the institution of the Crabtree Exhibitions, which played an important role until their usefulness was terminated by the Butler Act of 1944. Since these have given rise to many misunderstandings and some vilification, it is as well to consider their history and functions. They were developed by F. M. Rushmore early in his Senior Tutorship,[25] in memory of a former Tutor, E. W. Crabtree. The philosophy behind them was that many admirable men, who ought to be given an opportunity to come to a university, were unable to put a final 'edge' on their scholarship because of their considerable responsibilities and activities during their last year or so at school. A candidate might be, typically, captain of his school, a good athlete, perhaps an all-rounder with a record of running various school societies, the magazine, and so forth. Their qualities were in fact very much those leading now to entry, say, to the Atlantic College or some Outward Bound Course, and often to the various Colonial Services. Candidates were nominated by their schools, submitted extensive testimonials, and were interviewed by a

---

[24] These were first held in 1927. They have produced, for these two subjects, a remarkable list of academic achievements. Some seventy senior academic posts in geography, here and abroad are held by St Catharine's men: and rather more than half that in English.

[25] For the original Crabtree benefaction cf. p. 239.

committee of the Governing Body while they were sitting for the examination. On the evidence of their performance in this they were supposed to be capable of getting at least a Second in the Tripos. (Some did rather worse than this; some better.) Out of perhaps a score of candidates five or six would be selected and given small exhibitions of £30 or £40; these often acted as 'amplifying valves' for other grants of many different kinds.

One result was to produce annually from 1927 onwards, a core of men of exceptional character and leadership. They were sometimes, but not always,[26] excellent games-players which gave rise to the accusation that the College was giving 'games scholarships'. St Catharine's was by no means the only college with this reputation, but others, perhaps, did it less officially; the practice is by no means dead. It could be defended on many grounds; at a period when the 'house full' notice was never set up, and the main problem of the average undergraduate was that of money, it gave opportunity to many wholly admirable men, whose emotional and intellectual maturities were already in balance. Some day it may be possible to do some research into the distinguished careers and achievements of the Crabtree Exhibitioners.[27]

The Crabtree, like several of the closed 'awards' for particular schools, finally became obsolete because of the new grants system. The last award was made in 1954 to a man who is now a distinguished diplomat. For a while the College continued to examine, with Selwyn, as a lone effort during the Lent Term, adopting a system by which the papers were worked at the schools and marked in Cambridge before the 'possible' candidates were summoned for interview. (This practice has since been adopted, though with less thoroughness, by the December groups.) But in 1962 pressure was brought on all colleges to conform to a new timetable, in order that Oxford and Cambridge should complete their admissions by February of each year, thus allowing other Universities to complete their own

[26] A remarkable case was the Captain of a very large Secondary School in Liverpool, who had a withered right hand.
[27] e.g. of five elected in 1934, two got 2:1's, two 2:2's and one a 3rd.

lists. St Catharine's joined a 'December Group', and now examines jointly with Queens', Christ's, St John's, Emmanuel, Sidney Sussex, and Fitzwilliam.

The number of 'Firsts' rose steadily during the inter-war years, and became stabilized at about forty or fifty a year in the post-war period.[28] Statistics are misleading, and the academic 'crop' seems to vary, for no very clear reason, from year to year. An examination of the 'league tables' suggests that the College is, usually, in the 'top ten' in the University: the most successful subjects being Natural Sciences, Geography, English, and Modern Languages; and the least prominent Classics, Mathematics, and Engineering. Matters of this kind are never simple: but it is probably true to say that academic class-lists reflect the amount of money which a college is prepared to spend upon its annual awards, the quality of its teaching 'within the walls', the staff–student ratio, its contacts with particular schools which have outstanding teachers, and the reputation, difficult to define, which draws the ablest candidates to those colleges which have built up reputations for specific subjects.

We may notice in the records the College's large number of University Prizes that are associated with individual Triposes, and awarded on those examinations: among them the Philip Lake and William Vaughan Lewis Prizes for Geography, the Frank Smart Prize for Zoology, the Harkness Scholarship for Geography, the Prize for Aeronautics. The record in prizes, scholarships and studentships in Classics has been poor. Between the wars there was an excellent record in the Charles Oldham Shakespeare Scholarship, the Members' English Essay Prize, and in the Chancellor's Medal for English Verse (which has been won twice, as has the Seatonian Prize), the John Stewart of Rannoch Prizes for Hebrew, and for Music; with many others. A significant feature of the University today is the considerable number of 'traditional' scholarships and prizes which go unawarded; partly because the average undergraduate of ability is no longer under financial pressure; and,

---

[28] As random examples, there were thirty-nine in 1936, forty-two in 1948. In 1960 the College came third in the Tripos 'table' with 13% of Firsts.

if this should exist, he knows that he can make the equivalent of even the noblest endowment by a few weeks' work in a factory or as a postman. Nor is an array of awards and distinctions the passport that it once was to a Fellowship or to a University post; the Ph.D., and perhaps a Research Fellowship, have become the obligatory rungs on the academic ladder.

It is relevant to mention briefly the scholarship of the Senior Members. In the 1920s Chaytor alone had a European reputation as a modern linguist and Provençal Scholar, a reputation for which he never received full credit during his lifetime. W. H. S. Jones was recognized as a leading Classic of great if somewhat eccentric authority in a limited field. Of the previous generation the College had passed by without recognition or reward the work of Sir Norman Moore, Neville Figgis, and, above all, G. G. Coulton, in his time perhaps the leading medievalist in Europe. Sir Rowland Biffen had acquired the highest reputation for his work in plant genetics, though he took little part in College affairs. Among the major contributions[29] during the period under review were those of J. A. Steers,[30] first to the reputation of the College as the nursing-mother of most of the leading geography professors, and then for his own work on Scolt Head, the coastlines of Britain, the Great Barrier Reef: of E. E. Rich[31] in the History of the Hudson Bay Company, and subsequently in his editorship of *The Cambridge Economic History*: Dr Sydney Smith in his work on Darwin and as Sandars Reader in Bibliography: Professor J. H. Hutton[32] in his important work on Indian castes. The late Professor Winton Thomas[33] made many contributions to Hebrew Studies, including the 'work in progress' for the Hebrew Dictionary, and served on the Commission for

[29] As Master and as Editor I must add here a note on the contribution of T. R. Henn himself. Apart from the personal stimulus and enthusiasm which gave the College an outstanding place in English studies, his publications have won him a great reputation and have reflected much credit on the College. Particularly notable has been his work on Anglo-Irish literature, with *The Lonely Tower* marking a period in the study of W. B. Yeats; and his study of *The Bible as Literature*.–E.E.R
[30] Professor of Geography, 1945–68.
[31] Vere Harmsworth Professor of Imperial and Naval History, 1952–70.
[32] Professorial Fellow, 1937; and Bursar during the Second War. *d.* 1968.
[33] Professorial Fellow, 1943. Fellow of the British Academy.

the Revision of the Prayer Book Psalter. R. N. Gooderson[34] has contributed much to legal studies. On the science side F. S. Dainton,[35] elected to a Fellowship in 1945 and subsequently the holder of a Chair at Leeds, followed by the Vice-Chancellorship of the University of Nottingham, was among our most distinguished scientists; a tradition maintained in the 1960s by R. S. Comline[36] and A. G. Maddock.[37]

Finally, and of infinite importance in the life of the College are those who have ministered in the Chapel. Chaytor was followed for a quarter of a century by Christopher Waddams, whose memorials are elsewhere. He was assisted by a succession of full-time Chaplains: Harold Harding (1946–8), Hartley Bird (1948–55), David Shapland (1955–61), Alan Wilkinson (1961–7) and David Sparrow (1967–   ). It is in the nature of history that the Chapel, consecrated in 1704 to serve a foundation of perhaps fifty men, should now be adequate for a College of eight times that number. Compulsory Chapel, which was abandoned in 1921, was a relic of more ceremonious days, but not necessarily of greater spiritual concern. Yet it is clear that the Chaplaincies have always been vital contributors to the well-being of the College, and St Catharine's has recently marked this by elections to Fellowships.

VII

SOCIETIES AND GAMES

No historical sketch can afford to neglect these aspects of college life during the period, and I have deliberately set them out in this order.

Undergraduate societies rise and fall in relation to the interest and leadership at any one period. Thus all colleges

---

[34] Fellow, 1948: Reader in English Law, 1967.
[35] Fellow, 1945: Fellow of the Royal Society. Professor of Physical Chemistry, Leeds: Vice-Chancellor, University of Nottingham. Now Professor of Physical Chemistry at Oxford: K.B.E.
[36] Fellow, 1943: Reader in Veterinary Physic, 1965.
[37] Fellow, 1952: Reader in Radio-Chemistry.

have, in varying degrees of vitality, a Classical Society (this was of importance in the time of W. H. S. Jones), a Debating Society (now known as the Lightfoot, and somewhat intermittent in its operations), and Societies for Music, Law, and Economics. But two particular societies have been more continuous in their history and wider in their scope: the Shirley and John Ray Societies.

The Shirley Society was re-formed after the First War, taking over some of the functions of the old Literary Society, which went back at least half a century before. This was still in operation in 1920–1, and consisted, perhaps a little strangely, of the resident dons and the captains and secretaries of games. Its members drank beer and smoked, as a ritual, churchwarden pipes; the undergraduate members read in turn a paper on some cultural subject of their choice. On its ruins the Shirley Society came into being, with a wide charter which included painting, sculpture, and drama. All colleges have literary societies, usually named after some distinguished artist or writer in their past: the Shirley was alone in acquiring a wide reputation throughout the University. Between 1926 and 1965 it is hardly possible to name an important writer who had not been a guest of the Society.[38]

Equally, the John Ray has been remarkable for the number and reputation of its distinguished visitors; and today, with seven scientists among the Fellows, the range of interest is remarkable and varied.[39] Both the Shirley and the John Ray have always thrown their meetings open to the University as a whole, so that this form of intercourse has been of particular benefit to the College. The Music Society, refounded in 1919, has always been a feature of the life of the College, and is now fortunate in having two Fellows to oversee its interests. A

[38] A selection from our records includes Sir Arthur Quiller Couch, G. C. Coulton, W. P. Ker, Harold Monro, Lowes Dickinson, S. P. B. Mais, Philip Guedalla, Stephen Spender, F. L. Lucas, C. Day Lewis, L. A. G. Strong, Walter de la Mare, T. S. Eliot, G. M. Trevelyan, Sybil Thorndike, Roy Campbell, E. M. Forster, J. I. M. Stewart, Donald Davie, Pamela Hansford Johnson, F. R. Leavis, Patric Dickinson, Kathleen Raine, William Plomer and the late Poet Laureate.

[39] As examples, A. S. Eddington, Joseph Needham, C. D. Broad, B. C. Saunders, Sir George Thomson, Sir James Gray, D. Keilin.

concert party, 'The Midnight Howlers', resurrects itself sporadically to entertain the College in satire and song.

Perhaps the St Catharine's Society should be mentioned here: for although its membership includes the undergraduates currently in residence (who receive its magazine) it is primarily a fellowship of the Old Members of the College. It has co-operated with the College in providing a register, and this, together with past numbers of the magazine (begun in 1926) now forms an important source for the history of the College. The Society too was Rushmore's creation, in 1923, and is now some four thousand strong. Its most notable achievement, other than the sense of unity confirmed by its annual gatherings, has been the immense achievement of its contribution to the Quincentenary Fund in raising a quarter of a million pounds, with a total target, already in sight, of £350,000. Much credit is due to the work of its Appeals Committee, and in particular to A. A. Heath. The Society has branches, and holds meetings, in Australia, the Channel Islands, Canada, Uganda, as well as in London, Bristol, Yorkshire, and Manchester.

We may perhaps congratulate ourselves that Cambridge has never suffered from the hysterical adulation of the athlete that obtains (for example) in certain North American universities, where the success or failure of football and other teams are important factors in stimulating the generosity of the alumni. But the success or failure of a college in games, athletics, rowing, still has an effect upon its reputation in the university; and, even more important, among the schools from whom it draws its men. At worst this success is a tribute to vitality, to discipline and even to patriotism; rugger cup finals still draw large crowds. In the period before the First War a college of sixty men struggled manfully to put on a showing, so that members of the cricket xi used (we are told) to break off from a match to row in the one college boat. At any rate it is certain that our history records only a single Blue for rowing, and one for hockey, before that date.

After the First War the situation changed profoundly, and this was not merely due to the four-fold rise in numbers. The Tutors, with the help of some Old Members, established important contacts with the public schools, especially those in Wales. There were several notable athletics Blues in the early 1920s. But it was the St Catharine's rugger which began to attract attention: the cup was won in 1927, 1929, for three consecutive years in 1931–3, in 1938; but not again until 1954. At one period (1934) the whole of the College three-quarter line were Internationals, and there were in the same year, in addition, two Blues for soccer and for cricket, and one each for athletics, fencing, and boxing. Boxing has until recently been a strong interest, no doubt because of the redoubtable shadow of Donald Portway and the encouragement of C. R. Benstead. In 1936–7 the captains of all three University sides — rugger, soccer, and cricket came from the College: in 1936 there were thirty-five firsts, and thirty-six in 1938.[40] In 1967 — a more up-to-date random sample — there were twenty-one Blues and Half Blues. The rowing has been equally impressive: prior to 1946 there were two Blues in our history, R. Davies (1912) and W. L. R. Carbonell (1934). Since then there have been seven, including two Presidents of the C.U.B.C. During the same period, the College has been intermittently successful on the river, but has never won an event at Henley. Among the more remarkable feats was a year in which three boats achieved thirteen bumps between them; in 1967 the Second May Boat was the highest of those of all colleges, and confirmed its excellence by bumping the First Boat.

At the same time it is pertinent to note a changing attitude towards both societies and games. Until the post-Second War period the entertainments and distractions of a college were largely 'home-grown', proceeding out of the initiative of its own members, and related to the social habits of the under-graduates. In the last two decades the tendency has been to go further afield. The vast proliferation of University Societies— there are nearly two hundred — which exhibit their attractions to freshmen each October, has inevitably drawn off a number

[40] These are figures from years chosen at random. Lest they should be thought unduly selective, other figures of Firsts are: 1946—46; 1948—42; 1967—48. Today such figures would be misleading, since several Preliminary Examinations are not included.

of men from college life. The undergraduate calendar is now overcrowded with every imaginable kind of social, political, and cultural event, so that meetings like that of the Shirley Society (formerly every Sunday evening) may now clash disastrously with a speaker of some political or ecclesiastical prominence at Great St Mary's. In general, it seems that undergraduates are reluctant to read papers themselves to the various societies, preferring, misguidedly, to listen to visitors whose stature and significance appear to have been already achieved.

In somewhat the same way the status of all athletics, and the participation of the average undergraduate in them, seem to have decreased considerably. We may suggest various reasons. There is a pressure, real or imagined, to 'do well' in examinations, and the vacations, often given up to making extra money, are no longer periods of study to supplement the work in term-time; which has traditionally left room for 'extra-curricular activities'. There is much laboratory work in the afternoons, so that for many men rowing becomes an impossibility, and there is a corresponding emphasis on games of quick exercise, such as squash. Of recent years a great deal of time has been taken up in the afternoons with political discussion, confrontations, 'teach-ins' and the like, as well as film societies and dramatic productions. And with men of a particular social background the habit or tradition of bodily exercise in the afternoons has weakened: many aspects of university teaching do not observe the former magical period of 1–5 p.m. that was once sacrosanct to the open air.

A further divergence of customs and myth may be seen in the passing of the traditional 'rag'; November 5th tends to a degree of hooliganism, complicated by invaders from the youth of the industrial cities within motor-cycle range. The University found it necessary to issue a warning to undergraduates not to walk except in pairs in the streets at night. In 1969 an Exhibitioner was badly beaten up by skinheads or the equivalent, outside Great St Mary's Church. Clashes between these invaders, undergraduates and townsfolk, have become more frequent, and conditions seem to have reverted to those of the middle ages. The Poppy Day Rag, which many will

20

remember with pleasure and which used to bring out much good humour and ingenuity, was abandoned for political reasons. Its place has been taken by a day of collections and exhibitions in the Lent Term, in imitation of the civic universities, the London hospitals, and similar bodies. Minor exploits of the type that will be remembered between the wars as being both humorous and ingenious have been replaced by episodes which oscillate between violence and vulgarity, though there are welcome signs that a sense of humour may be returning to undergraduate life.

VIII

THE FUTURE

It is not the intention of this essay to attempt to prophesy what the future may bring. Clearly there are important landmarks in the past. The Society Magazine has noted that in our history these landmarks seem to have been erected some twenty years after the turn of each century: 1520, 1620, 1820, 1920. Two of these apparently coincided with the influx of new students at the conclusion of a major war. Again, we may note the significance of the phased rebuilding plans of 1930–5,[41] and the effect of the university reorganization of 1925–6 on the Fellowships. The decision of 1950 to stabilize the College at about three hundred and sixty undergraduates, thus bringing it into line with all the 'medium-sized' colleges at Cambridge, made possible the great rebuilding projects of 1946–67. In common with most other foundations, we have resisted pressures to enlarge beyond this limit (always excepting the steady growth of research students) on the grounds that the target of two-thirds of men within the walls can thus be met, and that accommodation of both Hall and kitchens is not to be extended further, and that there is a number of men (and perhaps of Fellows) beyond which cohesion becomes difficult. At the time of writing, the University Grants Committee has proposed, and

[41] Hobson's, 1930; the new (since demolished) Senior Combination Room, 1931; Gostlin House, 1933; Johns', 1935.

the Council of the Senate has recommended, that the total undergraduate strength of the University should be raised, during the quinquennium 1972–7, from 10,500 (in 1970) to 13,500. And while 3,000 men divided among the colleges may not appear too large, it is certain that even this increase will add greatly to many of our problems, and may modify still further the traditional character of Cambridge.

The College, therefore, may be thought of as having entered on a period of consolidation. This takes many forms. Not least among the problems of the last five decades has been the problem of maintaining the structures of the seventeenth and eighteenth centuries. All timber yields to time. Many buildings resent modernization by such devices as electricity, central heating, the washing of brick and stone. Much of the College roofing has had to be replaced; the noble staircase on Old Lodge has been preserved only by a remarkable feat of engineering. The Sherlock Library was never designed to carry its present weight of books, nor the present traffic in their use. The buildings on Queens' Lane have suffered (and 'E' staircase most of all) from the vibrations of heavy traffic. And all this in addition to the normal annual maintenance of the rooms.

Another, and perhaps the most important of all the problems, is the building-up of Fellowships and Scholarships to bring us into line with wealthier or more fortunate Societies. At the time of writing there are twenty-nine Fellows; our friends in comparable foundations range from forty upwards, and have achieved corresponding strength in their resources of teaching and scholarship. Growth is necessarily slow; and the slower because the College has, in the last two decades, been forced to make a choice between the immense capital investment represented by the new buildings, and the vital augmentation of its Fellowship. History tells us that the same dilemma confronted us at the end of the seventeenth century and in the middle of the eighteenth. Now, as then, the debts incurred take time and effort to liquidate. And for the prospect of this final discharge the College is indebted beyond measure to the generosity and the energy of its old members; without whose support the project could not have been brought to fruition.

What happened in these five decades, say 1920–70? The answer is of course complex, but some at least of the historical factors are clear. The flood of admissions — that often included men and schools that had no previous connection with Cambridge — was a powerful determinant of the resurgence. It was fortunate too that there were enough of the pre-war 'vintage' returning into residence to pass on some of the most valuable of the College traditions. Among them we may count friendliness and co-operation, virtues that arose, perhaps, from the very smallness of the old College, and forced the majority to take part in so many activities. This was a leaven which went on working. Whatever aspects of our past history had affected adversely the reputation of the House were of little consequence to those new generations. Wrong things had been, or were being, put right; the labours of C. H. W. Johns and the administrative gifts of F. M. Rushmore had already done much to clean the slate. There was the presence of five Fellows of whom three were wholly new to the College. And there was the rest of the University, with its traditional divisions, exclusiveness, even snobbishness, suddenly made aware of the 'new men', their variety, maturity and potentialities. The schoolboys too — the first considerable intake was in 1920 — were on the point of breaking away from the patterns of their traditional College allegiances. If one were to attempt some kind of graph of the progress of St Catharine's over these five decades it would show a steady rise, with, perhaps, a peak in 1933–6: the College wrestling with the ever-conflicting claims of Fellowships *versus* buildings, the building-up of scholarship and its funds, and the many improvements and improvisations on the cramped site. From 1934, that turning point in the history of Europe, there was the shadow of war; and the war took, as always, the best of those generations.

If we were to measure ourselves against other colleges, we should be aware that St Catharine's was gradually assuming its numerical place among the medium-sized Houses, no longer spoken of as 'small'. No doubt others were subject at the time to similar pressures, problems; though in less acute forms. Colleges which by foresight, benefactions, or the mere accidents of fortune, had wealth and space to expand, were able to do so gradually; the fever of Cambridge building is in the main a post-Second War phenomenon. And the University itself was adjusting to innumerable changes in teaching and organization. The senior members of the College were taking an ever-increasing part in the many boards, syndicates, committees by which the University is governed. Much of the energy of Fellows is spent, not merely in college teaching and administration, but in this double service; and a succession of able administrators among the younger men brought the College into prominence thereby.

There are many factors which make it impossible to extrapolate past events into the future. Many universities are now in competition with Cambridge as regards scholarship, teachers, administrators and undergraduates. It is certain that St Catharine's is set in a university which has suffered profound changes since 1919 and radical ones since 1965. The factors are economic, social, political, and ideological.

Any society that grows too rapidly tends to lose something of its traditional ethos; and hence its homogeneity. That is observable in certain of the newer universities. There are those who believe that these disintegrating forces will ultimately change the traditional nature of all colleges; so that they will eventually become little more than expensive and inefficient hostels; that the responsibility for teaching, whether of graduates or undergraduates, will pass even more rapidly into the control of the university; and that the traditional relationship of the individual pupil with his tutors and supervisors will no longer be possible or relevant. There are others who believe that the hierarchical structure of a college, originally modelled on the ecclesiastical foundations of five centuries ago, is now wholly obsolete. Events appear to have forced a reconsideration of the functions of those picturesque and useful survivals, the Proctors, and many ceremonious features of Cambridge life are being challenged.

There are arguments for all these points of view. It is certain that in the past half-century, change has been progressive and that its tempo is now accelerating, perhaps violently. The

College appears to have solved, once and for all, the main problems of its irregular and constricted site, and has provided itself with a complex of buildings adequate to any purpose that we can foresee. No doubt future generations will consider carefully the south-eastern boundaries of the College; there may be, one day, a south court facing inwards from Trumpington Street and Silver Street, with a new Master's Lodge. But whatever may be the future, the past fifty years of the resurgent, re-formed and renewed St Catharine's has no parallel in the history of any university.

INDEX

Ablett, J. F. A., 286
Addenbrooke, John, 135, 274
Adelaide, 281
Adlingfleet, 174, 200
Ainard, Abbot, 44, 46
Akenside, Mark, 137
Albert, Prince, 172–3, 182–3
Alcock, John, 16
Alderbury, 225
Alderton, Sid, 285
Alexandria, 36–7, 40–1, 43
—Bishop of, 41, 45
Allison, C. R., 283
Alston, Peter, 144, 146
—Thomas, 144
Alumni Cantabrigiensis, 138, 146
America, 105–6, 137
Andrewes, Lancelot, 59, 91–2, 97, 100
Anne, Queen, 112, 114, 128–9, 131, 133
Arminianism, 137
Armitage, R. C. D., 276n.
Arrowsmith, John, 95, 147
Arques, Joscelin de, 44
Ashley with Silverley, 207
Askern Colliery Co., 241
  see St Catharine's, Coal
Assembly of Divines, 86, 95, 115, 143
Aston, S. C., 268, 274, 281
Athanasius, 43, 46
Atkinson, Fello, 274
—William, 191–3, 195, 201
Atterbury, Francis, 130–3
Attorney General, 174–5
Aubrey, John, 93, 117
Auckland, University, 282
Ayeray, Thomas, 54–5
Ayerst's College, 257

Bacon, Francis, 73
—Nathaniel, 106, 137n
Bacton, Edmund, 141
Bainbridge, Reginald, 64, 77–80
Balderstone, Richard, 74, 76–7, 87
Balsham, Hugh de, 28
Bancroft, Thomas, 94
Bangor, Bishop of, 110, 112, 132

Bangorian controversy, 110 et seq.,
  132, 137
Barking, abbey, 46
Barnardiston, Sir Thomas, 154
Barbara, St, 48
Barkeston, Messrs, 163
Barnes, Robert, 79
Barnwell, 204
Barrier Reef, 292
Bartlett School of Architecture, 269
Barton, 200, 230
Basil I, Emperor, 42–3
—II, Emperor, 43
Bateman, Bishop, 33n
Baxter, Richard, 97, 117
Bayliss, J. C., 283
Beddingfield, Thomas, 156
Bede, the Venerable, 45
Bedford, 86
Bellarmine, Cardinal, 117
Bellfounders, 49–50
Bence, Alexander, 156
Berrill, Sir Kenneth, 374
Biffen, Sir Rowland, 246, 292
Bilney, Thomas, 79
Bird, Hartley, 293
Black Death, 8
Blackall, Offspringe, 124, 128–32, 134–5
Blakelock, Ralph, 206
Blount, William; Lord Mountjoy, 66
Bocking, 168
Bokenham, Osbern, 47 and n., 55–6
Boleyn, Anne, 80
Bonnell, James, 124, 134
Bonner, Bishop, 80
Bost, Henry, 7
Boston, Massachusetts, 106–7
Boyde, C. P., 159
Brabner, Rupert, 282
Brackenbury, Robert, 160
Bradford, John, 69, 82–3, 85, 97
Bramford, 144
Brentwood School, 283
Brighton College, 232
Brinkley, 200
Bristol, 107
—Bishop of, 184, 207
—University, 281

Britannia metal, 157
Brograve, Augustus, 154
Browne, G. Forrest, Bishop, 50 and *n.*,
    53–4, 115, 118, 136, 163, 178,
    184, 187, 204, 206–9, 212, 217,
    220, 224, 226–8, 234, 236
Brownrigg, Ralph, 66, 68, 74–5, 83,
    85–6, 99–103, 105, 118, 126,
    142
Brunel University, 281
Bucer, Martin, 69, 81–2
Buchanan, George, 117
Buck, Thomas, 94, 140, 153
Buckinghamshire, 88, 149
Bull Inn, *see under* St Catharine's College
Bullinger, Henry, 85
Bunbury, Sir Thomas, 158
Burgh, Thomas, 56
Burleigh, William Cecil; Lord, 71, 73–4
Burnet, Gilbert, Bishop, 113, 128–9
Burrell, Charles, 190–2, 195–8, 200–2,
    217, 251
Butler Education Act, 289
Byers, Frank, 161

Caesar, Sir Charles, 155–6
Cafe, William, 158
Caius, John, 21, 26–7, 73, 142
Calamy, Benjamin, 104, 118, 123–4, 126,
    134
—Edmund, 104
—James, 104, 124
Calcutta, Archdeacon of, 161
Calvin, John, 82, 85
Calvinism, 91–2, 95
Cambridge
    Carmelite Friars, 1, 80
    Christ's Church, Barnwell, 204
    Corporation, 198
    Fordham's Place, 79
    Great St Mary's, 59, 80, 83, 86–7, 95,
        297
    Holy Trinity, 98
    King's Lane, 225, 273
    —Mill, 273
    —Parade, 273
    Market Hill, 84
    Market Place, 59
    Milne St (Mill St), 1, 53, 61, 77, 88,
        94, 271
    Newnham, 234
    Parker's Piece, 234
    Perse School, 237
    Platonists, 100
    Queens' Lane, 61, 198, 217, 271, 299
    Rapham's Messuage, 54

Cambridge — *continued*
    Romsey Town, 266
    St Andrew's, 95
    St Andrew the Less, 204
    St Bene't's, 99
    St Botolph's, 198
    St Michael's Lane, 54
    Silver St, 61, 94, 198, 200, 217, 272–3,
        302
    Small Bridge St, 61
    Tennis Court Rd, 232
    Trinity Church, 94
    Trinity Lane, 54
    Trumpington St, 61, 94, 199, 230, 239,
        272, 302
    White Horse Tavern, 79
Cambridge University
    Act, 1956; 172
    Anatomical Schools, 198
    Caput, 169, 172
    Chancellor, 6, 32, 69, 71–2, 78, 83–4,
        89, 102, 172, 182, 272
    Church, *see* Cambridge, Great St
        Mary's
    Colleges, *see* under individual titles
    College lectures, 29, 76
    Collegiate system, 12, 15, 23–5, 27–8,
        75, 81, 262–3
    Commissary, 77
    Council of Senate, 169, 172, 299
    Curricula, teaching and Triposes,
        76–7, 80, 169, 218, 245, 252,
        255–6, 258–9, 262–3, 267
    Disney Professor of Art and
        Archaeology, 224
    Doctors of Divinity, 209, 260
    Downing Professor of Law, 202
    Entrance Examination, 260, 263
    Heads of Houses, 102, 104, 169, 171,
        181–2, 205, 209, 219
    Inter-collegiate lectures, 238, 245, 263
    Injunctions, 1535; 76, 80
    Lady Margaret Professor of Divinity,
        88
    Lecturers, 218, 227, 231, 252, 263,
        267, 278
    Library, 61, 132, 275–6
    Local Examinations Syndicate, 207
    Lodging houses, 286
    Lucasian Professor of Mathematics,
        189, 202
    Matriculation records, 65, 139, 142
    Non-Regent House, 172
    Norrisian Professor of Divinity, 186,
        202, 215, 228, 231
    Numbers in residence, 65–6, 252–3,
        255, 259, 263, 299

Cambridge University — *continued*
  Old Schools, 76
  Printer, 94
  Prizes, 177, 232, 291
  Professor of Anglo-Saxon, 214
  —of Chemistry, 135
  Professorial stipends, 218–19
  —fellowships, 219, 267
  Public Orator, 101
  Regent House, 73, 79, 84, 89, 172
  Registrary, 177, 185, 187, 205, 282
  Regius Professor of Divinity, 92, 95,
    189, 202
  Report on college chapels, 1636; 99
  Reporter, 207
  Revenue, 169, 171, 173, 218–20,
    262–3
  Royal Commissions, *see under* Royal
  Royal mandate, 124
  Sandars Reader in Bibliography, 292
  Senate, 169
  Senate House, 209
  Smith's Prizemen, 253
  Statutes, 89, 163, 170, 203, 220
  Stipends Ordinance, 1947; 267
  Survey, 1546; 63–5
  Traditionalism, 117
  University Sermon, 95
  Vice-Chancellor, 77, 83–4, 87–9, 92,
    121–2, 124, 132, 168, 172, 182,
    187, 206
  Visitation, 1529, 78; 1549, 80; 1557,
    86; 1636, 147; 1644, 105
  and the Royal Divorce, 79
Camden, William, 78
Cammaerts, F. C. A., 282
Canberra, 281
Canterbury, Archbishop, 191, *see also*
    Laud, Chichele, Cranmer,
    Parker
—Convocation, 92
Capell, Edward, 134
Capgrave, John, 47 and *n.*, 55–6
Capon, William, 79
Carbonnel, W. L. R., 296
Carlisle, Bishop of, 4, 88
Carmelite Friars, 1, 80
Carpenter, Bishop Boyd, 224
Carr, E. T. S., 213–14, 221, 230, 237–8,
    242–4, 246, 257–8
Carter, John, 158
Cartwright, Thomas, 88–9
Catering and Wages Act, 1943, 287
Catharine Hall (Hostel), *see* St
    Catharine
Catherine of Valois, 53–4
Catherine of Aragon, 78

Cavendish Hall, 236, 257
Caxton, William, 47, 275
Celibacy, 202 et seq., 222
Cecil, Robert, 72–4, 97
—William, 89
Ceylon, University of, 281
Chadderton, Laurence, 65
Chambers, Edith, 54
Champkin, P., 283
Chancellor, the Lord, 174–6, 179, 181,
    190, 195, 197, 250; *see also*
    St Catharine's College, *Visitor*
Chancery, Master in, 194
—suits, 165, 174
Charitina, St, 41
Charles I, King, 72, 92, 94–5, 100–3,
    114, 148, 150
—II, King, 105, 114, 116
Chauncy, Charles, 107
Chaytor, H. J., 246, 268, 276–8, 292–3
Chedworth, John, 4
Chesney, Robert, 45
Chester, 91, 146
—Bishop of, 87, 128
Chesterton, 200
Chevalier, Temple, 202, 253, 256
Chichele, Archbishop, 24
Chichester, Dean of, 111, 131
Christ's College, 30 *n.*, 35, 59, 62, 64, 66,
    76, 91–2, 94, 96, 142, 168, 179,
    192, 204, 281, 291
    see also God's House
Christie, William, 162
Church of England, 112 et seq., 188
Churchill College, 281
Clapham, 'Captain', 177
Clare, Lady Elizabeth de, 66
Clare College, 59–60, 62–4, 66, 87–8,
    104, 169, 185
Clare Hall, 3 and *n.*
Clarendon, Lord, 67
—Code, 116–17
Classical Tripos, 184, 252
Claypole, Sir John, 94
Clemence of Barking, 46
Clinton, Lord, 149
Close, Nicholas, 3
Cockburn, Lord Chief Justice, 219
Colchester, 107
Coleman, Philip, 160
Colonial Service, 289
Comline, R. S., 293
Connecticut, 108
Convocation, 92, 110, 126, 130, 132
    see also Canterbury
Conway, R. R., 232, 257–8
Cooke-Yarborough, G. B., 241

Cooper, C. H., *Annals of Cambridge*, 60n.
Cork, University, 281
Cornish, Henry, 123
Corpus Christi (Bene't) College, 6n., 87,
    142, 179, 181, 199, 259–60, 271
Corrie, D., 161
Corrie, G. E., 162, 181–2, 184–6, 202,
    205, 208, 249, 256
Costus, King, 36–7
Cosin, John, 99, 100, 104
Cosyn, Edmund, 83, 86
Coton, 77, 91, 193–4, 196–7, 201, 204,
    206, 225, 230
Cotton, John, 97
Council of State, 95
Coventry, 197
Crabtree, E. W., 166, 207
Crabtree scholarships and exhibitions,
    239, 289–90
Cragg, John, 91–2
Cranmer, Archbishop, 69, 77, 80, 99
Creighton, Robert, 101–2
Cressy, David, 72
Crimean War, 163
Cromwell, Oliver, 100–2, 104–5, 116,
    139
—Oliver, junior, 73, 102
—Thomas, 76, 80
Crosse, Thomas, 133–4
Cumberland, 77, 80
Curtis, J. B., 162
Curtis, Sarah (Mrs Hoadly), 113
Cutts, Sir John, 134

Dainton, Sir F. S., 268, 292
D'Arcy, Frances, 127, 129–30
Darby, H. C., 281
Darnal, Thomas, 157
Dartmouth, Royal Naval College, 277
Darwin, Charles, 292
Davie, D. A., 281
Davies, W. H., 89
Davies, R., 296
Dawes, Sir Robert, 127
—Sir William, 127–35, 156
Declaration of Indulgence, 124–5, 130
Dee, John, 73, 76
Denton, Robert, 108
Derby, the, 158
Derbyshire, 94
Dering, Sir Edward, 117
Dickinson, P., 283
Dilke, Sir Charles, 219
Diomed (racehorse), 158
Doket(t), Andrew, 16
Dominican Order, 48

Donellan, Nehemiah, 91
Donne, John, 97
Dove, Charles, 157
Dover, New Hampshire, 106
Downing College, 185, 199, 220, 260
Dowsing, William, 99
Drury, T. W. Bishop, 246–7, 266, 277
Dryden, John, 120
Dublin, Trinity College, 134
Duckfield, Daniel, 149
Dudley, John, Duke of Northumberland,
    83–4
—Robert, Earl of Leicester, 90
Dulwich College, 214
Dunstable, 45
Duport, J. M., 78
Durham, 47, 86
Durham, Thomas, 202
Durham, Bishop of, 231
Durham University, 202

Eachard, John, 119, 121, 124, 127,
    134–5, 151–3, 155
East India Company, 161
Ecclesiastical Commission, Court of, 124
Edward IV, King, 5, 16, 54, 71
—Charter from, 10, 20, 33
Edward VI, King, 80, 82–3
Eldon, Lord, 194, 251
Elizabeth, Queen, 70, 80, 87–8, 90, 141
Elliott, Sir G. N., 283
Elliston, G., 283
Elwen, Whitwell, 213
Ely, 88, 93
—Bishop of, 16–17, 28, 34, 128, 189
Elyot, Thomas, 68
Emmanuel College, 59, 61, 66, 70, 78,
    94, 96, 98–100, 102, 104, 106,
    108, 147, 217, 291
Enclosure Acts, 200
Erasmus, Desiderius, 66, 69, 75–7, 81
Erastianism, 137
Eton College, 5, 8, 15, 88, 113
—Provost of, 6–7, 87
Eusebius, 40
Evans, W. E., 283
Evelyn, John, 59, 61, 100
Exeter, Bishop of, 86, 99, 103
—St Luke's College, 236

Fawcett, W. M., 216
Fawdery, William, 157
Fellow Commoners, 17, *and see under*
    St Catharine's
Felsted School, 214

Ferrar, Nicholas, 97
Fiennes, Theophilus, Lord Clinton, 149
Figgis, J. N., 232–4, 236, 292
Fisher, John, 78
Fitzwilliam Hall (College), 236, 238,
         257, 281, 291
—Museum, 281
Fleming, Richard, 23
Fockerby, 200
Foster, William, 91, 146
Fourteen Holy Helpers, 48
Foxe, John, 79
Francis, Alban, 124
Frankland scholars, 197
French, Dr William, 200
Frencham, Edward, 84–5
Fulbourn, 77, 93
Fulham Palace, 134
Fuller, Thomas, 1, 6, 27, 60, 66, 99, 122

Gag Acts, 188
Gainsborough, 106
Galway, 91
Gardiner, Stephen, 86
Gardner, Philip, 190
Garrett Hostel, 35
Gascoigne, Thomas, 14
Geneva, 86, 89, 97
Genn, L. J., 283
George I, King, 110, 131–2
—IV, King, 160
Germany, Marian exiles in, 84, 109
Gerrard, Francis, 154
Gibbon, Edward, 188
Gilte Legende, 47
Gimingham, 193
Glenalmond, Trinity College, 184
Glendall, John, 166, 168
Godshouse (Christ's College), 17, 30n.,
         35, 76
Golden Legend, 47
Gonville and Caius College (Gonville
         Hall), 34, 62–4, 66, 71–2, 78–9,
         87, 89–91, 94, 199, 257, 259,
         262, 281
Gooderson, R. N., 293
Goodwin, C. W., 178–80, 252
Goodwin, Thomas, 73, 94, 96–7, 117, 156
Gostlin, Dr John, 66, 94, 98
Gothic Revival, 198
Goulding, Sir Irving, 282
Grand Remonstrance, 104
Great Munden, 114
Greek, 76–7, 80; see Cambridge
         University curricula
Green, Thomas, 61, 63, 76–8, 83, 94

Grey, Lady Jane, 83
Grey, General, 173
Grindal, Edmund, 80, 85, 89
Guilden Morden, 192, 197
Gunning, Henry, 204

Hali Meidenhad, 46
Halifax, 108
Hall, Peter, 283
Halls of residence, 16, 28–9, 34–5,
         54–5, 75, 257
Hamilton, Sir William, 254
Harding, Harold, 293
Hardwick, C., 43
Harrison, William, 70–1
Harsnet, Samuel, 100
Harvard, John, 73
Harvard College, 78, 107–8
Harveian Orator, 211
Harvey, L. M., 282
Hatcher, Thomas, 156
Hazlingfield, 120
Heath, A. A., 295
Hempstead, Massachusetts, 108
Henley Royal Regatta, 296
Henn, T. R., 276, 278
Hennell, David, 158
Henry VI, King, 4, 5, 9, 11–12, 20, 53–4
Henry VIII, King, 62, 69, 73, 79–80, 86
Herbert, George, 97
Hill, Christopher, 96
Hills, John, 74, 77–8, 83, 86, 93–4, 108,
         246
Hingham, Norfolk and Massachusetts, 106
Histon, 197
Hoadly, Benjamin, Bishop, 110–14, 118,
         129, 131–3, 136
Hoare, Richard, 151
Hobbes, Thomas, 117, 120
Hodgson, Philip, 146
Holdsworth, Richard, 102
Holland, 92, 95
Holwey, Moses, 128
Hooker, Richard, 86, 97
Hopkin, D., 283
Hopkins, W. Bonner, 179
Horam, J. R., 283
Hound, Edmund, 74, 78, 89–91, 93, 106
Howgrave, William, 88
Hudson's Bay Co., 292
Huguenot silversmiths, 150
Hundred Years' War, 8
Hurst, F. T., 166
Hussey, Peter, 155–6
Hutton, J. H., vii-viii, 268, 292
Hypatia, 40

Ireland, Accountant General of, 124
Isembert, Abbot, 44

James I, King, 93, 126
—II, King, 124, 130
Jameson, F. J., 204–6, 208, 210, 249–51, 256–7
Jarrett, Thomas, 253
Jefferies, Sir George, 123–4 and *n.*
Jennings, Sir Ivor, 281
Jesus College, 12, 16–17, 22, 26, 59–60, 64, 66, 77, 87, 93, 161, 169, 181, 187, 200, 238, 259, 281
Joan of Arc, 48
John the Baptist, 50
—the Evangelist, 50
Johns, C. H. W., 233, 238, 240, 242–4, 246–7, 300
—Mrs, 271
Johns Building, 271
Johnson, Francis, 92
—Reginald, 285
—Dr Samuel, 113
Jones, Inigo, 94
—W. H. S., 75, 81, 115, 121, 135, 164, 210, 235, 237, 245–7, 292, 294
Jowett, Benjamin, 182
Justinian, Emperor, 37

Kemp, George, 156
Kennedy, G. L., 271
King's College (College of St Nicholas; College of St Mary and St Nicholas), 4, 8, 22, 35, 51, 53, 55, 60, 62, 64, 69, 76, 84, 88, 91, 185, 199, 210, 217–18, 224–8, 230, 260–1, 273, 281
—Chapel, 59
—Label-stop in, 53
—Provost Wodelarke, 1 et seq., 32
—Statutes, 15, 51 and *n.*, 53
—Valuation, 22
—and foundation of St Catharine's, 4, 7
King's and St Katharine's College, 218, 225–31, 261
King's Hall, 4, 5–8, 27, 62, 64, 78, 86
Knollys, Hanserd, 106
Knowles, John, 107–9, 143–5
Knox, John, 85
Kolbert, C. F., 281
Knyvett, John, 154, 156

Lacey, W. K., 282
Lambert, E. and G., 285

Lambert, and Rawlings, silversmiths, 160
Lancashire, 78
Langbaine, Gerard, 21, 27
Laramie, Paul de, 157
Latimer, Hugh, 69, 71, 79, 82
Laud, Archbishop, 95–6, 118, 147
Lay, C. J., 231
Leeds, Theological College, 214–15
—University, 281, 293
Legenda Aurea, 36, 46–7, 50
Legge, Thomas, 90
Leicester, Robert Dudley, Earl of, 90
Leland, John, 26
Leng, John, Bishop, 125–6, 128
Lever, Thomas, 74, 83
Lightfoot, John, 63, 74, 78, 83, 107, 114–15, 118–20, 121*n.*, 124, 134, 140, 148
Lincoln, 86, 93
—Bishop of, 86, 93
—St Katharine's Priory at, 45
—Earl of, 149
Lincolnshire, 186, 189
Little Gidding, 97
Little Shelford, 196, 230, 242
Lloyd, David, 99–100, 103
—Thomas, 159
Locke, John, 117
Loggan, David, 59–60
Lollardry, 11, 51
London,
   bell-founders of, 49
   Bishop of, 85–6, 96
   Cathedral, *see* Paul's, St
   Harvard men at, 107
   Hospital School of Medicine, 269
   Inns of Court, 68, 71, 117, 139, 143–4
   —Gray's Inn, 96–7
   —Middle Temple, 82, 86, 124, 131–2
   Lord Mayor, 123
   Puritan lecturers of, 96
   Recorder, 123
   St Catherine's Hospital and Church, 45, 50–1, 55
   St Peter Poor, 131
   Silversmiths, 150, 158, 162
   Sheriff, 123
   Tower, 84
   University, 269, 281–2
Long Island, 108
Long Parliament, 139–40
Lord Chancellor, *see* Chancellor
Lord Chief Justice, 196
Lords, House of, 241, 244
Lothian, John, 101, 147

Lucasian Professor of Mathematics, 189
Luckett, Richard, 108
Lumby, Professor J. R., 167, 214–15, 224, 229, 258
Lupset, Thomas, 77
Luther, Martin, 79

MacDonagh, Oliver, 281
McKellen, I. M., 283
Madingley, 196
Maddock, A. G., 293
Madras, Bishop of, 161
Magdalene College, 60, 62–6, 106–7, 124, 185, 214, 220, 258, 260, 281
Maitland, C., 161–2
Malaysia, Prime Minister of, 282
Manchester, 82
Margaret, St, 48
—of Anjou, Queen, 16, 53
Marlborough College, 231
Marlow, Christopher, 73
Marnhull, 196, 232
Maplet, John, 89–90
Mary, the Blessed Virgin, 33n., 34–5 and n., 50, 81
—Queen, 63, 83–5, 125–6
Massachusetts, 106–8
Mathematical Tripos, 184, 252, 255, 260
Mather, Cotton, 108–9
Mathilda, Queen, 45
Maxentius (Maximius), Emperor, 36–7, 40, 43
May, John, 78, 83, 85, 87, 89–90
Memoriale Nigrum, 2, 4, 10, 33n., 52–3
Meeres, Robert, 147
Merton, Walter de, 28
Messenger, Edmund, 89
Michael House, 35, 53, 62, 64, 75
Middleton, Thomas, 156
Midnight Howlers, 295
Millington, William, 51
Milner, Joseph, 164, 205
Milton, John, 68, 73, 104, 117
Mirfield, 233
Monasteries, 68, 80
Montagu, Edward, Earl of Manchester, 105
Moore, Norman, 211–13, 233, 292
Morison, Samuel Eliot, 107–8
Morley, George, 166, 168
—Robinson, 158
Moyle, —., 152
Moule, H. G. C., 231
Mulley, F. W., 283
Muser, Peter, 147

Nairobi, 282
Nantwich, 152
Nashe, Thomas, 73
Neale, Thomas, 134
Nelson, Richard, 63, 65
Nether Whitacre, 200
Newcastle, Duke of, 159
Newcomen, Stephen, 104, 118
New England, 95, 105, 108, 118, 143
Newent, 196, 230, 237
Newman, L. F., 246, 277–8
Newton, Isaac, 124
Nixon, J., 286
Non-collegiate establishments, 257
Non-jurors, 111, 125
Norcrosse, Nathaniel, 108
Norfolk, 86, 88
Norrisian Professor of Divinity, 187
North, Lord, 191
North English Legendary, 46–7
Northumberland, Duke of, see Dudley, John
Norton, 200
Norwich, 191, 212
—Bishop of, 93, 125
—Canonry, 131, 192, 228
—Holy Trinity, 34
Nottingham University, 293
Nuremberg, 48

Overall, John, 74, 85–6, 92–3, 95, 99–100, 125–6
—Mrs, 93
Owen, John, 154
—Sir Roger, 117
Oxford,
    collegiate development in, 23–5, 27, 57
    Fellows from, 278
    Lollardry at, 10
    outlook of, 117
    Royal Commission, 1850; 169
    scholarships examinations, 288
    unions of colleges, 220, 229
    Colleges:
        All Souls', 8, 24
        Christchurch, 59
        Lincoln, 23
        Magdalen, 24, 30–1, 66, 95
        Merton, 27, 30–1
        Queen's, 7–8
        St John's, 127
        Worcester, 282
Oxford and Cambridge Act, 1877; 218–19, 226, 229, 262

Paris University, 48, 53n.
Parker, Archbishop Matthew, 26, 83,
        85, 88–9
—Richard, 21, 27
—Mr, silversmith, 160
Parker Society, 82, 85
Parliament, 255
—Members of, 71, 104, 112, 143
Parliamentary Enquiry, 1886; 258
Parr, William, 155, 168
Partherick, Edward, 154
Patrick, Symon, 128
Payne, Rosamund, 66
Paul's, St, Cathedral, 51, 82, 86, 92–3,
        123–4, 131
Peachell, John, 124
Peck, Robert, 106
Peacock, Reginald, 50–1, 55
Peel, R. F. W., 281
Pemberton, R. T., 287
Pembroke College, 35, 59–64, 66, 79–80,
        82, 91, 100–1, 179, 182, 185,
        202, 217, 259
Pepys, Samuel, 154
Percival, W. I., 283
Perkins, William, 91, 95, 97
Perne, W., 78
Perse School, 237
Peter, Hugh, 97
Peterborough, Dean of, 189
Peterhouse, 28, 34, 59–64, 66–7, 78, 80,
        86, 89, 99, 185, 191, 210
Pewter, 145
Phillips, Arthur, 239
Phillipson, A. T., 281
Philpott, Henry, 164, 168–86, 206, 211,
        218–20, 224, 249, 253, 256
Piggott, Gervase, 144–5
Pile, Sir W. D., 283
Pine, J. P., 178
Piper, D. T., 281
Plymouth Colony, 106
Plymouth and Mannamead College, 246
Poland, 63
Poll Tax, 142
Pope, William, 113
Porphyrius, 37
Porter, Charles, 285
Portway, D., 246, 269, 277–8, 296
Pretor, Alfred, 214, 231, 236
Price, Waterhouse and Co., 243–4, 246
Privy Council, 70, 220
Proctor, Francis, 178, 205, 258
—Joseph, 186–8, 190, 192–3, 195, 197,
        199–201, 217, 250–1, 253, 256
Purton, J. S., 179
Pym, John, 96

Queens' College, 1, 12, 16, 22, 35, 53, 55,
        60–2, 64, 66, 76, 78–80, 87–9,
        98–9, 142, 148–9, 189, 198,
        200, 291
Quincentenary Fund, 295

Radnor, Earl of, 168, 254
Ramsden, Mrs Mary, 136, 165, 174
    Bequest, 194
    Building, 174
    Estate, 174–5, 194, 197, 200, 239
    —revenue from, 222
    Foundation, 189
    Will, 195
    see also St Catharine's, Norton Coal,
        Fellows, New Foundation, and
        Skerne Fellows and Scholars
Rangoon, University, 281
Ray, John, 89, 102, 116
Redpath, R. T. H., 281
Rich, Hatton, 156
—Henry, Earl of Holland, 102
—E. E., Professor, 268, 270, 278, 292
Richard II, Duke of Normandy, 44
Richardson, Sir Albert, 269
Ridgewell, 193–4
Ridley, Nicholas, 80, 82
Ridley Hall, 231
Ripon, Bishop of, 224, 246, 277
Robinson, Charles Kirkby, 164–5,
        204–6, 208–13, 224, 229, 231,
        233, 237, 248–50, 256, 261,
        265, 267n.
Robson, Simon, 92
Roche, Richard, 10
Rochester, Bishop of, 78, 133
Rolls, Master of, 177
Roman Catholics, 112
Romilly, Joseph, 177, 205
Rooke, P. J., 285
Rosse, Dowager Countess of, 241
Rouen, 44–6
Rous, John, 26
Rouse, Sir John, 155–6
Royal Academy, 269
—College of Physicians, 135
—Commissions, proposals, 1837, 254;
        1844, 254; 1845, 254
    —report, 1852, 167–8, 170, 172, 202–3,
        218, 255; 1856, 172–3, 176,
        179–82; 1872, 218, 226; 1877,
        207, 218–22; 1924, 224, 245,
        267
—Shakespeare Company, 283
—Society, 117
Rufinius of Aquilea, 40

Rugby School, 283
Rundell and Bridge, silversmiths, 160
Rupp, Gordon, 79
Rushmore, F. M., 231, 236–8, 240–2, 245–6, 258, 266, 268, 277–8, 289, 295, 300
Russell, Lord John, 170

Sacheverell case, 130
St Alban's, Abbey, 45
St Barbara, 48
St Bartholomew's Hospital, 211
St Bees, 80
St Catharine of Alexandria, pp. 33 et seq.
—and bell-founders, 49–50
—and craft-gilds, 48
—and King's College Chapel, 53
St Catharine's College; Catharine Hall;
    St Kateryn's Hall
  Admission Book, 140
  Admissions and numbers, 27, 65–6, 102–3, 105, 116, 141–3, 149, 151–2, 159, 161, 185, 189, 208, 214, 223, 226, 233, 236, 252, 256–7, 260, 266, 269–70, 282, 298
  Amalgamated Clubs, 234, 238
  Amalgamation with King's College, 218 et seq., 225, 227–9
  Armitage Library, 276
  Arms, 140, 144, 160–1
  Army officers at, 161, 163
  Audit account, 197
  —books, 139–40
  —meetings, 175, 230, 243
  Autonomy of, 169–70, 246
  Bible Clerks, 65
  Boat Club, 185, 195–6
  Buildings, 60–1, 77, 94, 98, 107, 121, 138, 145–6, 150–1, 155, 174, 216, 239–40, 253, 261, 266, 270 et seq.
  Building Fund, 239
  Bull Inn, and Hotel, 66, 94, 199, 225–6, 230, 269, 271–2
  Burrell Fund, 242
  Bursar, 75, 149–50, 158, 186–7, 193, 197, 200, 208, 216, 225, 230–1, 242, 245, 257, 278
  —Assistant or Junior, 241–2
  Buttery, 146
  Caution Money, 236, 243–4
  Chantry duties, 9
  Chapel, 52, 61, 80, 99, 128, 129–30, 157, 163–4, 187, 233–5, 244, 271, 277, 288, 293

St Catharine's — continued
  Chaplain, 207, 222–3, 232, 235, 246, 293
  Charter, 1475; 10, 20–1, 33, 56
  Coal dispute, 239, 241, 244
  College Acts, 280
  College Lecturers, 184, 193, 222, 227, 236–7, 256
  Collegiate status, 76
  Combination Room, 146
  Common Stock (General Stock), 174–5, 194, 197
  Conclusion Book, 140, 156
  Crabtree Exhibitions, 289
  Curricula, courses and teaching, 170–1, 184, 207, 214, 227, 231–2, 256, 259–60
  Dean, 186–7, 193, 206–7, 242, 245–6
  Directors of Studies, 276, 291
  Estates, 186; see also Guilden Morden, Histon, Ramsden, Therfield
  Fees, 139, 159, 183, 185, 242
  Fellows
    Bye-Fellows, 136, 168, 175, 207, 213n.
    Conduct, 128, 207, 222
    Frankland, 128
    Honorary, 211, 222, 224, 233, 282
    Permutit, 287
    Prize, 221
    Professorial, 180, 187, 191, 200, 206, 242
    Research, 281
    Skerne, 136, 165–8, 173–6, 184, 189, 194, 197, 201, 207, 214, 222, 228–9
    Supernumerary, 222, 246
    dividends and stipends, 63, 81, 180–1, 195, 222, 230, 237–8, 240, 243
    duties, 70
    numbers, 64, 165–8, 201, 220, 222, 226, 237, 258, 270, 277–8, 299
    pernoctation by, 279
    and celibacy, 135, 176, 180, 202 et seq., 215–16
    and Holy Orders, 70, 178–80, 203, 222
    see also Old Foundation and New Foundation
  Fellowship Estates, 201, 208
  Fellows' Garden, 198
  Finances, 140, 150, 194, 197–201, 216, 220, 222, 226, 230, 236, 238, 240–5, 258
  Foundation of, pp. 1 et seq., 141
  Frankland Fellows and Scholars, 128, 197, 213n.

St Catharine's — *continued*
Furniture Fund, 243–4
General Fund, 221, 222, *see also*
    Common Stock
Graduate composition, 18, 30, 141
Grove, the, 239
Guilden Morden estate, 197
Hall, 216, 230, 233, 239, 262, 272
Histon estate, 197
Hobson's Building, 271
Improvements Fund, 208
Island Site, 198, 266, 270
Junior Combination Room, 234, 271
John's Building, 271
Library, 61, 134–5, 138, 197, 230,
    274 et seq., 299
Masters, 61, 63, 77–8, 89, 92–3, 95,
    99, 101–3, 105, 107, 111, 115,
    119, 125, 127, 131, 133, 140,
    146, 151, 164, 177, 188, 193,
    214, 218, 221, 224–5, 230, 233,
    238, 244–6, 258, 260, 266,
    268–70, 277
  Bishops, 85, 93, 99, 114, 128–9, 164
  elections, 86, 90, 92, 101–3, 115 and
    n., 131, 133, 140, 142, 164 et
    seq., 186–7, 189–90, 204 et seq.,
    209, 233, 238, 246, 248–51, 268
  expulsion, 148
  Lodge, 146, 154, 191, 198, 217–18,
    230, 262, 271, 302
  stipend, 181, 192–4, 197
  Vice-Chancellors, 83, 87–9, 93, 102,
    121, 128, 132, 168, 172, 182,
    191, 208
Memorandum Book, 167, 250
Midnight Howlers, 295
Midsummerians, 145
Migrations, 278, 281
Music Society, 234–5
New Foundation, 166
Noblemen, 139, 149, 183
Norton Coal Act, 242
Norwich Canonry, 131, 192, 222, 268
Oaths, 180, 188
Old Court, 61
Old Foundation, 136, 166, 168, 175–6,
    196, 229
Old Lodge, 182–3, 198, 238, 299
Order Book, 140, 154
Organ, 235–6
Patronage Fund, 175, 191, 193–8,
    200–1
Pensioners, 139, 140–1, 143, 151–2
Plate Money, 144, 159, 161–3
Playing field, 177, 234
Post-graduate students, 270, 278

St Catharine's — *continued*
President, 181, 187, 191, 200, 206, 242
Queens' Lane site, 198, 200, 216
Quincentenary Fund, 295
Ramsden: building, estate, Fellows,
    Scholars, *see under* Ramsden
Registers, 72 and *n.*, 140
Rugby Football Club, 296
Scholarships, 81, 167, 173, 178, 220,
    222, 288, 291
Seal, 181
Servants, 64, 200, 283 et seq.
Silver, 138 et seq.
—Fund, *see* Plate Money
Sizars, 120, 139, 143, 151–2
Skerne Scholars, 174
—Fellows, *see under* Fellows
Society, 283, 286, 295
Societies, 294 (Music, Shirley, John
    Ray, Literary)
Statutes: Founder's, 10, 17, 21, 33*n.*,
    53–4, 56, 101, 164–5, 171, 181,
    202; 1549, 21, 70, 81, 86, 164,
    171, 181, 202; 1854, proposals,
    171; 1860, 164–8, 173, 178,
    180, 182, 203, 213*n.*, 214,
    220–1, 229; 1882, 215, 221–4;
    1921, 224; 1926, 224
Steward, 187, 193, 197, 200, 208, 216,
    230, 242—5, 278
Swimming Bath, 272
Teaching, 76, 152–3; *see also under*
    curricula
Ten Marcs Rule, 176, 196
Tenure of Office, 230, 242
Therfield Estate, 134–5, 197
Treasury, 144, 146, 150
Tutors, 140, 143, 151, 184, 186, 190,
    193, 202, 207, 212–14, 216,
    227, 230, 237, 242, 245, 258
Tutorial System, 142–3, 184, 256,, 277
Tutorial Fund, 237, 240, 242–4
Undergraduates, 18, 25, 56, 64–5, 139,
    208, 233–4, 238, 242, 259, 269,
    275, 277 et seq., 284, 291,
    293 et seq.
University Lecturers, 233, 258
University Tax, 220–1, 223
Valuation, 21, 62
Visitation, 1549, 80; 1557, 87; 1564,
    141–2
Visitor, 169–70, 174, 176, 189–96,
    201, 222, 233, 244, 268*n.*
Walnut Tree Court, 98
Wine Fund, 244
Woodlark Building, 272
Yorke Fund, 177, 234, 237, 242

St Catherine's Hospital and Church, *see under* London
St Gennaro, 41
St George, 41, 99
St Germain's, 129
St Jerome, 66
St John, Oliver, 102
—Sir Rowland, 102
St John's College, 60–4, 66, 74, 78–9, 84, 88, 91, 95–7, 144, 168, 177, 179, 191, 217, 224, 252, 253, 262, 281, 291
St Katherine's Hostel, 35, 54, 75
—Priory, Lincoln, 45
St Lorenzo, 41
St Margaret, 41
St Mary, Aldermanbury, 123
St Nicholas, 41
St Paul's, *see under* Paul's
Salcot, William, 79
Salem, Massachusetts, 108
Salisbury, Bishop of, 114, 135
—Diocese, 232
Sambrook, John, 158
Sancroft, Archbishop, 93, 125–6
Sandars Reader in Bibliography, 292
Sandys, Edwin, 69, 74, 78, 80–6, 89, 103, 109
—Mrs, 85
Sawston Hall, 63, 217
Sayers, Professor R., 281
Schism Bill, 130
Scolt Head, 292
Scottish Verse Legendary, 47
Scrivener, Matthew, 120
Segal, Professor J. B., 281
Selby, Yorkshire, 158
—Sir John, 93
Selwyn College, 282, 288, 290
Shanghai, 178
Shapland, D., 293
Shelford, 196, 230, 242
Sherman, John, 107–9
Sherlock, Thomas, 111, 113–15, 126, 131–3
—William, 124–6, 131, 134–6
—Library, 197, 275
Shilleto, R., 210
Shirley, James, 274
—Society, 294
Shore, Jane, 7
Sibbes, Richard, 60, 66, 68, 72, 74, 78, 86, 94–101, 103, 106–8, 126–8, 142
Sidney Sussex College, 59, 63, 71, 105, 139, 185, 227, 260, 262, 291
Silberston, A., 281

Silver,
an investment, 151, 155
price, 144–5, 148, 150, 154–5, 157
standards, 157
tax, 159
Simeon, monk, 44
Simeon Metaphrastes, 43
Simpkin, George, 285
Sinai, Mount, 37, 42, 44
Slader, John, 150
Smectymnus, 104, 118
Smith, Mrs N., 285
Smith, S., 268, 292
—S. A. de, 281
Smyth, Canon C., vii, 113–14 and *n*.
Snow, Charles, 101
Society for the Promotion of Christian Knowledge, 129
—Christian Morals, 129
Sodor and Man, Bishop of, 91, 146, 277
Somerset, Duke of, 69
Soper, Lord, 282
Sotheby, James, 153, 158
South, Dr, 125
South English Legendary, 46
Southold; and Southold, Massachusetts, 108
Southward, W. T., 214, 222*n*, 227, 229, 235–8, 240, 242, 244, 246, 257–8
Sparrow, D., 293
Spate, Professor O. K., 281
Spear, T. G. P., 282
Spearing, N. J., 283
Spratt, A. W., 212–15, 221, 225, 227–31, 233–6, 238, 242–4, 246–7, 257–8
Spurrell, James, 162
Spurstow, William, 68, 74, 86, 101–5, 115, 118, 123, 148
—Robert, 154
Stafford, George, 79
Stanley, James, 17
Stanton, William, 89
Stapleford, 192
Starkie, Thomas, 202
Steers, Professor J. A., 278, 281, 292
Stepney, Bishop of, 207
Stockdale, William, 63
Storr, Paul, 160, 162
Stow, John, 27
—Archdeacon of, 93
Strachan, W. J., 283
Strype, John, 121, 124, 134
Stuart, James, Duke of Lennox, 101
Suffolk, 101, 108
Sussex, Thomas Ratcliffe, Earl of, 88, 90, 141–2

Swift, Jonathan, 112, 119, 134
Switzerland, Marian exiles in, 84, 109

Taylor, James, 84–5
—Joseph, 158
Tedder, Lord, 272
Tenison, Archbishop, 128
Test Acts, 128, 188
Therfield, 197
Thirty-nine Articles, 172
Thomas, Professor D. Winton, 268, 292
Thornely, Thomas, 219, 231
Thorpe, Joseph, 190
Tillyard, A. W., 262
Timber Development Association, 272
Tories, 111–12
Trinity College, 35, 54–5, 59–60, 62–4,
    66, 68–70, 78, 81, 86, 88–9, 92,
    95, 97–8, 101–2, 104–6, 116,
    134, 170, 182, 204–5, 210, 222,
    224, 231, 249, 252–3, 281
Trinity Hall, 22, 33n., 34, 60, 62, 64, 66,
    86–8, 185, 219, 281
Trunch, 193
Turnbull, W. P., 258
Turton, Bishop Thomas, 181, 187, 189,
    202, 253, 256
Tutorial system, 29; see also under
    St Catharine's

Undergraduates, 28–30, 34, 70–1, 73–4;
    see also under St Catharine's
Uniformity, Act of, 116, 118
University Grants Committee, 298
Urlin, Samuel, junior, 157

Vaizey, John, 281
Venn, J. A., 138, 142, 265
Vergil, Polydore, 26
Victoria, Queen, 182–3
Victoria and Albert Museum, 157
Vigani, J. F., 135
Virginia, 105–7
Voragine, Jacobus de, 36

Waddams, C. D., 268, 293
Wakerley, 3, 53 and n.
Walker, Sir G. A., 282
Walsingham, 108
Walters, D. M., 283
Warner, F. R. le P., 283

Walton Izaac, 97, 100
Waterhouse, Joshua, 190–1, 195, 197,
    251
Watertown, Massachusetts, 107–8
Waynflete, William, 24
Wayper, C. L., 281
Welde, Peter, 53n.
Wellington, Duke of, 183
Wells, 79
Wesley, John, 159
West Indies, 105
Westminster, Dean of, 189
Westmorland, 63, 78
Whigs, 110 et seq.
Whewell, W., 170, 182, 204–5, 249
Whitaker, William, 91–2
White, J. M., 283
Whitgift, John, 70, 82, 89, 92
Wilbraham, 77
Wilbraham, Randle and Roger, 152
Wilkins, William, 199
Wilkinson, A., 293
Willard, Samuel, 107
Williams, William, 162
Willoughby, Sir Francis, 153, 156
Winchester, Bishop of, 86
Winstanley, D. A., 164 and n.
Winthrop, John, 105
Withers, Sir J. J., 268
Wodelarke, Robert, pp. 1–58,
    passim, 69, 81, 86, 274
—Joanna, 3
—Richard, 3
Wolsey, Thomas, 78
Wood, Joshua, 190, 193, 195–6
Woodhouse, J. S., 283
Woodville, Elizabeth, 16
Worcestre, William of, 26
Worcester, Bishop of, 85, 164, 206, 224
Worcester College, Oxford, 282
Wycliffe, John, 51
Wylleborde, James, 141

Yates, Lowther, 186, 189, 197
Yelverton, Henry, 96
Yokohama, 179
York, Mr, 158
York, 148
—Archbishop of, 85, 89, 130
—St Peter's School, 184, 207
Yorke, Edmund, 166–7, 177, 214
Yorkshire, 88, 189
Yorkshire Fellows, 177
    see St Catharine's, Fellows,
        Skerne
Youngs, John, 108